AF607811

The Rhetoric of Hiddenness in Traditional Chinese Culture

SUNY series in Chinese Philosophy and Culture

Roger T. Ames, editor

The Rhetoric of Hiddenness in Traditional Chinese Culture

Edited by

Paula M. Varsano

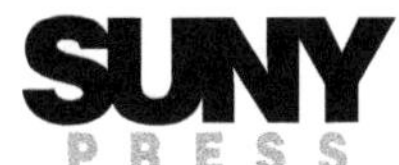

Published by State University of New York Press, Albany

Printed in the United States of America

For information, contact State University of New York Press, Albany, NY
www.sunypress.edu

Production, Ryan Morris
Marketing, Kate R. Seburyamo

Library of Congress Cataloging-in-Publication Data

Names: Varsano, Paula M., editor.
Title: The rhetoric of hiddenness in traditional Chinese culture / edited by Paula M. Varsano.
Description: Albany : State University of New York Press, 2016. | Series: SUNY series in Chinese philosophy and culture | Includes bibliographical references and index.
Identifiers: LCCN 2016007693 (print) | LCCN 2016038163 (ebook) | ISBN 9781438463032 (hardcover : alk. paper) | ISBN 9781438463049 (e-book)
Subjects: LCSH: China—Intellectual life—221 B.C.–960 A.D. | China—Intellectual life—960–1644. | China—Intellectual life—1644–1912. | Rhetoric—China—History. | Secrecy—China—History. | Hiding places—China—History. | Knowledge, Theory of.
Classification: LCC DS727.R48 2016 (print) | LCC DS727 (ebook) | DDC 951—dc23
LC record available at https://lccn.loc.gov/2016007693

10 9 8 7 6 5 4 3 2 1

Contents

Illustrations

Acknowledgments

The fourteen essays collected in this volume are revised versions of papers presented at a two-day conference held at the University of California, Berkeley, in September 2007. The title of the conference, like that of this book, was The Rhetoric of Hiddenness in Traditional Chinese Culture, and the impetus behind it was the recognition that the evocation of hiddenness—or, more precisely, the subtle interplay between the hidden and the manifest—pervades many aspects of premodern Chinese cultural production. From the earliest divination texts to the great novels of the late imperial period, from the practice of ritual to graphic representations of the body, some form of hiddenness can be counted on to appear, whether as a formal device, an interpretable theme, or—as in the most interesting and complex cases—both. Yet the role played by hiddenness in premodern Chinese culture had only been explored in its particular instances: as central to the study of allusion, gardens, eremitism, or disguises; or as implicit in the discussion of some broader topic, such as literary hermeneutics or studies of Daoist and Buddhist forms of enlightenment.

Perhaps the sheer ubiquity of this feature of cultural expression, and the reality that it is common in some form to all cultures and civilizations, made it unthinkable to attempt to examine it from an interdisciplinary or synthetic perspective. And so I am especially grateful that so many colleagues from such a wide range of disciplines responded immediately and enthusiastically to my call for papers, so many years ago. And, as we discovered over the course of our conversations, hiddenness—whether enacted rhetorically, poetically, or practically—can be thought of as marking the point where a range of epistemological, aesthetic, moral, political, and social issues converge: that place where various modes of knowledge (such as discernment, cognition, recognition, or intuition) can be observed as shaping—and being shaped by—aesthetic, social, and moral values and circumstances.

In the following pages, contributors have taken a particular instance of hiddenness as a starting point from which to examine their chosen texts with an eye to discerning: the motives and methods of concealment (as enacted by the authors, protagonists, or practitioners), the criteria guiding the choice of the "object" deemed worthy of dissimulation, or the implicit or explicit conditions for the revelation that object. The combined effect of this collection of studies is to illustrate how particular evocations or uses of hiddenness reflect, or even construct, notions of identity, ambition, friendship, loyalty, morality, enlightenment, beauty, or even—and perhaps most fundamentally—beliefs about the function and efficaciousness of language and signs.

Of course, the rhetoric of hiddenness, especially when it is central to the understanding of a particular text or practice, is bound to directly engage all readers and observers in the task—or game—of discernment, of interpreting the play of the hidden and the manifest. This group of readers necessarily includes us, latter-day scholars attempting to use a different language to decipher the uses of hiddenness, and the readers who undertake to engage in what is, by necessity, an open-ended and self-propagating project.

As grateful as I am to the contributors to this volume, and for their sustained support for its ultimate completion, I would also like to thank the other enthusiastic participants in this conference whose work is not explicitly represented here—Pauline Yu, Jack Chen, Wendy Swartz, and the late Alan Berkowitz—for their presentations and contributions to the discussions that ultimately enriched all of these essays. The conference itself was generously funded by the U.C. Berkeley Center for Chinese Studies, my own Department of East Asian Languages and Cultures, and the Doreen B. Townsend Center for the Humanities. Elinor Levine, the program director of CCS, was instrumental not just in making it happen smoothly, but in anticipating needs and details I never would have imagined.

I speak for all of the contributors, too, when I extend thanks to the anonymous readers who accepted the especially arduous task of evaluating and commenting on this somewhat unwieldy volume of essays. Without their comments and suggestions, it would have been much the weaker. And finally, we are especially indebted to the late Nancy Ellegate, senior acquisitions editor at SUNY Press, whose patience, responsiveness, and insight shaped this volume at each step until her untimely and sudden passing just before its completion. Had Jessica Kirschner not seamlessly taken the helm during this difficult period, this book would have fallen by the wayside.

❧

An earlier version of chapter 4, "Woman in the Tower: "Nineteen Old Poems" and the Poetics of Un/concealment," by Xiaofei Tian, was originally published in *Early Medieval China* 15, no. 1 (2009). www.maney.co.uk/journals/emc. We thank the publishers of EMC for permission to reprint the article here.

1

Lowered Curtains in the Half-Light

An Introduction

PAULA M. VARSANO

A Poem and an Explanation

The sensual surface of Li Shangyin's 李商隱 (813–858) poem, "Lamp," is like a gleaming piece of obsidian. Neither transparent enough to serve as a window nor reflective enough to be a mirror, it irresistibly attracts the eye only to withhold any compensatory promise of vision.

Lamp (Li Shangyin)

In gleaming purity, never to falter,
its ardent burning seeks to consume even itself.
In the season of blossoms, it lasts as long as the wine,
then rests after the rains, its back to the window.
Cold and dim: a yellow-thatched way station;
glowing and bright: a purple-cassia pavilion.
Wrapped in brocade bags are renowned paintings,
gathered up from the jade chessboard, the defeated pieces.
What place is free of such enticing dreams?
Who does not lie awake, suffering in the dark?
Shadows bend with the curtain-weights,
light flows along the pattern of the mat.

My guest, himself, surpasses the handsome poet, Pan Yue,
and now I am Mourn-no-more, good and beautiful.
Truly, one should keep a flame half-burning,
to turn back shining on the shyness of lowered bed-curtains.

燈 (李商隱)
皎潔終無倦, 煎熬亦自求。
花時隨酒遠, 雨後背窗休。
冷暗黃茅驛, 暄明紫桂樓。
錦囊名畫掩, 玉局敗棋收。
何處無佳夢, 誰人不隱憂。
影隨簾押轉, 光信簟文流。
客自勝潘嶽, 儂今定莫愁。
固應留半焰, 回照下幃羞。[1]

Readers who are familiar (to the extent that such a thing is possible) with the Tang Dynasty author of this poem will not be surprised by these qualities of sensuality and opacity. They are likely to intuit his hand, if not his mind, in the scarcely perceptible thread that leads from one seemingly unitary, iridescent image to the other; or, more accurately, in the scarce perceptibility of that thread.

Looking at the list of titles comprising this volume, which embraces subjects ranging from ancient poetry to modern art, and from medicine to philosophy, readers will no doubt confront a similar impulse to ferret out not so much an authorial hand as a unifying, implicit rationale. Surely there is a guiding thread that will lead us from one essay to the other; so, what sequence of apparently unrelated observations will ultimately lead us to a deeper understanding of the "rhetoric of hiddenness" named in the title? Knowing that the contributors to this volume participated in a conference called The Rhetoric of Hiddenness in Traditional Chinese Culture seems essential to making sense of this book. Yet simply reproducing here the initial questions to which each contributor was invited to respond would not necessarily illuminate the answer, because the invitation was, like hiddenness itself, designed to elicit as many perspectives as there were participants.

Instead, mimicking the process of discovery that the conference set in motion, this introduction will play with perspective. Structured in such a way as to echo the nature of our subject with the mode in which it is being explored, this introduction will foreground the very duality that characterizes hiddenness itself: as both a formal device (where it structures the selective presentation of information in a given work or practice) and a pervasive theme found in a range of literary, historical, philosophical, and religious texts produced in traditional China. This duality, which informs all of the essays included here, makes hiddenness (seemingly ironically) an especially powerful and supple hermeneutical tool, for its appearance marks the point where epistemological, aesthetic, moral, political, and social issues converge. Likewise, it is at that point of convergence that the various modes of knowledge (such as discernment, cognition, recognition, or intuition) can be observed shaping—and being shaped by—aesthetic, social, and moral values and circumstances.

This introduction, then, will guide the reader into the subject neither through a chronological narration of the findings included here, nor through a neat disciplinary schema, but from the position of one small point where many—although not all—of the issues raised by hiddenness can be seen to converge: in Li Shangyin's poem, "Lamp." This point of convergence is by design apt, arbitrary, and apt in its arbitrariness. Apt because, composed by one of the poets, if not *the* poet, most readily associated with interpretive difficulty, it is a poem that beautifully embodies the duality of hiddenness as both a formal feature and as a theme; indeed, it even layers this duality in especially revealing ways. Arbitrary, because the Chinese tradition is replete with texts, objects, and practices that lend themselves to this very purpose, and my own interest in poetry clearly played a large role in the choice. But arbitrariness is also part of what makes it useful, for, not unlike hiddenness itself, it invites the reader to play the endlessly informative game of substitution.

In what follows, I first offer a reading of how hiddenness functions in this one poem, and then gradually bring the insights of the contributors to bear on its further elucidation. In this way, the essays included here can be harmonized as hermeneutical instruments without being reduced to their most obvious points, bringing to light one hidden pattern of commonality while leaving wide open the reader's chances to find others. In the process, certain propositions about the role and workings of hiddenness in traditional Chinese culture will present themselves for consideration. Among the ones that emerge as dominant are: that the rhetoric of hiddenness, by virtue of its belonging to the domain of rhetoric, is never unilaterally imposed by a hider on a seeker, but creates and then thrives on their unspoken complicity (and flounders when that complicity is broken); that one of its primary roles is not just to convey meaning, but to signal what is meaningful; that the boundaries between the hidden and the manifest are not fixed, but reflect the real and unpredictable shifts that occur as the identity and perspective of the seeker change; and that the rhetoric of hiddenness and the substantive quality of the hidden have, at best, a tenuous relationship. As the different perspectives adopted by these essays variously bring into play these imbricated dimensions of the rhetoric of hiddenness, its roots in and implications for cultural practice in premodern China will, hopefully, become manifest.

Hiddenness of Qing? Or Hiddenness as Qing?

No less than "Lamp's" seductive play between the illuminated and the obscured, the known and the unknowable, the fact that this poem was written by the notoriously "hermetic" Li Shangyin has prompted many readers over the centuries to engage in the time-honored critical practice of connecting the dots in such a way as to turn frustrating figuration into pellucid, biographically verifiable meaning. Whether we subscribe to a traditional biographical approach or not, whether or not we find politically motivated coding in every erotic gesture, it remains that we readers strive, each in our own way, to turn the obsidian mosaic into a clear window onto the poet's—or, for those who prefer it, the speaker's—*qing* 情: that is, to posit some coherent subjectivity that corresponds to the elusive poet as he might have been, and to what he conceivably felt, at a given point in time. An understandable impulse, to be sure, if one that some contemporary readers tend to disdain, as though unaware that even modernist poetry (by some definitions born in the negation of the author as an "empirical person") ends up being personalized, in some fashion, by its most devoted readers.[2]

"*Qing*," depending on its immediate context, has engendered a range of definitions and translations, from "truth" to "emotion," with the latter being most closely associated with the world of literature. David Schaberg, in his contribution to this volume, implicitly reminds us that *qing*'s early morally inflected meaning of "truth" and its later lyrical connotations of "feeling," far from being mutually antagonistic, share a fundamental characteristic: that of hiddenness. Refraining from offering an easy (and misleading) translation of this term, Schaberg glosses the *qing* of early China as "any truth—objective or emotional—that is subject to hiding and that is brought into the open through human exposition" (p. 38). True, the *qing* he discusses refers to the psychological state of the ruler, treated as the primary object of exploitation by the persuaders of the Warring States period. But Schaberg also notes that later practices of reading and writing—that is, of both self-presentation and the discernment of the presented self by others–at least partly took root in the oratorical practices that this notion of *qing* inspired.[3] The judicious deployment of hiddenness by those elites of early China who are compelled to adopt public personas is also addressed in these pages by Michael Nylan. She demonstrates the increasing investment of the elite in hiding their *qing*, as the deceptively simple ideal of sagely transparency had to make room for an appreciation for its inherent dangers during the Qin and Han Dynasties. This is evident, she shows, in the increased prevalence of a mode of representation whereby "authoritative figures, male and female" are portrayed as epitomizing "just that auspicious balance of hiddenness and display" (p. 54).

Almost a millennium later, Li Shangyin, no one's idea of an "authoritative figure," much less a sage, played most skillfully with this balance and, consequently, with his readers. Few would deny that Li, especially in the poetry of his later years, had gone farther than most poets in enticing—and frustrating—the revelation-seeking exegete, and not merely by keeping his readers so flamboyantly at arm's length. Certainly his frequent invocation of the erotic was not done in ignorance of the age-old Confucian hermeneutics of reading politico-moral messages into scenarios of sexual desire. Nor could he have indulged his love of the fragmentary construct without some understanding that the resulting lacunae would only inflame a reader's thirst for narrative fullness. Even his choice to write an impressive number of "poems on things," or *yongwu shi* 詠物詩, seems a clear declaration that he relished the role of riddler.[4] So, if readers have characterized so many of the poems in his corpus as enigmatic, and exerted themselves to unlock them, their actions were not undertaken without his permission.

From the first, the title of Li's poem, "Lamp," casts an inviting, selective light. It tells us that what follows likely falls into the category of "poems on things," and so, that the poet will verbally display the properties of this particular thing in order to comment obliquely on some human truth, perhaps attained through personal experience. Widely accepted as an outgrowth of the Han Dynasty *yongwu fu* 詠物賦 ("rhapsodies on things"), poems on things constitute an especially clear example of what might be called "explicit hiddenness."[5] More than most, poems belonging to this genre are overtly designed to be decoded. They are structured, on the surface, along the syntagmatic lines determined by the properties, uses, and—as time went on—textual associations of the thing being described. At the same time, they are layered paradigmatically to suggest the poet's observations of some larger issue playing out in the world or, as it became adapted for use as lyric expression, in his life.

Many objects have been used as the focus of such poems; but there are some objects that, by their very nature, irresistibly invite both writers and readers to complicate this allegorical stance, and the lamp is one of them. As a thing, the lamp, like the candle and the mirror, presents a particular duality that lends itself to especially thought-provoking poetic acts of hide-and-seek. As it had been treated in literature up to the Tang, the lamp is both an object of perception—even an objet d'art—and an agent (if not fully a subject) that illuminates other objects of perception: a mediator of observation.[6] When treated by the poet as an object, the lamps in question are those that have been shaped to resemble something else: a dragon, a frog, or a bird. In such cases, the lamp's representation of yet another thing adds another level of referentiality; and a poem on a dragon-lamp, for example, can become a playful way of redirecting the reader's attention toward what the lamp—not to mention the animal shape into which it is formed—is not.[7]

As intriguing as that is, it is when the lamp is treated as an agent of illumination that it has the potential to bring into play the most complex configuration of relationships between the seen and the unseen, the visible and the invisible, the hider and the seeker. So, it is a bit surprising that, while many Six Dynasties poets excelled at playing with the atmospherics of light and dark that lamps produce, the world would have to wait for Li Shangyin to come along and show how the lamp can be deployed as a most exquisite vehicle for ruminations on the revelatory power of half-hidden hiddenness.

Li's poem adheres to the basic *yongwu* convention of omitting the thing's name from the body of the poem; the word "lamp" is never mentioned. If this practice was ever intended to intrigue, or even, simply, to incite the reader to fill in the blank in the most perfunctory way, that idea had been abandoned early on. One might even say that, by the time of Li Shangyin's writing, the conventional withholding of the object's name had become a perfect example of a "hiding" so obvious that it obfuscates its own hiddenness. Yet, here, in the hands of a poet for whom the rhetoric of hiddenness is a primary tool, the guessing game seems to have reemerged as an integral part of the process of meaning creation; if we were asked to read the poem without being shown the title, we would be hard pressed to divine the identity of the thing being described. We can briefly attempt just such a thought experiment here.

The poem begins with a parallel couplet that presents, in terms that border on the hyperbolic, two qualities that one may (or may not) associate with a lamp: light and heat.

> In gleaming purity, never to falter—
> Its ardent burning seeks [to consume] even itself.

> 皎潔終無倦，煎熬亦自求。

The opening phrase "gleaming purity" (皎潔 *jiaojie*) is not uncommon in Chinese poetry. A quick look in the Tang encyclopedia, *Yiwen leiju*, reveals that when it does occur, it appears most often in poems about romantic loss and yearning. In Ban Jieyu's 班婕妤's (ca. 48–6 BCE) famous "Yuan gexing"

怨歌行 (Song of resentment), it describes the pure white silk of the round, moon-like fan that, cut and resewn, represents her yearning for reunion with her love.[8] In Xie Lingyun's 謝靈運 (385–433) "Yuan xiaoyue fu" 怨曉月賦 (Resenting the dawn moon: a rhapsody), it is the frosty quality of the moonlight that fades with the rising sun[9]; and in the same poet's *yuefu* song, "Ri chu dongnan xing" 日出東南行 (The sun rises in the southeast), it is the gleaming pale skin of a beautiful woman, a reflection of her inner purity.[10] Bringing to mind such lunar, silken images of whiteness and luminosity, *jiaojie* is never used in reference to flames or fire. And so, its pairing with the "ardent burning" of the second line strikes one as more contrastive than complementary. What thing, one wonders, is both coolly luminescent and scorchingly hot? Without the aid of the title, the riddle-like quality of the first couplet brings to mind the ancient world of palace-style poetry: a world where the palpable purity of the eternally faithful heart pairs quite nicely with the desperate burning of erotic desire in the body of the desirous woman.

The answer to the implicit riddle—the hidden subject of this couplet—then, would seem to be a woman in love, most likely as observed and described by a man, even as the "ardent burning" of the second line also does evoke a lamp. The overall effect of these two lines is one of mutual transformation, the lamp and the woman each illuminating the other, neither of them quite dissolving into the other. This transformational juxtaposition is much more in keeping with the best parallel couplets of the regulated form of poetry (*lüshi* 律詩, of which Li Shangyin is a recognized master), than the unidirectional suggestion typical of *yongwu* poetry.

Having uncovered the identity of the subject(s) of the poem, we move on to the second couplet, only to discover that the link from the first to the second couplet is far more elusive than that between the first two lines.

> In the season of blossoms, she lasts as long as the wine,
> then rests after the rains, her[11] back to the window.

> 花時隨酒遠，雨後背窗休。

With this couplet, the poet amplifies the erotic associations set in place at the beginning. The anthropomorphic verbs in the second line, *bei* 背 ("to turn one's back to something") and, less definitively, *xiu* 休 (both "to rest" and "to cease"), intensify the image of the languorous woman in the boudoir. Taken in isolation, these two lines would seem to take a first step toward satisfying the reader's desire for narrative fullness, as they delicately render an erotic encounter the intensity of which is inextricable from its brevity. For all its blazing passion, or perhaps because of it, the moment of intimacy ends just as the effects of the wine that the lovers shared dissipate. The woman's desire, ignited and sustained by the wine, cools with intoxication's diminishment and the cessation of the erotic "rain"; the lamp, while tended throughout the initial period of their encounter, is ultimately left to burn out on its own.

Read in this way, with an exclusive focus on the goal of "decoding" the meaning of the thing being displayed, the second couplet seems to develop quite naturally from the first. Yet, while the poem's assemblage of images seems quite coherent, its discursive movement is not. In fact, the second couplet actually contradicts the first, asserting that the gleaming whiteness and intense heat of the woman/lamp are neither indefatigable nor unquenchable. The glimpse of eternity captured in the opening couplet is thus retracted almost as soon as it is proffered.

It is in crafting this particular tension between the experience of eternity and the hard fact of ephemerality that Li Shangyin creates the unifying thread that weaves together this "couplet collage."[12] Human perception, as the poet proceeds to show, is contingent on our (constantly shifting) place, not just in space, but also in time; yet these acts of perception are themselves transparent, remaining ever invisible to the perceiver. It is in objectifying the otherwise transparent framing mechanism of perceptual experience that the reader apprehends the ineffable emotion, the *qing*, of the speaking subject. and as we shall see, the rationale for the poet's choice of the lamp. The selective nature of a lamp's illumination, coupled with its own invisibility (just so long as it continues to cast its light on the things around it) is both rhetorically and substantially interwoven with the poet's *qing*. While it is clear that the poet is lamenting the loss of a past experience, the hidden *qing* points beyond the easily recognizable confines of mere nostalgia. This poem's lyrical power lies in the pathos of our inability to grasp, let alone accept, that our experience of the world is composed of a string of deceptively self-contained moments, linked together by nothing so much as a complex web of inexorable change. And nowhere is this mode of experience more palpable than in the boudoir, where the impression of eternity collides so powerfully with the ephemerality of the moment.

Cold and dim: a yellow-thatched way station;
Glowing and bright: a purple-cassia pavilion.

冷暗黃茅驛, 暄明紫桂樓。

At this point, the poet turns from the woman/lamp, the central object of the poem, to the space that both contains it and is illuminated by it. Side by side, or more accurately, one following the other, the lines of this couplet present the boudoir in two radically opposed states, as determined by the light and heat now emanating from—now withheld by—the woman/lamp at its heart. It can be an uninviting, humble stopping place where one tarries just so long before moving on toward some presumably more desirable destination, or it can be the abode of a goddess, which one would hope never to leave. This type of juxtaposition might seem to be an example of nicely wrought Tang parallelism lifting us out of the stream of time and into a timeless moment.

But the order of these two lines is more significant than their juxtaposition, and the mode of temporality it evokes is just the opposite of eternity. Instead, by reversing real-time experience, by placing the present scene before the past, this couplet enacts the helplessness of the lover grasping after what was, but a moment ago. The "yellow-thatched way station" captures the room at the *current* moment, attending the extinction of the light. The ensuing vision of the unattainable "purple-cassia pavilion" is, in effect, the mind's imaginative response to that moment—made all the more alluring by virtue of its inexplicable shift to the realm of memory.

This perversely indissoluble link between the visible and the hidden, or in this case, between the seen and the remembered, is immediately taken up in the ensuing lines.

Wrapped in brocade bags are renowned paintings;
Gathered up from the jade chessboard, the defeated pieces.

錦囊名畫掩，玉局敗棋收。

The pastimes of viewing paintings and playing chess were, if the boudoir poetry of the Southern Dynasties is to be believed, enjoyed by lovers in their chambers. As the speaker casts his eyes about the darkened, chill room, they fall on these objects that are—to him—all the more visible for having now been wrapped up, put away. Then, in a futile attempt to fall asleep and recover, if only in a dream, the recent pleasures made possible by those objects, he exclaims:

What place is free of such enticing dreams?
Who does not lie awake, suffering in the dark?

何處無佳夢，誰人不隱憂。

Whether the speaker's eyes are open or closed, the vanished dreamlike encounter is everywhere present and, by definition, stubbornly beyond reach.

Cruelly, instead of providing comfort, memory prevents him from sleeping . . . and from "returning" to his dream. The subtle reference in the second line to the ancient plight of sleepless lovers, first immortalized in the *Shijing*, hints that Li Shangyin just might allow himself to bring the evocative play of the visible and invisible to a conventional close, in the depiction of insatiable desire. Such an ending would bring the poem full circle, leaving the speaker tossing and turning, in much the same state as that in which we found the woman, and the lamp, in the beginning: burning so ardently as to be in danger of consuming it- or herself. But instead, it is the poem's focus on the play of light that prevails; the restless, insomniac eye continues to search the room. Alighting neither on the now-barely-illuminating lamp, nor on any of the objects of the lamp's illumination, the gaze fixes on the fluid light itself.

> Shadows bend with the curtain-weights,
> light flows along the pattern of the mat.

> 影隨簾押轉，光信簟文流。

Still in the identifiable space of the boudoir, the speaker has shifted his attention from the selected discrete objects in the room to a vision of vision's contingency. The light thrown by the lamp does not merely make things visible; rather, it is itself molded by those things or—because the verbs "bend" and "flow" here emphasize dynamism and change—is channeled, contained, and released by them. In responding to this image, it is not enough to say that light and shadow, the visible and the hidden, give rise to one another, or even that they complement each other, although both of these things are certainly true. More to the point, the undulating play of shadow and light depicted here returns us to the contemplation of how time and place condition vision, how what we "see" is only a matter of a moment's perspective.

The pathos of situatedness, the shifting conditions of vision and blindness that inhere therein, lies at the heart of the poem; and its couplet-collage structure enacts this experience. In thus stringing together successive, discrete moments of experience whose very irretrievability reflects the source of the speaker's pain—moments that successively cancel each other out even as they build on each other—the poem reveals that only by entering a static, permanent state of in-betweenness can one overcome the pain of loss. Only by entering a dream-state, wherein presence and absence are so fluid as to be one, can the speaker escape their unceasing and tortuous alternation between, and so free himself of his anguished quest to uncover, or recover, the hidden, once and for all.

And so, immediately before the poem draws to a close, the speaker enters just such a dream-state and, speaking in the first person, enacts the most dramatic transformation of the poem.

You, my guest, surpass the handsome poet Pan Yue,
and now I must be Mourn-No-More, good and beautiful.

客自勝潘嶽，儂今定莫愁。

Only because the *qing* of the poet is embodied not only in what he sees but in how he sees (and doesn't) can this couplet be smoothly integrated into the whole. With these performative words, the deeply satisfying invisible world of the imagination takes form, and takes the place of, the fragmentary, incomplete, desire-inducing visible world; what passion dictates *must* be true triumphantly subsumes what is truly possible.

It is no coincidence that this replacement of the real by the imagined is presented, not from the male speaker's perspective but from that of the woman/lamp. She is now the one speaking (albeit in free indirect discourse), and so emerges, if only for the short space of this couplet, as a, if not *the*, subject. It is possible that this is merely a shift of speaking subject; or that he is reporting what he "hears" her say. But another reading, one that makes good use of the play of light that is at the center of the poem, would dictate a brief merging of subjects. In this reading, the gaze of the male speaker, heretofore merely contingent on the "light" emitted by the woman/lamp, is now made to merge with it completely. Instead of continuing to look at her, the lamp, and the other objects that fall within the radius of their light, he now gives in, and adopts her perspective.

With this merging, the contingency of experience, and even of subjectivity itself, has been brought to its logical conclusion, the (re)union of the lovers fully achieved. In this dream-like state, it is possible not only to recapture the ephemeral moment of erotic union, but also to lift it out of its very ephemerality, both by taking erotic union to the extreme of the merging of seeing subjects, and by imbuing it with the permanence of legend (in the ancient, undying personages of the poet, Pan Yue (247–300), and the fictional beauty of the *yuefu* heroine, Mo Chou or "Grieve-no-more").

Like the couplet that preceded it, this one also could have functioned as a decent ending for this poem, but not without betraying the poem's *qing* in an important way. That is, to end the poem with this declaration would leave the reader with the sense that the transmutability of subject and object is achievable (and perhaps even sustainable), and that the desire that gave rise to the poem can thus be assuaged and made manifest. But such a conclusion would also lift the speaker out of the temporal flow that shapes all human experience. If left to stand, this ending would counterproductively resolve the (hidden) *qing* behind this poem that the desire produced.

It was not left to stand, clearly, and the ensuing and final couplet asserts—or, perhaps more accurately, confirms—that it is not desire's fulfillment, but desire itself that is eternal. Only desire escapes the ravages of passing time, and it does so not only by virtue of the ineluctable impossibility of its fulfillment, and but also through the perceptual world's power to evoke that desire, unceasingly and in myriad ways. Li Shangyin ends this poem with a tacit bow to the second-best solution; if eternal possession of what is desired is out of reach, then he can at least prolong the imminence of its acquisition:

Truly, one should keep a flame half-burning,
to reflect back on the shyness of lowered bed-curtains.

固應留半焰，回照下幃羞。

The half-burning flame is presumably longer-lasting and less likely to consume itself than one allowed to burn unchecked, just as it is also less likely to bring a too-bright illumination to bear on a fragile reality, or a cherished-if-incomplete vision. Behind the lowered bed curtains that filter the dim rays and render indistinct the lineaments of the lovers they veil, vision and reality, desire and truth can blend easily, free from scrutiny. And, as the poet well knows, even this barely visible scene can only be taken in in retrospect, with both the lamp and the lover "reflecting back" (*huizhao* 回 照) on the bed, recalling even as they observe.[13]

As with most strong poems, Li Shangyin's "Lamp" skillfully applies the meaning-making methods of its predecessors, so it is never a vain enterprise to try to tease out the specifics and figure out just what genre-determined paradigms and aesthetic practices it favors and which ones it rejects. On this subject, there is much to say, and indeed much as been said, as scholars bring to light Li's masterful transformations of such sources as those found in the workings of *yongwu* poetry, the erotic atmospherics of the "Ziye" songs of the Southern Dynasties, and even the earliest hermeneutic practices found in the *Shijing* and the *Chuci*. The reading I offer above, in contrast, is an attempt to observe up-close the workings of a poetic practice common to all of those, one that will show different sides of itself through the multiple lenses of the essays collected here.

Hiddenness and the Desire for Knowledge

Having completed our reading of Li's "Lamp," we become keenly aware of the poetry reader's natural desire for narrative fullness, the need to know who is expressing himself thus, and why, or to posit a possible subject in his place. Some of the best poems are those that pique that desire without fulfilling it; and apparently even by Li's time this had long been the case. Xiaofei Tian, in her contribution to this volume, titled "Woman in the Tower: 'Nineteen Old Poems' and the Poetics of Un/concealment," offers a fine-grained analysis of how, in that ancient grouping of anonymous poems, "articulation by suppression" functions precisely in that way. As she sees it, the sustained withholding of the (seemingly essential) narrative elements that would satisfy the reader's desire to know—elements such as the gender, location, or social identity of the speaker; the precise conditions leading to the state of separation lamented in any given poem; or the geographical location of the people involved—is directly responsible for the veneration that this body of poems, the "mother of all poetry (*shimu* 詩母)," has garnered. For, these poems, by suppressing "essential" information, create just the right measure of what Tian calls "perceived generality": the poetic quality that encourages readers to participate in the poem, make it their own, and (although Tian does not say as much) revive it periodically, in different ways, throughout the textured span of a lifetime.

Tian points out that this feature of the "Nineteen Old Poems"—the achievement of perceived generality through the suppression of narrative detail—is traceable as a continuous thread running through the history of Chinese poetry. Faced with the unabashed, even idiosyncratic, mysteries of the "The Lamp," some may well retort that suppression can sometimes go too far, and that in this and his other more elusive poems, Li Shangyin suppresses too much—or, perhaps, makes peculiar choices about what to suppress. As Tian herself points out, unlike the anonymous poems of the ancients, "signed" poems come to us with the lives of their authors firmly attached. It is as though the knowledge of the poet's name makes it impossible to indulge in the same degree of subjective identification that anonymous songs seem to invite. And so, when readers attempt to fill in the blanks of a Li Shangyin poem, they do so not with the undifferentiated palette of universal *qing*, but with the biographical details of Li's own, very particular life story.

Tian's point is supported by the fact that, working in the hermeneutical tradition of premodern China, readers of Li Shangyin's poetry who engage in the frequently futile task of pinning down the precise identities and circumstances behind this and many another of Li's poems do so in the belief that his practice of dissimulating such information was not rhetorical, but strategic. That is, like so many of his predecessors—from Qu Yuan on down—Li Shangyin would have felt compelled to code his political disgruntlements and personal career disappointments in the language of thwarted romance and, at least by the end of the poem, in a woman's voice. According to such a reading, Li's poems would be a latter-day instantiation of what Nylan here describes as a case of judicious hiding, implemented to ward off the dangers of too much transparency.

But even this is an incomplete reading of this poem's deployment of hiddenness, for it neglects to take the reader's role into full consideration. The texts expect readers to partake in the game of hide-and-seek in an active way, and not only by shining the lamp of our own experiences on the poem's hidden spaces. Certainly, by the time of Li's writing, if not before, there is a whole tradition of habits of reading that plays a huge role in determining what appears to be hidden in a text and why; and, as we know, these habits of reading, once they are articulated in commentaries, complicate the play of light and shadow in any text they attach themselves to. Wai-yee Li, in her essay "Hiding Behind a Woman: Contexts and Meanings in Early Qing Poetry," probes this very issue: "When," she asks, "is one justified to delve into 'metaphorical and allegorical meanings' (*bixing jituo* 比興寄託)?"; and "When is it justified to use [extrinsic] information as supporting evidence for unearthing hidden political meanings?" Her answer is as complex as the question itself is simple and direct, and its resonance with the poem we have been discussing here is striking. Without attempting to do justice to her detailed discussion here, I would like to highlight one essential concept that her essay brings to the table: the concept of "slippage." In the specific context of her subject—the motivations and interpretations of the poems of the Ming-Qing transition, in which male poets assumed, to varying degrees, the voice of a woman to express whatever was intently on their mind—slippage between the poet's intent and the readers' understanding seems unavoidable, and not just because a poet's intent is fundamentally unknowable. As Li shows, individuals living through the Ming-Qing transition shouldered extreme pressures on both the affective and the political levels; and, working so late in the tradition, they were subject to more layers of inherited assumptions about particular modes of expression. At that time, perhaps more than ever before, the reasons why a male poet would "hide" behind a woman would be surmised, not only on the basis of what the poem says, but on the context in which it is presumed to have been written; the meaning of the act of hiding is itself transformed, chameleon-like, by the background in which it is set. Wai-yee Li lays out specific cases where the matter of dating a poem results in a radical change in the understanding of the poet's intention, and in one instance, events that transpired long after a particular poem's composition indelibly transformed the ways in which the poet's choice of the female persona—and by extension, the very meaning of the poem, and the character of the poet—were retrospectively understood.

The Value of Distraction

In all of these cases—whether in our reading of "The Lamp," Xiaofei Tian's reading of the "Nineteen Old Poems," or Wai-yee Li's readings of the poets of the late seventeenth century—the sign that is being decoded is not itself hidden; rather, the sign is the "hiding" itself. In all three cases, one recognizes a sense of urgency, a sense that the feelings had to be expressed, and—for reasons that we are left to imagine—could not be directly articulated. In the poems discussed by Wai-yee Li in particular, value is only intensified by the traditional association of a woman's reticence with virtue; in Li Shangyin's poem, the type of hiding enacted by the "woman" invites quite a different type of valuation. Either way, to repeat Schaberg's definition, *qing* is that which is deemed important enough to hide; the import of what is hidden is embedded in the patterns of perception worked out between the text and its reader.

To take this matter of complicity between text and reader one step further, we might observe that the rhetorical effect of hiding is only as powerful as the text's ability to work with how its audience habitually "sees." Shigehisa Kuriyama's essay, "Hiddenness of the Body and the Metaphysics of Sight," examines how habits of seeing (and not) are exploited by documents that could not be more different than poems: the anatomical drawings used in the world of traditional Chinese medicine. Kuriyama shows that the medical illustrations of traditional China, in contrast with those of the West, do not peel away graphically layers of skin and tissue to reveal the hidden organs underneath. Instead, reflecting the "world of patterns" from which they emerge, a world where "sights are obscured less by obstacles than by distractions," these drawings aim at refocusing the attention on what is commonly overlooked. They tend to "spotlight" not the internal organs themselves, but the dangers of distraction, the reality of "how easily significant sights are overlooked." This means that, in practical terms, the usefulness of these pictures is not limited to illustrating the ways in which the human body manifests illness. They teach the diagnostician how to see past the usual distractions to what is truly significant. As teaching tools, then, these drawings are necessarily rife with distractions—distractions that effectively disappear as such before the trained eye. Eventually, the eye, so trained, sees a world that is not merely obstacle-free, but one in which the contingent relationship between the eye and its object is itself both salient and signifying.

The obvious differences between poems and medical illustrations notwithstanding, Kuriyama's work brings home the complicity between text and reader that is central to all representational patterns of light and shadow, explicitness and implicitness, showing and hiding. To recall Li Shangyin's lines: "Shadows bend with the curtain weights, / light flows along the pattern of the mat." When words and images shift our attention from what we see to how we see, the object of knowledge shifts accordingly from the deceptively stable content of the world to its dauntingly dynamic conditionality.

Some texts, then, go further than just acknowledging or even demonstrating the active role that the viewer or receiver plays in determining how the rhetoric of hiddenness is deployed. Such texts can and do use hiddenness, and the complicity between text and reader that makes it meaningful, to train the mind to "see"—to understand—in a particular way. The medical illustrations discussed by Kuriyama are one such example. Another one is the elusive set of poems known as the *Twenty-Four Modes of Poetry*, attributed to the ninth-century poet Sikong Tu 司空徒 (837–908). As I discuss in my own essay included here, "Worlds of Meaning and the Meaning of Worlds in Sikong Tu's *Twenty-Four Modes of Poetry*," the language of these poems, both individually and as a whole, conveys meaning, not by highlighting the (hidden) value of any particular poetic model, but by using the play between the hidden and the manifest to train and transform the meaning-making mechanism of the perceiver's mind into something that corresponds to the meaning-making mechanism of poetry. Specifically, through the use of what I call "decoy signposts" (and what Kuriyama might have called "distractions"), the *Modes of Poetry* trains the reader to perceive a variety of common rhetorical moves—from the enumeration and promise of classification indicated in the titles to the generic associations set in play by the text as a whole—as so many categories of knowledge to be acknowledged and immediately transcended. In the end, the reader is not only faced with the subjective and contingent nature of the categories on which she relies; she is further confronted with the heretofore hidden habits of mind that had allowed her to rely on them.

Returning to Li Shangyin's "Lamp" from this perspective, it is not hard to see how it deploys to similar effect the laying-out of objects that fall before the eye. With the naming of each piece of boudoir furnishing, with each phrase drawn from the lexicon of erotic poetizing, the reader is drawn into a specific scene that could not seem more concrete or more familiar. These decoy signposts are not merely numerous, but also, because of their erotic associations, particularly seductive, leading us to fall into the oldest habits of poetry reading there are: allegorization and biographical association. But, as Kuriyama demonstrates, in a world of pattern, it is not obfuscation but distraction that makes hiddenness speak; and the astute hider, familiar with the seeker's habits, will be most adept, not just at exploiting those habits, but also at making them salient. For Li Shangyin, unlike the creators of the medical drawings or Sikong Tu, pedagogy is the furthest thing from his mind, of course. The poet is simply sharing with his readers something they already viscerally understand: the pathos inherent in the essential conditionality of seeing, and of human experience.

The arguments raised thus far suggest that distinguishing between what is only apparently important and what is truly valuable, between the salient distraction and the hidden kernel of meaning, is the cooperative—and even transformative—work of a text's creator and its evolving community of infinitely varied interpreters. One possible conclusion to draw from this is that no text or image ever definitively means anything and that even hiddenness itself is a purely subjective matter. One could conclude that it is in all cases up to the reader to determine who is doing the speaking, why they are hiding, and what habits of thought must be avoided to apprehend what is important (just to recap our examples so far). While this may be a tempting conclusion, the sheer textuality of the tradition itself can be marshaled to argue the contrary; driving the incessant production of text and commentary is the belief that meaning can somehow be understood, and that hiddenness functions as an invitation—and not a barrier—to understanding, even if not everyone is equipped to receive, let alone respond to, the invitation.[14]

This tension between the belief in language's comprehensibility and the conviction that, as far as language goes, there is no there there is as old as Chinese writing itself, and is examined here in Cai Zong-qi's essay, "The *Yi-Xiang-Yan* Paradigm and Early Chinese Theories of Literary Creation." According to Cai, the epistemological and aesthetic foundations of Chinese literary thought took shape largely to fend off the dizzying possibility that linguistic signs do not exhaustively, or even reliably, convey meaning. This thread of what he calls "deconstructionist" belief, which stems from early Daoist thought, was ultimately woven into a complex paradigm that upholds the possibility of creating and recovering meaning, even as it acknowledges meaning's fundamental hiddenness. He terms this paradigm, at least insofar as it is relevant to the creation and reception of literary texts, the "progressively generative" model, highlighting the means whereby (hidden) meaning (*yi* 意), image (*xiang* 象), and language (*yan* 言) successively lead each to the next in increasing levels of explicitness and accessibility. And, if its earliest literary proponent, Lu Ji 陸機 (261–303), worried over the danger of the potential loss of substance that seems almost inevitable as he attempts to render his ideas, or *yi*, into words or *yan*, implicit in his anxiety is his belief that such loss is ideally avoidable. Cai shows that in choosing to elaborate this progressively generative model (rather than the deconstructionist one), Lu Ji and Liu Xie 劉勰 (ca. 460s–520s), the acknowledged progenitors of what we think of as early Chinese literary theory, did nothing less remarkable than preserve the value of literature itself. At the same time, they did not simply acquiesce to a Confucian "reificationist" model either. Indeed, far from expunging the element of hiddenness from literary expression, the successful model of the relationship between meaning and language, then, was the one that attributed to hiddenness its all-important role as the generative seed of the literary process.

Hidden at the heart of Cai's discussion of what we might call the earliest Chinese attempts to grapple with the metaphysics of meaning, is the all-important reader. Ultimately, if the text is successful, then the astute reader, who has learned—probably through long exposure to a variety of texts—not to be derailed by distractions or blinded by habits of thought, must appropriately respond to the invitation that hiddenness extends, and be able to retrace the steps taken by the poet to arrive at the correct, hidden meaning. And so, the question emerges: who are these ideal readers? What attributes must they possess if hidden meaning, or a writer's implicit intentionality, can become available to them, its valuable hiddenness nonetheless intact? The answer to this question lies in the oft-remarked implicit parallel, which Cai discusses at length, that Lu Ji draws between the poet and the Daoist (or more specifically, Zhuangzian) sage. The successful writer is one who, like the sage, can transcend, if only for a moment, the limits of space and time in an activity described as *xinyou* 心遊 (daimonic flight or "the roaming of the mind"). And the success of that writer implicitly depends on the existence, now or later, of an astute reader: one capable of discerning what was captured and set down as language in the course of that daimonic flight.

The Valued (Sometimes Hidden) Reader

Neither Lu Ji nor Liu Xie directly addresses this necessary symbiotic relationship between reader and writer; but this omission does not mean there is no textual precedent for recognizing the sage-like qualities of the discerning viewer of a text, image, or object. One need only think of the ancient story of Fu Xi 伏羲, who derived the hexagrams from the patterns he espied in the natural forms of the constellations and the grasses[15]; or, in a different key, of Mengzi, who prided himself on his ability to "know men" based on their words and actions.[16] What all this suggests is that hiddenness and its seemingly paradoxical, if selective, legibility confers value, not just on the thing hidden, or even only on the engineer of its hiddenness, but also on the person who possesses the discernment to recognize it and, ultimately, the wherewithal to put it to use. That is, to paraphrase Xiaofei Tian's description of the reader's role in the creation of meaning: to perform it, without reducing it to the realm of the perfectly manifest.

In the cases of the medical illustrations discussed by Kuriyama, and the poems on poetry examined in my own essay, this performativity is pedagogical in nature: the text exploits the mind's habitual mode of functioning only to bring it up to the level of discernment necessary to decode that very text. By implication, the trained mind thus becomes astute at reading deeper into all of the meaningful patterns, or *wen*, it encounters in the world. But there are probably many more texts that are intended, perhaps explicitly, for the eyes of those who already possess that capacity. Such texts (which include objects) deploy hiddenness in such a way as to confirm the reader's privileged relationship with the text and, sometimes, with the author. In some cases, such texts go so far as to confer on the reader the sage-like quality of discernment.

For example, a reader who can persuade others that he catches the meaning of one of the more hermetic Li Shangyin poems acquires a particular status. From a narrow perspective, he becomes the *zhiyin* 知音—"he who understands the melody"—of the great poet: not just his intended audience, but (should he attempt to communicate that understanding in his own writing) also an extension of his voice. Viewed more broadly, he ascends to the status of one who can see beyond what is obvious, or who can discern the patterns that make the obvious meaningful. How much more valuable, then, are readers who can penetrate the most recondite ideas buried in the texts of the ultimate authoritative figures: the sages.

Of course, no one can begin to fathom precisely what readers have understood unless they, in turn, become writers, committing their interpretations to the imperfect medium of language. In the textual tradition of premodern China, texts deemed important enough to require illumination spawned legions of readers: the commentators, whose transgenerational conversations shed a shifting spectrum of light on the ancient texts—and, not incidentally, on each other. In an unintended effect of this rich hermeneutical practice, the commentarial tradition also affords us a unique opportunity to examine the workings of the reader-writer complicity we have been discussing; for the commentator can be thought of as the site where the reader and writer coexist explicitly in the most intimately symbiotic of all relationships. What happens to hiddenness when a single mind explicitly combines the activities of both reading and writing, of both the discernment and deployment of patterns of transparency and opacity, in the transmission of the foundational philosophical writings of the tradition? And how does the commentator confer sufficient value on himself to warrant the reading of others?

Michael Puett's contribution to this volume is an exploration of precisely this phenomenon, as he discusses the peculiar example of the *Xiang'er* 想爾 commentary to the *Laozi*, a commentary that he dates to the second century CE. In his essay, "Manifesting Sagely Knowledge: Commentarial Strategies in Chinese Late Antiquity," Puett systematically lays out the variety of ways in which Han Dynasty commentators addressed the problem of ferreting out purportedly hidden meaning in purportedly sagely texts. The thorny issue confronted by all readers of transmitted texts had become tied up with determining who were the true sages, and which texts were written by them, a problem that gave rise to a wide range of complicated hermeneutic practices. Whatever stance these commentators assumed—from what he calls the arrogant "violent misreadings" perpetrated by early Eastern Han commentators (including the authors of the *Huainanzi*) to the humbler approaches of those who came later and proposed either to restore meanings that were either deliberately or carelessly obfuscated or to generate new meanings appropriate for the age—the commentators simultaneously depended on and carved out their own privileged position vis-à-vis writings that, they believed, could but be obscure to others.

In a study of what can only be called the exception that proves the rule, Puett shows how the *Xiang'er* commentary, in effect, blends to the point of blurring beyond recognition the familiar categories of arrogance and humility, and of readerly receptivity and writerly creativity. Specifically, the *Xiang'er* insistently and explicitly subordinates itself to the *Laozi*, claiming that there was never anything hidden in that text to begin with; that a proper reading is simply a matter of not being distracted by the ingenious, overly clever interpretations that have been appended to it. The *Xiang'er* directly presents itself, writes Puett, as "simply a paraphrase of a straightforward, clear, and completely correct text." But, and here is where the peculiarity of this commentary makes its appearance, it applies this method to the most elusive, linguistically playful of all ancient texts, and so engages in misreadings so violent, interpretations so at odds with even the most obvious and conventional syntactic and semantic dictates of the words, that it would make the authors of the *Huainanzi*, whom Puett identifies as the most violent of misreaders, blush.

In the process, the *Xiang'er* draws our attention to the "play" of hiddenness, the slippery quality of what we take for granted as a clear distinction between the explicit and the implicit. There is something fascinating about a commentator who positions himself as a naïve reader, content with spotlighting the already obvious meanings of a supposedly limpid text, while then putting forth a writing that provokes some mightily vigorous head-scratching among its own readers as a way to convey that limpidity. It bears stressing that the shadowy, vexing aspect of the *Xiang'er* does not derive from any ambiguities in the language. Quite to the contrary, as Puett shows, the writing is reminiscent of that of the Mohists, dull, boring, and obvious to the extreme. Therefore, the hiddenness here is posited neither in the text of the *Xiang'er* per se nor in the *Laozi*, but in the seam that joins them: a joining that is embodied in the single person of the reading/writing commentator, and that confers value on both. Hiddenness is rarely if ever a given; it is a joint creation with its own signifying valence.

The Hidden Language of Hiding Things

As odd—even perverse—as this commentary is, the *Xiang'er* stands as a striking example, perhaps the limit case, of the extent to which hiddenness can be positioned and repositioned at will to confer value as needed. But the explicit repositioning of the hidden and the manifest is not limited to poetic or philosophical texts. The world of objects, too, as shown by three of the contributors here (Lillian Tseng, James Robson, and Eugene Wang), presents a rich venue for exploring the play of hiddenness, its reliance on complicity between the presenter and the viewer, and its intimate connection to the process by which meaning and value are created.

Lillian Tseng, in her essay "Absence and Presence: The Great Wall in Chinese Art," traces, in reverse chronology, the trajectory of representations of the Great Wall in painting and photography, demonstrating along the way that the explicitness of its renderings develops in inverse proportion to its manifest usefulness as a military defense. In other words, as the real-world presence (understood here as usefulness) of the Wall diminished, its representation in the visual arts became more manifest. Although Tseng does not venture an explanation, many possibilities come readily to mind. Certainly, this phenomenon cannot simply be explained away as a predictable transfer of power from the manifest to the symbolic, or even as a nostalgic transformation of real effectiveness into remembered grandeur—although both of these explanations have some validity. The progression of modes of representation of the Wall from complete hiddenness to monumental display is complicated by the advent of new artistic media, and increased sophistication in making them work with and against how we see.

The exploration of the capacities and limitations of particular media culminates in the work of the contemporary artist, Xu Bing, whose oeuvre as a whole invariably draws the viewer's attention to just this problem. To what extent does the reproduction of a once-irreproducible monument keep alive what history has eliminated? And to what extent do particular modes of making the hidden manifest—not just visible, but also tangible—make a mockery of any such project? Xu encapsulates the diachronic narrative of the Wall's real-world diminishment in a spatial installation that compels the viewer to confront the perceptual capacities and limitations of her body, even as she encounters the simultaneous monumentality and fragility of the Wall. The Wall, like history itself, is as immense as it is textured; and as unassailable as it is volatile. Before it, the viewer's perception, like the circumscribed nature of the span of a lifetime, restricts us to forms of knowledge that can take in either immensity or texture, not both.

Implicit in Xu's immense installation would seem to be the converse argument of our recurring assertion that hiddenness is a matter of complicity between the hider and the seeker; for, as true as it is that the successful hider does not unilaterally impose hiddenness on the seeker, there are nevertheless conditions that impose hiddenness on corners of the world that encompass us all, hiders and seekers alike. The story of the Great Wall's history of visual representation, especially as it culminates in *Ghosts Pounding the Wall*, stands as a reminder of the realm of hiddenness that stands, impenetrably, just beyond the edge of the time and space that an individual body can inhabit. It reminds us, too, of our unending yearning for fullness, for complete illumination beyond that edge: the very yearning that grants hiddenness its value and its power. As we recall, Li Shangyin's lowered yet translucent curtains, illuminated by his carefully half-dimmed lamp, stand as the lyrical testament to the importance of preserving the yearning, since its object is inaccessible; Xu Bing's *Ghosts* confirms that yearning and wonder may be our only options.

The darkness that stands ineluctably at the margins of any one mortal's presence and perception is the focus of mystical rumination and theological inquiry, in traditional China as elsewhere. Those who study religion will inevitably find themselves drawn to this subject as well. As James Robson points out in the essay included here, religious studies has, in recent years, paid particular attention to the nature of hiddenness and secrecy; nevertheless, sometimes the most intense scrutiny can still unintentionally overlook the most carefully framed esoteric gesture. In "Hidden in Plain View: Concealed Contents, Secluded Statues, and Revealed Religion," Robson looks at the flip side of the unspoken accord that joins hiders and seekers in a common quest to define and discern what warrants interpretation: that is, the problems that arise when that contract is broken. What happens, he queries, when researchers, whose job it is to uncover hidden meaning, are distracted by the methodological blind spots that steer them away from what hiders framed for discovery?

The question is apt. True, accusations of wrongheadedness are part and parcel of the world of hermeneutics as it is practiced across all fields; and considering the close link between hiddenness and valuation, one might even argue that this type of antagonism is a necessary part of the process of imparting value as we uncover meaning. Yet Robson successfully isolates a case where the blind spot is especially troubling: our sustained and puzzling inattention to a particularly widespread type of deity statue. These statues contain a cavity in its back in which objects and documents—believed to animate the deity statue—are secreted. This essay affords us a look at two layers of hiddenness: one on the part of the seekers, inhabited by a cultural prejudice against "iconoclasm," and the other created, with ritual intentions, by the makers of the statues.

These two forms of hiddenness dovetail in a way that shows that, just as certain types of hiddenness lend value to their object, that value can be reduced—or even erased—when the rhetoric of hiddenness itself becomes obfuscated in the course of transmission. Robson's explorations, then, are doubly productive, for by explicitly establishing new grounds for complicity between the hider (the religious community that makes and circulates the statues) and seeker (the researcher trying to make sense of them), he succeeds in both restoring to the statues the value that hiddenness provides and bestowing on their hidden contents the long-untapped power to animate them.

As the essays by Li, Puett, and Robson suggest, complicity between writers and readers (or, more broadly, hiders and seekers) can be vexed and fragile; and the locus of hiddenness will shift accordingly. Sophie Volpp takes on the precise nature of that quality of slipperiness in yet another context: one where it might be said that the burden of recognizing—or even creating—hidden value rests squarely with what we have thus far called the seeker. In her essay, "The Vernacular Story and the Hiddenness of Value," Volpp analyzes a vernacular tale written by Ling Mengchu 淩濛初 (1580–1644), where she brings into a productive dialogue the traditional bipolarity of *xu* 虛 and *shi* 實 with the Americanist Bill Brown's analysis of the elusive unintelligibility of the thing and the concrete intelligibility of objects. In the process, she changes the terms we have been relying on thus far.

As if to counter any unchallenged assumptions that there is a necessary and uncomplicated connection between hiddenness (or, in her terms, unintelligibility) and value, Volpp marshals Ling's tale to show the futility of establishing value on that basis. Hiddenness, opacity, and unintelligibility shift in accordance with the larger cultural, economic, and linguistic contexts through which the hider, seeker, and thing constantly travel; transparency and ready intelligibility do not reliably signal the absence of value. By presenting to us the literary mechanisms through which Ling exposes the mutability *and* inextricability of meaningfulness and meaninglessness, of illusory value and real value, Volpp—in her own way acting like Sikong Tu, the author of the *Twenty-Four Modes of Poetry*—finally, but not incidentally, compels us to reconsider our own habits of reading. Are vernacular stories, which we have long held to be transparent narratives of reality, necessarily free of hidden recesses of unexpressed meaning? Conversely, one might then ask, are poems—especially hermetic ones such as those by Li Shangyin—necessarily repositories of richly meaningful hidden depths? And finally, are our own scholarly attempts to bring hidden textual significance to the surface just so much transparent explication, impervious to the kind of mining to which we habitually subject ostensibly literary writings? If Robson has shown us the ease with which an unintentionally broken contract between hiders and seekers can mute the rhetoric of hiddenness, Volpp shows that, at least by the late sixteenth century, there arose some recognition that the intentions of either party do not play as definitive a role in the rhetoric of hiddenness as one might have thought: that things—and the value they seem to bear—have a fate of their own.[17]

Making and Remaking Connections

The reality of broken or unformed complicities, and the overdetermined fate of objects both hidden and manifest, far from negating the signifying force of a rhetoric of hiddenness, confirm the degree to which hiddenness should be thought of as something that, by its very nature, is ever in a state of "play." Furthermore, since indeterminacy itself is subject to patterning, it is worth investigating the mechanisms of that play. In practical terms, it bears asking whether there is a nonreductive way to identify the patterns and codes that readers, beholders—all seekers working within the Chinese tradition—apply when attempting to discern the presence, nature, and value of the hidden. The import of this question is obvious, for it attempts to understand and find a flexible formula for the ubiquitous human endeavor of hermeneutics in the context of a particular culture and language. Can we identify a pattern according to which traditional Chinese readers of texts wrest meaning from signs?

A couple of decades ago, Stephen Owen and Pauline Yu formulated a controversial response to this question when they demonstrated, each from a slightly different standpoint, that traditional Chinese poetics tends toward the metonymical structure of synecdoche, with metaphor—if and when it does occur—taking a secondary position. In this volume, Owen revisits this idea in an essay titled, "Synecdoche of the Imaginary." In this study of "poetic mist," and the increased signifying weight it came to bear in the poetry of the ninth century, Owen shows that in fact mist had a relatively short life as a strong poetic signifier. It gradually changed from an infrequent evocative atmospheric image to a resonant organizer of felt time and space, and finally to a poetic cliché—all in less than two centuries. This may strike the reader of these pages as surprising, not only because mist seems like the synecdochal sign par excellence, but also because, given the centrality of situatedness in the construction of a rhetoric of hiddenness, mist strikes one as a most apt signifier.[18]

As Owen shows, mist at its most eloquent activates the perceptual experience of recession and emergence, linking vision with memory on the one hand, and potentiality with hope on the other. Unlike the cover of darkness, it imbues space with three-dimensionality, and reminds us that, given our situatedness, we can only ever see a part of an otherwise inaccessible whole. Indeed, situatedness is the language of much of Chinese poetry itself, the language that signifies through the dynamic play between the hidden and the manifest, and not through the assertion of a stable equation between the two. Owen reminds us that even when mist can be metaphorically equated with the resistance to empire, as it is in the many ninth-century poems that foreground the legendary Fan Li's 范蠡 disappearance into the "misty waves," that is not where its poetic power lies. Rather, it is to be found in its capacity to render the whole into its parts, and to thereby ignite some form of desire in the reader, the seeker: the desire to know, the desire to re-experience, the desire to follow.

Li Shangyin, himself a ninth-century poet, did not use mist in his poem "Lamp." But, he did use the mist-like technique that Owen calls "couplet collage" to similar effect. Just as poetic mist stirs up the desire to connect what has just disappeared from view to what is on the point of emerging, so Li's enigmatic leaps from image to image, couplet to couplet, teach the reader about the nature of that desire, and, in the end, about the wisdom of acquiescence to the pleasure and pain of only partial vision.

Owen notes that poetic mist would fulfill its poetic potential in the medium of painting in later centuries. Eugene Wang's contribution to this book, " 'The Disarrayed Hills Conceal an Old Monastery': Poetry/Painting Dynamics in the Northern Song (960–1127)," captures the complexities of that moment, when painters were called on to translate an aesthetic derived directly from poetry, the "the sense of concealment" or *cangyi* 藏意. The centrality of visual imagery in traditional Chinese poetry might lead one to assume that such a translation would be easy; Owen's discussion of mist implies as much. And yet, competing social, ethical, and religious connotations of particular images and modes of representation made the requirement surprisingly difficult to fulfill. Furthermore, "suggestive concealment"—whether through obstructing hills, tree branches, or mist—served many purposes, including, but not limited to, the obedient display of poetic consciousness by would-be artisanal painters. Ultimately, by the mid–twelfth century, the best way, the most poetic way, to paint the desolated monastery is judged to be not to paint it all. Paintings belonging to the subgenre known as "The Disarrayed Hills Conceal an Old Monastery" do not convey the monastery, but its concealment; for a depicted monastery would only be, at best, a distraction (to borrow, once again, Kuriyama's observations) and, at worst, a crass testament to the lurid, empty ornamentation characteristic of so many real Buddhist monasteries of the time. Whether the selected mode of concealment is applied to Fan Li's boat or the old monastery, the arbiters of "good" poetry and painting help keep the makers and the readers engaged in the complicated dance of hiddenness, where the yearning to see trumps the satisfactions of merely seeing. Almost as if taking Li Shangyin's advice, they keep the curtains lowered, the flame only half-burning.

How to Read This Book

Turning, at last, to the book at hand, readers will already have noted that the range of topics is broad, encompassing fields of human endeavor that include early Chinese politics, medicine, literature, religion, philosophy, and the visual arts. The chronological reach is deep as well, spanning the two millennia from the Warring States period up through the Qing Dynasty, and comes full circle with a discussion of a contemporary representation of an ancient icon. By the end, it turns out that the most consistently productive concept in thinking about the rhetoric of hiddenness is not reliably rhetorical, but a matter of "play": play as performance, yes, but also and more importantly, play in the sense of all that is interactive, dynamic, and in process.

The purpose of this introduction has not been to provide easy access to the project at hand, but to inspire a complete reading of the volume by putting the reader in a particular frame of mind. Since the workings of hiddenness in premodern Chinese culture are better revealed through the process of discovery than through synthetic formulation, the hope is that, after patiently working their way through this multilayered discovery of the rhetoric of hiddenness, readers will be incited to read on and experience the juxtaposition of its different modes—for it is only in their cumulative juxtaposition that its full rhetorical force becomes evident. It seemed a more helpful way to convey what happens when "the yearning to see trumps the satisfactions of merely seeing."

For the reader who works her way through this introduction, the structure of the volume will then serve as an additional guide through the material. If hiddenness is both a kind of hermeneutical contract between the makers of texts (broadly defined) and their "readers," and shaped by shifting perspectives occupied by a shifting readership, then a chronological or even disciplinary organizational schema would only obfuscate that essential characteristic. Instead, this volume is organized along the lines of selected strategies that play on and mirror particular modes of writer/reader interaction and readerly perspective—not as they are activated within particular media or disciplines, but across them. Among these are: withholding, distraction, the manipulation and creation of blind spots, and the use of synecdoche. The final two chapters, by Michael Puett and Zong-qi Cai respectively, form an apt "epilogue," meditating as they do on the consequences and complications that arise from our irrepressible tendency to espouse one or another language in the quest to make accessible what we hold to be essential.

Note on Language Conventions

- Individual contributors to this volume have been encouraged to maintain their own considered translations of key Chinese terms, expressions, and even proper nouns, rather than submit to one unifying rendering across the volume. Readers may consult the index for pinyin renderings of the Chinese as well as for all translations used in this volume, which will permit them to cross-reference any given term or expression among the chapters.
- Traditional Chinese characters have been used throughout this volume, including in the notes, regardless of whether the cited work was published in traditional or simplified Chinese characters.

Notes

1. Liu Xuekai 劉學鍇 and Yu Shucheng 余恕誠, eds., *Li Shangyin shige jijie* 李商隱詩歌集解 (Beijing: Zhonghua shuju, 2007), 810–14. Cf. Stephen Owen's translation in his *The Late Tang: Chinese Poetry of the Mid-Ninth Century (827–860)* (Cambridge, MA: Harvard University Press, 2006), 474.

2. One cogent discussion of this phenomenon is to be found in an essay by Jonathan Culler, who points out that "Depersonalization, instead of eliminating the category of person, leads to the construction and explication of a speaker." See his "On the Negativity of Modern Poetry: Friedrich, Baudelaire, and the Critical Tradition"

in Sanford Budick and Wolfgang Iser, eds., *Languages of the Unsayable: The Play of Negativity in Literature and Literary Theory* (Stanford, CA: Stanford University Press, 1987), 193.

3. Schaberg rightly points out that the "mediation of *qing* in language and settings, and the value placed on concealing *qing* from potential exploiters, is perhaps early Chinese oratory's legacy to the . . . literati of later times" (p. 48).

4. In normative *yongwu* poems dating as far back as the Han, even this formulaic gesture of hiding is balanced with an enumerative fullness: a meticulously logical ordering of the thing's constituent properties. The combination of thoroughness and orderliness would, inadvertently or not, emphasize both the objective givenness of the thing being verbally constructed before our eyes, and trace the underlying unifying principle—indicative of the (hidden) writer's perspective—bringing those features together in a recognizable whole.

5. For some helpful discussions of the continuity between *yongwu fu* and *yongwu shi* see Kang-i Sun Chang, *Six Dynasties Poetry* (Princeton, NJ: Princeton University Press, 1986), 93; Liao Guodong 廖國棟, *Wei Jin yongwu fu yanjiu* 魏晋詠物賦研究 (Taipei: Wenshizhe chubanshe, 1990); Cynthia Chennault, "Odes on Objects and Patronage During the Southern Qi" in *Studies in Early Medieval Chinese Literature and Cultural History: In Honor of Richard B. Mather and Donald Holzman*, eds. Paul W. Kroll and David R. Knechtges (Provo, UT: T'ang Studies Society, 2003), 331–98; Lin Tianxiang 林天祥, *Bei Song yongwu fu yanjiu* 北宋詠物賦研究 (Taipei: Wanjuanlou tushuguan, 2004). Most recently, and of greatest relevance to the subject at hand, see Xiaofei Tian, *Beacon Fire and Shooting Star: The Literary Culture of the Liang (502–557)* (Cambridge, MA: Harvard University Press, 2007), 214–24.

6. For the most thorough treatment of Six Dynasties poems on lamps and candles, see Xiaofei Tian's chapter, "Illusion and Illumination: A New Poetics of Seeing" in *Beacon Fire*, 211–59.

7. See esp. Tian's discussion of such poems in her *Beacon Fire*, 214–20.

8. *YFSJ*, 42.616.

9. *YWLJ*, 1.

10. *YFSJ*, 28.419.

11. At this point in the discussion, it seems helpful to change the translation of the indeterminate subject of this line from "it" to "she" and "its" to "her"; both, of course, are implied.

12. Stephen Owen makes this point in his essay below (pp. 267–68).

13. It seems likely, too, that Li had in mind the well-known story in which Emperor Wu of the Han who is tricked by a magician into thinking he sees, through a curtained enclosure lit by lamps and candles, the spirit of his beloved deceased Lady Li. The vision intensified his pain and longing such that he composed a poem. See *Hanshu* 97.3952.

14. Closely related to this question of the use of hiddenness to create, legitimize, and capitalize on the connection between knowledge and power is the highly developed discourse on the sociology of secrecy in esoteric cults. For a thoughtful review and emendation of the scholarship as it pertains to China, see Robert Campany, "Secrecy

and Display in the Quest for Transcendence in China, ca. 220 BCE–350 CE" in *The History of Religions* 45, no. 4 (May 2006): 291–336.

15. *Zhouyi zhengyi*, 8.74.

16. *Mengzi* V. B. 8.ii.

17. Pauline Yu, in an essay that presents examples of the many ways in which hiddenness functions in the Chinese literary tradition, probes the difficulties of delimiting both the cause and the effect of its presence in any given text. See her "Hidden in Plain Sight?: The Art of Hiding in Chinese Poetry," in *Chinese Literature: Essays, Articles, Reviews (*CLEAR*)* 30 (Dec. 2008): 179–86.

18. For a relevant discussion of how clouds function as a sign or "graph" in the history of Western painting, see Hubert Damisch, *A Theory of /Cloud/: Toward a History of Painting*, trans. Janet Lloyd (Stanford: Stanford University Press, 2002). See esp. the chapter "Syntactical Space," 82–124.

The Art of Withholding

2

The Ruling Mind

Persuasion and the Origins of Chinese Psychology

DAVID SCHABERG

In China, no less than in Greece, psychological theory has its deepest roots in the practicalities of oratorical method. Early Chinese narratives, a huge number of which purport to recount episodes of persuasion, bespeak a keen interest in the emotions of the hearer, the seeming character of the speaker, and the matching of subtle psychological manipulation with verbal argument. Just as for Aristotle and a whole lineage of European rhetoricians, the early Chinese oration, its arguments, and its performative accoutrements were designed to create conviction rather than truth.[1] Several influential accounts of the individual emotions and of *qing* 情 ("state of affairs," psychological or other) read less convincingly as disinterested depictions of the human psyche than as user's manuals and guides to the obscure inner territory that the learned individual is to discover and cultivate. This is not merely a matter of self-cultivation, though self-cultivation has regularly been understood as the implicit aim of much early Chinese philosophical writing and reading. Self-cultivation belongs with the cultivation of others, for example, of students by their teachers in pedagogical persuasion, or of a ruler by his subjects in deliberative persuasion; emotional models and manipulative savoir-faire serve in every case. The needs of the orator may not account entirely for the genesis of psychological models in China, but they cannot be neglected as a contributing factor.

It would be an exaggeration to say that the ruler was the sole decision-maker in early Chinese courts, since key policy matters were frequently or regularly submitted to groups of councilors for discussion. Yet decision and execution were as a rule attributed to the ruler as an individual, and persuasion was understood to be addressed to and routed through the mind of this individual. Where Aristotle's plural "hearers" were subject to the relatively open and observable emotions of the group, the early Chinese target of persuasion was less perfectly knowable and, potentially at least, entirely hidden. The ruling mind became the most crucial mind, the one whose pleasures and passions mattered most and the one to which, more than to any other, enticements and admonitions were addressed. Long after the heyday of Chinese oratory, the hidden psyche and its true *qing* would retain some of the qualities they acquired in this first era of persuasion.

Psychology in Anecdotes of Oratorical Expertise

The notion of a psychological manipulation that goes on around the edges of the speech proper presumes an adversative relationship between speaker and hearer. If the persuader succeeds in turning his ideas into the ruler's actions, then his wisdom will have replaced the ruler's original inclinations, and these in turn will be revealed in retrospect as wrong or shortsighted. Anecdotes often award praise and success to rulers who accept advice, far less often to rulers who rightly reject bad advice. The emphasis is on how advisors can make up the ruler's mind.

But the early Chinese corpus differs from some others, including the Greek, in assigning a slightly more prominent role to archaic rulers who had minds of their own and needed no correction. Because these sages combine in themselves the best plans and the most attractive and effective psychological makeup, little opposition can build up around them. Especially in the mode associated with Ru 儒 thinkers, the sages' minds are perfectly open to the inspection of all their subjects. Their aides work for them like their own limbs, and the common people follow them out of a conviction born from affection. No one plays on the sage's emotions. He is his own orator, and his emotions play on those of the world he rules.

In sagehood's idealized collapse of all rhetorical hiding and plotting, the ruler makes his own emotions and character inseparable from those of his subjects. The *Shuoyuan* 說苑 of Liu Xiang 劉向 (79–8 BCE) attributes an exaggerated version of this vision to the Western Han lover of antiquity, Prince Xian 獻 of Hejian 河間 (r. 155–129 BCE), who is reported to have said, "Yao set his mind on the world and imposed his aims upon the needy people. He felt pain when any in the ten thousand clans was implicated in some crime and felt sorrow when any among the many living things did not get ahead. If there was one man who suffered hunger, Yao said, 'This is because I made him hungry' . . . Yao's humaneness shone forth and his dutifulness stood firm; his virtue was broad and his transformations widespread."[2] The vision advanced is ultimately the familiar one of transformation through moral example. But the emphasis on emotional vulnerability and the effect of character are interesting specifications. As Yao "sets his mind" (*cun xin* 存心) upon the world, he makes his mind the index of the world's emotional events and his character the mold for all its characters. For mournful sages from Yao and Yu 禹 to King Wen 文 and the Duke of Zhou—to judge from the anecdotal accounts—ruling was a matter of constant responsibility and constant worry. Along with an openness to the petitions and complaints of subjects, sorrow and fear were regarded as the hallmarks of the excellent ruler.[3] This ruler is his own persuader, and he persuades perfectly by asserting an identity of emotion and character between himself and the audience he represents.

But excellent rulers of this kind, held up as examples in Warring States texts, were always a thing of the past. As idealized alternatives, they point up the qualities regarded as most important and problematic in the Warring States ruler: his opacity, his apathy, his fecklessness, and his ruthlessness. Yao had identified with his subjects so as to correct their character flaws, but contemporary rulers were simply as poorly made and unreformed as anyone else.

Among the hundreds of accounts of persuasions before Warring States rulers there are many that feature a canny grasp of psychological opportunity. Sometimes it is simply a matter of sharing the ruler's sorrow or worrying on his behalf. An anonymous Yan envoy addresses the Qin king: "Should you now cause Zhao to advance northward and annex Yan, then Yan and Zhao with their combined strength are sure to stop accepting [commands] from you. I presume to worry about (*huan* 患) this on your behalf."[4] An unspecified persuader recites for the Wei king a plot he has learned of: "When I heard these words, I presumed to sorrow (*bei* 悲) for you, your highness: Qin is certain to use this against you."[5] The orator regularly and implicitly claims to share the ruler's worries and to use all his skills of calculation to remove the source of these worries. The intellectual content of any speech, its overt strategic recommendation, is thus framed as part of an overall effort to manage the ruler's emotions and to maximize his pleasures. The *Mengzi*, discussed below for its scheme of the human psyche, likewise shows an abiding concern with maximizing the pleasures of the listener.

The potential for manipulation is obvious, and the sorts of persuaders and strategists who are celebrated in the *Zhanguo ce* and other handbooks of guile are quick to capitalize on their psychological expertise. The readiest emotional tool is anger. Aristotle's observations are relevant to the Chinese case: anger results from a "conspicuous slight at the hands of men who have no call to slight oneself" (1378a). Warring States persuaders counted on rulers' and others' fundamentally social sense of hierarchy, spurring action where honor was called into question.

The renowned persuader Cai Ze 蔡澤 raises himself from extreme destitution by a masterly play on anger. Arriving in Qin and having heard of the prime minister's errors and his secret shame (*nei can* 內慚) about certain offenses he has committed, Cai Ze sends people around to spread a rumor: "The visitor from Yan, Cai Ze, is one of the towering heroes of the world, a man broadly learned and discerning in his judgments. If he should have one audience with the king of Qin, the king is sure to appoint him minister and deprive our lord [i.e. the Ying Marquis] of his position." The Ying Marquis, whom Cai Ze does plan to replace, summons him to an audience and asks for an explanation.[6] But by the time the Marquis asks for reasons, he has already been bested on the psychological field. In order to gain the audience, Cai Ze has exploited the Marquis's secret shame and conspicuously attacked his pretension of unmatched mastery and power, provoking exactly the kind of anger Aristotle would have predicted. In his explanation, then, Cai Ze argues that everything that reaches its acme must thereafter fall, and that the Marquis has reached his acme; if he goes on any longer, he must resemble ministers like Shang Yang 商鞅 (fl. 359–338 BCE), who rose to the heights only to die miserably. Thus Cai Ze recognizes that power brings a jealous sense of honor; piques his target's shame, jealousy, and anger to gain access; and then offers his target a plan to preserve his power. As predicted, the Marquis does yield his position to Cai Ze within days, though not for reasons that he himself could entirely understand.

The confidence that persuaders were thought to have in the psychological manipulability of their targets is captured in the term *bi* 必 ("must," "is certain to," "cannot but"), with which these persuaders often link chains of predicted consequences. At one point King Huai 懷 of Chu (r. late fourth c. BCE) imprisons the great pro-Qin persuader Zhang Yi 張儀 and prepares to put him to death. A Chu man, Jin Shang 靳尚, secures Zhang Yi's release with a double appeal. First he addresses the king: "If you imprison Zhang Yi, the king of Qin is certain to be angry. And when the world sees that Chu lacks Qin's help, Chu is certain (*bi* 必) to lose the weight of its influence." He reinforces this by a more secretive approach, an appeal to the king's favorite woman, Zheng Xiu 鄭袖. "Are you aware that you are about to fall low in the king's favor?" To free Zhang Yi, the Qin king will give a beloved daughter of his own (*ai nü* 愛女), plus trinkets and treasures and territory as her dowry, and with these she will work on the Chu king to release Zhang Yi. The Chu king "is certain to love her" (*bi ai* 必愛); the more intoxicated he becomes with the wealth and Qin backing she has brought, he "is certain (*bi*) to revere her and love her richly," while forgetting about Zheng Xiu. But if Zheng Xiu herself urges the king to release Zhang Yi, then "the Qin woman is certain (*bi*) not to come and Qin is certain (*bi*) to give great weight to" Zheng Xiu. And with domestic honor, foreign connections, and the gratitude of Zhang Yi, Zheng Xiu will win the favorite's fondest goal: her "sons and grandsons are certain (*bi*) to be their heirs to Chu."[7]

One might argue that predictions of the sort Jin Shang uses do not resemble the psychological manipulation that Aristotle had in mind in the *Rhetoric*. Jin Shang details psychological reactions openly in his various hypotheticals, and in certain cases—such as Chu's likely loss of influence with its allies if Qin abandons it—the predictions require little in the way of psychological insight. If all of the psychology is there to see in the very words of the speech, then this is something other than the unacknowledged provocation that the Greek orators favored. But in fact, the psychology is both on the surface of the persuasions and below the surface. Jin Shang's prediction of psychological effects elsewhere is what permits him to achieve his psychological aims here and now. None of the other predictions will be put to the test; all that matters is that Jin Shang correctly predict the effects of his words on his present targets. Once the king and Zheng Xiu believe that Jin Shang's hypotheses are correct, they will do as he proposes. Thus the real locus of psychological certainty is the persuaded person, who is created as a predictable psychological subject by being convinced of a specious predictability in others.

In contrast to the sage and to persuaders who (like Mengzi) hold themselves up for emulation, the practical persuader is closed to observation. He may know much about how the human mind works and can be made to work, but his character does not bear imitation. In their role as teachers and ritual guides, the Ru duly sought to create a certain kind of predictable subject through character example and empathy (if we may translate *shu* 恕 that way), encouraging a communication of emotion up and down the social hierarchy. They further emphasized constant standards (*chang* 常, *jing* 經, *li* 禮, and the like) that could serve as the outward settings and supports for the cultivated character and that would minimize hiddenness in individuals and changes in society. Meanwhile, persuaders who did not identify with *Ru* teachings were guided by the exigencies of whatever plot they were pushing. The only constants that mattered were verities of human psychological response and of cause and effect in the social and natural worlds. Other truths were only the sorts of temporarily effective truths that could be created in the minds of hearers.

As it happens, *qing* 情 is the word that in early Chinese denotes these three varieties of truth: psychological constants, underlying social and natural dynamics, and personal responses to situations. It is a grasp of *qing* that persuaders count on when they set about calculating hypothetical consequences and manipulating hearers. The *Han Feizi* 韓非子 warns against too precipitous an attempt to get close to a ruler and to divine his private *qing*, though as we shall see the same text offers an unmatched program for the manipulation of *qing*.[8] Yu Qing 虞卿 begins an appeal to the king of Zhao with these words: "Is it the *qing* of a human being to prefer to receive a court visit from others? Or rather to pay a court visit to another person?" 人之情，寧朝人乎？寧朝於人也.[9] Bu Pi 卜皮, suspicious of a corrupt underling, directs his own young son to feign love for the underling's beloved concubine (*ai qie* 愛妾), and in this way learns all the hidden facts (*yin qing* 陰情) of his household.[10] *Qing* may be specifically emotional or simply secret; the main thing is that it is something subject to hiding, and therefore to the threat of exposure, and therefore to exploitation. As in the case of Bu Pi's stratagem, the connection with strong emotions such as love makes the truths more important to hide and easier to exploit.

All of the several emotions normally listed in résumés of *qing* are at one point or another used as secret sources of persuasive leverage. Anger (*nu* 怒) and love (*ai*) we have seen already. The Yan king is "certain to be pleased" (*bi xi* 必喜) if a rebellious general returns, suggests a persuader plotting on behalf of the general.[11] Signs of mournfulness (*ai* 哀) and love alike are invoked in a persuasion before a queen dowager of Zhao.[12] Fear (*ju* 懼) is a reliable quantity in the military calculations of a Chu persuader strategizing against the statelet of Western Zhou.[13] A Chu consort destroys a rival by manipulating impressions of the king's loathing (*wu* 惡).[14] By his very character (*wei ren* 為人), a certain Chu king has a fondness (*hao* 好) for warfare and can be counted on to behave predictably; calculations based on desire (*yu* 欲) work similarly.[15]

Emotional effect and response do have a public face, as in those texts that urge rulers to count on the emulousness of their subjects: because resources always gather at court and subjects always seek to attract favor by imitating the king's taste, the latter can institute moral change simply by showing a fondness (*hao*) for it. The *Mozi* 墨子 makes this point most straightforwardly, but it also underlies Ru notions of the effectiveness of sages.[16] Such hopes for an open, beneficent emotional leadership linger even as a competing model of the ruler comes to dominate realistic discourse on governance. In this competing model, the ruler controls his subjects through selective displays of taste and, more often, through complete opacity. The *Han Feizi* carries the clearest technical advice on these methods, with the *Laozi* 老子 advocating them less directly.[17] The ruler cannot afford to be a public personality or to make any of his emotional truths—his *qing*—known, since every one of them is a potential source of psychological leverage. With the triumph of this vision of the hidden ruler, the ruler is himself forced to adopt the position of expert manipulator, and the persuaders' model of a closed and private personality is established as the norm.

Schemes of *Qing*

Just as exemplary tales of persuasion betoken a mastery of *qing* and its uses, systematic (that is, nonnarrative) accounts of *qing* likewise show a certain adaptation to the needs of manipulators. More generally, early Chinese thinkers' and writers' efforts to develop models of the invisible human psyche do not arise ex nihilo, but reflect in concrete ways some of their external motivations for speaking and writing.

It is useful to begin with the *Han Feizi*, which as noted above names *qing* as something that the speaker must never seem to be probing when he pursues his aims.[18] The text does not otherwise offer a catalog of *qing* or a model of the psyche.[19] Yet because of its concern with practical oratory, it does offer a guide to the intricacies of the ruler's psychological and emotional responses. The "Shui nan" 說難 ("Difficulties of persuading") chapter holds that the real challenge in oratory lies in "knowing the mind of the person being persuaded and in being able to match one's persuasion with it" 知所說之心，可以吾說當之.[20] There follows a uniquely sophisticated analysis of this mind (*xin* 心), with emphasis on its specious pretenses and its hidden truths. Many of the latter are by definition emotional in nature. The ruler has some fondness or desire that motivates him, and the speaker must know what it is. No one will succeed by promising the profit-loving ruler good reputation, or the glory-loving ruler profit: one who does so will "appear mindless and divorced from the truth of affairs, and [the ruler] will certainly not accept his case." Further, the speaker must avoid endangering his own life by stumbling on something the ruler has hoped to keep secret or by seeming to fawn. "The key in all types of persuasion," Han Fei writes, "is to know how to beautify whatever the target is proud of and to smother anything he is ashamed of." For example, if he has some private matter that is pressing to him (*si ji* 私急), support it with an appeal to some public duty (*gong yi* 公義). Speak of admirable goals and noble motivations, but appeal quietly to his baser attachments and aims. Never disturb his image of himself, whether he considers himself potent or resolute or cunning. Ultimately, by this approach, the persuader will enjoy the ruler's dear confidence and will be able to "give free rein to his wit and discernment" (*ji pin zhibian* 極騁智辯) and "fully have his say" (*jin ci* 盡辭).[21]

Stable models of the psyche are apparently irrelevant here, either because they are too speculative to be useful or because they offer no sure rhetorical purchase. For Han Fei, as for the persuader, the psyche is largely invisible. One proceeds not by a road map, but by a series of educated shots in the dark. The persuader must have the wherewithal to address a ruler's private motivations in terms suitable for all in court to overhear. He must be able to play confidently on both sides of the divide between private (*si* 私) and commonly shared (*gong* 公). He is quite literally a master of the *yin* 陰 ("shaded, hidden") and the *yang* 陽 ("open, overt"); in the literature of persuasion and strategy, the latter term was also written *yang* 佯 ("pretended, fake").[22] His expertise is entirely a matter of reliable intelligence and *ad hoc* psychological acuity.

The *Han Feizi*'s approach might be deemed stochastic: one aims carefully and hopes to hit something useful. Most other Warring States texts that address the psyche prefer a schematic approach, and it is this approach that has dominated later scholarly investigations of early Chinese notions of mind. The attention that twentieth-century philosophers have given to the question of *xing* 性 ("human nature"); their interest in *qi* 氣, in the "heart-mind" (*xin* 心), and in the Chinese take on the mind-body problem; even the efforts to understand the two-part soul, the *hun* 魂 and *po* 魄, that some early texts mention: all these reflect a desire to capture or reconstruct some characteristically pre-Buddhist Chinese model of the psyche. But even as they downplay nonschematic and pragmatic approaches to the psyche—like the *Han Feizi*'s guide to manipulation—they neglect certain clues as to the practical utility of the schematic models themselves. The philosophy of mind, as it appeared in fits and bursts in Warring States texts, was not the product of an unconditional quest for the truth, any more than Aristotle's account of the emotions was. It had its uses, and these were not limited to self-cultivation or the effort to create the "gentleman" (*junzi* 君子); schemata of the mind show a real connection with the aims of persuasion and manipulation.

The *Mengzi* 孟子, which is all too rarely read for its celebration of practical oratorical skills, foregrounds the thinker-persuader's psychological discernment, his role as a sage-like transforming moral model, and his promise to secure happiness for the ruler who would heed him.[23] In view of the text's emphasis on emotional management, it is not surprising that the *Mengzi* also contains one of the most influential early models of the human mind. This model is the familiar exposition of the "four germs" or "four starting-points" (*si duan* 四端) (*Mengzi* 2A.6).[24] Mengzi states that every person has a heart that cannot bear to treat others cruelly. Since the issue of bearing to be cruel (*ren* 忍) is raised primarily in connection with kings elsewhere in the *Mengzi* (1A.7, 4A.1), one must wonder at the outset whether Mengzi's thesis on human beings is not most pertinently a statement on the emotional susceptibilities of kings.[25] Mengzi continues by observing that the former kings had hearts of this sort and practiced governance of this sort; for rulers like them, governing the world would be like rolling something in the palm of one's hand. This preamble immediately suggests an appeal to kings, whom Mengzi often cajoles with promises of the effectiveness of moral display in governing. Mengzi may well be proposing a general psychological principle for human beings, but he is also offering his readers and imitators an authoritative vision of the good king's psychology. Knowing what one's target can and cannot bear to do—or being able to define those things for him—is a powerful sort of leverage, and is in fact used in discussion of the sacrificial ox at *Mengzi* 1A.7. Mengzi's vision of the former kings matches the *Shuoyuan*'s depiction of Yao as emotionally open; but Mengzi will exploit his insight in his appeals to the closed minds of contemporary rulers.

Mengzi's basis for claiming that everyone has a heart of this kind is his well-known observation that anyone in the world would rescue a baby from the edge of a well, and would do so without consideration of profit, simply because of a feeling of alarm and compassion. This feeling of compassion is a defining characteristic, a sine qua non, of the human being, as are three others outlined in parallel with it (though without experiential demonstrations corresponding to the baby test): the feeling of shame and loathing; the feeling of deference and yielding; and the feeling of correctness and incorrectness. These are the famous "four starting-points," of humaneness (*ren* 仁), rightness (*yi* 義), ritual propriety (*li* 禮), and knowledge (*zhi* 智), respectively.

The four *duan* are indeed basic to human psychology: "People have these four starting-points just as they have their four limbs; anyone who has these four starting-points and yet claims he is lacking in ability [to achieve the four virtues] is maiming himself." But they are also immediately guides to the prescriptive psychology of the ruler under persuasion: "Anyone who claims his ruler is lacking in ability is maiming his ruler." Mengzi concludes: "For anyone who has the four *duan* in himself and who knows how to enlarge (*kuo* 擴) them and fill them out (*chong* 充), they are like fire when it first catches or a stream of water when it first trickles through. Just as long as one is able to fill them out, they are sufficient for the guarding of all within the four seas; but if one does not fill them out, they are not sufficient for serving one's parents." Throughout the passage, running in parallel with a general human psychology and a general project of self-cultivation or education, there is the particular theme—apparently the one psychological project that merits marking in this way—of the ruler's attitude toward cruelty, the ruler's four starting-points, and the ruler's ability to "guard all within the four seas," that is, to govern a unified world.

A. C. Graham was the first to propose the translation "starting-point" for the term *duan*, though he did so only in the case of a Later Mohist definition. For *Mengzi* 2A.6 he preferred "shoots."[26] The decision is hard to understand. In Mencian terms, one who "enlarges" and "fills out" shoots could hardly be better than someone who, like the old man of Song, "pulled up" (*ya* 揠) his seedlings (2A.2).

Clearly the *si duan* are not the starting-points of lines, as in the *Mozi*. Instead, they may be the starting-points of opinions of the sort reached through persuasion and argumentation. In the *Han Feizi*, *duan* is used in parallel construction with *qing* and appears to refer to a point of access for the persuader: "Now if the ruler of men does not conceal his *qing* and hide his starting-points, and in this way causes the subjects to have a route by which to attack their ruler, then it will not be difficult for his subjects to behave like [the usurpers] Zizhi and Tian Chang."[27] These starting-points may have a special connection with the ruler's process of study: "What is more, as the ruler of men gives his ear to studies, if he affirms someone's words, then it is fitting that he should assign him an official position and employ his person, while if he denies his words, then it is fitting that he should remove his person and put a stop to his starting-points."[28] It is possible that these are to be understood literally as the beginnings of speeches.[29] Given the moral tenor of the speeches Mengzi is said to have delivered before kings, and given the *Mengzi*'s preference for arguments based on models of the hidden psyche, it seems less likely that the *si duan* are "shoots" than that they are points of access for the Mencian persuader and starting-points for his speech.

Following the lead offered by the *Mengzi*, we may look for other traces of the orators' psychological expertise in models addressed to pedagogues. The Ru made their way in the world as ritual specialists and as teachers, and their work required an account both of the educable psyche and of the perfected state that education could bring. A speaker who won a hearing as a teacher—whether as companion to the ruler of a state or head of a family, as tutor to a son, or as lecturer to a group of children—also won, besides his special access and authority, an opportunity to evoke in his student the very psyche he would then go on to exploit.

The *Xunzi*'s vigorous refutation of the *Mengzi*'s case for the goodness of human nature (*xing*) can read like part of a narrowly academic dispute. But the *Xunzi*'s psychology fits the text's overall project of demonstrating the political utility of *li* 禮, just as the *Mengzi*'s psychology supports arguments for generous and lenient governance. Where the *Mengzi* offers a reader a model of the good *xing* and numerous examples of how to appeal to this *xing* in practical oratory, the *Xunzi* holds up the bad *xing* and the cure for it, promising the reader worldly success as a master (and teacher) of *li* in all its dimensions.[30] It is easy to see how psychology, pedagogy, and public policy come together in such models of cultivation. Diagnosis and cure go hand in hand, and the most persuasive diagnostician will bring to light precisely those personal and public truths—*qing*—that allow him to practice his trade.

In the psychological schemes of the *Xunzi* and other texts from the middle Warring States and after, the particular aim of teaching one other man, the ruler, largely disappears into the generic project of cultivation, usually presented as self-cultivation. Nonetheless, there are traces in these schemes of the special importance once attached to convincing the ruler of their validity. In the *Xunzi*, for example, at the end of the "Xing e" 性惡 ("Human nature is bad") chapter, after the most rigorous exposition of the title's thesis, the discussion grows slack, loosely treating the sort of milieu or conditioning (*mi* 靡) that can influence a man's moral development. There is room here for a little hierarchy of knowledge, from the sage's knowledge (*shengren zhi zhi* 聖人之知) down to the laborer's knowledge (*yifu zhi zhi* 役夫之知).[31] This passage in turn recalls a hierarchy of discernment (*bian* 辯) in "Fei xiang" 非相 ("Against Physiognomy"), from the sage's discernment (*shengren zhi bian* 聖人之辯) down to the connivings and slick talk of the rogue (*jianren* 姦人).[32] The two passages show near thematic and verbal parallels, and both rank men on their skills in speech. For the *Xunzi* as for the *Mengzi* (3B.9), discernment and disputation (*bian*) are justified by the need to defend the way of the former kings against the perverse theories that have arisen in recent times. Thus both the "Fei xiang" and the "Xing e" end with reflections on the role of a milieu of speakers in the moral cultivation of a man figured as a ruler in the making. The *Xunzi*'s famous analysis of human nature and its rhetoric alike come around at last to the fashioning of a ruler in the mode of the former kings, and of any man in the mode of a ruler.[33]

A third early psychological scheme, the so-called "Xing zi ming chu" 性自命出 ("Nature derives from the decree"), likewise makes a place for a normative psychology of the ruler and for a reproduction of ancient rulers in the context of a general project of cultivation and self-cultivation.[34] The text's model of the human psyche is more elaborate than anything found in the *Mengzi* or the *Xunzi*, beginning as it does with a series of observations on the links between human nature (*xing*), *qi*, *qing*, and the cultivation of *qing* and moral response through learning of the *Shi* 詩 ("Songs"), *Shu* 書 ("Documents"), *li* 禮 (rites), and *yue* 樂 (music). As Michael Puett argues in his analysis of this section of the text, the practices that would ultimately issue in the Ru classics are the sages' reworkings of old traditions, based on true human psychological dispositions but adapted to use in moral education: "*Qing* . . . becomes the basis of the ethical system in the text: by defining it as the inherent emotional disposition of humans, the authors are able both to explicate the emergence of the traditions of *Poetry*, *Documents*, *Rituals*, and *Music* and to defend their importance."[35]

A later section of the "Xing zi ming chu" focuses on the psychology of the man who would govern or be used in government. The context demands that *qing* here be understood both as a component in the human psyche and as the opposite of "artifice" (*wei* 偽), that is, as something like "genuineness":

> The *qing* of human beings is in every case something that can be delighted in. As long as one goes by one's *qing*, even if one errs one is not hated for it; but if one does not go by one's *qing*, then even what is difficult is not esteemed. As long as one has the relevant *qing*, even if one has not yet performed the deed, others will believe one. One who is believed even before he has spoken is a person of fine *qing*. One who inspires constancy in the people even before he has begun teaching is a person of excellent *xing*. One who brings encouragement to the people even without having rewarded them is a person who preserves his blessings. One who strikes awe in the people without having punished them is a person who has something awesome in his own mind.
>
> 凡人之情為可悅也。苟以其情，雖過不惡；不以其情，雖難不貴。苟有其情，雖未之為，斯人信之矣。未言而信，有美情者也。未教而民恒，性善者也。未賞而民勸，含福者也。未刑而民畏，有心畏者也。[36]

Since it was the sages who first understood the cultivation of *qing* and its uses in governance, there is inevitably a cybernetic element to the perfection of *qing*, which was presumably key to the sages' own political success and, in passages like this one, opens the way for a new effectiveness in social organization.[37]

Whether the reader addressed here is a ruler-in-training, a would-be functionary, or simply someone who wishes to persuade or educate, the science of *qing* and the whole psychological model surrounding it depend on the assertion that society is bound by *qing* as "genuineness in emotional commitment." This *qing* will necessarily begin with the ruler's own commitments, and it will have a fundamentally rhetorical character in that it is based not on demonstrable truths but on induced convictions. As a tool of teaching, this psychological model prepares everyone, including the prince, as receptive hearers of Ru-style rhetorical appeals. It will be up to the Ru themselves, teachers of tradition and of normative psychology, to make the ruler ready for this project of genuineness.

The Ruling Mind: Legacies of *Qing*

By way of conclusion, we may consider the ways that orators' and educators' psychological models influenced later notions of *qing* and of the hidden human mind. The problem of defining and translating the term *qing* has formed a minor topos in intellectual history in recent decades. The trouble is that when its whole semantic range is taken into account, *qing* can as readily designate objective states of affairs as it can invisible psychological states such as anger, sorrow, and love. A. C. Graham stressed the aspect of "genuineness" in the word, moving from there to "essence" and, in the case of emotions, "essential desires": "The *ch'ing* of × is what × cannot lack if it is to be *called* 'X.' "[38] For Chad Hansen, *qing* "are all reality-induced discriminations or distinction-making reactions in *dao* executors"; they are both "reality inputs" and "reality responses." This definition serves Hansen's distinction of classical Chinese philosophical views from traditional Western views, which he takes to be typified in Greek accounts, especially that of Aristotle.[39]

Both Graham and Hansen wrote with an expressed interest in understanding the *qing* problem through a presumptive East-West divide in the apprehension of reality and the role of language. Both cite Aristotle as a sort of founding hero of Western notions of essence. But neither cites the *Rhetoric* at all, and the implications of this originary text for the rhetorical and manipulative dimensions of emotion theory are left unaddressed. Michael Puett, offering his own review of Graham's and Hansen's efforts, sets aside the project of finding a unified meaning of *qing* (and the project of marking the East-West divide) and instead considers the debates that can be reconstructed around the term. His treatment of "Xing zi ming chu" shows the success of this approach. Especially useful for a consideration of rhetoric and emotions is Puett's demonstration of the negotiable status of the term: "As a term with a broad semantic field including various internal qualities, *qíng* came to be employed by different figures who wished to exploit particular shades of meaning in the term."[40] This argument focuses attention squarely on the rhetorical utility of the word and invites us to consider how and why *qing* achieved this status.

Christoph Harbsmeier's approach to the term opens the way for a summary view of rhetoric, emotions, and the ruling mind.[41] Examining materials from the entire pre-Buddhist history of Chinese writing, he identifies seven distinct senses of *qing* from "factual" to "emotional." Without directly engaging Graham's and Hansen's hypotheses about *qing* and the East-West divide, he does make room for a "metaphysical" sense of the term.[42] But it may be in connection with the "personal" sense of the term *qing* that he offers an insight into the more fundamental functioning of the term. He notes that "In HANFEI the word currently refers to the real propensities or basic convictions of the ruler which one might try to spy out, and which the ruler should take care not to disclose. . . . In contexts like these *qíng* 情 comes close to meaning 'ultimate real motives, underlying motives.' "[43] Harbsmeier has rejected at the outset the effort to impose on the material any of several familiar schematic oppositions, including "manifested versus hidden,"[44] and his observations about the *Han Feizi* are intended to identify only one species of *qing*. Nonetheless, they have implications that extend beyond the *Han Feizi* and may ultimately lead to a schematic underpinning for all the senses of the term. The dynamic of hiddenness that Harbsmeier identifies in the "personal" sense of *qing*—the sense that *qing* is never simply patent, but must be brought to light through investigation and verbalization—would appear to subtend any possible use of the term.

Defined more specifically in the light of persuaders' uses of emotions, *qing* is any truth—objective or emotional—that is subject to hiding and that is brought into the open through human exposition. Whether they are psychological constants, social or natural dynamics, or personal responses to situations, *qing* are the sorts of things that might remain hidden or unknown, and that require discovery to be called *qing*. The moment of exposure or interpretation is apparently crucial, as things that are simply and patently the case rarely earn the name *qing*. Both the aspect of hiddenness and the role of revelation come to the fore in various ancient efforts to define the term. For Xu Shen 許慎 (ca. 55–ca. 149), for example, *qing* was "the hidden (*yin*) *qi* of human beings that carries their desires" 人之陰氣有欲者; the reference to *yin* parallels a correlation of *xing* with the *yang* or "apparent," but of course also recalls the persuaders' exploitation of hidden (*yin*) truths.[45]

The role of discovery in the definition of *qing* means that as an expressed truth *qing* is inevitably social and often verbal in nature. The discovery implied in *qing* is a revelation to another person, in the case of emotions, or the explanation for another person, in the case of some hard-to-know state of affairs. An idealizing passage on the ritual management of the seven emotions (*qi qing* 七情) from the "Li yun" 禮運 ("Processes of Ritual") chapter of the

Liji 禮記 captures this social aspect: "Drink, food, men, women: in these lie human beings' great desires. Death, exile, poverty, suffering: in these lie human beings' great dislikes. Thus desires and dislikes are the great starting-points for the mind. When the human being hides his mind, and it cannot be fathomed, and when the things he finds to admire or dislike are all there in his mind, but he shows no color of them, then if you wish with one stroke to exhaust all these things, what tool will you adopt if not ritual propriety?"[46]

> 飲食男女・人之大欲存焉・死亡貧苦・人之大惡存焉・故欲惡者・心之大端也・人藏其心・不可測度也・美惡皆在其心・不見其色也・欲一以窮之・舍禮何以哉・

The mention of "starting-points" (*duan*) recalls the problematic use of the same term in *Mengzi* 2A.6. Desiring and loathing are points of purchase for the action of ritual on the individual mind, and by seizing on desire and loathing in the occasions it orchestrates (from weddings to funerals), ritual brings out and "exhausts" the hidden mind. In a manner familiar from Ru texts, potentially dangerous private emotion is relieved in normative social acts.

But beyond such programs of ritual, the revelation associated with *qing* is less often a relief than a danger. Although ritual programs and characters such as the *Shuoyuan*'s Yao or the Confucius of *Lunyu* 論語 2.4 ("At seventy I followed whatever my heart desired . . .") promise a *qing* that does not bear hiding, the oratorical literature suggests something very different, a *qing* that one must keep to oneself. The danger in making one's *qing* accessible is not only that they may be discovered and exploited by the flatterers, blackmailers, and manipulators that persuaders are. Worse still is that because of the social element in their making—because they are brought to light in a process of expression or conversation—*qing* can be created for one. A clever persuader does it by appealing at once to laudable goals and to base aims, and by in this way imposing his own project as the ruler's own. A more ambitious philosopher does it through education, by imposing and then operating a particular model of the psyche.

Rulers grand and petty are the targets of persuasion. In them is concentrated the wealth and power that make an effort at persuasion worthwhile. The persuader approaches the ruler with all the tools he has at his disposal, from the reason and beauty he may display in his speaking to the psychological insights and techniques he may deploy as he speaks. There is some evidence that thinkers who considered the makeup of the human psyche in early Chinese did, like Aristotle, have in mind the desirability and danger of psychological manipulation. But because the audience in China was no public assembly but typically the one man—however highly placed he might be and however dependent he might be on consultation with ministers—the understanding of the psyche and the techniques for guiding it differed in some basic ways from the Greek comparandum. Perhaps surprisingly, given certain commonplaces about the East-West divide, the Chinese case ended up laying more emphasis on emotions and the susceptibilities of the individual, with relatively little attention to the sorts of emotions that affect groups making decisions. The result was a hidden *qing* of uncertain status, subject to efforts of all kinds to cultivate it as something admirable or to exploit it as something base, and created as an avowed truth through confidences and conversations. The mediation of *qing* in language and in social settings, and the value placed on concealing *qing* from potential exploiters, is perhaps early Chinese oratory's legacy to the students, philosophers, and literati of later times.

Notes

1. See Aristotle, "Rhetoric," in *The Complete Works of Aristotle: The Revised Oxford Translation*, ed. Jonathan Barnes, trans. W. Rhys Roberts. 2 vols. (Princeton, NJ: Princeton University Press, 1984), 2153–2269, especially 1377b on "looking right" and managing hearers' emotions. On conviction versus truth, see Renato Barilli, *Rhetoric*, trans. Giuliana Menozzi, in *Theory and History of Literature* (Minneapolis: University of Minnesota Press, 1989), vol. 63, 4.

2. Liu Xiang, *Shuoyuan jiaozheng* 說苑校證, ed. Xiang Zonglu 向宗魯 (Beijing: Zhonghua shuju, 1987), 5. Compare *Xinshu jiaozhu* 新書校注, eds. Yan Zhenyi 閻振益 and Zhong Xia 鍾夏 (Beijing: Zhonghua shuju, 2000), 360.

3. For more on the theme of ancient fearfulness, see my *A Patterned Past: Form and Thought in Early Chinese Historiography*, Harvard East Asian Monographs 205 (Cambridge, MA: Harvard University Asia Center, 2001), 295–96.

4. *Zhanguo ce* 戰國策 (Shanghai: Shanghai guji chubanshe, 1978), 1127. I have accepted the editors' proposed emendations.

5. *Zhanguo ce*, 827.

6. *Zhanguo ce*, 211–12. Cf. *Shiji* 史記 (Beijing: Zhonghua shuju, 1959), 79.2419–25.

7. *Zhanguo ce*, 528.

8. *Han Feizi jishi* 韓非子集釋, ed. Chen Qiyou 陳奇猷 (Shanghai: Renmin daxue chubanshe, 1974), 48.

9. *Zhanguo ce*, 748.

10. *Han Feizi jishi*, 566.

11. *Zhanguo ce*, 455.

12. *Zhanguo ce*, 770.

13. *Zhanguo ce*, 50. Cf. 190.

14. See the story of Zheng Xiu 鄭袖 in *Han Feizi jishi*, 588–89; *Zhanguo ce*, 553–54.

15. *Zhanguo ce*, 836. Persuaders can also adopt the tactic (best known to us from *Mengzi*) of pointing out that the king is fond (*hao*) of several things, and could just as well be fond of something better, such as talented men (*shi* 士). See *Zhanguo ce*, 414–17. On desire (*yu*), see *Han Feizi jishi*, 602.

16. *Mozi jiaozhu* 墨子校注, ed. Wu Yujiang 吳毓江 (Beijing: Zhonghua shuju, 1993), 159–60.

17. For the ruler's manipulation of subjects through displays of taste, see *Han Feizi jishi*, 655.

18. See again *Han Feizi jishi*, 48.

19. The *Han Feizi*'s handling of such terms as *xing* 性 is consistent with that of the *Xunzi* 荀子, perhaps reflecting Han Fei's debt to his teacher. See *Han Feizi jishi*, 887, 1134.

20. *Han Feizi jishi*, 221.

21. *Han Feizi jishi*, 222.

22. E.g., *Zhanguo ce*, 509: Su Qin "secretly (*yin*) plotted with the king of Yan to destroy Qi and divide up its lands between them; he therefore pretended (*yang*) to have been accused of a crime and fled, entering Qi" 陰與燕王謀破齊共分其地。乃佯有罪, 出走入齊.

23. On Meng Ke 孟軻 as persuader, consider *Zhanguo ce*, 1061, as well as the activities and abilities implied in such passages as *Mengzi* 2B.8, 2B.9, 2B.12, and 3B.1. Key passages on pleasure include 1A.2, 1B.4 (on the worthy man's pleasures) and 1B.1 (on the ruler's pleasures). Mengzi is said to have discerned rulers' hidden motivations and desires (1A.7, 4A.15), to have served as a sort of counselor to them (1B.1, 1B.3, 1B.5), and to have reformed others by displaying his own character and emotional responsiveness (2B.10).

24. Text in *Mengzi zhengyi*, 232–36.

25. Other uses of *ren* 忍 and *bu ren* 不忍 in the *Mengzi* differ from the passages cited here in that they are verbal constructions—"to bear to do X," some specified action—in contrast to the absolute *ren* of the ruler-related passages.

26. A. C. Graham, *Disputers of the Tao: Philosophical Argument in Ancient China* (La Salle, IL: Open Court, 1989), 126, 160.

27. *Han Feizi jishi*, 112–13.

28. *Han Feizi jishi*, 1091.

29. See *Han Feizi jishi*, 297 for the phrase *yan wu duan mo* 言無端末, "in his speech there is neither starting-point nor ending," i.e., one could make neither head nor tail of it. A. C. Graham proposed, besides "starting-points" and "shoots," that *duan* might mean a pause within a sentence; see A. C. Graham, *Later Mohist Logic, Ethics and Science* (Hong Kong: The Chinese University Press, 1978), 479.

30. Especially relevant for this claim are the *Xunzi* chapters "Ru xiao" 儒效, with its conversation on the advantages to be derived from the employment of Ru in government; "Yi bing" 議兵, with its emphasis on the organizational efficiency of *li*, even for military matters; and "Qiang guo" 強國, with it reliance on the power of *li* and other virtues to attract migration. See *Xunzi jijie*, 117–21, 265–90, 295–300. Also worth mentioning here is the *Zuozhuan*'s account of a Zheng noble's explanation, before the head of the powerful Zhao line of Jin, of the role of *li* in managing all the human emotions and social relations; see Yang Bojun 楊伯峻, ed., *Chunqiu Zuozhuan zhu* 春秋左傳注 (rev. ed., Beijing: Zhonghua shuju, 1990), 1457–59 (Zhao 25.3).

31. Wang Xianqian 王先謙, ed., *Xunzi jijie* 荀子集解 (Beijing: Zhonghua shuju, 1988), 445–46. One hint that the speech of each type of man is directed to a political superior is the reference to *chan* 諂, "fawning," in the case of the petty man's knowledge (*xiaoren zhi zhi* 小人之知), 446.

32. *Xunzi jijie*, 88–89. Clues that *bian* is to be directed to political superiors or in official functions are the mention that the "discernment of the gentleman of service" (*shi junzi zhi bian* 士君子之辯) is "worth heeding" (*zu ting* 足聽), perhaps as a persuasion is, and the mention that the rogue, when employed (*yong qi shen* 用其身), is liable to be deceptive and unproductive.

33. Note too that *Xunzi*'s direct oratorical advice in "Fei xiang" (*Xunzi jijie*, 84–86) presages some of the complex psychological manipulation found in *Han Feizi*, "Shui nan."

34. The text is one of several discovered at in a tomb at Guodian 郭店, Hubei, in 1993. See Jingmen shi bowuguan 荊門市博物館, *Guodian Chumu zhujian* 郭店楚墓竹簡 (Beijing: Wenwu chubanshe, 1994), 59–66, 177–84. The strips "Xing zi ming chu" were written on were originally bundled with strips containing three other texts, all having to do with the principles of Ru education; see Li Ling's 李零 grouping of the four texts in *Guodian Chu jian jiaodu ji* 郭店楚簡校讀記 (Beijing: Beijing daxue chubanshe, 2002), 103–44. Another version of the text, now referred to as "Xingqing lun" 性情論 (Discourse on human nature and emotions), is among the bamboo texts purchased by the Shanghai Museum in 1994, and had probably been buried in another tomb in or near the Guodian tomb. See Ma Chengyuan 馬承源, ed. *Shanghai*

bowuguan cang Zhanguo Chu zhushu 上海博物館藏戰國楚竹書 (Shanghai: Shanghai guji chubanshe, 2001), 1:215–301.

35. Michael Puett, "The Ethics of Responding Properly: The Notion of *Qíng* 情 in Early Chinese Thought," in *Love and Emotions in Traditional Chinese Literature*, ed. Halvor Eifring, Sinica Leidensia, Vol. 63 (Leiden: Brill, 2004), 51.

36. *Guodian Chumu zhujian*, 181. The section immediately before this one begins: "Artificiality in humans is in every case something to be detested" 凡人偽為可惡也.

37. It should be noted that the section immediately following this one covers men who are clearly not in the position to govern, such as the low-placed and the poverty-stricken. Again, the cultivation of the ruling mind is part of a more general project of cultivation.

38. A. C. Graham, *Studies in Chinese Philosophy and Philosophical Literature* (Albany: State University of New York Press, 1990), 59–65.

39. Chad Hansen, "Qing (Emotions) 情 in Pre-Buddhist Chinese Thought," in *Emotions in Asian Thought: A Dialogue in Comparative Philosophy*, eds. Joel Marks and Roger T. Ames (Albany: State University of New York Press, 1995), 181–211, esp. 196.

40. Puett, "Ethics of Responding," 43.

41. Christoph Harbsmeier, "The Semantics of *Qíng* in Pre-Buddhist Chinese," in Eifring, *Love and Emotions*, 69–148.

42. Harbsmeier, "Semantics of *Qing*," 76–82.

43. Harbsmeier, "Semantics of *Qing*," 100.

44. Harbsmeier, "Semantics of *Qing*," 72.

45. Zhu Junsheng 朱駿聲, *Shuowen tongxun ding sheng* 說文通訓定聲 (Beijing: Zhonghua shuju, 1984), 858.

46. *Liji jijie* 禮記集解, ed. Sun Xidan 孫希旦 (Beijing: Zhonghua shuju, 1989), 607.

3

Beliefs about Social Seeing

Hiddenness (wei 微) and Visibility in Classical-Era China

MICHAEL NYLAN

The good man obeys the promptings of his heart
Displaying himself or keeping quiet, as the times require.
仁者用其心，何嘗失顯默。

—Tao Yuanming, "Drinking Wine," Poem XVIII
陶淵明，《飲酒二十首並序，其十八》

Nothing is revealed more than what is hidden,
and nothing more obvious than the subtleties.
莫見乎隱，莫顯乎微

—*Zhongyong*

Over the past few years, my research has tried to tease out the various ways that early thinkers in China, their counterparts in classical Greece and Rome, and the modern neuroscientific community have construed the complex related processes of seeing, visualizing, and thinking. Beliefs about seeing constitute a fascinating topic on its own, but this essay focuses on the sociopolitical context for assertions about social status and status-related proclivities and, in particular, the social valences attached to hiddenness and visibility in early

China. Several recent works, including those of Zheng Yan 鄭岩 and Miranda Brown, have discussed the importance of public display in the Han mourning rites, and many more have written about the aesthetics of emptiness (*xu* 虛), referring to "phenomena above [i.e., prior to] form," a specific cosmogonic stage thought to predate that highly differentiated world we credit with "reality." However, scholarship to date has paid remarkably little attention to the social advantages or disadvantages accruing from hiding and display outside of these limited contexts.[1] This essay argues that acts designed to hide or display oneself—the very choice to position oneself along a spectrum of possible degrees of visibility—reflect the attitudes and commitments shared by members of the governing elite during the classical era (423 BCE–316 CE) in China.

Recently, Nathan Sivin, the historian of science, challenged scholars to look for what he dubs "cultural manifolds" (i.e., mutually dependent notions, institutions, identities, and ambitions), since ideas do not exist in a vacuum, but rather as "part of a continuum that includes what thinkers want out of life, who they consider their colleagues to be, . . . how they make sense of the world around them, and what political and social choices they make."[2] A review of the cluster of terms employed to denote a sense of what is hidden, rather than revealed—the most important being *wei* 微, the hidden, and *wuxing* 無形, the formless—allows us to begin to disentangle the different valences implied by the words used for "seeing," "gazing," "contemplating," "peering," and "watching."[3] As we thus sensitize ourselves to some of the nuances that classical-era readers and writers brought to their own compositions, several impressions immediately emerge, three of which, being particularly germane to the topic at hand, will be discussed below: (1) while the original connotations for *wei* ("the hidden") tend to be very negative, they gradually become much more positive by the early unified empires of Qin and Han, thanks in part to literary depictions of the mysterious activities and marvelous capacities of the sage-king and his advisors; (2) lively discussions during Zhanguo, Qin, and Han, building on parallel discussions about cultural and cosmic patterns, repeatedly raise the topic of public ridicule, asking who deserves it, who does not, and why, in the process implicitly posing the larger question, what is conventionally shameful and what truly shameful?; and, as a result, (3) the visual and literary rhetorics eventually seek to provide convincing portraits of authoritative figures, male and female, who epitomize just that auspicious balance of hiddenness and display.

Specialists in the early China field will see immediately that the first of these three hypotheses about hiddenness and visibility depends to some degree on the correct dating of key texts in the received literature (a highly controversial matter), but an essay of this length can hardly resolve complex questions about dating for each and every text in the received tradition. Of more immediate utility to readers, perhaps, may be the opportunity to see for themselves the most ingenious and vivid proofs for the third hypothesis regarding the need for members of the Qin and Han elites to parade their exemplarity via a fine balance of display and reclusiveness. One begins with the topic of "knowing men" simply because a preoccupation with this topic evidently underlies so much of the extant rhetoric handed down from members of the governing elite in this period.

"Knowing Men"

In the pre-Han and Han periods, the chief subject of epistemological inquiry for those in power was not "knowing facts" but "knowing men": knowing how to gather and weigh evidence about the character and proclivities of potential and actual candidates for office. That helps to explain why the governing elites were determined to see and be seen. Members of the governing elite had a solemn duty to construct, primarily through their persons and secondarily through the writings that they left behind, highly visible and visually arresting exemplary models for the benefit of their peers and those of lower status. Retinues of clients,[4] solemn funerary processions and tours of inspection, the intense scrutiny that went with rating candidates for office—all these activities aimed to render visible to groups far beyond the family circles both the inward state and outward status of claimants to power. The centralizing states had an interest in promoting the advantages of social visibility to members of its ruling elite, in part because the rapidly expanded scale of the early empires made it otherwise next to impossible for the court and its subjects to know its local officers and minor functionaries well,[5] and in part because smart powerholders well understood the limited utility of force or threats of violence to compel others to act or submit. As it was not enough to wield brute force, authorities at every level somehow were to display their charismatic powers (*de* 德) within their own political spheres. And charismatic power was purportedly best communicated—to discerning eyes, at least—as much through ritualized displays of dress and gestures, of mien and demeanor, and of decor and decorum, as through wise policies or rhetoric about the standard virtues. The rites demanded visible "embodiment" (*li* 禮 = *ti* 體), as the standard gloss went.[6] There is a good reason why "decor," "decoration," and "decorum" all derive from the same Latin root, signifying both "appropriate form" and "adornment." Similarly, classical Chinese employs comparably rich punning plays on the word for "banners" or "standards."[7]

One chapter of Liu Shao's 劉邵 (early 3rd c.) *Renwu zhi* 人物志 (Treatise on characters) provides a stunning example of just how central the language of hiddenness or its reverse was to the conventional language of "knowing men," for in Liu's "Jiu zheng" 九徵 (Nine manifestations) chapter, every single one of a total of fourteen stratagems for the successful evaluation of potential candidates for office utilizes tropes of visibility vs. hiddenness—vision, exhibitionism, insight, illumination, and perspicacity—to delineate the innate worth of a person's nature or second nature.[8] In one conventional formula, the *junzi* makes plainly visible what is subtle (*junzi biao wei* 君子表微),[9] exemplifying and propagating it, while the sage kings "investigate" or "analyze" the finest points that are "difficult to know."[10] Therefore, the early Western Han compilation, the *Hanshi waizhuan*, celebrates good judges who can "hear the subtle and decide the doubtful" (*ting wei jue yi* 聽微決疑) when deciding cases. Similarly, ritual, music, and divination are all praised in one *Rites* classic for "in discerning improprieties, making plain-as-day what would otherwise remain hidden" (*biexian mingwei* 別嫌明微).[11]

Many of the most sophisticated thinkers of the age took it for granted that formal appearances staged outside the family home, for instance court speeches, would not only *not* deceive onlookers, but would also prove to be transparent revelations of both the person and his or her family traditions.[12] The total effect engendered by the person's speech, conduct, and look made a "human portent" (*ren yao* 人妖) that would be no less indicative of the person's basic underlying patterns than animal entrails or strange signs in the sky.[13] The prevalence of such beliefs hardly forestalled severe conflicts over the reigning paradigms of viewing, however. If our paltry records may be trusted, earlier aristocratic eras had given a uniformly positive ethical valence to the nobility's visual prominence, but by the late Zhanguo (475–222 BCE), this was no longer as true. Presumably strategic necessities—the desire to avoid assassination, the need for fraud and deception in war—undermined some of the enthusiasm for celebrations of display. In any case, in their respective seats of power, members of the governing elite had become more aware of competing priorities, and quicker to seek to control the motivation, origin, and direction of the gazes of others, in order to reserve for themselves the right to fend off potentially intrusive and aggressive looks.[14] Anxiously, authors acknowledge that anyone longing to become the cynosure of all eyes would do well to take the requisite steps to avoid being viewed, not with admiration, but with the contempt that stems from overexposure to prying eyes.[15]

Such cautions notwithstanding, the goal of the powerful was still to create a vivid yet highly stylized impression by the careful staging of unfaltering exemplarity. Hence the focus on ritual, which, if carefully done, could induce a thrilling sense of immediate connection between onlookers and participants, correspondingly enhanced when access to certain venues became narrow or exclusive. Han society placed a premium on living up to the judgment of authoritative viewers,[16] whose honorable ranks included the dead ancestors and certain gods to whom regular reports were issued and who legitimated the high-ranking in return. Clearly, in the eyes of statesmen and thinkers of late Zhanguo and the two Han periods, the establishment of collective memory and cultural reproduction, and finally the very stability of society, depended directly on first staging and then imparting the correct interpretation of such edifying spectacles. (Unfortunately, we know next to nothing about how public monuments and public inscriptions were used in this early society to build up favorable impressions, since our best source for monuments in the classical era in China comes centuries later in a text, Li Daoyuan's 酈道元 (d. 527) *Shuijing zhu* 水經注 [comp. 526 CE?], a compilation surprisingly resistant to straightforward readings.)[17]

Perforce we fall back on the received literature,[18] especially that subsumed today under the categories of "history" and "philosophy," to see what it can tell us about the relative social advantages perceived to come from hiddenness and display. Not surprisingly, given the official or semiofficial nature of most of the Qin and Han sources, the majority of political comments about the hidden allude to mayhem at the imperial courts, where loyal remonstrants are mistaken for traitors, and sycophants and slanderers thrive. Yang Xiong 揚雄 (d. 18 CE) articulates the atmosphere of fear in his *fu* entitled "Dispelling Ridicule" 解嘲賦: "One false step may end up bloodying my entire clan" 不知一跌將赤吾之族也.[19] So seriously is ridicule taken in the classical era that superiors threaten subordinates with execution or exile when they hear they are the object of scornful laughter.[20] The mere threat of ridicule suffices to prevent a wary ruler from taking unwise actions;[21] and the most keenly felt forms of public shame reportedly exposed noble persons and their lines to the caustic gaze of their social, moral, and gender inferiors.[22] The jeering, whispers, and catcalls could prove unbearably painful, as we know from Sima Qian's 司馬遷 (145?–86? BCE) famous "Letter to Ren An" 答任安書, whether in this life (most horribly, in public execution in the marketplace) (figure 3.1) or the next (when readers and reciters of texts would be apt to sneer at historical figures who disgraced themselves or their progeny).[23]

Since captives and base criminals had their bodies exposed,[24] to be "manhandled" was thought more awful than death itself. Utter degradation was thus conveyed through such four-character phrases as *shensi renshou* 身死人手 ("killed by another's bare hands") or *luogong shou chi* 裸躬受笞 ("stripped naked and flogged"). The degradation associated with exposure should hardly

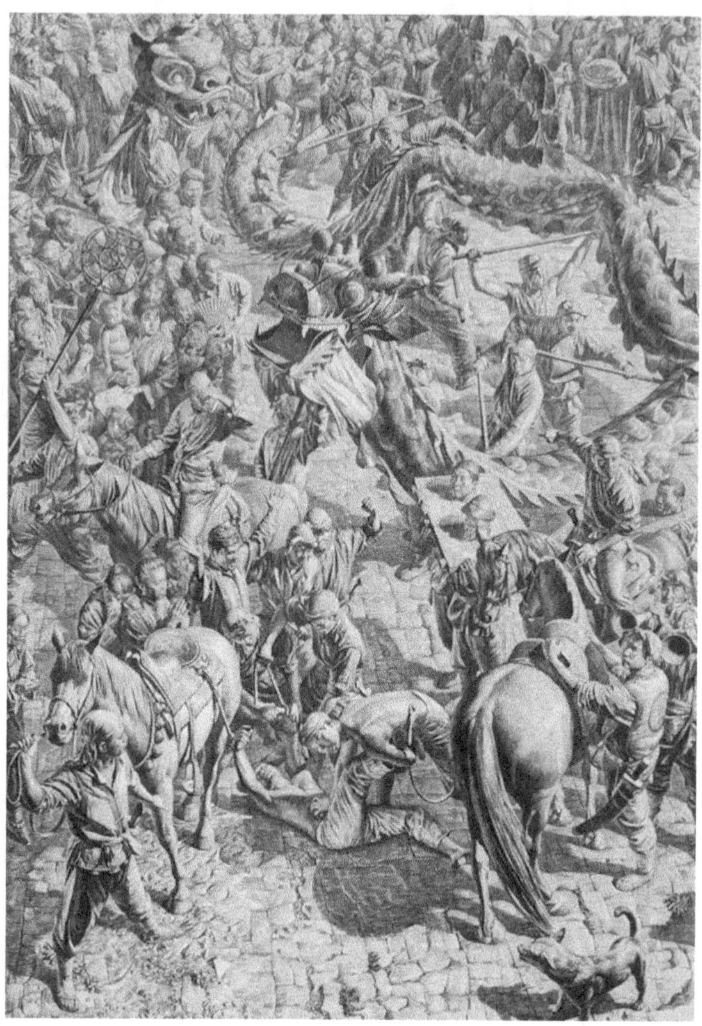

Figure 3.1. Zhi Lin (b. 1959), *Drawing and Quartering*, from the series *Five Capital Punishments in China*, 2000–2003. Place made: China. Hanging scroll, mounted as a *thangka*; charcoal on canvas, screen-printing on ribbons. Painting: 269.2 × 188.0 cm (106 × 74 in.); mount: 365.8 × 213.4 cm (144 × 84 in.). Museum purchase, Fowler McCormick, Class of 1921 Fund, with gifts from P. Y. and Kinmay W. Tang Center for East Asian Art, Alisan Fine Arts, Ltd., Alice King Gallery, and Thaw Charitable Trust, 2005-131. Princeton University Art Museum, Princeton, New Jersey. Photo credit: Princeton University Art Museum/Art Resource, NY.

While no Han work depicted criminals or their execution unless they were barbarians (the subject being too inauspicious), this contemporary work captures the profound shame of prisoners being readied for drawing and quartering in a marketplace.

surprise us, since the prevailing optical theories considered the eyes no less capable of violating a person than the hands.[25]

Essentially, inhabitants of the early empires equated noble standing with the unusual ability to *choose* when and how one will show oneself or not.[26] Thus the class and status attributes typically ascribed to visibility and hiddenness are key to understanding the deeper ironies threading through a host of wonderful anecdotes dated to the Han period, as when that wily commoner, Liu Bang 劉邦, against all odds overturns the aristocratic Xiang Yu 項羽 by the shameful ruse where he hides himself like a cowardly peasant. Continual manipulations of the prevailing presumptions about display are no less central to the portrait of Kongzi 孔子 (aka Confucius), the uncrowned king, supposedly a teacher who—quite uniquely for his time—proves willing to overexpose himself to his social and moral inferiors and refuses to heed the mockery of his peers who cannot understand his eagerness to teach.[27] Such adages and legends presumed the advisability of carefully calculating the odds when wagering shameful visibility against eventual success: heroes more than once chose to cower in undignified postures in order to enjoy the last laugh when they upended societal expectations by scrambling to the top.[28] Clearly, the need for the *junzi* 君子 (as ruler, official, or "gentleman") to display graceful sociability as a sign of his cultivation was never easy to reconcile with the noble man's expectation of protection from prying eyes.[29] Hence the variety of models (some of them quite contradictory) put forward that claimed to insure the requisite level of enviable conviviality.[30] Doubtless, a large part of the attraction of ritualized behavior was that it promised a disciplined person might learn to achieve the two desirable effects simultaneously, reducing the number and severity of the risks of transgressing in social situations while advertising membership in a small, protected in-group, the better to warn others off from scoffing.[31] By some theories, that training was so rigorous that the supremely "great man" or "sage" masked all his feelings, neither laughing nor smiling.[32]

To Be Seen or Not: The Visual and Linguistic Evidence

Han murals and pictorial stones routinely depict members of the governing elite in such a way that their formal gestures, postures, appointments, and arrangements together convey that "impressively authoritative, yet expressively opaque"[33] quality that elites hoped to pull off when turning to face the world. The first figure (figure 3.2a–b) shows two details of a mural where an imposing power couple, almost certainly the tomb occupants, are sumptuously dressed and seated on a dais, as if waiting to receive important guests and clients. The couple is positioned at one focal point of the tomb, near an arched doorway,

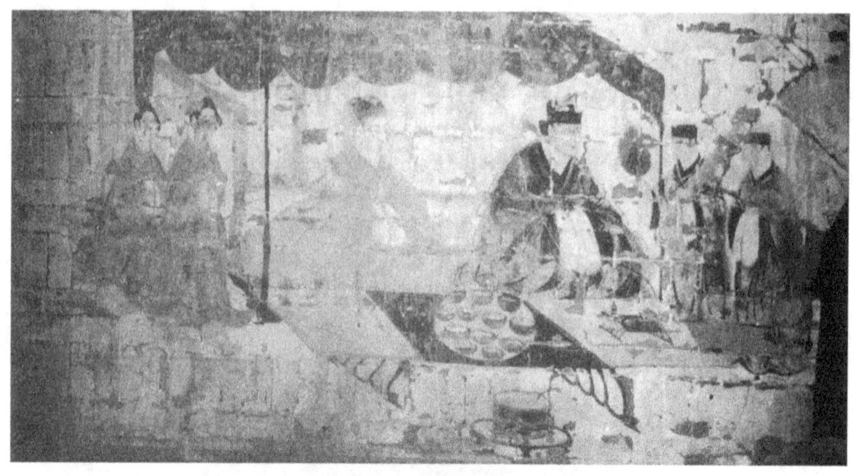

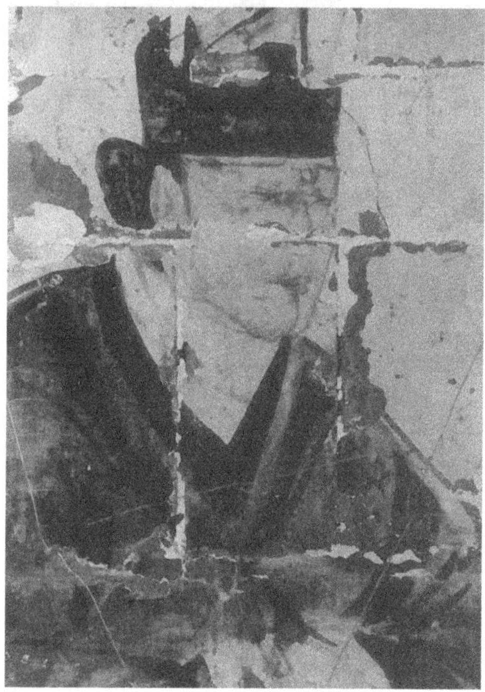

Figure 3.2a, b. Painted tomb mural (color) of the tomb occupants poised to receive guests. Height 1.46 m, length 2.5 m. Late Eastern Han or Cao-Wei period (early third century CE). Excavated in 1991 from Henan Luoyang, Zhucun. From *Luoyang Hanmu bihua*, eds. Huang Minglan and Guo Yinqiang (Beijing: Wenwu chubanshe, 1996), 190, pl. 1.

yet their masklike faces and absence of gesture offer no hint of their inner thoughts as they gaze blandly if expectantly outward on the several guests and servants hastening toward them. Notably, the impressive couple is somewhat shielded from the full force of the onlookers' prying gaze, both by the angle at which they sit and the canopy that partially covers them. As art historians have remarked, in Han times few except the gods dared to meet another's gaze squarely, in a full frontal pose.[34]

Figure 3.3 depicts a female figure whose posture is equally typical of Han-era pictorial stones, from Shandong in the northeast to Sichuan in the southwest, a figure who attracts the viewer's gaze by her appearance half-

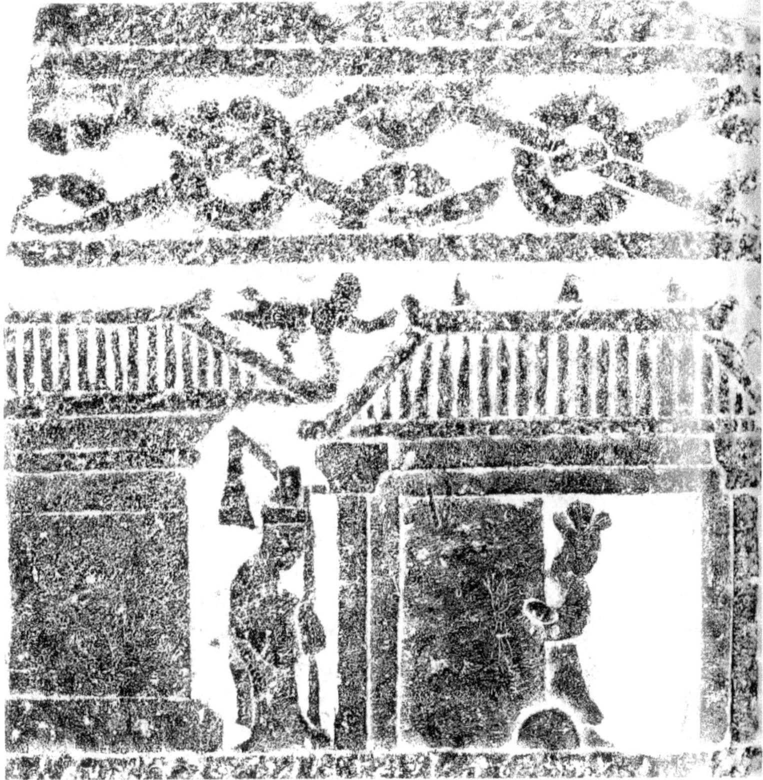

Figure 3.3. Rubbing of a pictorial stone (detail), Han Dynasty, Shandong Province. 63 × 133 cm for the stone in total, half of which is shown here. Excavated in 1976 from Yishui 沂水 County, Shandong, Houcheng zi 後城子. After *Zhongguo huaxiang shi quanji* 中國畫像石全集 (Shandong, vol. 3) (Jinan: Shandong meishu chubanshe, 2000; Beijing Wenwu Press), 65, pl. 77.

hidden behind a partly open door. Paul Rakita Goldin has argued that such women (winged or not) are always prostitutes luring men in, but in a great many instances the pictorial stones are simply not amenable to that reading.[35] Such designs may evolve from an individual artisan's desire to experiment with rendering volume and depth, but they evidently were popular with classical-era patrons because they allowed a good woman of the house (witness her full-blown cap) to be seen peering around, without offending any of the norms of modesty. (Peering is an activity that Han artisans delighted in depicting, for it imparted intense liveliness to the most ordinary acts. Perhaps the most famous example is the Eastern Han pictorial stone from Sichuan that shows monkeys, a bird, and two nearby males peering intently at a wildly copulating couple.)[36]

Figure 3.4, a brilliantly colored mural, depicts either a small city or a mortuary complex from three views simultaneously (a bird's-eye view, a horizontal view, and one tilted up). Despite the varied perspectives, onlookers would have been hard put to make out what people and objects the architectural units contain. Yet all the architectural features in the complex testify handily to the tomb occupant's wealth and status. To my mind, each of these three classical-era artifacts brilliantly conveys a sense of the governing elite's profound ambivalence about seeing and being seen. On the one hand, they had to exhibit their status and wealth, if they hope to be credited with possessing them. On the other, too much display was unseemly, if not downright dangerous.[37]

Those powerful depictions mixing hiddenness with visibility prepare us for the complex ways that the logograph *wei*, meaning "hidden" or "dimly seen," is deployed in the literary sources of the period. In our earliest texts, *wei* appears to be uniformly negative. In the pre-Han texts, it occurs in such compounds as *shuai wei* 衰微 (decline and weaken); *wei ruo* 微弱 (insignificant and weak), and *jian wei* 賤微 (low and debased) or as verbs meaning "to be eclipsed" or "to slight" (*wei bo* 微薄). Very much on the Chunqiu and Zhanguo thinkers' minds is the potential for dire calamities to begin from the smallest actions—mere slips of the tongue or careless gestures.[38] Crucially, the noun *wei* (meaning, "commoner") is played off in the early texts against nouns signifying high rank. *Wei* is moreover the antonym of *sheng* 盛 ("florescence") and of *ming* 明 (brilliance).[39] Often it refers to what is tabooed, being too shameful to mention.

Under the unified empires of Qin and Han times, however, the extant works come to use *wei* in a significantly more positive manner. *Wei* comes to signify the "small nascent signs" or "subtleties" of an unfolding event that the gentleman (*junzi* 君子) or the sage reads for himself and then interprets

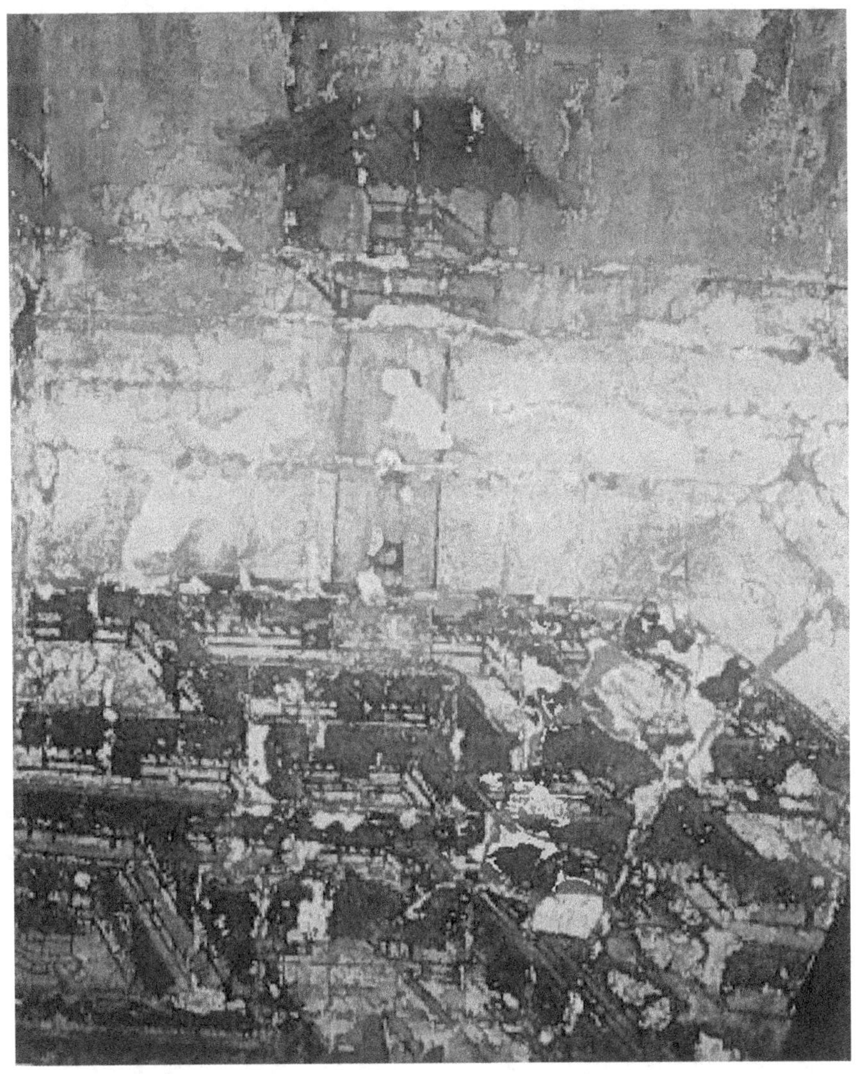

Figure 3.4. Painted tomb mural (color) showing a walled compound, variously identified as either a city or a mortuary complex. Height 230 cm, length 135 cm. Dated CE 176. Excavated in Anping, Hebei Province. This mural appears in one small chamber in the tomb, which also features a portrait of the deceased, tentatively identified as a relative of Zhao Zhong, the most powerful eunuch during Han Lingdi's reign (168–89). After *Anping Dong Han bihua mu* 安平東漢壁畫墓 (Beijing: Wenwu chubanshe, 1990), 27, pl. 9.

for those inferior to him in understanding (who may, of course, still be his superiors in society or at court). During the Han, conscientious attempts to stitch together the negative and positive valences of the logograph *wei* in a single narrative prompted the theory that the more hidden an object of vision, the more developed the seer's faculty *beyond* sight; after all, when things are hidden from view, only the perfect moral and practical "clarity" of the seer lends itself to that extraordinary level of "seeing." The ties between the seen, the seer, and the act of seeing, the object of vision and the viewing faculty, not to mention realms within and beyond sight, did not end here. If ontologically, all material things are partial replicas or emanations of the one immanent Dao, the source of life that remains ever shrouded in mystery, then, in theory, those who imitate the Dao may partake of its divine hiddenness, however visible they are. Thus, whatever person or behavior is deemed godlike (*shen* 神) is in possession of *wei*, a "subtle, verging-on-ineffable quality"[40] that supposedly permits sympathetic understanding of all other "hidden" (*wei* 微) patterns—those that are too subtle, ineffable, volatile, or incipient to be easily apprehensible to ordinary people.

As analogies between the unseen Dao and the highest political leaders proliferated among the court propagandists, the idea that the sages and the *junzi*, like the Dao, would conceal their fundamentally beneficent activities, so as not to draw undue attention to themselves, begins to dominate the political rhetoric. Even "rationalist" thinkers such as Xunzi had been known to dabble in such ideas,[41] and eventually, the sage was said not only to "know the formless" but also to assume "formlessness" himself,[42] becoming a triune power with the Dao in all its aspects, past and present.[43] Perhaps this explains why communication with the highest-ranking gods routinely took place at night, until the attacks of bandits and thieves on the imperial cortège put an end to such practices; also why the imperial countenance was never reproduced on coins or in statues at cult sites, despite the integrative force such ubiquitous portraits might have exerted in a society with high levels of functional illiteracy.[44] The effect on court practices was bound to follow. To take one obvious example, whereas the politics of display in late Zhanguo, Qin, and early Western Han meant frequent imperial progresses to stage the distribution of fantastic amounts of largess outside the capital region (hence the multiple extended tours of the First Emperor of Qin and Emperor Wu of Han all over their realms) (figures 3.5a–b), by late Western Han times the emperors seldom ventured for long outside the Chang'an palaces, preferring to send envoys to conduct prayers at the ancestral shrines or dispense charity.[45]

In one extreme form, this trope of deliberate masking alleges that the true sage never allows others to see him resorting to divination, lest others notice and marvel at his uncanny ability to predict events on the basis of his profound

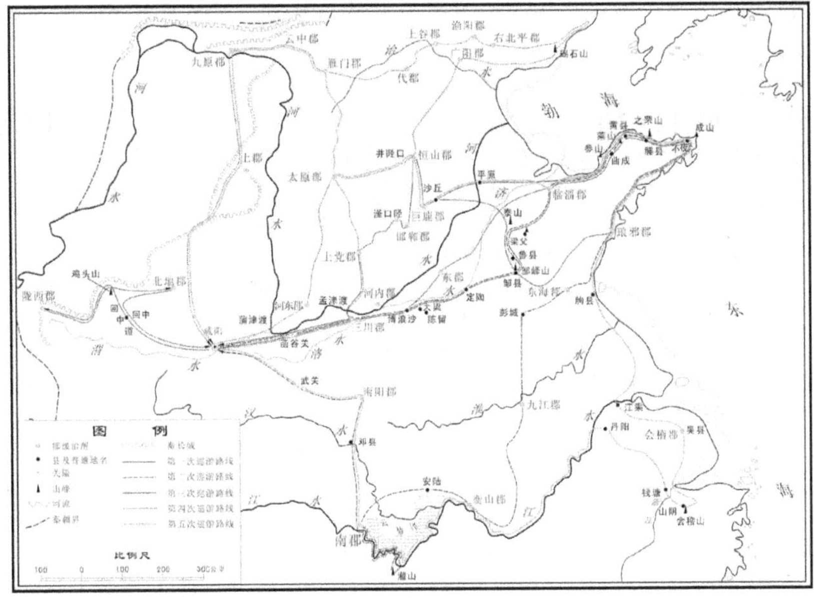

秦始皇巡狩路线

Figure 3.5a. Map showing imperial progress of the First Emperor.

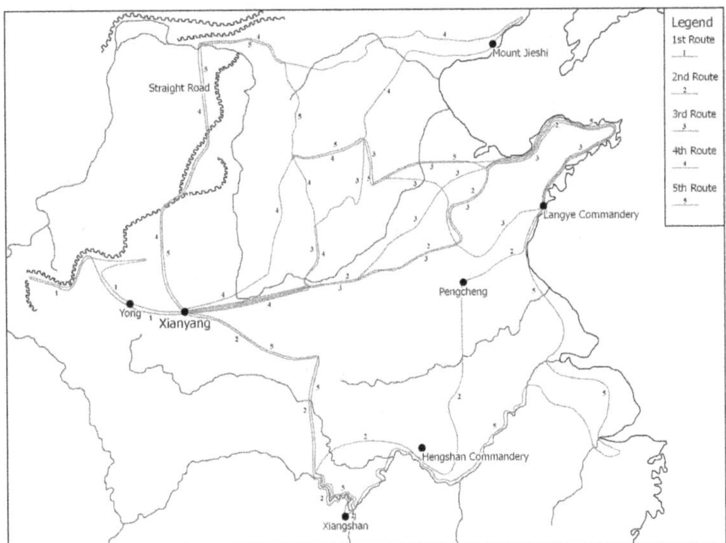

Figure 3.5b. Map showing imperial progress of Han Wudi, generated by Griet Vankeerberghen and Daniel Shultz (McGill University), on the basis of an earlier map generated by Michael Nylan.

appreciation of cosmic and societal patterns.[46] And with the best minds of the era busily constructing for the ruler's pleasure the tropes that cast the ruler as a simulacrum of the shadowy Dao, it was not long before those same minds began fashioning their own literary personae in the same mode, aided in this by the double meaning of *junzi* as "ruler" and "gentleman." After all, "every man could fancy himself a [wise minister] Gaoyao / When those sporting hairnets with ribbons dangling held their parlays."[47] Not coincidentally, a new series of compounds appear that stress refinement, subtlety, virtuosity, and marvelous artfulness, with *jing wei* 精微 (the finest, most subtle parts of distilled *qi*), and the binomes *wei miao* 微妙 and *qiao miao* 巧妙 favored the most. Such compounds often limned the *junzi*'s dislike of showiness and glibness; hence the characterization of the *junzi*'s words, for instance, as "subtle yet pregnant with meaning" (*wei er zang* 微而臧).[48]

Accordingly, charismatic conduct for the ruling class turned Janus-faced, at once hidden and visible. Language edging toward paradox asserted that the true gentleman's exquisite-yet-bold patterns may go unnoticed by all but men like himself, the most astute readers of people.[49] What is unambiguously true is that "the hidden" in Han times became an artifact or sign of elite refinements "closed off to the masses," but open to the "subtle messages" (*weiyan* 微言) employed by sages such as Confucius in speech and in writing.[50] We can trace the gradual parallel shift in the connotations of this phrase from negative to positive in the legends about Confucius, with the earliest stratum of the "Gongyang" 公羊 tradition using *weiyan* to refer to "tabooed information" too shameful to mention, but with Han-era "Gongyang" theorists, including Dong Zhongshu 董仲舒 (d. 104 BCE?), twisting it to mean the "subtle messages" pronounced by Confucius for all time in his capacity as Supreme Sage.[51]

Of course, the shift from negative to positive could never be completed in the classical era in China, as too many preunification classics and masterworks remained in circulation, and some of the newly elevated Han elites sought to imitate older models of heroism. Thus quite a few Han writings reflexively reiterate earlier warnings about the likelihood that bad habits will arise from the smallest misstep, even as the same texts alert readers to the social cachet attached to hiddenness. Meanwhile, the "hiddenness" motifs continued to reflect grave concerns over what is shameful in the public eye and what invites ridicule in consequence. It certainly looks as if anxiety about life's unpredictability continued unabated, exacerbated by the sudden dramatic reversals of fortune that accompanied wars, coups, factional disputes, and rebellions during the five centuries or so spanning the late Warring States, Qin, Han, and immediate post-Han periods.

It is rather uncommon in classical Chinese for words to start out with bad connotations and end up with good. How did this near-reversal of social valences come about? We can but speculate: perhaps the "pivot" aspect of *wei*—the aspect of *wei* that seems to have allowed it to swing between connotations of good and bad—arose from the meaning of *wei* as "target." (Targets function as objects of attack, yet they also signify the goals toward which we strive.) In like manner, *wei* simultaneously suggests desirable or privileged access and encryption. Moving beyond speculation, historians can with greater assurance link improvements in the social valence of *wei* to other well-attested phenomena during the Han and immediate post-Han period, beginning with the early Han rulers' claims to transparency as a means of distinguishing themselves from the previous Qin dynasty; the increasing determination to sort out the philosophical and medical implications of theories of the senses and percepts; successive decisions by later thinkers to define the *junzi* in terms of his dedication to serving or accommodating unseen forces (elaborating on Xunzi); stiff competition among literate groups vying for court patronage, which inevitably inflated the virtues ascribed to men in the recommendations, eulogies, and autobiographies of the period; and even perhaps, after the first century or so of Han rule, the rhetorical fashion for playing with the paradoxical.[52]

Social Remedies: Light in the Dark

In the classical models, a mere handful of sources (*Zhuangzi* 莊子 and Sima Qian among them) had the audacity to dwell on the harsh notion that neither the mind's eye nor history's mirror may adequately perceive or reflect reality.[53] For, absent a reliable way to panoptically survey the self and one's place in the world, it is unclear how a person is to employ the body and its resources to avoid shame and live in undisturbed peace.[54] Most of the extant sources portray ritual action and social cultivation as the most effective ways to facilitate an immature person's gradual development from solipsism to profound ethical responsibility. What was needed was a slight adjustment, a turning inward to employ the appraising self as eye or mirror, especially when the common wisdom failed to enlighten, as it did so regularly. For these reasons, though the goal of ethics within the classical cultures was more to distinguish propriety from impropriety than to discern the opposition of reality/appearance or true/false (as in modern science),[55] tropes of vision, light, and the mirror were repeatedly mobilized by those intent on acquiring and coordinating accurate knowledge of the world, of others, and of the self.

Of course, having the capacity of sight is no guarantee that people will really take the trouble to learn how to see.[56] The profusion of sensory percepts flooding in at every moment could so bedazzle the senses that the person would find it nearly impossible to sort out what is true, let alone what priorities should be upheld. Far better, then, to replace the usual befuddlement associated with the turbulent riot of sensations with the sort of soft radiant dimness cast by the wax candle.[57] For practical wisdom is the candle that illumines the Way, allowing the person to keep to the main road during the arduous journey.[58] Huan Tan 桓譚 (d. 28) was one of several classical masters to elaborate the candle's symbolism in the examined life (*sheng* 生).[59]

Meanwhile, the most lucid of Han thinkers began to try to accustom their followers to the notion that even the best and most moral human life must confront an ultimate Mystery, despite the person's determined efforts to gain more perfect clarity.[60] One exchange in the *Fayan* maintains the comforting idea that even the faintest light still can visibly shine, as in the following dialogue:

> Someone asked me about light.
>
> "It is faint."
>
> Someone asked me, "But if that is the case, then why compare it to something very bright?"
>
> "If something faint becomes visible at all, then how is its inherent brilliance negated?"[61]
>
> 或問明。
>
> 曰微。
>
> 或曰微。何如其明也。
>
> 曰微而見之。明其誶乎。

However poignant such defiance in the face of life's vicissitudes may seem, it could offer no effective remedy for the stark realization that the befuddlement of life yields far too soon to that "great obscurity," the eternal darkness of death.[62] In the twinkling of an eye, the irrevocable blackness of the tomb envelops even the high and mighty forever. In addition, repeated visits to those underground tombs on the horizontal plains that spread across the land from late Western Han on might well have caused mourners to quail at the thought of overmuch contact with the newly dead. How welcome, then, the faint light thrown off by candles or torches below. Still, as spook stories made clear, the newly dead whose lives were still sputtering out sometimes retained enough residual power to appear to terror-stricken people as flickering lights, too, at least if they were high-ranking revenants who once derived their vital *qi* 氣 from the stars.[63] But was this any comfort to those confronting certain death? We cannot know for sure, but it seems unlikely.

Perhaps the best that could be hoped for was this: that the writings suffused with the light of the Ancients would serve those who craved lasting fame "enduring beyond the grave" (*buxiu* 不朽). Their unfailing light would serve as a mirror in which the good could see themselves or have others see their true spirit reflected (with both kinds of seeing indicated by the single binome, *zijian* 自見).[64] For, as one text averred, simply "to open them [the sages' works] renders visible all the vast space within the four seas."[65] Moreover, through artful neoclassical writings modeled on the exquisite productions of the Ancients, one might learn a graceful method to "hide in court," avoiding present dangers while awaiting the unstinting praise of later generations. No need existed for actual reclusion—retreat from the public eye and removal from the court—to demonstrate the purity of one's devotion to upright principles;[66] it was enough to "live open to the world, . . . in good spirits and free."[67] And so, first in mid-Western Han, with Sima Qian, and then more emphatically with the *haogu* 好古 reformers of late Western Han, lovers of antiquity spelled out the critical importance of reading old writings and composing new classicizing works, which embodied certain Enlightenment.[68] Once again, the concept clusters relating to hiddenness and visibility had resonated powerfully with the men and women of the governing elite, this time in the form of an ever-increasing emphasis on visible literary accomplishments (*wen* 文), which would eventually come to define relative "worth" even more than good breeding itself.[69]

Yet even to the classicists most committed to the *haogu* ideals, doubts remained as to whether applying one's soaring intellect to life's mysterious ebb and flow would bring a final surcease of care. But they could always hope, as did the Eastern Han classicist Zhang Heng 張衡 (78–139) in his famous *fu* on the "The Bones of Zhuangzi":

> . . . Suddenly I looked and by the roadside
> I saw a man's bones lying in the squelchy earth,
> Black rime-frost over him; and I in sorrow spoke

And asked him, saying, "Dead man, how was it?
Fled you with your friend from famine, and for the last grains
Gambled and lost? Was this earth your tomb, or did floods carry
you from afar?
Were you mighty? Were you wise? Were you foolish and poor? A
warrior, or a girl?"
Then a wonder came: for out of the silence a voice
Thin echo only—in no substance was the Spirit seen—
Mysteriously answered, "I was a man of Song,
Of the clan of Zhuang; Zhou was my name.
Beyond the climes of common thought
My reason soared, yet I could not save myself.
For at the last, when the long charter of my years was told,
I too, for all my magic, by Age was brought
To the Black Hill of Death. . . ."
Then I responded:
"Let me plead for you at the tops of the Five Marchmounts,
Let me pray for you to the gods of heaven and of earth,
That your white bones may arise,
And your limbs be joined anew . . .
Would you not have it so?"
The dead man answered me:
"O Friend, how strange and dreadful are your words.
In death I rest and am at peace; in life, I toiled and strove . . .
Shall I now once again desire, whom death
Already has hidden in the Eternal Way . . . ?
. . . .
Of the Primal Spirit is my substance; I am a wave
In the river of Darkness and Light . . .
With Nature am I conjoined . . ."[70]

❧

As late as Eastern Han, the world was seen to be real, and its people either capable of discerning both the overt and the underlying realities, or liable to misperceive them. Sages intuited the larger social and cosmic patterns, whose general outline they passed on to others, whereas miscreants intentionally distorted reality for self-advantage. In the centuries after the fall of the Eastern Han in the early third century, however, a new discourse positing the greater "reality" of the unseen as against the illusory nature of everything visible came to overlay the older visions purveyed by the Han visual and literary conventions, at which point a more intense interiority and a "cult of non-Being" (in place of the Formless) attained logical priority over the social. The discrepant meanings attached to the same Chinese character *wei* in the post-Han, Buddhist world are the subject of other essays in this volume. This essay simply serves as a reminder that no less interesting discussions concerning the hidden vs. the displayed were not premised on a strong sense of inner-directedness, in the manner of later writings in classical Chinese.

Bernard Williams's *Shame and Necessity* laments modern scholars' propensity to approach the study of classical Greece through a Christian lens, whether they are believers or not, "measuring Greek attitudes by the standard of a Christian . . . outlook, which associates morality simultaneously with benevolence, self-denial, and inner directedness or guilt (shame before God or oneself)."[71] The same impulse, strange to say, strongly colors the study of early China today, with the result that some modern students of early China, East and West, either rush to find Christian-like values within the early Chinese writings or devalue Chinese philosophy and history because of what they see as a puzzling "lack" of interest in disinterested altruism, asceticism, and inner-directedness.[72] Nietzsche articulated a saner alternative of studying the antique, to my mind, gauging the precise value of a classical culture to lie in its "untimely" or "unmodern" character; for study of such a culture may reveal the limitations of our own habitual ways of thinking and acting to the degree that it is *not* of our world[73] and yet evinces that consummate sophistication in visual and literary rhetoric that constitutes the subject of this essay.

Notes

1. Miranda Brown, *The Politics of Mourning* (Albany: SUNY Press, 2007); Zheng Yan 鄭岩, "Guanyu Handai sangzang huaxiang guanzhe wenti de sikao" 關於漢代喪葬畫像觀者問題的思考, *Zhongghua Hanhua yanjiu* 中國漢畫研究 2 (2006): 39–55. I date the classical era in China from ca. 323 BCE to 316 CE, with the first date corresponding to the time when all the contending states signaled their independence from Zhou by their rulers' adoption of the term "king," and the second date, to the loss of the North China Plain to invaders from the north.

2. "Cultural manifold" is a term devised by Nathan Sivin in Lloyd and Sivin, eds., *The Way and the Word: Science and Medicine in Early China and Greece* (New Haven, CT: Yale University Press, 2002), xi–xii. David Keightley's was one of the early works to contrast and compare classical Greece and Shang China. See his "Clean Hands and Shining Helmets: Heroic Action in Early Chinese and Greek Culture," in *Religion and Authority*, ed. Tobin Siebers (Ann Arbor: University of Michigan Press,

1993), 13–51. Others believe that all cross-cultural comparisons are pointless, since China is unique in world history.

3. Xiaofei Tian, *Records of a Dusty Table: Tao Yuanming and Manuscript Culture* (Seattle: University of Washington Press, 2005) organizes the discussion around two variant readings of a line in Tao Yuanming's poems, one that talks of "seeing" (*jian* 見) and one that talks of "gazing" (*wang* 望).

4. The presence of clients, friends, and family—the escort as sign of collective strength—was one of the chief markers of the noble and notable man. As the *Analects* 4/25 says, "Virtue never dwells alone; it will always bring in neighbors."

5. The result of this was that the court became dependent on the local officers and elites to assess and recommend suitable men for office, with predictably disastrous consequences for the dynasty.

6. This is a standard Han pun. For one example, see Han Jing 韓敬, ed., *Fayan zhu* 法言注 (Beijing: Zhonghua shuju, 1992), citing *FY* 4/3: "ritual decorum is what allows him to embody it. These render a person as powerful as heaven."

7. These are ubiquitous, but for one example, using biao 表. See *Huainanzi* 9, "Zhu shu xun" (the opening lines): 言為文章,而行為儀表於天下 ("His [the perfect ruler's] words represent a cultivated show, and his conduct is the standard for decorum in the empire.").

8. See J. K. Shryock, *The Study of Human Abilities: The* Jen wu chih *of Liu Shao* (New Haven, CT: American Oriental Society, 1937), 83. Shryock and others tentatively date the text to 244 CE, about two decades after the downfall of the Eastern Han Dynasty.

9. Similarly, *Xunzi* 14/67/20 defines a person fit to be a "teacher" or "model" as one who "knows the nascent and can speak of it systematically" 知微而論, 可以為師. A transition period seems to be posited, where both "hiddenness" and "display" are required of the *junzi*, as in *Xunzi* 8/30/2 ("The *junzi* hides yet makes his name; he is subtle yet clear; he cedes to others and yet wins." 君子隱而顯, 微而明, 辭讓而勝); cf. *Han Feizi* 38/122/13 ("He can, in his clarity, shine his light on faraway traitors, and yet appear hidden." 明能照遠姦而見隱微).

10. See, for example, *Xinshu* 8.5/61/27 ("What is fine and subtle is difficult to recognize. Only the former kings were able to examine such things." 細微難識, 唯先王能審之).

11. See chapter 2 of the *Hanshi waizhuan*. For divination, see *Liji* 271/133/30.

12. Jiuan Heng, "Understanding Words and Knowing Men," in *Mencius: Contexts and Interpretations*, ed. Alan K. L. Chan (Honolulu: University of Hawai'i Press, 2002), 151–68, collapses the inner/outer dichotomy, as does Jane Geaney, "Grounding 'Language' in the Senses: What the Eyes and Ears Reveal about *ming* 名 in Early Chinese Texts," *Philosophy East and West* 60, no. 2 (2010): 113–42.

13. See, for example, *Zuozhuan*, Lord Zhuang 14; *Lüshi chunqiu* 15.1 ("Shen da" 慎大). Anecdote after anecdote in the *Shujing, Zuozhuan, Hanshi waizhuan*, and *Shuoyuan* (not to mention the *Fayan*'s emphasis on the outward appearances) presume the relevance of the outward appearance to "knowing men" (*zhi ren* 知人).

14. One thinks, for example, of several stories in the *Zuozhuan* where nobles feel compelled to uphold their honor by killing those who have glimpsed them or their wives naked. Compare Shadi Bartsch, *Mirrors of the Self: Sexuality, Self-knowledge, and the Gaze in the Early Roman Empire* (Chicago: University of Chicago Press, 2006), 116–21 (esp. 116), speaking of the Roman elite. The evocation of antiquity itself was largely shaped by the presentation of exemplary deeds (good and bad).

15. See below for a discussion regarding the publicity and exposure attached to mutilating punishments.

16. See Michael Nylan, "Beliefs about Seeing: Optics and Moral Technologies in Early China," *Asia Major* 21, no. 1 (2008): 89–132. Cf. Bartsch, *Mirrors of the Self*, 124.

17. Michael Nylan, "Wandering in the Land of Ruins: The *Shuijing zhu* 水經注 (Water Classic Commentary) Revisited," in *Interpretation and Literature in Early Medieval China*, ed. Alan K. C. Chan (Albany: SUNY Press, 2010), 63–102, disputes the commonplace that the *Shuijing zhu* (Water course classic) is a transparent record of above-ground edifices; it also shows the degree to which editions of this classic have been emended to make them more amenable to improvements in geographical knowledge. Meanwhile, our best evidence for classical Greece and Rome suggests that the potential of such monuments in those cultures was not fully exploited until the time of Augustus. See Paul Zanker, *The Power of Images in the Age of Augustus*, trans. Alan Shapiro (Ann Arbor: University of Michigan Press, 1988), as emended by Tonio Holscher, in *The Language of Images in Roman Art*, trans. Anthony Snodgrass and Annemarie Künzl-Snodgrass (Cambridge, UK: Cambridge University Press, 2004).

18. The excavated texts tell us almost nothing about this topic, since the overwhelming majority are either administrative documents, texts of the classics, or commentaries on them. At this remove, we can only note that these literary depictions shaped and reflected thinking on this issue, so that it would be impossible to untangle which came first, changes in behavior or changes in the prescriptions for behavior.

19. See *HS* 87B.3565.

20. Numerous examples could be given, including *SJ* 42, where Zigong's laugh so angers the duke that he wants to kill him; cf. *Shui yuan* 9 ("Zheng jian"正諫), passim.

21. Typical is *SJ* 69.2250, where a speech warning the king that he will soon become a laughingstock (為天下大笑) causes him to rethink his actions.

22. The expectation is that all inferiors laugh at what is great; hence, the proverb, "When inferior men in service hear of the Dao they have a good laugh at it" 下士聞道大笑之, in *Laozi* 41. Therefore, the "crass Ru" laugh at the "great Ru" when they are in straits, as seen in *Xunzi* 8/32/12 (是大儒 . . . 其窮也, 俗儒笑之).

23. For example, in Jia Yi's 賈誼 (d. 167 BCE) "Guo Qin lun" 過秦論, cited in *SJ* 6.276–84, Qin is said to become the "laughingstock" of the known world (為天下笑者). A surprising number of anecdotes show women criticizing men, and servants (civil and household) criticizing their superiors, and in nearly every case, this is said to infuriate the object of the remonstrance.

24. *Wenxuan* 51, "Sizi jiangde lun" 四子講德論, attributed to Wang Ziyuan 王子淵, for example, describes the residents in the frontier lands as "naked, having

'patterns' [tattoos?] on their persons" 文身裸袒. The ultimate disgrace for a person is not to be buried properly, and thus to be exposed to prying eyes and animals. See *Xinshu* 10.3/74/20 ("He died, was left unburied, and became a laughingstock to the world" 身死不葬, 為天下笑; also repeated statements in the *Mozi*, such as *Mozi* 12.2/110/9–10: "If you [as son] do not bury [the father] properly, then others will sneer at you" 子不葬, 則人將笑子.

25. For this, see Nylan, "Beliefs about Seeing." The ultimate act of violation is suggested by the phrase: "the mouths of the masses point and [or, pointedly] laugh" 眾口指笑, a sentiment repeated in the *Jiaoshi Yilin* 焦氏易林 (4/18/25; 18/87/23). See ibid., 14/66/24, 21/99/13, 59/283/5, for the shame engendered by "being observed closely and being laughed at" 為人觀笑, see *Yijing* 10/Hexagram 13/ 5). One of noble rank or pretensions was said to be "wide-eyed with fear" (懼) at the prospect of being laughed at.

26. *SJ* 111.2922: "Someone born a slave thinks it enough to avoid canings and scoldings" 人奴之生, 得毋笞罵即足矣.

27. See, for example, *Lüshi chunqiu* 10.3/49/24: "Other men would surely mock him, thinking he was quite deluded" 人必相與笑之, 以為大惑; and for the older view, *SJ* 92.2610, when "an entire marketplace full of people laughed at Xin, thinking him a coward" (一市人皆笑信, 以為怯). Here I also think of Xiao He's 蕭何 use of imposing palace buildings to create an aura of authority for Liu Bang before he gains power; and Shusun Tong 叔孫通, an influential figure at the early Western Han court, who cynically remarked on the supreme idiocy of those with social pretensions who failed to see that the "times had changed" (若真鄙儒也,不知時變). See *SJ* 99.2723. In the old eras prior to the Qin and Han Empires, cowardice earned a man sniggers, but in those early empires, cowardice came to be condoned on occasion (but stupidity never).

28. For one example see Yang Xiong's "Jie chao" 解嘲 (Dispelling Ridicule), recorded in *HS* 87A.3566–73, which mentions Fan Ju's stowing himself in a sack and Yan He's boring a hole in the wall to escape.

29. For sociability as a precondition for human happiness, see *Jiaoshi Yilin* 52/250/3: "None with whom to talk and laugh; with the autumn winds, many sorrows; these make my heart sore aggrieved" (莫與言笑。秋風多哀, 使我心悲).

30. See Nylan, "Confucian Piety and Individualism," *Journal of the American Oriental Society* 116 (Jan.–March, 1996): 1–27; Brown, *Politics of Mourning*, Introduction, esp. 5, on the "remarkably varied and contradictory beliefs about political life."

31. For "ways to avoid being laughed at by others," see *Huainanzi* 9/77/6.

32. See Wang Chong, *Lunheng*, *pian* 26 ("Ru zeng" 儒增): "Now the Master did not speak or laugh" (夫子不言, 不笑), which quotes *Lunyu* 14/3.

33. The expression is modified from Maggie Bickford's discussion of Huizong's bird and flower paintings in Patricia Buckley Ebrey and Maggie Bickford, eds., *Emperor Huizong and Late Northern Song China: The Politics of Culture and the Culture of Politics* (Cambridge, MA: Harvard University Asia Center, 2006), 457.

34. Here I think specifically of Dora C. Ching, *Icons of Rulership: Imperial Portraiture During the Ming* (PhD thesis, Princeton University, 2011), but one may also

consult on these conventions Audrey Spiro, *Contemplating the Ancients: Aesthetic and Social Issues in Early Chinese Portraiture* (Berkeley: University of California Press, 1990) and Jan Stewart and Evelyn S. Rawski, *Worshiping the Ancestors: Chinese Commemorative Portraits* (Washington, DC: Freer Gallery of Art, 2001).

35. See Paul Goldin, "The Motif of the Woman in the Doorway and Related Imagery in Traditional Chinese Funerary Art," *Journal of American Oriental Society* 121, no. 4 (2001): 539–48. For a considerably more sophisticated reading of "peering," see Keith McMahon, *Causality and Containment in Seventeenth-Century Chinese Fiction* (Leiden: E. J. Brill, 1988), 9–11, 19–21, 26–27, 36–41, 43–50.

36. See Robert Bagley, *Ancient Sichuan: Treasures from a Lost Civilization* (Princeton, NJ: Princeton University Press, 2001), color plate 107 (p. 293).

37. See Hsin-Mei Agnes Hsu, "Pictorial Eulogies in Three Eastern Han Tombs" (PhD thesis, University of Pennsylvania, 2004), for a lengthy discussion of the Anping tomb.

38. See, for example, *Hanshi waizhuan* 9/19 ("Disaster arises from the smallest [incident]" 禍起於纖微); *Shuiyuan* 10/30/84/10.

39. A typical phrase in the *Guliang zhuan*, for example, bemoans the fact that the "Son of Heaven is slighted, while his vassals do not serve him well" 天子微，諸侯不享覲. See *Guliang zhuan* 5.5.5./40/13. In the *Jiaoshi Yilin*, *wei* is almost unrelievedly bad, a sign of decline.

40. See, for example, *Chunqiu fanlu* 13.3/59/28 (而疑於神者，其理微妙也); or *Xinyu* 2/4/21 describing *qi* 氣 as 纖微浩大 ("of the very subtlest [substance], yet powerfully flowing." That such fine *qi* is more susceptible to transformation than things with well-defined "forms" is obvious and articulated in many texts, including *Qianfu lun* 33A/69/6 ("Now the form and bodily structure are firm and strong; still, it seems they do change according to government policy. How much more is this true when the refined and subtle *qi* of the heart is not nourished? 夫形體骨幹為堅彊也，然猶隨政變易，又況乎心氣精微不可養哉?"). By late Western Han and Eastern Han, a fully developed cosmogony has the original fine *qi* declining as it evolves and proliferates types of being.

41. See *Xunzi jijie* 19.2c (p. 355); Knoblock, III, 60.

42. *Guanzi* 3:8–11: "Without form, without sound; one only sees his perfection" 無形無聲，而唯見其成.

43. See, for example, *Shui yuan* 20.20/179/9; cf. *Han Feizi* 8/1//5, "Now the Way is great, but without form" 夫道者弘大而無形). A turning point seems to come with the thinkers often seen as Daoist or Legalist: *Laozi*, certainly, given his love of paradox, but also the *Guanzi*, *Shangjun shu*, etc., given their attention to details and preoccupation with the slow inculcation of habits. It is Han Feizi, for example, who urges the ruler to become "formless" (i.e., not seen), even as he acts in such a way as to perform bold deeds of great scope. See, for example, *Han Feizi* 21.43/9 ("When phenomena arising from the formless greatly contribute to the empire; this we call "subtle illumination" 起事於無形，而要大功於天下，是謂微明).

44. The dynastic histories make it clear that the court had access to coins sporting the ruler's face. That the Han court refused to run the risk that images would

be mishandled seems likely. For further information, see Michael Nylan, "Empire in the Classical Era in China (323 BCE–316 CE)," in *Conceiving the Empire: China and Rome Compared*, eds. Fritz-Heiner Mutschler and Achim Mittag (Oxford, UK: Oxford University Press, 2008), 34–64.

45. This is the picture I derive from *HS* 25A–B, the treatise recounting the development of the Western Han imperial cults. Comparisons between Emperor Wu (r. 141–87 BCE) and Emperor Cheng (r. 33–7 BCE) show that Emperor Wu's trips were both more extensive and of longer duration, while Emperor Cheng barely left the palace precincts.

46. See, for example, *Bohu tong* 22/46/17. Most have misread the term *xian zhi* 先知, thinking it always refers to the sages' "prescience." Rather, in most Han texts, the sage "knows what will transpire ahead [of events]" because he has mastered the underlying patterns; only in that limited sense is he "prescient." A few Han texts, however, attribute to the sage the ability to predict events.

47. See Yang Xiong's "Dispelling Ridicule" in *HS* 87A.3566–73. The hairnets and ribbons mark the high official.

48. See, for example, *Liji* 18.7/97/16.

49. See, for example, *Shenzi* 8/7/17 ("Yi wen" 逸文): "Now virtue is refined, subtle, and unseen; [the sage] is perceptive yet he does not initiate activity" 夫德精微而不見，聰明而不發.

50. Kongzi, or Confucius, was said to employ *weiyan* when editing the *Chunqiu*. The *Chunqiu fanlu* 1.1/2/4–12 (partly Han and partly post-Han) says that Kongzi only used "subtle messages" about the events he personally witnessed; the further back in time, the more plain and obvious his meaning reportedly was ("In reporting what he had personally seen, he made his phrasing subtle" 於所見，微其辭). For elite refinements, see, for example, *Zuozhuan*, Duke Cheng 14, which describes the *junzi* as "subtle yet obvious; committed yet dark" or Zhang Heng, "Contemplating the Mystery" 思玄賦 lines 19–20 ("My raiment is truly fair . . . / But it is not prized in this present age"), as translated by David Knechtges in Xiao Tong, *Wen xuan or Selections of Refined Literature*, trans. David Knechtges. 3 vols. (Princeton, NJ: Princeton University Press, 1982–), vol. 3:107. For one of the clearest articulations of the idea, "closed off to the masses," see *Yantie lun* 鹽鐵論 10.1/69/13 ("The subtle is what cannot be known by the masses" 微者，固非眾人之所知也.).

51. Chen Suzhen 陳蘇貞, *Handai zhengzhi yu Chunqiu xue* 漢代政治與春秋學 (Beijing: Zhongguo guangbo diantai chubanshe, 2001); Michael Loewe, *Dong Zhongshu, A "Confucian" Heritage and the* Chunqiu fanlu (Leiden: Brill, 2010). Hans van Ess has written an interesting unpublished paper linking *wei yan* to Confucius's (late) designation of "uncrowned king."

52. See *Xunzi* 19/98/9, which has the Great Man acting "without form while perfecting his patterns" 狀乎無形影，然而成文. Somewhat surprisingly, it is Xunzi also who insists on the godlike and consequently "formless" quality of the sages' effective acts. See *Xunzi* 3/10/1; 26/124/1: "The Great Man forms a triad with Heaven, being refined and subtle and without form" 大參于天，精微而無形.

53. Lucretius equates the statesman's desire to construct an image as a cynically wielded "cloak for the pursuit of wealth and power," in *De rerum natura* 5.1120–35.

Of course, my phrase "there there" conjures up Gertrude Stein's (1874–1946) acerbic assessment of her home town.

54. That this is the goal of a person is made plain in the "Hongfan" chapter of the *Documents*, which makes the "good end" one of life's supreme blessings. For further analysis of that chapter, see Michael Nylan, *The Shifting Center: The Original "Great Plan" and Later Readings* (Monumenta Serica Monograph Series 24, 1992).

55. A. C. Graham, *Later Mohist Logic, Ethics, and Science*, 39, notes: "The Mohist does not use a single term corresponding to English 'true.' A name or series of names applied to an object either 'fits' (*dang*) or it 'errs' (*guo*)" [Wade-Giles converted to pinyin].

56. Many of Yang Xiong's works play on notions relating vision to seeing. David Knechtges, *The Hanshu Biography of Yang Xiong (53 BC–AD 18)* (Tempe: University of Arizona, 1981), 19–22, translating *HS* 87A.3529–32.

57. For these themes, see Albert Dien, "Lighting in the Six Dynasty [sic] Period," *Early Medieval China* 13–14 (2007): 1–32; cf. Ban Gu, "Communicating with the Hidden," in Knechtges, trans. *Wen xuan*, 3, 83–103.

58. *FY* 3/12 defines "wisdom" as the candle (智，燭也).

59. See Huan Tan, *Xin lun*, cited in *Hsin-lun (New Treatise), and Other Writings by Huan T'an (43 B.C.–A.D. 28)*, trans. Timotheus Pokora (Ann Arbor: University of Michigan, 1975), 76–79.

60. *FY* 8/10: "The brilliant light of day—that is of use to everyone's eyes. And the vast mystery that is the sages' way—that is of use to everyone's hearts and minds!" 赫赫乎日之光。群目之用也。渾渾乎聖人之道。群心之用也.

61. *FY* 6/1. However, one commentator reads *bei* 誖 as *pengbo* 蓬勃 ("flourishing," "prospering"). See Han Jing, 123, n. 2.

62. On this point, see many stele inscriptions, which liken death to the "bright sun returning to the dark *yin*" 將去白日，歸彼玄陰 (from "Jinxiang zhanghou chengbei" 金鄉長侯成碑); as well as other writings, which speak of it as "sinking into great obscurity" 潛白日于玄陰兮 (from the "Qiusi fu" 愁思賦); or as "extinguishing the lamp and candles" 燈燭既滅 (from the "Jibei Xiang Cuijun furen lei" 濟北相崔君夫人誄) by Cai Yong 蔡邕 (133–192)).

63. This is the main idea of *Lunheng, pian* 65 ("Ding gui" 訂鬼) and *pian* 66 ("Yandu" 言毒). See the translation in Wang Chung, *Lun-heng*, Alfred Forke, trans. and ann. (New York: Paragon Book Gallery, 1962), 1, 241, 299.

64. The-Ancients-as-mirrors is a theme that appears in the *Documents* (e.g., in the "Shaogao," "Wuyi," and "Taishi" chapters) and the *Odes* (e.g., Mao nos. 235, 255). For *zijian*, see for example, *Shiji* 47.1943, 2376; *Hanshu* 57B.2580. Some Han inscriptions on mirrors contain the phrase 金之青 (? = 清) 視我形 ("The metal's polish makes visible my form."), as reported in Kong Xiangxing 孔祥星, *Zhongguo tongjing tudian* 中國銅鏡圖典 (Beijing: Wenwu chubanshe, 1992), 279.

65. See *FY* 4/7. Such passages draw on the "Xici" 繫辭 ("Great Commentary" 大傳) to the *Yijing*. See Willard Peterson, "Making Connections: 'Commentary on the Attached Verbalisations' of the *Book of Changes*," *HJAS* 42 (1982): 67–116.

66. For hiding in the crowd, see Pokora, 65–71; and Poem 18 of Tao Qian's "Twenty Drinking Poems." On eremitism, see Aat Emile Vervoorn, *Men of the Cliffs*

and Caves: The Development of the Chinese Eremitic Tradition to the End of the Han Dynasty (Hong Kong: Chinese University Press, 1990); and Alan J. Berkowitz, *Patterns of Disengagement: The Practice and Portrayal of Reclusion in Early Medieval China* (Stanford, CA: Stanford University Press, 2000). Vervoorn tends to read the recluse stories as historical accounts, and Berkowitz, as literary archetypes. Perhaps the fullest and most subtle treatment of the issue to date is to be found in Robert Ashmore, *The Transport of Reading: Text and Understanding in the World of Tao Qian (365–427)* (Cambridge: Harvard University Asia Center, 2010).

67. Translation of Yang Xiong's "Poverty," modified from that of Arthur Waley, 1923, in *Madly Singing in the Mountains: An Appreciation and Anthology of Arthur Waley*, ed. Ivan Morris (New York: Walker and Company, 1970), 173–74.

68. For Sima Qian, see Stephen Durrant, *Cloudy Mirror: Tension and Conflict in the Writings of Sima Qian* (Albany: SUNY Press, 1995); Wai-yee Li, "The Idea of Authority in the *Shih chi* (*Records of the Historian*)," *Harvard Journal of Asiatic Studies* 54, no. 2 (Dec., 1994): 345–405; Michael Nylan, "Sima Qian: A True Historian?" in *Early China* 24 (1998) [published 2000]): 1–44. On the *haogu* movement, see Nylan, *Yang Xiong and the Pleasures of Reading and Classical Learning in Han China* (New Haven, CT: American Oriental Society, 2011). Michael Loewe, *Crisis and Conflict* (London: Allen & Unwin, Ltd., 1974), has called many in this movement simply "the Reformists." I employ the term "Enlightenment" in full awareness that some reserve that laudatory term for European thinkers, because I read some of the values of the *haogu* leaders as comparable to aspects of the early modern traditions in Europe. Bernard Williams, *Shame and Necessity* (Berkeley: University of California Press, 1993; rev. ed. 2008), esp. 127–29, 166, concludes first that we are more like the ancients than we care to admit: we are fragmented, we have given up a search for a lost unity, and yet some things of a special beauty and power have survived. He secondly insists that the ethical thought of some ancients (for him the early Greeks) was "not only different from most modern thought . . . but was also in much better shape" (p. xvii) than "modern thought influenced by Christianity."

69. Nylan, "Calligraphy: The Sacred Test and Text of Culture," in *Calligraphy and Context*, eds. Cary Liu and Dora Ching (Princeton, NJ: The Art Museum, Princeton University, 1999), 1–42; Nylan, "Textual Authority in pre-Han and Han," *Early China* 25 (2001): 1–54; and Martin Kern, "Ritual, Text, and the Formation of the Canon: Historical Transitions of *wen* in Early China," *T'oung pao* 87, nos. 1–3 (2001): 43–91.

70. Arthur Waley, 1923 translation (mod.), in Morris, *Madly Singing*, 179–80.

71. Williams, *Shame and Necessity*, xvi.

72. Hence the consignment of some sophisticated works in classical Chinese to a "pre-moral" phase, which implies an inferior step on the developmental scale. Williams says (1) there has been no progression (unilinear or otherwise) toward "developed moral consciousness" (the progression being a "myth" in Williams eyes); and (2) our underlying conceptions about ethics have changed less than the "progressivists suppose" (p. 7).

73. Friedrich Nietzsche, "Vom Nutzen und Nachteil der Historie für das Leben," *Unzeitgemäße Betrachtungen*, translated by Gary Brown in William Arrowsmith, ed., *Unmodern Observations* (New Haven, CT: Yale University Press, 1990), 88.

4

Woman in the Tower

"Nineteen Old Poems" and the Poetics of Un/concealment

XIAOFEI TIAN

Like all origins, the origin of classical Chinese poetry is a retrospective construction. Although *The Classic of Poetry* is commonly regarded as the fountainhead of Chinese literature, the "Nineteen Old Poems" 古詩十九首 are often considered to constitute the true origin of classical Chinese poetry.[1] That this group of poems occupies a uniquely important place in the development of Chinese poetry can be clearly seen in the remarks of many a premodern critic. In a phrase that summarizes the case, Lu Shiyong 陸時雍 (fl. 17th c.) makes the intriguing claim that these poems "may be called the remaining trace of the 'Airs' as well as the mother of all poetry" (謂之風餘, 謂之詩母).[2]

No other definition seems to capture the nature and status of "Nineteen Old Poems" more precisely than this double metaphor. The implication of considering "Nineteen Old Poems" as the "remaining trace" of the venerable "Airs" is that "Nineteen Old Poems" directly descends from *The Classic of Poetry*; and this certainly befits the temporal scheme, as *The Classic of Poetry* precedes the "Nineteen Poems" by many centuries. But then, in an incestuous rhetorical move, the "Nineteen Poems" as "mother of all poetry" are elevated to the position of the spouse of the "Airs," which now must be identified as the unspoken "father of all poetry." The elevation of "Nineteen Old Poems" is undercut by the remark on its being the "remaining trace" or, literally, "remnant" (餘 *yu*)—something extra, superfluous, a leftover; and yet, the simultaneous praise and disparagement are nothing but an accurate reflection of the status of the feminine in a patriarchal culture. What deserves note is that the femininity of the "Nineteen Poems" is configured as that of Mother: indeed, nothing could bespeak the profoundly authoritative (hence threatening) *and* profoundly marginalized (hence reassuring) position of this group of poems better than the Mother figure.

Ironically, the origin of "Nineteen Old Poems" itself is a murky one. All we know for certain about these poems is that they were singled out from a larger corpus of anonymous poems in five-syllable lines circulating in the early sixth century, and included in the influential *Wenxuan* 文選 compiled by Crown Prince Xiao Tong 蕭統 (501–531) under the collective title "Nineteen Old Poems."[3] There are debates about the dating of individual poems, but they are usually dated to the Eastern Han (although this does not mean the poems were actually written down as fixed texts in the Eastern Han); it is most likely that they were not composed by a single author.

For a literary tradition that prizes "knowing what kind of persons authors were and considering the age in which they lived" (*zhiren lunshi* 知人論世) and that spends significant effort digging out biographical information about an author, it is a surprise that critics and scholars throughout the history of reception have been largely content to let the poems remain anonymous.[4] In fact, "Nineteen Old Poems" are the only anonymous poems after *The Classic of Poetry* to be granted such a prominent status in the traditional literary discourse. *The Classic of Poetry* has at least a putative editor/author, namely Confucius himself; as a matter of fact, even *The Classic of Poetry* had acquired contextualizing prefaces to individual poems as early as in the Han, which would provide a hermeneutic "footing" for later readers to either agree with or reject. In contrast, "Nineteen Old Poems" are not only more or less "left alone," but their very anonymity is turned into a positive value by premodern Chinese critics. Why is this? Stephen Owen argues that anonymity could become positive only in a story of origin; that is, anonymity is seen as a sign of "oldness" (i.e., predating a work by a known author), which helps make "Nineteen Old Poems" a foundational text in Chinese literary history.[5] This is certainly true. In this paper, however, I want to discuss the other aspect of this issue: that is, how anonymity functions as a decisive factor in the perceived generality of these poems. This perceived generality is as important in appreciating "Nineteen Old Poems" as in understanding traditional Chinese poetics and the uses of poetry in imperial China.

Anonymity is only one of the dark qualities of "Nineteen Old Poems," "dark" here being used in the sense of mysterious. Closely associated with it is another level of darkness enshrouding these lyrics: namely, their resistance to any assignment of definitive meaning. This may come as another surprise, since the poems in "Nineteen Old Poems" are well known for their linguistic simplicity and lucidity. Liu Xie 劉勰 (ca. 460s–520s) describes them as "direct" (*zhi* 直).[6] More than a millennium later, Xie Zhen 謝榛 (1495–1575) points out that the poems "do not prize difficult diction" and sound as if "a scholar chats informally with a friend." Two metaphors, both stressing the transparency of "Nineteen Old Poems," are particularly worth mentioning. In the first case, the Tang monk poet Jiaoran 皎然 (fl. 8th c.) states that "[the poems'] meaning is bright" (*yi bing* 義炳). In the second case, Chen Yizeng 陳繹曾 (fl. 14th c.) says of the poems: "As they achieve the greatest transparency of meaning, they manage to express the poet's utmost feelings" (*cheng zhi qing, fa zhi qing* 澄至清, 發至情).[7] The first clause, *cheng zhi qing* 澄至清, refers literally to the purification of water, and the play on words of *zhi qing* (supreme clarity 至清/utmost feelings 至情) is obvious.

Bright fire and limpid water, two figures of the transparency of "Nineteen Old Poems," ostensibly dispel any hermeneutic opacity, and yet, these comments on the verbal clarity of "Nineteen Old Poems" form a curious contrast with premodern and modern critics' extremely diverse and often conflicting interpretations of individual poems, stanzas, and lines. We will examine a few individual cases in the following sections.

Gift-Giving, Blockage, Disconnectedness

Poem VI offers a good example of the ambiguity of these lyrics:

I cross the River to pluck lotus flowers,
in the orchid marsh there are many fragrant plants.
To whom do I want to give the flowers?
The one I long for is on a distant path.
Turning around and gazing at former home:
the long road is vast and endless.
We are of the same heart, but live apart—
filled with sorrows, we thus end our days.

涉江采芙蓉　　蘭澤多芳草
采之欲遺誰　　所思在遠道
還顧望舊鄉　　長路漫浩浩
同心而離居　　憂傷以終老

There is no doubt that the "Nineteen Old Poems" are "a poetry of dislocation,"[8] or, in the words of the Qing critic Shen Deqian 沈德潛 (1673–1769): "The Nineteen Poems by and large voice the feelings of exiled subjects, abandoned wives, and separated friends; feelings about parting in life and parting by death or about old and new relationships."[9] The theme of disconnectedness nevertheless finds expression in attempts to establish connection across spatial and temporal distance. These attempts at communication and exchange include gift-giving and letter-writing; they sometimes prevail, but more often than not they fail. When they fail, there is discontinuity, and as in the poem cited above, discontinuity as a poetic theme is mirrored in the blockage of meaning, for there are widely divergent explications of what exactly the poem says and who is speaking.

Classical Chinese poetry rarely uses pronouns, and there is no distinction between plural and singular forms. My translation above supplies the first-person pronoun "I" out of necessity, but it does not help us to decide who this "I" is. Is the speaker a woman or a man? While the act of "plucking lotus flowers" is often associated with women in the later tradition, it has no specific gendered connotation in the early period. Indeed, since the poem is full of echoes of the *Chuci* 楚辭 ("Crossing the River" 涉江 being the very title of one of the *Chuci* poems), the speaker of "Li Sao" 離騷 who decorates himself with fragrant plants easily comes to mind. If the speaker in the "Old Poem" is a man, is the man traveling away from his home, or is he the one left behind by a dear friend?

The Yuan commentator Liu Lü 劉履 (1317–1379) believes that it is the former: "A traveler lives afar, missing his kith and kin but unable to see them. Though he wants to pluck flowers to send to them, the road home is too long for him to do that, so he can only grow old in sadness." Zhu Yun 朱筠 (1729–1781) likewise states that "the one who travels wants to send flowers to the one who stays."[10] This reading is challenged by Jiang Renxiu 姜任修 (1721 *jinshi*): "[The speaker] plucks the flower to send to the one far away, because the one who is 'on the distant path' is also gazing back toward home and sharing the same feelings with the speaker."[11] Zhang Yugu 張玉轂 (1721–1780) takes the same position: "This is a poem about longing. The first four lines. . . . point out that one's beloved is far away; the couplet beginning with 'turning around' is [her] speculation about his feelings, as she posits that he must also be gazing at his hometown and lamenting the long road home."[12] The debate continues well into the twentieth century. For instance, Ma Maoyuan 馬茂元 reads the poem as uttered by the male traveler,[13] whereas Pan Xiaolong 潘嘯龍 identifies the speaker as a lotus-picking girl, a common image in later poetic tradition.[14]

The gender identity of the speaker is ambiguous, and the exact relation between the gift-giver and the potential recipient is yet another source of uncertainty. Some take the recipient as the speaker's "kith and kin"; some are more specific and identify the recipient as the spouse or a very close friend. Rao Xuebin 饒學斌 (d. 1841), in his attempt to read "Nineteen Old Poems" as an interconnected political narrative, assigns the role of a slandered minister to the speaker of the series, and takes the potential recipient in Poem VI as the speaker's "fellow-sufferer," in other words a fellow-member of his faction who has likewise been slandered and sent into exile in the South (while the speaker himself is supposedly exiled to the North).[15] Wu Qi 吳淇 (fl. seventeenth century), on the other hand, believes the poem is about the relationship between a slandered minister and his estranged ruler ("the one I long for").[16] Zhang Geng 張庚 (1685–1760) develops Wu Qi's idea but refines it, construing the speaker as a minister pining hopelessly after the ruler (the one "on a distant path") and finding it impossible to turn back and go home ("the long road is vast and endless").[17]

The greatest enigma eventually comes from within the poetic text itself, as the poem ends with this couplet: "We are of the same heart, but live apart—/ filled with sorrows, we thus end our days" 同心而離居，憂傷以終老. Wu Qi, a keen critic of poetry, calls our attention to the oddness of the first line: "Now that they are 'of the same heart,' why should they 'live apart'?" He concludes, in the vein of constructing a political allegory, that "there must be a small-minded person who has come in between them."[18] The second line is, however, no less shocking than the preceding line, as we realize that this is no temporary parting, but a separation that the speaker anticipates will last till the end of their lives. The length of time matters: even a ten-year or twenty-year severance would one day end, and the hope of reunion would illuminate the vast space of despair; a lifelong separation is something else, for it will never become the past, but is simultaneously one's present and future: a temporal vastness that matches the spatial distance that separates the speaker and the object of his or her desire.

We ask, as Wu Qi does: what indeed causes two people "of the same heart" to live apart? Thanks to the suggestive *er* 而—and/but—that connects *tongxin* 同心 and *liju* 離居, the couplet is phrased in such a way that it makes this question inevitable, and there is an unmistakable hint that this separation is imposed on the lovers by someone or something beyond their control. The externality of the reason, as opposed to a change of heart and betrayal, whispers loudly of a story, but the story itself is suppressed. We are shown the tip of an iceberg only to be prohibited from seeing the mass submerged underneath the water. Herein lies the whole point of this lyric, for every reader may now claim the untold story as her or his own. In other words, we are given the outline of a story so that we may freely fill in our own experiences or imagination. The story, hinted at but remaining vague, is loosened from the framework of an individual life full of particularities and specifics: it thus becomes every man and woman's story. We are denied the narrative opulence because this is the only way we can fully participate in this poetry.

Rampant Plants Metaphors, Variants, Articulation by Suppression

The "Nineteen Old Poems" offers a special mode of story-telling: articulation by suppression. Suppression is deployed as a way of uttering rather than silencing, and there is constant tension between what the poem says and what the poem *shows the reader* it does not say. A great example is the opening couplet of Poem XI: "I turn back my wagon and venture on, / embarking on a long journey, my destination far-flung" 迴車駕言邁悠悠涉長道. The very first word is disorienting: "turn back" from where? What has prompted the poet's change of mind and change of direction? The poet then uses four characters within the space of ten characters—*mai* 邁, *youyou* 悠悠, and *chang* 長—to emphasize the length of his return journey (which of course also tells us how far he has come): such descriptive extravagance forms a sharp contrast with his narrative terseness, as we are never told exactly where the traveler is heading now and where he was going before. The rest of the poem laments the brevity of human life, and ends abruptly with praising "honor and fame," the only road to immortality; but the gloomy view of the transience of human life expressed in the first part of the poem casts a shadow over the ostensible endorsement of the pursuit of worldly glory.

Compared with the *Wenxuan* version cited above, the early Tang encyclopedia *Yiwen leiju* 藝文類聚 (comp. 624) provides an interesting variant for the first line of the couplet: "*I drive my wagon and go far away in service* embarking on a long journey, / my destination far-flung. 驅車遠行役, 悠悠涉長道" [my italics].[19] The same first line also appears in No. 39 of Ruan Ji's 阮籍 (210–263) "Songs of My Cares" ("Yonghuai" 詠懷), in which *yi* 役 (service) refers specifically to a military campaign.[20] The early Song encyclopedia *Taiping yulan* 太平御覽 adopts "drive my wagon" rather than "turn back my wagon," though the rest of the line in *Taiping yulan* remains the same as in the *Wenxuan* version.[21] Of course almost every text would have multiple versions in a manuscript culture; it is nevertheless of interest to note that textual variants always, if not exclusively, occur in places fraught with semantic difficulties, and that for an obscure line there is often a clear, easily understood version, which conveniently solves all hermeneutic problems.

Indeed, how one understands the phrase "turn back my wagon" may set the tone for the entire poem. Zhang Geng associates the image with Confucius's decision to "go home" after an unsuccessful three-year stay in the Domain of Chen; he further makes a distinction between the hypothesized failure in the speaker's public career and his determination to establish fame by pursuing a private enterprise.[22] Similarly, Zhu Yun believes that the poem focuses on the speaker's "post-enlightenment" state, and reads the phrase "turning back my wagon" as an expression of disillusionment with the world; he then explains away the last line of the poem, "honor and fame are to be treasured," as indicative of the desultory, less-than-earnest compromise that the speaker reached as a way to deal with mortality.[23] Ma Maoyuan reinforces this reading by quoting these lines from "Li Sao": "I turn my coach around along the same path, / it was not yet too far I had strayed in my going" 迴朕車以復路兮，及行迷之未遠.[24] But Zhu Yun's clumsy attempt at reconciling an image of disillusionment with the final resolution of "treasuring honor and fame" only illuminates the deep ambiguity present in the gesture of "turning back." In the end, though, it is both impossible and unnecessary to decode this gesture with any certitude: all we can tell is that it is meant to be a bridge connecting the past and present, the invisible history beyond the text and the visible moment within. It points to, but never reveals, a story, which we are made aware of but forbidden to look at closely.

Poem VIII gives us a more discernible outline of a story, with more signposts along the road, but in many ways the story is even less clear than that alluded to in the poem cited above:

Swaying is the bamboo growing in solitude,
forming its roots at the bend of a great mountain.
To form a marriage alliance with you:
the dodder plant attaches itself to the creeping vine.
There is a time for the dodder plant to grow,
and there is a time for husband and wife to come together.
Traveling across a thousand miles to marry,
far off, separated by the slopes of the hill.
Longing for you makes me old;
how late in coming is the curtained carriage.
I feel wounded by flowers of orchid and basil,
holding its blossoming within, ready to shine forth.
Now if one does not pluck it in its prime,

it will wither with autumn plants.
If you truly hold on to noble principles,
what, after all, can this humble concubine do?

冉冉孤生竹　結根泰山阿
與君為新婚　兔絲附女蘿
兔絲生有時　夫婦會有宜
千里遠結婚　悠悠隔山陂
思君令人老　軒車來何遲
傷彼蕙蘭花　含英揚光輝
過時而不采　將隨秋草萎
君亮執高節　賤妾亦何為

The translator faces an impossible task here, as the Chinese language has no tense markers. The third line of the poem, for instance, could be understood as a past action: "I have recently married you"; or as anticipation of the future: "I shall become your new wife"; or as a statement of a fact: "Being recently married to you [is like the dodder plant attaching to the creeping vine]"; or a hypothetical "If you and I become newlyweds, then we shall be like . . ." Much depends on which version we choose, as commentators have debated vehemently whether this poem expresses resentment about a belated wedding or about parting soon after wedding. The "slopes of the hill" in line 8 could be either separating the girl's native home from her married home or the insurmountable barrier between herself and her husband, who embarks on a journey soon after she married him; similarly, the curtained carriage in line 10 could be either the coach sent to fetch her for the wedding or *his* coach returning home after a long period of absence.

The plant metaphors in this poem are fraught with uncertainty, like the poem itself. The lone bamboo "forming its roots" at the bend of a great mountain is a striking image, for bamboo usually grows in clusters, not in isolation. It may be taken as a figure of the woman speaker and her relation with her husband (or alternatively, with her native family), but the next plant analogy effectively subverts the opening couplet, for unlike the pliant but essentially firm bamboo, both dodder plant and creeping vine are soft, fragile, and of the clinging sort that must attach themselves to other things to grow. While the great mountain provides protection for the lone bamboo, a creeping vine can offer no such solid support to the dodder plant.

The transfer from the firm, solitary bamboo to fragile and spreading vines is taken one step further in the second half of the poem, as the woman speaker sees her fate in the sweet-smelling orchid and basil: if one does not pluck the flower of her youth and beauty in time, it will fade with all other plants. The line describing the orchid embodies the very ambiguity of her identity: "Holding its blossoming within, ready to shine forth" 含英揚光輝. The phrase, *han ying* 含英 ("holding its blossoming . . ."), is to contain the blossoming within the bud, while the verb *yang* 揚 designates the motion of sending forth, thus an opening up, a spreading out. Once again, the translator has to make the line sound sensible in English by differentiating the two stages—present and future—and add "ready to [shine forth]," but in the original Chinese text the two phrases, *han ying* and *yang guanghui* 揚光輝, appear side by side, two contradictory terms bound to each other in one line and seemingly on the same temporal plane. The tension created by this pairing provides a perfect linguistic mirror of the profound indeterminacy of the woman herself. Is she a maiden waiting for her fiancé to take her away from her parents' home? Or is she a bride whose husband leaves her soon after their wedding night? Both interpretations have been vigorously defended by commentators from the premodern to the modern period. There is no resolution. Nor, perhaps, does there need to be.

What we know for sure is that the woman wants to be "plucked" (*cai* 采); otherwise she predicts that she will "wither" with other autumn plants. Even here we face hermeneutic difficulty. Since orchid and basil are well-known "Li Sao" plants, another interpretative possibility, much more sinister than simply fading away, is concealed right underneath the surface of these resonant images. Consider these "Li Sao" lines in which orchid and basil are mentioned together: "Orchid and angelica change, and are sweet no more; / iris and basil are transformed into straw. / How come these fragrant plants of old days, / have now turned into stinking weeds?"[25] While loss of fragrance (i.e., youth and beauty) is an external change that does not affect one's true nature, turning into straw and stinking weeds indicates a much more disturbing change, one that bespeaks a fundamental difference from what one once was. We already witness the metaphorical transference of the bamboo into dodder plant into orchid/basil in the Old Poem, each being more fragile than the other (orchid and basil being more fragile than dodder plant because they have more to lose—that is, their sweet-smelling blossoms); it would not be far-fetched to imagine a further, more troubling, metamorphosis from fragrant plant to stinking weed, hinted at through the textual echo of the well-known "Li Sao" lines.

To detect this subtext in Poem VIII is not a fanciful reading unjustified by the text itself. The final couplet caps the ambiguity that permeates the entire poem: "If you truly hold on to noble principles, / what, after all, could this humble concubine do" 君亮執高節，賤妾亦何為. Some commentators take "noble principles" to mean that he keeps faith with her, but this is not clear. It could just as easily mean that he maintains his integrity in public life, in his service to the community, and so forth. Once again, there are many narrative possibilities. As for the last line, virtually all commentators understand it as an expression of her acquiescent acceptance of the situation and a vow of fidelity; but then all those commentators were male, and it is certainly self-serving to read a declaration of faithfulness into the last line, which is formulated as a question. "Nineteen Old Poems" are not prudish, as testified by the well-known Poem II, "Green, green is the grass by the river," in which a beautiful woman, all made-up and dressed up in her husband's absence, climbs the tower, looks out, puts a hand out the window, and declares, "An empty bed is hard to keep alone." The point is that one can easily hear very different insinuations in the last couplet of Poem VIII if one is not bound by self-serving and self-fulfilling traditional commentaries, which are eager to dissolve hermeneutic and moral ambiguity by means of "politically correct" interpretations exactly because such ambiguity is so threatening.

The last line has a textual variant, cited in Li Shan's 李善 (fl. 630–689) *Wenxuan* commentary. Instead of "what, after all, could this humble concubine do?" we have, "What does this humble concubine plan to do?" 賤妾擬何為.[26] In the third position we have *ni* 擬 rather than *yi* 亦. This is an apparently minor change, but *yi* is an essentially "empty" particle that enhances the tone of "after all, what else could I do," while *ni* seems to make the question less rhetorical and more probing. The suppressed and potentially troubling reading, whereby a woman is considering taking her fate into her own hands, finds expression in a textual variant that is not adopted in most versions of "Nineteen Old Poems."

Covered by Brocade Bedding (yichuang jinbei zhegai 一床錦被遮蓋)

The last example to be considered in this paper is Poem XVI, a poem that meshes dream and reality. Just as a love-longing dream is the focus of the poetic narrative, a dream-like ambiguity prevails throughout the poem. Once again, we have difficulty determining the gender of the speaker. Once again, we are given an outline of a story whose details keep eluding us. We also have difficulty deciphering an enigmatic line involving a brocade coverlet, which in this case serves nicely as a figurative "coverup."

The poem begins with a general setting for the story:

With shivering chills, the year is coming to an end,
crickets cry sadly in the evening.
The cool wind has become austere everywhere;
the traveler suffers from cold, having no clothes.
Brocade bedding is left by the Luo River;
the one sharing my greatcoat is not with me.

凜凜歲云暮　　螻蛄夕鳴悲
涼風率已厲　　遊子寒無衣
錦衾遺洛浦　　同袍與我違

The season is autumn; the weather is chilly; the lovers are separated from each other, as they always are in "Nineteen Old Poems." That much we know about the waking reality in the poem; the rest is all blurry. The confusion begins to set in with the fourth line: "The traveler suffers from cold, having no clothes." Is the speaker male, talking about himself? Or is the speaker female, thinking of her man traveling far away from home?

The imagery of cold and covering continues into the next couplet, which is so obscure that it completely defies comprehensibility: "Brocade bedding is left by the Luo River; / the one sharing my greatcoat is not with me" 錦衾遺洛浦, 同袍與我違. On a purely verbal level, "the one sharing my greatcoat" seems to have been directly inspired by the foregoing mention of "having no clothes" in the poem, for both phrases appear together in one of the "Airs" entitled "No Clothes" (*Wu yi* 無衣). The first stanza of "No Clothes" is as follows: "How can you say, 'I have no clothes?' / I will share my greatcoat with you. / The king is raising his army, / we will make ready pike and spear, / and I will share all foes with you" 豈曰無衣, 與子同袍. 王于興師, 脩我戈矛, 與子同仇.[27]

The *Classic of Poetry* poem "No Clothes" is, however, a poem about comradeship between fellow soldiers; its speaker is clearly male, and the male bonding is testified to by the sharing of clothes *and* of enemies. The softness of the fabric, embodying the comfort and warmth of friendship, is contrasted with the sharpness and coldness of the pike and spear, weaponry of violence and death. And yet, many critics assume that Poem XVI has a female speaker and that "the one sharing my greatcoat" indicates her husband, and the Tang Dynasty "Five Ministers" commentary to *Wenxuan* (presented to the throne in 718) glosses "sharing my greatcoat" as a reference to "[the relation between] husband and wife."[28] *Tongpao* 同袍, however, is used, then and now, primarily for male relationship. It is, of course, not impossible that a wife borrows the term to refer to her husband, but in such a context, the textual echoes of "No Clothes" at best add to the gender ambiguity of the Old Poem; and, indeed, this is partially why Poem XVI has been interpreted by some critics as being about male friendship rather than love between man and woman.[29]

To adopt the mainstream "female speaker" reading does not solve the hermeneutic problems that arise in this couplet. The verb in the second line of the couplet, *wei* 違, presents another instance of doubt because of its multiple connotations: does it simply mean "separate," or does it imply a betrayal (as in "going against")? This, in a way, depends on how we construe the foregoing line: "Brocade bedding [is left] by the Luo River" 錦衾遺洛浦. *Yi* 遺, to leave behind, is also pronounced as *wei*, to present something as a gift. The Luo River is resonant with the lore of the Goddess of the Luo River, the bewitching but flirtatious Fufei 宓妃, with whom the speaker of "Li Sao" hesitates to form an alliance. A romantic involvement is implied in this line, but the nature of such an involvement remains undisclosed. Is the female speaker suspecting her husband of an adulterous dalliance during his trip? Might the "goddess" even be the reason of his prolonged absence? Is this simply an innocent way of saying that "that poor man, he does not have winter clothes or proper cold-weather bedcovers in his luggage, for he has left behind his brocade bedding here with me"? Or a bitter statement, "Of course he suffers from the cold, because he has given/left behind his brocade bedding on the bank of the Luo River!" Or, if we consider the ambiguity of classical Chinese poetic grammar and the multiple meanings of the verb, we could understand the line as saying "A brocade bedding was presented to him by the Luo River"; in other words, her worries about his having no winter clothes are interrupted by speculations that in fact he is being well taken care of—by some other woman. In a reading that takes the speaker to be male, we could interpret the couplet as stating that he has left his brocade bedding with his wife at home, and that he now has neither winter clothes nor warm coverlet, being separated from the one "sharing my greatcoat." It could also easily be a case of the man lamenting the faithlessness of the Goddess of the Luo River (just as the "Li Sao" speaker does). In a word, we are faced with numerous narrative possibilities. As the modern scholar Ma Maoyuan says with some exasperation, "The past interpretations of this couplet are extremely messy."[30]

Leaving this couplet for the moment, we shall first take a look at the second section of the poem, which centers on the dream:

> Sleeping alone on many a long night,
> in a dream I see the shining countenance of my love.
> The husband has his former sweetheart on his mind,

turning aside his carriage, he offers the mounting strap of old.
I wish this sweet smile would stay forever;
holding hands, we would return in the same coach.

獨宿累長夜　　夢想見容輝
良人惟古歡　　枉駕惠前綏
願得常巧笑　　攜手同車歸

The mention of "husband" (*liangren* 良人) seems to strongly indicate a woman speaker, who dreams of *her husband*, but then again *qiaoxiao* 巧笑, a sweet smile, is famously used in one of the *Airs* to describe a woman, and it would seem a little odd to have the woman say this either of her husband or of herself. Handing over the mounting strap is what a bridegroom does for his bride, but of course it could simply a gesture of helping her into the carriage and share the ride together. "*Former* sweetheart" and "mounting strap *of old*" fuse the past with the present in the dream, but the dream world is smashed as soon as the dreamer wishes to prolong the dream state. Time, or rather an awareness of time, breaks the spell in the last section of the poem:

My love is here for only an instant,
and does not linger in the deep chambers.
In truth I have not the wings of a dawn-wind hawk,
how could I fly away, riding the wind?
I look sideways to ease my feelings;
craning my neck, I gaze afar.
Pacing to and fro, I feel sadness within;
tears fall and soak the double-gate.

既來不須臾　　又不處重闈
亮無晨風翼　　焉能淩風飛
眄睞以適意　　引領遙相睎
徙倚懷感傷　　垂涕霑雙扉

"Dawn-wind hawk," a "poetic bird" that appears frequently in the *Airs*, works particularly well here semantically, as the word "dawn" denotes the end of night, dream, and fantasy (the first word, *liang* 亮, truly, also means "bright," and serves double purposes in this context). The following couplet beginning with "I look sideways" is missing in Li Shan's *Wenxuan*, perhaps because it does not make easy sense: two modes of looking, one close-range and one distant, are listed side by side. It might, however, very well describe the waking of the speaker: looking sideways at the beloved only to see the empty side of the bed, she or he gets up from bed and gazes afar, as if trying to catch a glimpse of the departed dream lover. The tears in the last line are the after-effect of the dream experience: a displaced wetness.

As the modern scholar Wu Xiaoru 吳小如 observes, Poem XVI is the archetypal text for numerous dream texts in the later tradition.[31] As is only appropriate for a dream poem, the focus of attention turns out to be the brocade bedding that covers and conceals. This brings us back to the premise posed at the beginning of this paper: when a text sketches a mere outline of a narrative that points to multiple plots and subplots, it offers an open invitation to fully realize the narrative.

Performativity and the Meaning of Lyric

The seventeenth-century critic Chen Zuoming 陳祚明 gives an admiringly cogent elucidation of the significance of "Nineteen Old Poems," which straddles the boundary between poetics and hermeneutics: "The reason why the Nineteen Poems are the ultimate writings of all times is because they manage to articulate the feelings shared by all people. . . . Upon reading them, everyone feels the pain as if it were one's own. This is precisely because poetry is something born of human nature and human emotions. And if feelings are shared by all people and everyone possesses them, then everyone naturally has poetry in oneself."[32] The above passage, though specifically speaking of the "Nineteen Old Poems," underscores an important tenet in traditional Chinese poetics: poetry is a mode of individual *and* collective expression. Ideally, theoretically, it belongs to *everyone*. Of course Chen Zuoming immediately has to grapple with the "evil twin" of this theory, for, after all, not everyone is a poet, and Chen Zuoming must account for a poet's special ability to articulate feelings commonly shared with all humanity and to articulate them well—that is, as poetry. Chen solves the problem imperfectly by arguing that "human emotions are naturally tortuous" and so the tortuousness of these poems is only following the contours of human emotions. Chen thus reconciles the idea of poetry as nature and that of poetry as artifice by arguing that the "tortuousness" of "Nineteen Old Poems" is both the result of "conscious and painstaking efforts" *and* a faithful, natural reflection of feelings shared by all humanity. "Nineteen Old Poems" is promiscuous and democratizing. This, however, is precisely what a traditional Chinese poem was believed to be.

The quirky and brilliant commentator Jin Shengtan 金聖嘆 (1608–1661), Chen Zuoming's contemporary, voices a similar definition of poetry.

In a letter to a friend, he writes: "Poetry is but a sudden cry from a person's heart. No matter whether it comes from a woman or a child, whether it is at dawn or in the middle of night, it could come from anyone and at any time."[33] To emphasize that poetry could come from "even" women and children is simply a seventeenth-century male elite member's way of saying that illiteracy or poor education has little bearing on the genesis or perception of poetry.

Jin Shengtan's observation is particularly relevant in the case of "Nineteen Old Poems," some of the earliest poems in five-syllable lines produced at a time when poetry in five-syllable lines was considered a "low" form (with poetry in four-syllable lines, *fu*, and other prose genres occupying the literary high ground). There was, moreover, no clear dividing line in this period between "old poems" (*gushi* 古詩), including "Nineteen Old Poems," and "songs" (*yuefu* 樂府), as lines of an "old poem" frequently appear in a *yuefu* song or are cited in a later source as a *yuefu* fragment, and vice versa. Many scholars have discussed the possibility that "Nineteen Old Poems" or at least some of the "Nineteen Old Poems," are part of the *yuefu* tradition.[34] If some of the Old Poems were indeed performed as songs, they would be performed many times by different singers and to different audiences, and ambiguity would augment the generality of these poems and maximize the possibilities of participation by singers of both sexes as well as by the audience. If, as Stephen Owen argues, "old poems," *yuefu* ballads, and Jian'an poetry by known authors were "one poetry," with shared topics, themes, lines, and segments, then ambiguity could also very well be the consequence of composition by piecing together lines and segments on an appropriate occasion.[35]

Performativity is the key to understanding "Nineteen Old Poems." By performativity I refer not only to the possible performance of the "old poems" or of segments of the "old poems" by singers of both sexes in front of an audience, but to the act of meaning production by members of the audience and eventually, in a textual tradition, by readers. In other words, singers, members of an audience, and readers help realize this poetry's narrative fullness. The word "narrative" is crucial here, for although the poems are considered the origin of Chinese "lyric poetry," "Nineteen Old Poems" almost always presents a dramatic situation and hints at a hidden but more complete narrative, and the very power of this poetry comes from the singer, listener, and reader fully entering the virtual narrative and playing the leading role in it.

Here we must also take a moment to reconsider the meaning of the term *shuqing* 抒情. The term was used often in traditional discourse, but simply as a verb-object construction—to voice one's feelings—without ever becoming a set phrase and a conceptual category as it has in the twentieth century. The modern investment of value and significance in the term *shuqing* stemmed from the need and desire to translate into the Chinese context the term "lyric," a word of Greek origin that initially signified a song accompanied by a lyre. "Lyric poetry" is used in a binary scheme to contrast with "epic poetry," which is one of the major forms of Indo-European narrative literature. Just like *shuqing*, *xushi* 敘事 (literally, to narrate an event) was a term elevated from a simple verb-object construction to the prominent status of a conceptual category in Chinese literary discourse. Completely converted to the division of "lyric poetry / epic poetry" as if it were a *natural* binary construction, modern Chinese men of letters—writers, scholars, and critics—have long been troubled by the "lack" of epic poetry in Chinese literary tradition, which leads to the attempt of making *more* out of "Chinese lyric poetry" to fill up the acutely felt "absence" of the epic.

In the Chinese context, the creation of these two modes of *shuqing* and *xushi* as inherently opposite and complementary and so mutually dependent categories is, however, misled as well as misleading. The feelings expressed in classical Chinese poetry are always contextualized by narrative circumstances: these circumstances are constructed on the basis of contextualizing the poet as a historical person—the larger narrative context of the poem; they are also frequently substantiated by a situation presented within the poetic text (often indicated by the occasional title from the fifth century on). Tao Yuanming 陶淵明 (365?–427) is a good example: his autobiographical poetry, often marked by the dates given in long and chatty titles (something new in literary history), demands to be read within the narrative context of his life. Even though we regard the impassioned attempts to provide a more specific context for Tao Yuanming's poetry as flawed, we must at the same time recognize that this sort of contextualizing impulse is intertwined with traditional Chinese critical discourse. Simply put, the binary scheme *shuqing*/*xushi* represents a modern effort to understand and articulate Chinese literary tradition; the neat split, however, remains alien and inadequate to the Chinese context.

In the case of "Nineteen Old Poems," "expression of feelings" *shuqing* is tightly interwoven with a special mode of narration. The anonymous "Nineteen Old Poems" cannot claim any historical contextualization by reconstructing the circumstances of its author or authors, but there are always stories being told in the poems, which constitute a narrative context for the poems. The "expression of feeling" in "Nineteen Old Poems" is inseparable from the narrative situation presented in the text itself, such as parting from one's beloved, sending gifts, an outsider coming to the big city and seeking his fortune, and so forth. These narrative contexts, in turn, depend on the "performers" of the texts—singers, audience, readers—to be fully realized.

Once again, a couplet taken from one of the "Nineteen Old Poems" provides us with the perfect allegory of this poetry. In Poem V, the speaker stands outside a tower and listens, enraptured, to the singing of a woman in the tower. He wonders: "Who can sing a song like this? / Surely it must be someone like Qiliang's wife" 誰能為此曲，無乃杞梁妻. According to legend, Qiliang's wife had cried so bitterly over her husband's death in battle that even the city walls crumbled at her lamentation. Noticeably, on hearing the sad song of an invisible woman in the tower, the listener attempts to contextualize her song by giving the singer an identity and a dramatic life story. She is a widow whose husband died in battle: this narrative he pieces together from her song also becomes the narrative that enables him to understand her song and, by extension, understand *her*, a woman hidden behind the music. He is the "one who understands the sound" (*zhiyin* 知音), who brings into realization the narrative fullness that is fragmented and suppressed in her song. The song is at once the woman's self-expression and the man's, coming alive through her performance and his. The song of the woman parallels and mirrors the poem uttered by the male speaker, as feeling expressed in the song is understood by way of a story, just as the feeling expressed in Old Poem V can only be understood by way of a story. What happens in these lines is therefore symbolic of the dynamics of the performance and reception of "Nineteen Old Poems," which in turn furnish us with a basic model of how traditional Chinese poetry works.

The poetry critic Hu Yinglin 胡應麟 (1551–1602) describes the paradoxical nature of the poems: "The more shallow their sense is, the more profound it becomes; the closer the words, the further away they are."[36] The second clause has a certain ambiguity to it: Hu may be saying that the meaning of the words eludes the reader, or he may be saying that the words are far-reaching.[37] The ambiguity of Hu Yinglin's comment reflects the ambiguity of the poems he comments on. Indeed, although these poems are apparently straightforward and transparent on a linguistic level, they become illusive as soon as one tries to determine exactly who is speaking what to whom and tantalize the reader with a protean quality. Many signs seem to point to a narrative fullness lurking just underneath the linguistic surface; and yet, just as we think we have deciphered the covert messages, other hermeneutic possibilities emerge and confound the coherence of meaning. In the end, it turns out that the gesture of ellipsis in "Nineteen Old Poems" points to the very principle of hiddenness, and the woman in the tower, anonymous and concealed, is ultimately the perfect figure not only for the composers of "Nineteen Old Poems" but also for the poems themselves.

Notes

1. Such a view, whether justified or not, is widely held by scholars and critics from past to present. Wang Shizhen 王世貞 (1526–1590), for instance, calls these poems "the forebears of poetry in five-syllable line" in *Yiyuan zhiyan* 藝苑卮言. In Ding Fubao 丁福保, ed., *Lidai shihua xubian* 歷代詩話續編 (Beijing: Zhonghua shuju, 1983), 978. A modern scholar refers to the poems as "the true 'source'" of Chinese lyric poetry. See Lü Zhenghui 呂正惠, *Shuqing chuantong yu shehui xianshi* 抒情傳統與政治現實 (Taipei: Da'an chubanshe, 1989), 21.

2. Lu Shiyong, *Gu shi jing* 古詩鏡. Cited in Sui Shusen 隋樹森, ed., *Gushi shijiushou jishi* 古詩十九首集釋. In *Gushi jishi deng sizhong* 古詩集釋等四種 (Taipei: Shijie shuju, 1969 rpt), 4.5. Hereafter, Sui Shusen. "Airs" refers to the first section, "Airs of the Domains" 國風, in *Shijing*.

3. Xiao Tong 蕭統, ed., *Wenxuan* 文選 (Shanghai: Shanghai guji chubanshe, 1994), 29.1343–50.

4. "Zhiren lunshi" is a set phrase and a reformulation of Mencius's remarks. See *Mengzi zhushu* 孟子注疏 10b.188, in *Shisanjing zhushu* 十三經注疏, comp. Ruan Yuan 阮元 (Taipei: Yiwen yinshuguan, 1955). Although several names, most notably the name of Mei Sheng 枚乘 (d. 140 BCE?), are attached to some of the "Nineteen Old Poems" as early as in the fifth and sixth centuries, the attribution is generally not treated as serious.

5. Stephen Owen, *The Making of Early Classical Chinese Poetry* (Cambridge, MA: Harvard University Asia Center, 2006), 40–41.

6. Zhan Ying 詹鍈, ed. and annot., *Wenxin diaolong yizheng yizheng* 文心雕龍義證 (Shanghai: Shanghai guji chubanshe, 1989), 193.

7. Xie Zhen, *Siming shihua* 四溟詩話; Jiaoran 皎然, *Shi shi* 詩式; Chen Yizeng, *Shi pu* 詩譜. In Sui Shusen, 4.3, 4.1, 4.2.

8. Stephen Owen, ed. and trans., *An Anthology of Chinese Literature: Beginnings to 1911* (New York: W. W. Norton, 1996), 250.

9. Shen Deqian, *Gushi yuan jianzhu* 古詩源箋注 (Taipei: Huazheng shuju, 1986), 117.

10. Liu, *Xuanshi buzhu* 選詩補注. In Sui Shusen, 3.3; Sui Shusen, 3.50.

11. "Gushi shijiushou yi" 古詩十九首繹. In Sui Shusen, 3.40.

12. *Gushi shangxi* 古詩賞析. In Sui Shusen, 3.60.

13. Ma Maoyuan, *Gushi shijiushou tansuo* 古詩十九首探索 (Hong Kong: Wenhan chubanshe, 1969), 85.

14. *Han Wei liuchao shi jianshang cidian* 漢魏六朝詩鑒賞辭典 (Shanghai: Shanghai cishu chubanshe, 1992), 140–42. Pan's reading is directly challenged in recent years by two authors who propose yet another new reading of the poem. See Wang Jian 王健 and Wang Zequn 王澤群, "Qian shei 'Shejiang cai furong'" 倩誰涉江採芙蓉, *Xiandai yuwen* 現代語文 3 (2006): 30.

15. *Yuewu lou gushi shijiushou xiangjie* 月午樓古詩十九首詳解. In Sui Shusen, 3.82–83.

16. *Liuchao xuanshi dinglun* 六朝選詩定論. In Sui Shusen, 3.14–15.

17. *Gushi shijiushou jie* 古詩十九首解. In Sui Shusen, 3.28–29.

18. *Liuchao xuanshi dinglun* 六朝選詩定論. In Sui Shusen, 3.15.

19. Ouyang Xun 歐陽詢 et al., comps., *Yiwen leiju* (Taipei: Wenguang chubanshe, 1974), 484.

20. Chen Bojun 陳伯君, ann., *Ruan Ji ji jiaozhu* 阮籍集校注 (Beijing: Zhonghua shuju, 1987), 321.

21. Li Fang 李昉 et al., comps., *Taiping yulan* (Taipei: Shangwu yinshuguan, 1975), 1071.

22. Sui Shusen, 3.32–33.

23. Ibid., 3.53.

24. Ma Maoyuan, *Gushi shijiu shou tansuo*, 100; see Hong Xingzu 洪興祖, ann., *Chuci buzhu* 楚辭補注 (Taipei: Tiangong shuju, 1989), 16. Owen's translation, from *An Anthology*, 166.

25. *Chuci buzhu*, 40.

26. *Wenxuan*, 1220.

27. *Maoshi zhengyi* 毛詩正義, in *Shisanjing zhushu*, 244. Owen's translation, from *An Anthology*, 52. I have underlined the overlapping parts of the "Air" with Poem XVI.

28. *Liuchen zhu Wenxuan* 六臣注文選 (SKQS edition), 12a.

29. Zhang Geng asserts: "This poem is about a luckless traveler longing for help from his old friend" 客游無賴而思故人拯之. In Sui Shusen, 3.36. Zhang Qi 張琦 (1764–1833) states: "These are the words of missing one's friend" 此思友之辭. In Sui Shusen, 2.25.

30. Ma Maoyuan, *Gushi shijiu shou tansuo*,167. Other notable interpretations include Wu Qi's and Fang Dongshu's 方東樹 (1772–1851) comments. Wu Qi regards the "brocade bedding" as a rhetorical device, not an "actual" incident. See Sui Shusen, 3.22. Fang Dongshu regards the Goddess of the Luo River as a figure for the female speaker herself, arguing this is a "flashback" to the time when she was first involved with the traveler. See Sui Shusen, 3.71.

31. *Han Wei liuchao shi jianshang cidian*, 161.

32. Sui Shusen, 4.5–6.

33. Cao Fangren 曹方人 and 周錫山標點, eds., *Jin Shengtan quanji* 金聖嘆全集 (Nanjing: Jiangsu guji chubanshe, 1985), 4:39.

34. See, for instance, Daniel Hsieh, "The Origin and Nature of the 'Nineteen Old Poems,'" *Sino-Platonic Papers* No. 77 (1998); Liu Xuqing 劉旭青, "Gushi shijiushou wei 'ge shi' bian" 古詩十九首為"歌詩"辨 in *Zhongguo yunwen xuekan* 中國韻文學刊 19.4 (2003): 10–13.

35. Owen, *The Making*, 73.

36. 意愈淺愈深, 詞愈近愈遠. *Shi sou* 詩藪. In Sui Shusen, 4.4.

37. I thank Paula Varsano for pointing this out to me.

5

Hiding Behind a Woman

Contexts and Meanings in Early Qing Poetry

WAI-YEE LI

For a male poet to adopt a female persona is one of the least surprising gestures in the Chinese poetic tradition. This choice is perhaps above all else a matter of aesthetic surface—I use the word *surface* advisedly, since "speaking as a woman" often means communicating finely wrought perceptions and sensations, which put us squarely in the realm of fabrics, skin, reflections, light and shadows, screens and curtains. It is when we move from surface to meanings that fissures and uncertainties can appear. A poet may choose a woman's perspective simply because he is interested in the emotional and perceptual horizons it opens up, of course, in many cases we are supposed to infer hidden sociopolitical functions and meanings. When is one justified to delve into "metaphorical and allegorical meanings" (*bixing jituo* 比興寄託)? Among the contexts that facilitate their construction are titles, historical situations, biographical circumstances, and anecdotes about the composition and circulation of the works in question. When is it justified to use such information as supporting evidence for unearthing hidden political meanings?

In this essay, I focus on why male poets assume female personae and perspectives, especially in moments of national crisis that render both poetic expression and communication more urgent and more difficult. My examples will be taken from the Ming-Qing transition, a period when censorship necessitates subterfuge, and when ambivalent or contradictory emotions are entrusted to indirect expression (*shenqu* 深曲, *yinqu* 隱曲), even as politicized readings become a pervasive practice among the poets' contemporaries as well as their posterity. When does "hiding behind a woman" convey a clearly coded, albeit indirectly expressed, political message? Under what circumstances does that poetic choice convey real ambivalence about historical changes or the poet's attitudes and situations? When does the female persona function as a cipher affirming common grounds or negotiating differences in poetic exchanges within male literary communities? One thing is certain: this acknowledged convention can have the effect of framing the interpretive act as the focus of attention (even, at times, dramatizing it), and in the process, it allows us to see how and why a time-honored formula can inspire a range of different readings.

The tradition of conveying "metaphorical and allegorical meanings" through feminine perspectives suggests the aesthetics of indirectness and reticence, yet it encompasses self-revelation in varying degrees of transparency. When the poetic "I" in "Encountering Sorrow" ("Li Sao" 離騷, attributed to Qu Yuan 屈原, ca. third c. BCE) declares, "The throng of women, jealous of my fair brow, / Slanders me with charges of licentiousness" 眾女嫉余之蛾眉兮，謠諑謂余以善淫,[1] most readers readily decode this as a lament that jealous rivals block the poet's access to his ruler. The Tang poet Zhu Qingyu 朱慶餘 (fl. 820s) writes in the voice of a woman getting ready to pay her respects to her in-laws the morning after the wedding: "Having finished my makeup, I ask my husband: / The way my eyebrows are painted—dark or faint—is it modish or not?" 妝罷低聲問夫婿，畫眉深淺入時無 The poem's title ("Boudoir Thoughts, Submitted to Minister of Water Management Zhang" 閨意上張水部) allows us to construe the young woman as Zhu's self-representation as he seeks recognition, approval, and direction from his superior Zhang Ji 張籍 (ca. 767–ca. 830).[2] In contrast to such relative clarity, the possible analogy between the language of ineffable loss and romantic longing in Li Shangyin's 李商隱 (813–858) "Untitled Poems" (Wuti 無題) and his political aspirations and frustrations or Tang factional politics is very much open to debate.[3]

In the following examples from the Ming-Qing transition, we see a comparable spectrum of opacity and transparency. What is different is the richness of contextual materials and circumstantial details that give us insight into how the interplay of concealment and revelation in the use of a female voice or persona is realized as a social process: through this device poets adjudicate each other and negotiate their political differences. Hiding behind a woman has always facilitated a poetics of indirectness that addresses complex and contradictory emotions, but by the seventeenth century the very gesture of hiding is built into a culture of performance and theatricality. The heightened consciousness of audience—be it the contemporary community or posterity—lends drama and pathos to the idea of self-definition through a woman's fate and choices. One may say that, expecting judgment and varying interpretations, the poet dramatizes the urgency of revelation through concealment by drawing attention to the perils and contradictions of his historical situation. I will begin with a particularly extreme example, in which a male poet attempts to "pass" as a woman.

Passing for a Woman

Around 1657, a young poet, Wu Zhaoqian 吳兆騫 (1631–1684), under the feminine name Liu Susu 劉素素, put up twenty quatrains on the walls of a temple in Tiger Mound near Suzhou. In an autobiographical preface, Liu is made to tell of her sad fate during the Ming-Qing transition.[4]

> I, Liu Susu, am a native of Yuzhang. Following my mother, I have since childhood been raised by my maternal grandparents. My elder sister Qianniang, admirably skilled in literature, often taught me the art of composing and intoning poems when taking a break from embroidery. As a result, we had frequent poetic exchanges within the inner chambers. In the year Dinghai (1647), my sister got married at the age of eighteen. I was at the time sixteen and just beginning to tie my hair back. My mother arranged my marriage with Licentiate Xiong from the same prefecture. He was a noble young man with distinguished pedigree. That year great chaos broke out in Yuzhang. I followed my mother and sought refuge in the mountains. And then the northern troops plundered and ravaged with abandon—I was [abducted and] thus trapped under an overarching yurt. Grieving over separation from my mother and sister, and mourning the devastation of family and realm,[5] I am heartbroken as tears of blood stream down. To suffer ill fate like this—truly I am no different from earthen figurines and drifting duckweed.[6] This year the man [who owns me] is serving in Zhejiang. He has been detained because of military campaigns in Nanjing, and we stopped our boat outside Changmen (the west gate) of Suzhou, awaiting his return. As I sat still by the boat's window, a hundred sorrows came together. I thus sought brush and paper and composed twenty quatrains to vent my lament and anguish. By midnight the poems were completed. Accompanied by a maid, we secretly rowed the boat to Tiger Mound, and mourned the legendary courtesan, Zhenniang, at her grave. I then pasted the poems on the wall of the temple, hoping that, to the talented ones

of the Wu area, my feelings can be made known. Alas! The cries of gibbons in the gorges, the simurgh's shadow in the mirror—the lament of all ages is in these poems!

Anecdotes about abducted women leaving poetic testimonies on walls and inspiring responses proliferated during the Ming-Qing transition.[7] These are stories that answer the need for redeeming victimhood. Following the pattern of such accounts, the Liu preface links personal misfortune to political lament. We note only two points of divergence from the usual pattern: the lamentation at Zhenniang's 真娘 grave and the explicit appeal to "the talented ones in the Wu area." Abducted women who left poetic testimonies on walls almost never compared themselves to famous courtesans, and while they bare emotions and often express the wish for ransom, rarely do they make collective appeals to an entire literary community.

The grave of Zhenniang, the famous ninth-century Tang courtesan, has since her death been a favorite poetic topic.[8] In most cases, she features as an eternally absent object of desire, her early death symbolizing evanescence and unattainability. As in poetic treatments of the grave of Su Xiaoxiao 蘇小小, another famous courtesan, her allure is often personified in the beauty of nature where she is commemorated.[9] (According to legend, the youths of the Wu area carried out her deathbed wish to have numerous flowers planted at her grave.) A Tang scholar, Tan Zhu 譚銖, opines that, alone among the innumerable graves at Tiger Mound, Zhenniang invites poetic attention because men mostly "value sensual beauty" (*zhongse* 重色).[10] Imagining Zhenniang's seductive charms at her grave seems to have been a favorite male literary pastime and the basis of many poetic exchanges; but there are also poems that point up the absurdity of such preoccupations by pitting the romantic longings associated with Zhenniang's grave against tragic devastation, such as Lu Wenkui's 陸文奎 (1256–1340) poem, dated 1291, lamenting the fall of the Song dynasty at Tiger Mound.[11]

As mentioned above, extant poems on walls by (or attributed to) abducted women almost never refer to Zhenniang. Indeed, her grave rarely came up as topic in women's poetry, although Suzhou was at the center of female literary networks in the late imperial period. When women poets wrote about it, they did not adopt a tone of romantic longing. A notable exception is a song lyric on Zhenniang's grave (to the tune "Qin lou yue," composed ca. 1670s) by the courtesan Chen Susu 陳素素, whose romance with the poet Jiang Shijie 姜實節 (1647–1709) is said to have been sparked by the song lyric.[12] Wu Zhaoqian's deliberate invocation of Zhenniang's grave, inasmuch as it is somewhat untypical of women poets and also summons incongruously romantic associations, is either an inadvertent betrayal of, or oblique reference to, the use of "Liu Susu" as a mask. "Her" direct appeal to "her" prospective audience is likewise uncharacteristic. We sometimes find pleas for help in this genre of poetic testimony, but the self-revelation of "Liu Susu" sounds like an implicit invitation for poetic exchange or commentary. These differences speak of an incomplete masquerade, or perhaps a hidden desire to be found out.

These divergent points notwithstanding, the twenty "Liu Susu" quatrains invoke imagery often found in poetic testimonies of abducted women—being taken away on horseback, sent into exile, subjected to endless peregrinations, and encountering the desolation of the frontier and the strangeness of northern or nomadic customs. Many of these testimonies invoke comparisons to the legendary Han Dynasty figures, Wang Zhaojun 王昭君 (first c. BCE) and Cai Yan 蔡琰 (ca. late second–early third c.).[13] Wang Zhaojun (also called Mingjun 明君 or Mingfei 明妃, the Bright Consort), the Han palace lady sent off to marry the ruler of the Xiongnu as part of a policy of appeasement, has through the ages become the emblem of a range of often-poeticized experiences, including exile, nostalgia, longing for home, recognition and its failure, and public duty that takes precedence over private inclinations. She is also sometimes invoked to question the very notion of loyalty, as in the subversive poems by Wang Anshi 王安石 (1021–1086) and Xu Wei 徐渭 (1521–1593).[14]

Cai Yan (Cai Wenji 蔡文姬), an aristocratic woman abducted and detained by the Xiongnu for twelve years, was forced to leave her two half-Xiongnu sons behind when she was ransomed. Like Zhaojun she emblematizes exile, but acquires additional associations with poetic testimony, ethical dilemmas, and separation from one's children, because she experienced the return from exile as another displacement. Cai Yan in particular is commonly remembered as the prototype of a woman poet whose account of personal suffering also chronicles her tumultuous times, despite the fact that scholars have questioned the authenticity of the works attributed to her, "Poem of Grief and Rancor" (Beifen shi 悲憤詩) and "Eighteen Beats of the Barbarian Fife" (Hujia shiba pai 胡笳十八拍).[15] But from another perspective, stories about Cai Yan also show how political disorder can suffice to authenticate and legitimize writings. This may explain why Wu Zhaoqian's son, Wu Zhenchen 吳振臣 (b. 1664), would claim that the title of his father's collection, *Autumn Fife* (*Qiujia ji* 秋笳集), alludes to Cai Yan's songs of barbarian fife.[16]

Indeed, in these quatrains references to Zhaojun and Cai Yan thread through the longing of "Liu Susu" for home and family. Even as she mourns the famed courtesan Zhenniang, she considers Zhaojun, whose Green Grave Mound lies beyond the frontier, more pitiable:

Deep, deep among the fragrant grass, the fair one is buried.
Wind-blown flowers everywhere, like so many tearstains.
Do not say that Zhenniang suffered such ill fate—
It is still better than a Green Grave Mound way out in Yinshan.[17]

深深芳草葬紅顏　　滿地飛花染淚斑
莫道貞娘多薄命　　猶勝青塚在陰山

In the fifteenth quatrain, "Liu Susu" compares herself to Cai Yan, whose sad fate and writings are said to appeal to the sympathy and discernment of "the talented ones of Wu," among whose ranks Wu Zhaoqian must count himself. Wu is both the author and the ideal reader, healing the division through role-playing. By inventing a poetic persona for whom he feels perfect empathy as reader, he also bridges the gap between the fictional imagination and its historical context. This is a hide-and-seek game that allows him to be both inside and outside the mask:

East wind scatters willow strands, as far as the eyes can see.
At the mountain temple of Tiger Mound, I inscribe poems, all alone.
There cannot be a lack of talented men in this land of Wu,
They too must be heartbroken over the fate of Cai Yan.

滿目東風散柳絲　　虎邱山寺獨題詩
吳下才人知不少　　也應腸斷蔡文姬

According to the late Qing writer and revolutionary Chen Qubing 陳去病 (1874–1933), Wu Zhaoqian's authorship was not revealed until later, and "Liu Susu" was celebrated as the paradigmatic talented and ill-fated woman: "By daybreak, when various scholars saw them, they were all very surprised. They thought these were truly by a woman, and at the time there were many who wrote poems in response" 厥明, 諸文士見之, 咸甚驚異, 以為真閨閣中筆也, 一時和者甚眾.[18] Chen does not cite his source for the story, which does not appear in extant early Qing writings. Although the exact circumstances of the composition and circulation of the "Liu Susu" quatrains remain unclear, their authenticity is not in doubt. Wu Zhaoqian's son, Wu Zhenchen, grouped them with poems composed before 1658 in Wu Zhaoqian's collection, *Autumn Fife*, where they appear under the title "Twenty Quatrains on the Walls [of a Temple] at Tiger Mound, with Preface" (Huqiu tibi ershi jueju youxu 虎丘題壁二十絕句有序).[19] This much is clear: the "Liu Susu" quatrains follow the mode of "speaking in another's voice" (*daiyan* 代言). In other poems in the same *daiyan* mode, Wu makes clear the context and logic of impersonation, as in "Gazing Afar, Twelve Songs" (Wang yuan qu shi'er shou 望遠曲十二首) or the series of poems composed in the voice of earlier poets, "Imitating the Ancients, Later Poems in Miscellaneous Styles" (Nigu hou zati shi 擬古後雜體詩).[20] In contrast, he provides no explanative context for the "Liu Susu" quatrains, and the silence suggests that he did indeed leave these poems on the walls under the assumed name.

What prompted Wu Zhaoqian to adopt this fictive or allegorical mask? Was this merely a youthful prank designed to enhance the reputation of a rising literary talent? Did he use the female persona to facilitate a more dramatic literary exchange or to provoke greater interest? Did he personally identify with the pathos of the victimized woman's story, or, instead, did he consider it broadly symbolic of his times? Is he using the emblematic power of the displaced and victimized woman to lament the fall of the Ming? We will never know for sure: all these are plausible motives that could have come together in varying combinations. If the poetic testimony of the abducted woman has special resonance during this period (although it would not fully explain Wu's choice), it may be because exile (whether "inner" or actual, voluntary or involuntary) had become a potent metaphor that captured the imagination in the postconquest world. Images of exile and alienation are ubiquitous in poetry from this period. Wu Zhaoqian himself wrote about the strangeness of postconquest Jiangnan:

> The Gusu Terrace, overrun by deer, is not my land,
> East of the river are gowns and caps different from travelers of old.[21]

> 胥臺麋鹿非吾土　　江左衣冠異舊游

Instead of clear explanations regarding the motives behind the composition of the "Liu Susu" quatrains, we are left with the irony of their role as the inadvertent omen of Wu's fate as the exiled victim of the new regime. Wu was implicated in the examination scandal of 1657, when allegations of corruption in the Shuntian and Jiangnan civil service examinations led to the execution of the examiners and exile for the successful candidates. The case became an excuse for the Qing court's draconian persecution of the literati of Jiangnan, where anti-Qing resistance lasted longer than in the north. Under the surveillance of armed guards, Wu Zhaoqian turned in blank sheets when he had to retake the examination in Beijing in 1658. Interpreted by some as a gesture of protest, it was more likely simply the toll of trauma. Branded guilty, Wu was exiled to Ninguta (in Manchuria) in 1658 and was only allowed to return in 1681 through the concerted help of some of the most prominent literati and scholar-officials at the time.

In the course of his northward journey in 1659, Wu again assumed the persona of the suffering woman, and wrote one hundred quatrains on the walls of a post station at Zhuozhou (in Hebei), signing himself "Wang Qianniang, a woman from Jinling" 金陵女子王倩孃. Those poems are not included in *Autumn Fife*, but Xu Qiu 徐釚 (1636–1708) records two of them in an anecdote in *Sequel to Poems in Context* (*Xu benshi shi* 續本事詩):

I recall the carved windows of bygone days that enclosed the
 jade-like beauty.
In the bright mirror with coiled dragons, she had just painted
 her brows.
And now, adrift and fallen, on the roads of mountain passes,
In vain, the fair one tries to entice springtime to the frontier.
The felt-wool tents sag heavily, the night air chills.
Frosty moonlight fills the courtyard, soaking the balustrades.
The morn of the morrow, again toward Yuyang we go—
White grass and yellow sand, from horseback surveyed.

憶昔雕窗鎖玉人　　盤龍明鏡畫眉新
如今流落關山道　　紅粉空嬌塞上春
氈帳沈沈夜氣寒　　滿庭霜月浸闌干
明朝又向漁陽去　　白草黃沙馬上看

According to Xu Qiu, "These heartfelt words are so wrenching that, from the regions of the two rivers and around the capital, many wrote poetic responses. That is why the poem by Ji Gaiting Fucao [Ji Dong 計東 (1625–1676)] says, 'Most of all, in Qianniang's lines inscribed on walls / Are the Wu lad's unbearable feelings at the frontier's extreme reaches'" 情詞淒斷, 兩河三輔多有和之者, 故計改亭甫草詩云: 最是倩孃題壁句, 吳郎絕塞不勝情.[22] We cannot be certain whether the "Liu Susu" quatrains were composed as an elaborate ruse, but the "Wang Qianniang" poems suggest that the "hiding" can be transparent and effective: Wu's friends had no trouble decoding the assumed persona.

There is little reason to doubt the authenticity of this anecdote. For one thing, Xu Qiu is a credible source; he married Wu Zhaoqian's sister and the two studied together in their youth, and Xu wrote the only extant epitaph for Wu on the latter's death.[23] In addition, the poet Ji Dong, whose friendship with Wu is well documented in *Autumn Fife*,[24] also took care of Wu Zhaoqian's family after his exile.[25] The first "Wang Qianniang" quatrain that Xu Qiu cites is the same as the sixteenth quatrain in the "Liu Susu" series. The nineteenth-century scholar Wu Chongyao 伍崇曜 (1810–1863), who republished *Autumn Fife* in his collectanea (*Yueya tang congshu* 粤雅堂叢書, 1852), confused the two stories and thought that Xu Qiu's anecdote referred to the "Liu Susu" poems.[26] Indeed, both figures serve as a fictional focus that gives a voice to collective victimhood. Keeping them separate, however, yields the unplanned satisfaction of an inadvertent omen and its deliberate fulfillment: whereas images of abduction and exile in the "Liu Susu" poems promise indefinite allegorical meanings that would eventually accidentally tally with Wu Zhaoqian's life, their repetition in the "Wang Qianniang" poems indicates self-conscious conflation of the poet and his persona.

The element of a possible ruse or practical joke in the Liu Susu story tallies well with anecdotes about Wu's youthful arrogance.[27] By contrast, Wu's banishment authenticates the pathos of Wang Qianniang's story, just as her figure universalizes Wu's personal misfortune, reminding his audience of the emblematic fate of displacement, in its many guises and ramifications, suffered by so many in that era. In that sense, our interpretations of these two sets of poems are determined by the contexts of composition.

Wu's assumption of the guise of the victimized woman in both the "Liu Susu" and "Wang Qianniang" poems may suggest a persistent desire to protest the new order and, possibly, lament the fallen dynasty—a stance that, in the latter case, would be fully justified by his having suffered wrongful accusation and exile.[28] Such a reading finds further justification in other poems by Wu, such as "The Song of the White-Haired Palace Lady" (Baitou gongnü xing 白頭宮女行, 1658) written on the eve of his exile, in which Wu displays his anguished empathy for the woes of a former palace lady who had served the last Ming emperor.

In contrast, there are other cases when Wu Zhaoqian follows the convention of using the abandoned and pining woman to seek favor and sympathy, without expressing anger or protest.[29] The imperative of suppressing rancor, driven by his anxiety to avoid further charges and, if possible, to secure a pardon, is evident in many of his metaphorical invocations of the self-abnegating female, as in Wu's letter to Ji Dong (dated the fifth month of 1658): "The palace lady from Handan, though married to a lowly menial servant, dreams of the depths of the palace as she faces spring flowers and autumn moon." 邯鄲宮人，嫁身厮養，而春花秋月，尙夢深宮.[30] The figure of Wang Zhaojun, too, appears in eponymous poems in *Autumn Fife* as the emblem of sorrow and longing divested of resentment.[31]

Wu was not the only one to see himself in the role of ill-fated beauties; the same pathos obtains in his friends' characterizations of him, as in Gu Zhenguan's 顧貞觀 (1637–1714) famous song-lyrics, addressed to Wu in 1676: "Compared to the fair-faced ones, even more ill-fated, / How then to bear now what is ever more unbearable?" 比似紅顏多命薄, 更不如今還有. Chen Weisong 陳維崧 (1625–1682) also laments Wu's fate using the familiar tropes of the abandoned woman and the "distant marriage" of Wang Zhaojun in his poem.[32] Indeed, Wu Zhaoqian's exile is remembered in literary history in part because of the famous poems lamenting his fate by, among many others, Wu Weiye, Gu Zhenguan, and Nara Singde.[33] (The latter two, along with some other prominent literati and scholar-officials, eventually secured his pardon.)

There are uncanny parallels between Wu Zhaoqian writing as a displaced woman and the ways in which his exile becomes a collective cause. In both cases—the assumption of a female guise and the collective adoption of an individual's lamentable fate—the processes of empathy and identification derive momentum from the symbolic quotient of exile and displacement and how they "translate" across categories of experience. They evoke emotions that speak to the concerns of the era and facilitate imagined analogies in writing and reading. Further, some critics have opined that Wu Zhaoqian's poetry would not have achieved lasting fame had it not been for his tragic story and the ways it became a topic in early Qing literature. The same may be said of the very idea of a woman leaving traces of her victimhood on walls. Some poems travel because of the stories surrounding them. Sometimes one even has the disconcerting feeling that some poems depend entirely on sensational stories of pathos and martyrdom for their circulation. Wu Zhaoqian may well have mastered and manipulated this logic, but he also became the victim who embodied it. Victimhood—both imagined and actual—can be made to speak through a female persona, and the revelations achieved through this mode of "hiding" are demonstrably effective in generating responses from, and consolidating ties within, the literary community.

A Woman's Choices: Transparent and Hidden Analogies

Actually pretending to write as a woman is an extreme gesture. Much more common is the practice of referring to oneself and other men in one's cohort as women, so as to dramatize the literati's dilemmas in the new political landscape. The term *jie* 節 or *kujie* 苦節, which describes both female chastity and uncompromising political integrity, was often invoked during the Ming-Qing transition. This shared lexicon illustrates the ease with which, in some literary representations, the female body merges with the body politic. In like manner, service in the new regime is sometimes compared to a widow's dishonorable remarriage, through the shared application of the terms *shijie* 失節 and *shishen* 失身.

The analogy between chastity and political integrity, which had appeared intermittently in literary writing since the Song, became ubiquitous in the self-representation and mutual judgment of men of letters during the Ming-Qing transition. Xia Yunyi 夏允彝 (1596–1645), for example, went so far as to define his duty and destiny in terms of the chaste woman's imperative of martyrdom. Xia Yunyi, as one of the leaders of the Revival Society,[34] vociferously attacked the corrupt elements of the late-Ming court. After the fall of the Southern Ming in 1645, Xia was involved, together with Chen Zilong 陳子龍 (1608–1647), in the anti-Qing resistance in Songjiang (near present-day Shanghai). After the failure of the Songjiang insurrection, he was urged to escape and join the resistance in Fujian, but he refused. The commander of the Qing army in Songjiang nevertheless tried to entice him to agree to a meeting: "If Mr. Xia is willing to join us, he will be granted an important position right away; even if he is not willing, he should just meet me once" 夏君來歸我, 即大用之. 即不願, 第一見我. Xia inscribed the answer on his door: "Suppose there is a chaste woman, and someone wants to marry her off (to another). She refuses. And then someone says to her, 'Even if you are not willing, just show your face.' Should the woman then raise the curtain and come out? Or should she protect herself by dying?"[35] 有貞婦者, 或欲嫁之, 婦不可. 則語之曰: 爾即無從, 姑出其面. 婦將搴帷以出乎? 抑將以死自蔽呼? To protect (or cover) oneself (*zibi* 自蔽) by means of one's own death is to claim the moral high ground of martyrdom by eliminating any room for compromises or uncertainties. Shortly afterwards, Xia drowned himself.[36]

The Cantonese poet Qu Dajun 屈大均 (1630–1696), who died as a loyalist of the Ming, tried to dissuade his friends from serving the Qing by tauntingly referring to them as women who yield to seduction and give themselves in marriage with indecorous haste:

> I sigh that you, along with Zhu the Tenth of Lovebird Lake,
> While not yet married, have at the front hall sealed the pact
> with your gaze.[37]
>
> 鴛湖朱十嗟同汝　　未嫁堂前已目成

The poem is addressed to Li Yindu 李因篤 (1631–1692), a well-known scholar and poet who initially refused to serve the new dynasty but eventually took the examination for "Outstanding Scholars of Vast Learning" in 1679, which was expressly designed to heal the rift between the Qing government and the intellectual elite. "Sealing the pact of mutual gaze" (*mucheng* 目成)

is a direct borrowing from the tradition of the *Verses of Chu* (*Chuci* 楚辭), in which the inconstant goddess forms such a pact with the shaman only to break it. Qu Dajun is implying that Li and Zhu, having betrayed their initial intention to remain loyalists of the Ming, are only entering into a fragile pact with the Qing court and negotiating new political dangers.

Zhu the Tenth is the renowned poet and scholar Zhu Yizun 朱彝尊 (1629–1709), who also obtained office through the examination in 1679. Qu and Zhu were both involved in anti-Qing resistance in the Zhejiang area in the 1650s. In another poem, Qu refers to their erstwhile comradeship, as well as the lost cause of resistance, in romantic and marital terms, presenting himself as the patient and long-suffering wife:

Twenty-five years, and yet I wait for you,
Hair graying, I still refuse to marry in the rays of the setting sun.[38]

二十五年還待汝　　白頭未肯嫁斜暉

Whereas the above analogies are transparent, the female persona or perspective can also be summoned to secretly convey the poet's ambivalence when faced with the contradictions of political choices, as in Deng Hanyi's 鄧漢儀 (1617–1689) poem, "On the Temple of Lady Xi" (Ti Xi furen miao 題息夫人廟).[39] In contrast with Wu Zhaoqian, Deng does not write in the first person, although it is also possible to read the style of narration as "free indirect speech." Lady Xi, who committed suicide to preserve her chastity, may function as a transparent mask, but Deng's ambivalence between empathy for and censure of her choice is not resolved by such "hiding." Deng Hanyi was himself very much an "in-between" figure: he befriended many Ming loyalists as well as Qing officials—his wide circle of acquaintance was important to his anthology projects. He sometimes expressed lament and nostalgia for the fallen dynasty, but he himself served under the Qing when he became a successful candidate in the aforementioned examination of 1679.[40]

Deng Hanyi, "On the Temple of Lady Xi"

In the Chu palace, she languidly brushes her dark eyebrows anew.
Inexorably, without a word, she faces late spring.
Through the ages the greatest test: to embrace death—
When it comes to grief, how could there only be one Lady Xi?

楚宮慵掃黛眉顰　　祇自無言對暮春
千古艱難惟一死　　傷心豈獨息夫人

"Lady Xi" refers to Xi Gui (consort of the Xi ruler), who appears in a story from *Zuozhuan* (ca. fourth c. BCE). In 680 BCE, Chu destroyed the small state of Xi, in part because he heard report of Xi Gui's extraordinary beauty and coveted her:

> [King Wen of Chu (r. 689–677 BCE)] took Xi Gui back home, and she eventually gave birth to Du Ao and the future King Cheng. But she had not yet spoken a word. The Master of Chu asked her about this, and she replied, "I, one woman, have served two husbands. Even though I have not been able to die, why should you expect me to speak?"
>
> 以息嬀歸, 生堵敖及成王焉. 未言. 楚子問之. 對曰:「吾一婦人, 而事二夫, 縱弗能死, 其又奚言?」(*Zuozhuan*, Zhuang 14.3)[41]

Opening up debates on political choices and definitions of political integrity (including its figural ties with female chastity), Lady Xi has continued to exert her hold for centuries. Like Wang Zhaojun and Cai Yan, she is the victim and the displaced woman; unlike them, she is associated with silence and hidden emotions, lending her story a special resonance. Among the many who attend to this particular aspect of her persona are the Tang poets Wang Wei 王維 (699–761) and Du Mu 杜牧 (803–ca. 853):

Wang Wei, "Lady Xi" 息夫人[42]

Do not think, just because of today's favor,
She can forget the ties of yesteryear.
Looking at the flowers, her eyes filled with tears,
She would not speak with the king of Chu.

莫以今時寵　　能忘舊日恩
看花滿眼淚　　不共楚王言

Du Mu, "On the Temple of the Peach Blossom Lady" 題桃花夫人廟[43]

In the palace of Chu is the peach tree by the well, newly planted:
Her heart full, her words lacking, how many springs has she passed?
But then Xi was destroyed, and for what reason?
Pity the one who fell from the tower in the Gold Vale Garden.

細腰宮裡露桃新　　脈脈無言度幾春
至竟息亡緣底事　　可憐金谷墜樓人

In Wang Wei's poem, the idea of emotions too intense or contradictory for words, of not speaking or of speaking only to explain silence, is enacted by the aesthetics of reticence underlying the quatrain form. Wang Wei's restraint in "Lady Xi" is sometimes adduced as proof of his compromises with the rebels during the An Lushan Rebellion[44]—a critique that typically conjoins the evaluation of poetry with moral judgment over political choices in real life.

More than a century later, Meng Qi 孟棨 (*jinshi* 875), in his *Poems in Their Contexts* (*Benshi shi*, completed in 886), elaborated an anecdote that purports to explain Wang Wei's poem in a different light. According to Meng, Prince Ning took into his harem a cake vendor's wife. When asked whether she still thought about her former husband, she would not say a word. The prince summoned the cake vendor, and his wife seemed stricken with grief when they met. Wang Wei supposedly wrote the quatrain on witnessing this meeting. In some versions of this story, Prince Ning was moved by Wang Wei's quatrain to restore the wife to the cake vendor.[45] In this way, a poem about silence is turned into an implicit and effective remonstrance about loyalty.

More often than not, however, this same poem is admired for rising above judgment. The early Qing poet Wang Shizhen 王士禛 (1634–1711) concludes that reticence is "why the high Tang style is exalted" 此盛唐所以爲高 when he compares Wang Wei's refusal to judge with Du Mu's more explicit critique of Xi Gui.[46] In Du Mu's poem, her silence becomes heavily sensual and tinged with guilty pleasure, and she is more pointedly criticized for failing to expiate her "guilt" and embrace martyrdom like the Jin minister Shi Chong's 石崇 (249–300) concubine Green Pearl 綠珠, who threw herself from a tower when Shi Chong was implicated in treason on the instigation of Sun Xiu 孫秀, a rival who coveted Green Pearl.[47]

In various poetic anecdotes, Deng's quatrain is said to pointedly criticize Ming officials who served under the Qing. But it is also possible to read more troubling ambiguities into the poem. Lady Xi languidly brushing her eyebrows (line 1) may indeed invoke the sensual image of a woman, implicitly criticized in Du Mu's quatrain, who has chosen pleasure over principle. But whereas Du Mu depicts her silence as compromising or perhaps even complacent and oblivious, in Deng's poem (line 2) it suggests sorrow and helplessness in a manner reminiscent of Wang Wei—"inexorably" (*zhizi* 祇自) implying the lack of choice or freedom; "she faces late spring" (*dui muchun* 對暮春) marks temporal duration as being characterized by melancholy and purposelessness. The battle between seduction and repulsion, feelings that are routinely juxtaposed in poems about Lady Xi, is here not resolved with the usual charges of hypocrisy or inconstancy; rather, the ideal of martyrdom is said to be a challenge throughout history, and the failure to embrace it has undone so many, who all share Lady Xi's grief.[48] The poet's voice thus veers from indictment to empathy, as he ponders difficult choices of participation or withdrawal, inner resistance or outright opposition in the postconquest era. As mentioned above, Deng's ambivalence was very much a function of his own circumstances and his historical understanding.

Revelations through Hiddenness: Contexts of Reading

Whereas the contexts of Qu Dajun's lines are stated in his poem, the frame of reference for Deng Hanyi's poem is only inferred. Both types of contextualization are common. Indirectness is no barrier since the process of encoding and decoding political interpretations is a deeply ingrained habit. This means that, with poets whose biographical circumstances, dilemmas, and choices of martyrdom or compromise are better known, dating becomes an all-important factor in interpretation. As examples we may consider the works of Chen Zilong, who died in anti-Qing resistance in 1647 and is widely hailed as one of the greatest poets during the Ming-Qing transition, along with those of his close friend and exact contemporary Li Wen 李雯 (1608–1647), who served under the Qing, albeit only briefly, and with great anguish and soul-searching.[49] The delicate, feminine diction of their song lyrics, which may delineate romantic emotions or convey political sentiments, pose special problems for the reader. The validity of a political interpretation often hinges on whether a song lyric can be dated to after 1644, although there is no decisive stylistic break before and after the fall of the Ming. To better facilitate comparison between different readings, I have chosen a cluster of song lyrics that all treat the topic of willow catkins, conventionally associated with dispersal, separation, helplessness, and the melancholy of late spring.

Li Wen, "Willow Catkins, to the Tune 'Langtao sha'"
〈浪淘沙。楊花〉

On golden strands, catkins fading in the morning breeze,
Pure snow swirling in the bright sky.
For whom does it fly up to the jade balustrade?
What shame—in the wake of the new rain at Zhangtai—
To be trodden into mud.

Tainted for no reason,
The blue bird picks them up in vain—

A springtime full of hidden dreams, where the green duckweeds
grow—
In dim corners, heartbroken in thin silken sleeves,
I furtively shake them off in tears.

金縷曉風殘
素雪晴翻
為誰飛上玉雕欄
可惜章臺新雨後
踏入沙間

沾惹忒無端
青鳥空銜
一春幽夢綠萍間
暗處消魂羅袖薄
與淚偷彈

In an eloquent exposition, Ye Jiaying 葉嘉瑩 shows how, in comparing himself to the willow catkins, Li Wen conveys the anguish and shame of being a hapless victim of fate—service under the new regime is a kind of involuntary elevation ("fly up to the jade balustrade") that inevitably ends in dishonor and degradation ("trodden into mud") impossible to reverse ("the blue bird picks it up in vain").[50] Traditional lore has it that willow catkins turn into duckweeds in water—here the transformation beckons as a provisional, albeit elusive, escape where at least hidden dreams will be possible. The last two lines shift attention to the female persona whose identification with the willow catkins is confirmed by her furtive tears, thereby alluding to Su Shi's 蘇軾 (1037–1101) famous song lyric on catkins with the same title (To the tune: "Shuilong yin" 水龍吟), which concludes with the image of willow catkins turning into "tears of parting ones."[51] The persona's action is "furtive" in the last line because his compromises have deprived Li Wen of the right to mourn outright those who died trying to reverse the tide or to directly lament the lost world of the fallen dynasty. Had this song lyric been included in *Orchid Compositions* (*Youlan cao* 幽蘭草, ca. 1632–1637), the late-Ming anthology drawn from the poetic exchanges and literary gatherings of Li Wen, Chen Zilong, and their younger friend Song Zhengyu 宋徵輿 (1618–1667), our reading would have been radically different. We would have relegated the poet to the position of observer, albeit one who writes with intense empathy for the ennui and helpless grief of his female subject.

Our reading of a hidden political reference implied by the female persona in Chen Zilong's case also depends on dating. As with Li Wen, the stylistic divide in Chen's song lyrics before and after the fall of the Ming is uncertain. This is evident when we compare his two song lyrics on willow catkins, one found in *Orchid Compositions* and the other in the early Qing collection *Poetic Communications* (*Changhe shiyu* 倡和詩餘, ca. 1646–1647; 1650 preface by Song Zhengbi 宋徵璧).[52]

"Willow Catkins, to the Tune: 'Huanxi sha'" 〈浣溪沙。楊花〉

Through a stretch of Zhangtai Road, a confused flight—
Layers of curtains tease the rays of spring.
I pity their drifting, but they cannot help but fly.

They whirl the pale sun to exhaustion beneath catkin shadows,
A waft of gentle wind sends them west of Jade Tower.
Here at sky's edge, my heart is so little known.

百尺章臺撩亂飛
重重簾幕弄春暉
憐他漂泊奈他飛

淡日滾殘花影下
軟風吹送玉樓西
天涯心事少人知

"Willow Catkins, to the Tune 'Yi Qin'e'" 〈憶秦娥。楊花〉

The misty expanse of spring—
Fragrant clouds of catkins blow through the red-patterned curtains,
Red-patterned curtains.
Broken dreams rolled up in the shade—
Let loose and drifting.
A lighthearted willfulness no match for the spite of spring,
Along with the bits of flowers borne by bees and butterflies, equally worn and torn.
Equally worn and torn—
Everywhere, duckweed on water,
Pavilions in the setting sun.

春漠漠
香雲吹斷紅文幕
紅文幕

一簾殘夢
任他飄泊
輕狂無奈春風惡
蜂黃蝶粉同零落
同零落
滿地萍水
夕陽樓閣

The dating of the first song lyric on catkins can be determined with a degree of certitude; it was probably written in the 1630s, when Chen Zilong was in the throes of a romantic relationship with courtesan-poet Liu Rushi. (Liu and Chen met in 1632 and separated in 1635 after a few months of cohabitation.) The reader is tempted to link willow catkins to Liu's name, in which case the association of willows with Zhangtai or pleasure quarters would also be a fitting reference.[53] "Drifting" (*piaobo* 飄泊) in line 3 would thus refer to the vicissitudes of a courtesan's uncertain fate—the poet's "pity" and empathy (*lian* 憐), in the same line, are tempered by a sense of helplessness—they "cannot help but fly" (*nai ta fei* 奈他飛). In brief, knowing the approximate date of this song lyric, we are prone to read it as addressing the confusion, uncertainties, and disappointments of love.

By contrast, the second song lyric, having been written after the fall of the Ming, is likely to invite a political interpretation, although a romantic reading is certainly also possible.[54] The "fragrant clouds of catkins" drift by the red-patterned curtains (line 2). It is a beautiful association that "breaks off" (*duan* 斷—translated in this line as "blows through"): this suggests lost love, but can mean also political failure. Following a political reading, the same compound that suggests a beloved woman's pitiable fate, "drifting" (*piaobo*), would summon associations with Chen Zilong's peregrinations as a resistance fighter and a fugitive after the conquest. Likewise, the words "worn and torn" (*lingluo* 零落) or "setting sun" (*xiyang* 夕陽), toward the end of the poem, would lament not merely personal helplessness but the sad fate of the country. Basically, however, the diction of the two song lyrics is similar enough to defy easy polarization of romantic and political readings *independent of contexts*, although the tone of the second song lyric is arguably more anguished. Even as astute and learned a reader as Chen Yinke 陳寅恪 (1890–1969) might have misread political lament as romantic longing because of mistaken dating.[55]

The choice of female personae and perspectives during the Ming-Qing transition thus allows us to probe how contextual evidence determines transmitted meanings. The gesture of hiding can be theatrical and self-dramatizing, as in the case of Wu Zhaoqian. But while self-dramatization implies authorial control, the fact that the female victim through whom he might have intended to convey political commentary coincidentally presages his fate and becomes a factor in decoding his works points to inherent slippage between authorial intent and hidden meanings. Hiding can seem transparent, as when male writers use the discourse of chastity for self-definition and mutual evaluation. Even in such cases, however, there is room for ambiguity, as demonstrated by the shifting margin between empathy and judgment in Deng Hanyi's poem on Lady Xi. To what extent, then, can readers assume that the extreme political pressures of the Ming-Qing transition guarantee that a poet's use of feminine perspectives justifies political readings? The song lyrics of Li Wen and Chen Zilong demonstrate the logic of context-driven interpretations. Hidden political meanings are ultimately not provable, but their possibility maps regret and longing onto the complexity and contradictions of the era, as evinced by the gap between intent and actions, the mixture of shame and self-justification inherent in moments of compromise, and the interplay of self-doubt and conviction accompanying acts of heroism.

Notes

1. Zhu Xi 朱熹, ed., *Chuci jizhu* 楚辭集註 (Hong Kong: Zhonghua shuju, 1987), 9.

2. This is the title included in Hong Mai 洪邁 (1132–1202), ed., *Tangren wanshou jueju* 唐人萬首絕句, *j.* 8, and also Gao Bing 高棅 (1350–1423), ed., *Tangshi pinhui* 唐詩品彙, *j.* 52. The poem has the alternative title "Submitted to Overseer of Water Management Zhang, As the Examination Approaches" 近試上張水部, in: Cao Xuequan 曹學佺 (1574–1647), ed., *Shicang lidai shixuan* 石倉歷代詩選, *j.* 69; Peng Dingqiu 彭定求 (1645–1719) et al., eds. QTS, *j.* 515; and in Hengtang tuishi 蘅塘退士 (1711–1778), ed., *Tang shi sanbai shou* 唐詩三百首, *j.* 8 The anecdote describing the circumstances of the poem's composition and circulation appears in Fan Shu 范攄 (fl. 877), *Yunxi youyi* 雲谿友議; Ji Yougong 計有功 (fl. 1121–1161), *Tangshi jishi* 唐詩紀事, *j.* 46; You Mao 尤袤 (1127–94), *Quan tang shihua* 全唐詩話, *j.*3.

3. For some examples, see Liu Xuekai 劉學鍇, Xu Shucheng 徐恕誠, eds., *Li Shangyin shige jijie* 李商隱詩歌集解 (Beijing: Zhonghua shuju, 1988), 1: 389–400; 4: 1439–84. Cf. Stephen Owen's discussion of Li Shangyin in *The Late Tang: Chinese Poetry of the Mid-Ninth Century* (Cambridge, MA: Harvard University Asia Center, 2006), 335–526.

4. Wu Zhaoqian, "Twenty Quatrains Inscribed on Walls at Tiger Mound" (Huqiu tibi ershi jueju, you xu 虎丘題壁二十絕句有序), in his *Qiujia ji* 秋笳集, ed. Ma Shouzhong 麻守中 (Shanghai: Shanghai guji chubanshe, 1993), 200–6; Qian Zhonglian 錢仲聯 et al., *Qingshi jishi* 清詩紀事 (Nanjing: Fenghuang chubanshe, 2000) (hereafter *QSJS*), 1958–60. In the second quatrain, Liu speaks of being separated

from her mother for ten years, which would date the poems to 1657. All of the translations in this essay are my own. On Wu Zhaoqian, see also *Qing shi gao* 清史稿, 484.13337–38; Xu Qiu's 徐釚 (1636–1708) epitaph on Wu Zhaoqian, in *Qiujia ji*, 341–43; Deng Zhicheng 鄧之誠, *Qing shi jishi chubian* 清詩紀事初編 (Hong Kong: Zhonghua shuju, 1976), 387–89.

5. The line puns with "The grand finale of the tune 'Nian jiashan.'" According to Chen Yang 陳暘 (twelfth c.), *rupo* 入破 (literally, "to enter and break up") is a Tang musical term that refers to the converging final notes of a tune. The fact that tunes during the Tang emperor Xuanzong's (r. 712–756) times are often names of frontier places is taken as an omen that these lands would be lost to barbarian invaders. The court of Li Yu 李煜 (937–978), the last ruler of Southern Tang, had a musical tune titled "Nian jiashan po" 念家山破, which means, literally, "thinking of the breakup of home and realm," and it is also said to portend the fall of the Southern Tang. See Chen Yang, *Yue shu* 樂書 in *Yingyin Wenyuange Siku Quanshu* 影印文淵閣四庫全書 [hereafter *SKQS*], 211:164.

6. Earthen figurines (*tugeng* 土梗) represent mere semblance. Guo Xiang 郭象 glosses it as "not the real thing" 非真物也. They are also easily destroyed by water and thus symbolize evanescence; see *Zhuangzi* 21, "Tian Zifang" 田子方 in Wang Shumin 王叔岷 comp., *Zhuangzi jiaoquan* 莊子校詮 (Taipei: Academia Sinica, 1994), 767, 770–71; *Zhanguo ce* 戰國策, *j.* 10, Qi 3; *j.* 18, Zhao 1. In Liu Xiang 劉向 comp., *Zhanguo ce* (Shanghai: Shanghai guji chubanshe, 1985), 374, 603. "Drifting" or "floating" duckweed is a conventional topos for homelessness.

7. For some examples, see *QSJS*, 15510–12, 15526–36, 15625–38.

8. A collection of poems on Zhenniang's grave (*Huqiu si ti Zhenniang mu shi* 虎丘寺題真娘墓詩, in one *juan*) is listed as "no longer extant" in the Song compendium *Chong wen zong mu* 崇文總目, compiled by Wang Yaochen 王堯臣 (1001–1056) and others.

9. A good example is Li Shangyin's 李商隱 (813–858) "Harmonizing with Another on Zhenniang's Grave" (He ren ti Zhenniang mu 和人題真娘墓), in *Li Shangyin shige jijie*, 1946–49. The principle of synecdoche here is comparable to Li He's 李賀 (790–816) poem, "Su Xiaoxiao's Grave" (Su Xiaoxiao mu 蘇小小墓), in Wang Qi 王琦 et al., comp., *Sanjia pingzhu Li Changji geshi* 三家評註李長吉歌詩 (Hong Kong: Zhonghua shuju, 1976), 46.

10. Tan Zhu's satirical quatrain, "On Zhenniang's Grave" (Ti Zhenniang mu 題真娘墓) is found in an anecdote from Fan Shu, *Yunxi you yi* in *SKQS*, vol. 1035, *juan* zhong, 27b: "On the foothills of Tiger Mound, endless graves pile on, / Pines soughing and desolate—all can stir lament. / Why then must men value sensual beauty, / And on Zhenniang's grave alone inscribe poems?" 虎丘山下塚累累, 松柏蕭條盡可悲, 何事世人偏重色, 真娘墓上獨題詩?

11. Lu Wenkui (1256–1340), "Inscribing a Poem at Tiger Mound, in the Third Month of the Xinmao Year, Written at Sword Pond" (Huqiu liuti xinmao sanyue shuyu Jianchi 虎丘留題辛卯書于劍池), in *Qiangdong leigao* 牆東類稿 in *SKQS* 1194:18.7b.

12. The romance between Jiang and Chen is dramatized in the *chuanqi* play *Qinlou yue* 秦樓月 by Zhu Suchen 朱素臣 (mid–seventeenth c.). Chen Susu's poems,

as well as poems on the romance by other woman writers (among them Wu Wenrou 吳文柔, Wu Zhaoqian's sister), are appended to the early Qing edition of the play.

13. On the representations of the abducted women in this period, see Li Wai-yee, "Ming mo Qing chu liuli daolu de nannü xingxiang" 明末清初流離道路的難女形象, in Wang Ayling, ed. *Kongjian yu wenhua changyu: kongjian yidong zhi wenhua xuanshi*《空間與文化場域：空間移動之文化詮釋》(Cultural interpretations of mobility) (Taipei: Hanxue yanjiu zhongxin, 2009), 143–86.

14. Wang Anshi: "The grace of Han is but shallow, that of the barbarians, deep: / In deep recognition of like minds is the joy of human existence" 漢恩自淺胡自深, 人生樂在相知深, from his "Song of Bright Consort" 明妃曲, in *Linchuan wenji* 臨川文集, *SKQS* 1105:4.11b; Xu Wei: "He who married you to the barbarian was the Han emperor, / He who ransomed Cai Yan, who was he to Han?" 嫁爾呼韓漢天子, 贖歸蔡琰漢何人? In Xu Wei, *Xu Wei ji* 徐渭集 (Beijing: Zhonghua shuju, 1999), 869. Cao Cao 曹操, who ransomed Cai Yan and allowed her return, was also traitor to Han. From the perspective of the victimized woman, the conventional evaluation of the embodiment of just authority and its betrayer is reversed.

15. See Lu Qinli 逯欽立, *Xian Qin Han Wei Jin Nanbei Chao shi* 先秦漢魏晉南北朝 (Beijing: Zhonghua shuju, 1983), 1:201; Hans Frankel, "Cai Yan and the Poems Attributed to Her," *Chinese Literature Essays Articles Reviews* 5, no. 2 (1983):133–56; Wilt Idema and Beata Grant, *The Red Brush: Writing Women of Imperial China* (Cambridge, MA: Harvard University Asia Center, 2004), 112–27; Kang-i Sun Chang and Haun Saussy, eds., *Women Writers of Traditional China: An Anthology of Poetry and Criticism* (Stanford, CA: Stanford University Press, 1999), 22–30.

16. Wu Zhenchen, "Postscript to *Autumn Fife*" (*Qiujia ji* ba 秋笳集跋), in *Qiujia ji*, 358.

17. Fourteenth quatrain. Legend has it that the grass at Zhaojun's grave stays green, despite the surrounding arid landscape.

18. Chen Qubing, *Wushizhi* 五石脂, in Suzhou Museum, Suzhou University History Department, Suzhou Gazetteer Committee, eds., *Danwu biji, Wucheng riji, Wushizhi* 丹午筆記、吳城日記、五石脂 (Suzhou: Jiangsu guji chubanshe, 1985), 277.

19. *Qiujia ji* was first published by Wu's friend, the Qing scholar-official Xu Qianxue 徐乾學 (1630–1694), in 1676, when Wu was still in Ningguta. When Wu Zhenchen republished it in 1726, he divided the Xu printing into four *juan*, and added four more. *Juan* 5, "Autumn Fife: Earlier Collection" (Qiujia qianji 秋笳前集), and *juan* 6, "Imitating the Ancients, Later Poems in Miscellaneous Styles" (Nigu hou zati shi 擬古後雜體詩) comprise poems composed before Wu's exile in 1658, "Autumn Fife: Later Collection" (Qiujia houji 秋笳後集), *juan* 7, includes his postexile poems. The Liu Susu poems are found at the end of *juan* 5.

20. *Qiujia ji*, 5.183–87; 6.207–20.

21. Wu Zhaoqian, "To Qi Yixi" (Zeng Qi Yixi, 贈祁奕喜), in *Qiujia ji*, 5.187. The poem is dated to 1655. Yixi is the cognomen of Qi Bansun 祁班孫 (d. 1673), son of the late-Ming scholar-official and writer Qi Biaojia 祁彪佳 (1602–1645). Wu and Qi belonged to the same Jiangnan literary circles. Exiled respectively in 1657 and 1661, they continued their friendship "beyond the frontier."

22. See Xu Qiu, *Xu benshi shi*, in Meng Qi 孟棨 et al., *Benshi shi Xu Benshi ci* 本事詩續本事詩本事詞, punct. Li Xueying 李學穎 (Shanghai: Shanghai guji chubanshe, 1991), 374; *Qiujia ji*, 343–44. On Xu Qiu, see *Qing shi gao*, 484.13342; Deng Zhicheng, *Qingshi jishi chubian*, 386–87.

23. See Xu Qiu, "Xiaolian Hancha Wu jun muzhiming" 孝廉漢槎吳君墓誌銘 in *Qiujia ji*, 341–43. See also Wu's letters to Xu and Xu's letter to Wu (*Qiujia ji*, 308–12, 369–70).

24. See *Qiujia ji*, 135, 158, 172, 192, 196, 268–69.

25. See Ji Dong's biography in *Qing shi gao*, 484.13337; Deng Zhicheng, *Qing shi jishi chubian*, 378–79; *QSJS*, 1944–48.

26. Wu Chongyao (1810–1863), "Postscript to *Autumn Fife*" (*Qiujia ji* ba 秋笳集跋), in *Qiujia ji*, 361–62. The fact that Liu Susu's sister is named Qianniang adds to the confusion.

27. See *QSJS*, 1949.

28. When Beijing fell in 1644, the precocious twelve-year-old Wu Zhaoqian wrote poems of political lament in the style of Du Fu, but by the 1650s he became reconciled enough to want to participate in the examination and join the new order. The nineteenth-century scholar Li Yuerui 李岳瑞 asserts that Wu's implicit lament for the fallen Ming in some of his works might have led to his persecution (*Chunbing shi ye sheng* 春冰室野乘, cited in *QSJS*, 1954). There is little solid evidence for this, however.

29. See, for example, "The Concubine of the Youth of Zhongshan" (Zhongshan ruzi qie 中山孺子妾), "Plaint of the Consort of River Xiang" (Xiang fei yuan 湘妃怨), "Plaint of Changmen Palace" (Changmen yuan 長門怨), "An Ill-fated Concubine" (Qie boming 妾薄命), in *Qiujia ji*, 107–9. Included in a 1676 edition published by Xu Qianxue, these poems cannot be dated with certainty. The sense of "pandering to those in power" (*meishang* 媚上) is also precisely what irks his critics.

30. Wu Zhaoqian, "Yu Ji Fucao shu" 與計甫草書 (Letter to Ji Dong), in *Qiujia ji*, 268–69.

31. See *Qiujia ji*, "Wang Zhaojun," 235; "The Song of Bright Consort" (Mingfei qu 明妃曲), 253. "Wang Zhaojun" was written after his exile; "The Song of Bright Consort" appears in the undated "Supplementary" section and is similar in tone to "Wang Zhaojun."

32. Chen Weisong, "Five Laments" (Wu ai shi 五哀詩), in *Qiujia ji*, 382.

33. Wu Weiye, "Song of lament, for Wu Jizi" (Beige zeng Wu Jizi 悲歌贈吳季子); Gu Zhenguan, "To the tune: Jinlüzi." See *Qiujia ji*, Appendix 6, 382–404, for a collection of contemporary poems about Wu's exile, many of them addressed to him.

34. Members of the Revival Society (Fu she), active during the reign of the Chongzhen emperor (1628–1644), advocated political and administrative reforms.

35. See Hou Xuanhan's 侯玄涵 (seventeenth c.) biography of Xia Yunyi, "Libu Xia Yuangong zhuan" 吏部夏瑗公傳, included in the modern printing of the collection of his son, the precocious poet and famous Ming martyr Xia Wanchun 夏完淳 (1631–1647), see *Xia Wanchun ji jianjiao* 夏完淳集箋校, ed. Bai Jian 白堅 (Shanghai: Shanghai guji chubanshe, 1991), 516–20. On Xia Yunyi, see also *Ming shi* 明

史, 277.7098–99; Chen Tian 陳田 (1849–1921), *Mingshi jishi* 明詩紀事 (Shanghai: Shangwu yinshu guan, 1936), 6, 1884–85.

36. See Hou's biography, in *Xia Wanchun ji jianjiao*, 519; Xia's biography in *Ming History* tells how "confusion and despair among mountains and marshes," as well as the examples of friends who had chosen martyrdom, drove him to suicide (*Ming shi*, 277.7099).

37. Qu Dajun, "Composition sent to Li Zide" (Fuji Fuping Li Zide 賦寄富平李子德), in *QSJS*, 871.

38. Ibid., 870.

39. Ibid., 2817.

40. For Deng Hanyi's social and literary circles, see Tobie Meyer-Fong, "Packaging the 'Men of Our Times,' Literary Anthologies and Political Accommodation in Early Qing," *Harvard Journal of Asiatic Studies* 64 (2004): 5–56; *QSJS*, 2815–20.

41. *Zuozhuan*, translated by Stephen Durrant, Wai-yee Li, and David Schaberg (University of Washington Press, 2016). In *Lienü zhuan* 列女傳 4.7, Lady Xi is said to have killed herself, and her suicide earns her a place in the "Chaste and Dutiful" (*zhenshun* 貞順) section.

42. Wang Wei, *Wang Mojie quanji jianzhu* 王摩詰全集箋註, comp. Zhao Songgu 趙松谷 (1683–1756) (Hong Kong: Guangzhi shuju, n.d.) 13.197. Zhao includes all the textual variants in his annotations.

43. Du Mu, *Du Mu xuanji* 杜牧選集, comp., Zhu Bilian 朱碧蓮 (Shanghai: Shanghai guji chubanshe, 1995), 197–99. By the Tang Dynasty, for reasons not totally clear, Lady Xi is also called "Peach Blossom Lady."

44. Zhang Biaochen 張表臣 (Song Dynasty), *Shanhugou shihua* 珊瑚鈎詩話 (*SKQS*, 1478:3.5a–5b). Using as criteria "learning" (*xue* 學) and judgment (*shi* 識), Zhang considers Du Mu's poem superior to Wang Wei's. Zhang's comparison of these poems follows an entry on his judgment of Wang Wei's lack of political courage during the An Lushan Rebellion.

45. *Benshi shi*, 8, in *Benshi shi, Xu Benshi shi, Benshi ci*.

46. *Yuyang shihua* 漁洋詩話, *juan xia*, no. 51, in Ding Fubao 丁福保 (1874–1952) comp., *Qing shihua* 清詩話 (Shanghai: Shanghai guji chubanshe, 1999), 212.

47. Fang Xuanling 房玄齡 et. al., *Jin shu* 晉書, 33.1008. The Gold Vale Garden was Shi Chong's estate.

48. The last two lines of Deng's quatrain are quoted in chapter 120 of *The Story of the Stone* to criticize Xiren. Xiren, first maid and then unofficial concubine of the protagonist Jia Baoyu, submits to a marriage with the erstwhile actor Jiang Yuhan after Baoyu renounces all worldly attachments and becomes a monk. Whereas Deng's lines arguably retain a measure of ambiguity, the author of the last forty chapters of *Stone* adduce them as unforgiving castigation of compromise.

49. Many poems in *Liaozhai houji* 蓼齋後集 testify to such sentiments; an especially moving example is the poem and letter Li Wen sent to Chen Zilong in 1647 ("Bingshu chuxi" 丙戌除夕). See *Liaozhai houji*, in *Siku jinhui shu congkan* 四庫禁毀書叢刊 (Beijing: Beijing chubahshe, 1997), 111:2.14a. On Chen Zilong, see

Kang-i Sun Chang, *The Late Ming Poet Ch'en Tzu-lung: Crises of Love and Loyalism* (New Haven, CT: Yale University Press, 1991). On the Yunjian (Songjian) literary community to which Chen Zilong and Li Wen belonged, see Yao Rong 姚蓉, *Ming mo Yunjian sanzi yanjiu* 明末雲間三子研究 (Guangzhou: Guangdong gaodeng jiaoyu chubanshe, 2004).

50. Ye Jiaying, *Qingci xuanjiang* 清詞選講 (Taipei: Sanmin shuju, 1996), 5–48.

51. See the last lines of Su Shi's song lyric on willow catkins, "To the tune: Shui long yin": "Look closely: / these are not willow catkins, / but drop by drop, / tears of parting ones" 細看來，不是楊花，點點是，離人淚. See Su Shi, *Dongpo ci* 東坡詞, ed. Cao Shuming 曹樹銘 (Hong Kong: Wanyou tushu gongsi, 1968), 109.

52. *Poetic Communications* represents the Yunjian literary community, and comprises song lyrics composed around 1646 and 1647 by Chen Zilong, Qian Gu 錢穀, and several poets from the Song clan of Yunjian—Song Cunbiao 宋存標, Song Zhengbi, Song Zhengyu, and Song Siyu 宋思玉.

53. Chen Yinke surmises that the *ci* should be understood in the context of the love affair between Chen Zilong and Liu Rushi, see his *Liu Rushi biezhuan* 柳如是別傳 (Shanghai: Shanghai guji chubanshe, 1980), 244.

54. Ye Jiaying, for example, reads this in the light of the Chen-Liu romance, see *Ye Jiaying zixuan ji* 葉嘉瑩自選集 (Jinan: Shandong jiaoyu chubanshe, 2005), 196–201.

55. Chen reads "Jiangcheng zi" 江城子 ("bing qi chun jin" 病起春盡) in the light of the Chen-Liu romance, but that *ci* is included in the post-conquest anthology. (Chen did not have access to *Youlan cao* and *Changhe shiyu.* He was working from *Chen Zhongyu quanji* 陳忠裕全集, which gives no information about dating.)

The Lessons of Distraction

6

Hiddenness of the Body and the Metaphysics of Sight

SHIGEHISA KURIYAMA

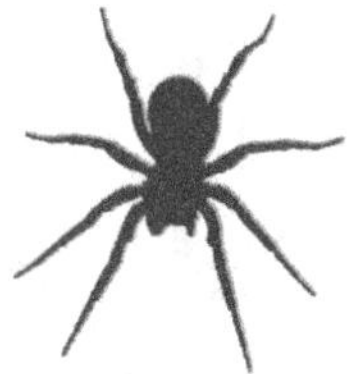

"What is this?"

"A spider," you answer easily.

But if I first enclose the spider in a box, and then ask about what is inside, you just shrug silently. How could you know? Stare as long and intently as you like, and you still face only the expressionless walls of the box. Its blank and opaque surfaces.

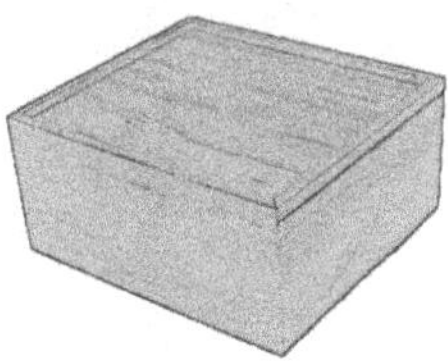

The spider is *hidden*. Such is the basic, ordinary sense of this word—when a visible object is made invisible by obstacles that block our view.

1

Anatomists have taught for centuries that the core of the human body is hidden in this way. And they have utterly convinced us: for us, the hiddenness of our internal organs is a plain fact, an indisputable given. Our sight stops at the body's surface, already blocked by the skin.[1] Nothing could be more obvious. Unless we cut open the body, the heart, kidneys, and other viscera are all invisible. Hidden, like the spider in a box.

This is the overarching lesson of anatomical illustrations. At the same time that they reveal the form and place of exposed structures, these pictures take great pains to remind us of all the skin, and muscles, and other surfaces that had to be peeled back or removed to expose them. They teach us, that is, not just about particular organs, but also and more generally, about the nature of the anatomical gaze—about how seeing is a form of unveiling, about how knowing the body requires an uncovering of the covered.

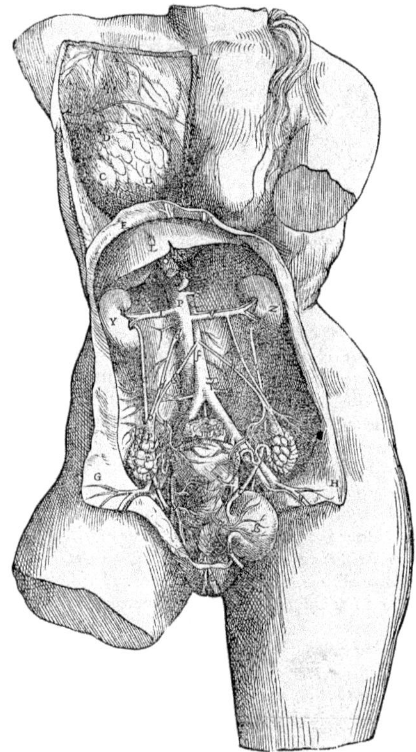

Figure 6.1. Torso, from Andreas Vesalius, *De fabrica corporis humanis* (1543).

2

So we are puzzled by the transparency of bodies in old acupuncture texts. Although they are often referred to as "anatomical" plates, images of the viscera in Ming and Qing medicine betray no trace of the dissector's labors, no hint of an original hiddenness. Examining the spleen, stomach, and intestines appears as casual, and effortless, and commonplace as glancing at the eye, or nose, or ear. It is as if Chinese doctors were strangely indifferent, or oblivious, to the opposition of visible surface and concealed contents. As if the very distinction of outer and inner did not signify.

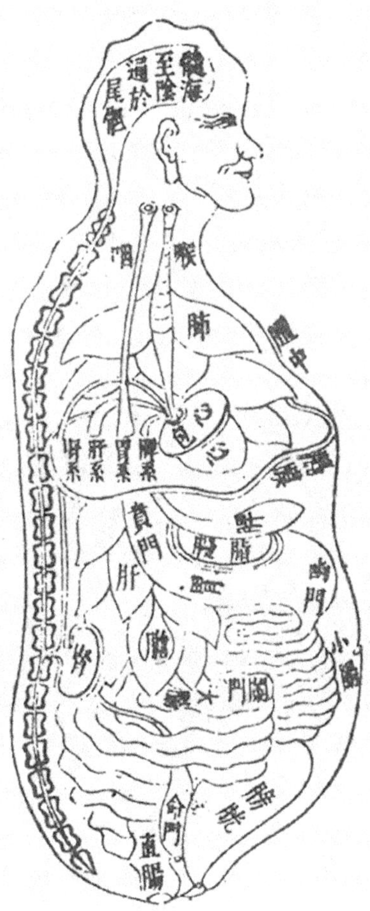

Figure 6.2. *Neijingtu*, from Zhang Jiebin, *Leijing tushuo* (1624).

What could this mean? How should we interpret this odd absence of hiddenness? Answering this question would presumably go far toward illuminating another, more familiar enigma in comparative medical history, namely, the absence in premodern China of sustained interest in anatomy. Historians and anthropologists of Asian and European medicine have long cited this neglect of dissection as the most salient trait separating traditional Chinese from Western approaches to the body. Transparency torsos such as these suggest a crisp explanation: doctors in China did not dissect, because they saw no need. There is no reason to cut open corpses if nothing is veiled from view. It is curiosity about what ordinarily can't be seen, after all, that impels the onlookers in Vesalius's *Fabrica* to crowd eagerly around the dissected corpse. Their intense absorption in anatomy is inseparable from an acute sense of hiddenness, the hope of glimpsing secrets.

Of course, this answer raises its own perplexities. Yes, if the viscera are already visible, and nothing is concealed—as the transparent torsos imply—then anatomy is pointless. But the reality is that the viscera *aren't* visible. How could Chinese doctors have imagined otherwise? This seems even harder to fathom than an indifference to anatomy. The transparent body is plainly a fiction; the hiddenness of the organs is solid fact. No one can see the heart and stomach nestled inside the body. Just as no one can perceive a spider concealed in a box.

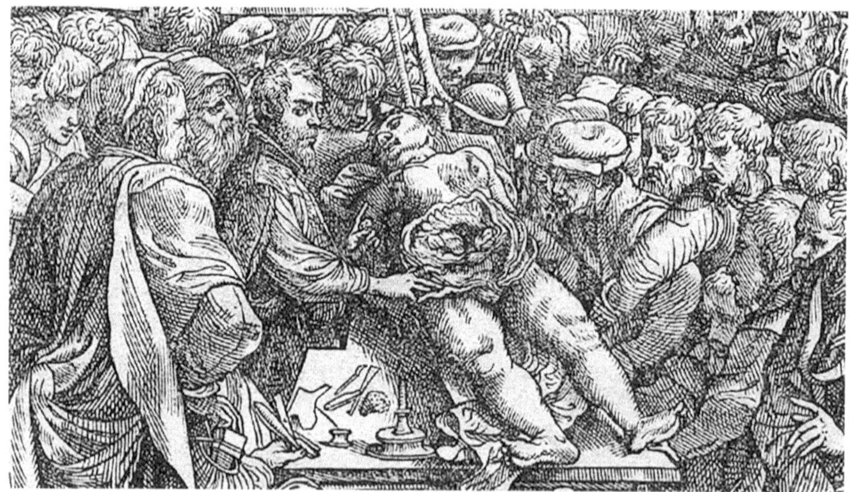

Figure 6.3. From Andreas Vesalius, *De fabrica corporis humanis* (1543).

3

Or can they? When Zhuge Yuan was appointed to a post in Xinxing, his friend Guan Lu 管輅 (209–259) came to bid him farewell, and found other well-wishers already there. Yuan left his guests briefly, the *Records of the Three Kingdoms* reports, and after collecting a spider, a swallow's egg, and a wasp's nest, he placed the three objects in a covered box. He then returned, and challenged Guan Lu to say what the box contained.

A spider, a swallow's egg, and a wasp's nest, replied Guan Lu, to the astonishment of all.[2] He, for one, apparently had no trouble espying a spider in a box.

On another occasion, one Xu Jilong, the prefect of Qinghe, tried to stump Guan Lu by secreting no less than thirteen things inside a large basket. "I count thirteen hidden objects," Guan Lu declared, and then he named them one by one, starting with a chicken's egg, and concluding with a silkworm cocoon. His sole mistake was to confuse a comb for a ladle.[3]

Guan Lu excelled at *shefu* 射覆, "shooting the covered"—the divining of secreted objects. He became the most celebrated master of the art in Chinese history, but he was neither the first nor the last. The *History of the Former Han Dynasty*, for instance, already relates how Dongfang Shuo 東方朔 (154–93 BCE) proved his *shefu* credentials by detecting a concealed gecko.[4] Numerous treatises were composed setting forth the techniques of the art, and later histories record a line of enthusiastic practitioners stretching into Qing times, including the eminent Neo-Confucian philosopher Shao Yong 邵雍 (1011–1077).

All of which now strikes us as vaguely unreal. Our impulse today is to dismiss offhand the tales of shooting the covered as just amusing fantasies, or evidence of premodern gullibility. We simply don't believe that human sight can pierce walls, not really, not in real life, just as we don't believe in seeing viscera without dissection. If we scratched our heads over images of transparent torsos, we are yet more baffled by tales of penetrating closed containers.

Two points merit emphasis. The first is that past Chinese historians themselves portrayed *shefu* insight as cause for amazement. They recorded the names and feats of Guan Lu and Dongfang Shuo, that is, precisely because they were thought extraordinary. *Ordinarily*, it was assumed, people can't know the contents of closed containers. In this, the common sense of traditional China was no different from ours. Where it departed slightly but puzzlingly from our intuitions was the allowance for exceptions—the belief in unusual people with special skills who could perceive what you and I cannot.

The second point is that these skills didn't actually entail a penetrating gaze, an ability literally to pierce occluding obstacles. Guan Lu didn't stare, as we might stare, at the boxes in which spiders, eggs, and the like were concealed, straining to peer through their opaque walls. In fact, he didn't even look in their direction. Instead, he cast milfoils, and interpreted their configurations in the mirror of the *Yijing*, the *Book of Changes*. He saw by divining.

Prompted by an official named Liu Bin to shoot the covered, Guan Lu correctly announces the presence of a seal case and a feather plucked from a mountain pheasant. Asked to explain his clairvoyance, he speaks of the shapes that he discerns in the hexagrams:

> The inside square, the outside round,
> Its patterns formed of many hues.
> The treasures enclosed under trusted seal,
> Revealed show a well-patterned print.
> This is a seal case.
>
> On the craggy heights of a towering range,
> Stands the scarlet shape of a bird.
> Its feathered cloak is black and brown,
> And it never misses the call of dawn.
> It's the feather of a pheasant.[5]

Guan Lu's insight thus turned, in other words, not on raw ocular force—some superhuman power to pass through walls, like X-rays—but rather, on a sensitivity to meaningful patterns. His gaze was akin to that of the astute doctor studying a skein of symptoms, the savvy hunter eyeing animal tracks, or the Serendip prince who surveyed the irregularities in grazed grass and saw the blindness in a camel's right eye.[6]

He saw in a way not unlike the way that you are seeing at this moment, when you scrutinize the marks on this page and see into my mind.

4

Shefu was an art of insightful reading. Reading is seeing—but with a sort of double vision. One must simultaneously look *at* the object at hand, and also see *beyond* it. The hunter looks at impressions on the ground and sees, with astonishing precision, the evasions of hunted prey. The scholar looks at black traces on scraped parchment and sees the labyrinthine thoughts of thinkers long dead. It is a form of seeing that to untutored eyes appears nothing short of magical.[7]

"Look," someone says, pointing to this figure. "What do you see?"

Glance casually, and you make out only a grainy blur of countless speckles, a vague, amorphous texture. After brief consideration, you likely pass on, seeing nothing of note. Even if I alert you to the latent presence of an image, and you stare intently for a long time, you still may not see anything.

Once you do see, however, once you recognize the shark swimming in the sea—yes, it is truly there, look again—everything is suddenly, magically transformed. The previously invisible figure now looks so astonishingly clear and vivid, that you wonder how they could have escaped you before. Incredibly, the blurry fog suddenly shines like a luminous mirror, and the shark almost floats off the page, in a startlingly deep, three-dimensional space.

Of course, if you still see nothing, you will be perplexed by this description, and may even get angry, suspecting a mean joke or a lie.

And yet everything is there, in plain sight, openly accessible to all eyes. There are no obstacles blocking your view. Whether you see or not depends solely on your ability or inability to apprehend the pattern on display, your skill in reading. Depending on how you look, the shark either shimmers brilliantly or is completely hidden.

❧

It seems, then, that there are at least two sorts of hiddenness.

There is, on the one hand, the hiddenness with which we began, hiddenness as we commonly conceive it in daily life: one object blocks the view of another. This is a hiddenness determined by the laws of optics and the disposition of things, an absolute hiddenness, in which it does not matter who is looking, or how. A spider scampering across the kitchen table is visible. A spider trapped under a clay bowl is hidden—to you as well as to me, to keen and obtuse observers alike. To everyone.

And then, there is the hiddenness exemplified by the sharks lurking amid the specks, the autostereogram[8]—a relative hiddenness, in which what is hidden to me may be apparent to you, and what is hidden to you and countless others may still be clear to some exquisitely trained eye. This isn't at all unusual. Autostereograms may themselves be exotic, but the form of hiddenness that they illustrate is one that we confront daily, as we try to fathom the inner lives of others.

People regularly conceal what they feel or think. They dissemble. They feign interest when they are bored, or feign boredom to disguise their interest. They mute their worries and eager hopes. They harbor plans. A woman carries on as usual, and casual acquaintances and strangers like me may notice nothing. But you, who have known her since childhood, discern the latent boredom, the fear, the unspoken intent.

What boredom? What fear? What plan? I ask, confused. And you yourself may be unable to say exactly how you see what you see. You may be unable to articulate the many subtle changes that form the telltale pattern—the flattened or rounded arch of the lips, the shine or dullness of the pupils, the faint tightening or droop of the shoulders. You simply see—the agitation, the boredom, the secret plot.

No one can completely hide all the telltale changes, not from everyone. Recall how the heroine in one of Stefan Zweig's novellas peers into a gambler's inner life—the wild hopes and despair that his willfully impassive face conceals—by noting the small jerks and twitches of his fingers.[9] There are always residual clues that betray the truth—at least to a mother, a spouse, an acute analyst. At least, that is what we tend to suppose.

We tend to suppose this, because to suppose otherwise would be to believe in disembodied passions—in fear or excitement as discrete *things* floating entirely free of the body, which could be secreted like a spider in a box. But surely they aren't like this. Surely, fear, anger, joy, boredom are more like tremulous webs of change, altering nearly every aspect of the person. And while it is true that people can pose and dissimulate, and that steely discipline may hush the most dramatic expressions of a passion, no one can suppress all the changes that occur, say, in someone who is intensely anxious—the strained voice, the constricted capillaries, the churning stomach, the cold sweat—without erasing the anxiety altogether. For these changes do not just express the fear. They are part of the felt experience, basic to what fear *is*.

Diseases are another example. They, too, are networks of intricately linked alterations. Which is why a gifted physician can diagnose an affliction early on, long before its ravages become apparent to all. The historian Sima Qian 司馬遷 (ca. 145–ca. 86 BCE) thus tells of how the perspicacious physician Bian Que 扁鵲 (fl. ca. 255 BCE) tracked the disease of the Duke of Huan—its slow and steady descent, over weeks, from the surface of the skin into the marrow of the bones—just by scrutinizing the patient from the outside.[10] Bian Que looked at the Duke and said, "A disease has pierced the skin," and later, "The disease has burrowed into the blood vessels," and finally, "Your disease has lodged in the flesh; you must treat it now, or die." And each time the Duke just scoffed, and blithely ignored the diagnosis. He felt fine, as strong as ever; and besides, how could a stranger know, just by looking from the outside, what was transpiring inside him? But of course the physician was right, and the Duke soon falls ill and dies.

How can someone strong and sound suddenly die? Such cases are baffling to laymen, the *Nanjing* 難經 (*Classic of Difficult Issues*) explains, but experienced doctors know that the deaths aren't as unexpected as they seem. These are patients whose inner store of vitality was exhausted. They are like plants severed from their roots.[11] For a while, before the inevitable wilting and withering become manifest to all, the person may talk and laugh as usual, and appear to flourish. But shrewd observers will spot the signs of the emptiness within—a faint dimming of the skin's luster, perhaps, or a spreading pallor, a subtle hollowing of the voice—and recognize this bloom as a momentary simulacrum of past vigor. Good doctors will know that, like cut flowers, such a person is as good as dead.

Life and death, the flourishing and faltering of the viscera, are all plainly visible for those who know how to see. There was no need here for either X-ray vision or for dissection. In traditional Chinese medicine, the viscera were never just discrete structures, never solitary things, but configurations of powers, interacting with other configurations of powers. Yes, organs called the heart, lungs, liver, spleen, and kidneys could be espied inside the abdomen; but their workings were manifest in a person's gait and posture, in the complexion of the face and the timbre of the voice, in the penchant for sweet or salty tastes, in the propensity to laugh, or sing, or cry. To observe the dynamically evolving configurations of posture, complexion, tastes, and the like was thus directly to observe the viscera as they mattered most, as powers in action, shaping and reshaping the horizons and feel of life.

Anatomy in such a body was thus not only superfluous, but even absurd. It made no more sense to dissect the body to know the liver than to cut open the body to see a blushing child's embarrassment. Just as we read a letter and peer into private thoughts, just as we glance at faces and see the clouding of doubts and clearing of confusions, so skilled physicians could see the waxing and waning of the viscera right there, on the surface. To expert readers, the inner lives of others—the activities of their organs as well as the shifts of feeling—were as perspicuous as a black spider momentarily frozen on a white page.

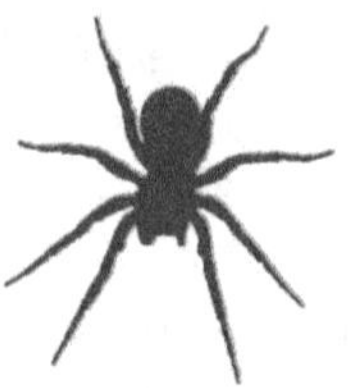

5

The belief in absolute hiddenness—the assumption that no one can perceive the spider in the box or the viscera in the abdomen—is rooted in a realistic vision of the world. I mean realistic in its etymological sense: I mean a vision that envisages a world of *things* (Latin, *res*).[12] Things impede our view of other things. Stone walls block our view of the house behind it. A wooden box conceals the spider inside. The body's skin hides the underlying muscles and viscera: Western anatomy is the application of a realistic gaze, a gaze focused on things—the model of the spider in the box—to the understanding of human beings.

The Chinese art of *shefu* was inspired by the opposite perspective. Its approach essentially applied the model of reading people—of diagnosing diseases and interpreting feelings—to the spider in the box. Guan Lu did not need to see through obstacles. He saw the secreted spider in the same way that Bian Que saw the faint beginnings of Duke Huan's disease—by espying expressive webs of propensities, by studying figured forces.[13] He was an experienced reader inhabiting a thoroughly readable world. Instead of confronting a universe of things, he contemplated a cosmos of *patterns*.

For you and me, and other laymen, sore sinews, tired eyes, irritability, and a sudden craving for sour pickles may be just so many separate developments, isolated signs; we may recognize no ties between them. Similarly, we glance at boxes, spiders, the diviner's milfoils, and see disparate objects, unrelated things. But just as the soreness, the anger, and the hankering for sourness all coalesced, in the eyes of the Chinese doctor, into the portrait of an afflicted liver, so the *shefu* master scrutinized the figures formed by milfoils, and saw a spider, a cocoon, a pheasant's feather.

My point is this: hiddenness and visibility are as much matters of metaphysics as of optics. What things are opaque and what transparent depend, crucially, on differing perceptions of what things *are*. If we approach a sealed box as an isolated object holding other isolated objects, we then find that its opaque surfaces indeed block our view and that its contents are beyond our ken. If we confront the human body as a thing secreting other things, we feel compelled to uncover the organs inside. Supposing a world of things instantly subtracts much of the world from our purview. Realism is blinding.

But Guan Lu and Bian Que saw instead a universe of patterns. Their key insight was precisely the recognition that there is no need for insight, no need to see *in*—that the world's secrets are hidden not as things occluded by other things, but as subtle designs, visible to all who grasp how to look, that hidden secrets are less like treasures locked inside a thick vault, than like our shark swimming in a sea of speckles.

6

The belief in a world of patterns goes hand in hand with the presumption of a world ruled by change. There are no truly opaque things in this world, no fixed, impenetrable solids, because nothing is permanent. The entire universe is in ceaseless flux. "In the transformations that affect all things," Guan Lu declares, "constant forms do not exist, and in the vicissitudes that affect men, there is no constancy of bodily shape."[14] Like the medicine of yin and yang and the five phases, the art of shooting the covered supposed constancy only in the patterns that rule inconstancy.

The *shefu* expert's mastery of these patterns meant that his clairvoyance reached beyond closed spaces, into the shadows of time. Just like a doctor, he could survey the past and future of disease.

Called in to diagnose a man's crippled foot, Guan Lu traces the problem back to a forgotten crime in the past: the man's ailment, he explains, owes to the vengeance of a woman who had been brutally murdered.[15] In Guangpin, he is consulted on the first month of the year about the wife of one Liu Fenglin. The woman is so ill that her coffin has already been prepared, but Guan Lu predicts that she has longer to live. "Her fate is to die during the eighth month on the twenty-eighth day of the sixty-day cycle. She will die at noon." Although the husband is incredulous, his wife improves, and events unfold exactly as the seer had foretold.[16]

In yet another case, Guan Lu illuminates the forgotten history entombed in a house. Asked to solve the mystery of a severe fright afflicting the women in the household of the prefect of Xindu, he prophesizes: "At the western extremity of the northern hall there are two dead men, one of whom clutches a spear and the other a bow and arrows." It is their buried bodies, he explains, that secretly underlie the women's terror. Again, everything turns out as Guan Lu says, and the women recover when two skeletons are exhumed from the old wall.[17]

7

In a world of patterns, all the sights that we confront on this spot at this moment—the closed box, the ailing foot, the women struck by terror—are inseparable from an intricate web of connections that bind it dynamically to countless other sights in other spots and other times. It is this connectedness that allows Bian Que to diagnose diseases and predict their outcome, and makes it possible for Guan Lu to shoot the covered. But this same connectedness also means that most of us suffer from chronic myopia. Most of the time, we are hypnotized by the sights immediately before us, and ignore the vast net of which they are but a few nodes. We have no idea how much eludes us. We are unaware that our seeing is a form of blindness.

❧

One object can block our view of another, we said. A wall hides the house behind it. In a world of things, placing obstacles is the natural way to conceal.

But there are other ways to hide. In a world of patterns, sights are obscured less by obstacles than by distractions. Despite the transparent torsos, hiddenness looms as a major concern in Chinese medicine as well. But the concern is of a different sort: while anatomical plates in Europe stress the labors required to uncover the covered, medical illustrations in traditional China spotlight, rather, how easily significant sights are overlooked.

Consider the illustrations in treatises of *waike* 外科, external medicine. Because these works specialize in afflictions that manifest themselves on the body surface, we would expect diseases here to be the exact opposite of hidden. Certainly Western surgical manuals abound in graphic close-ups, often quite frightening, of the tumors, wounds, and other conditions that the surgeon must treat.[18] Yet in the plates of a major Qing dynasty compendium such as the *Yangyi daquan* (瘍医大全), the pathologies are remarkably hard to spot.

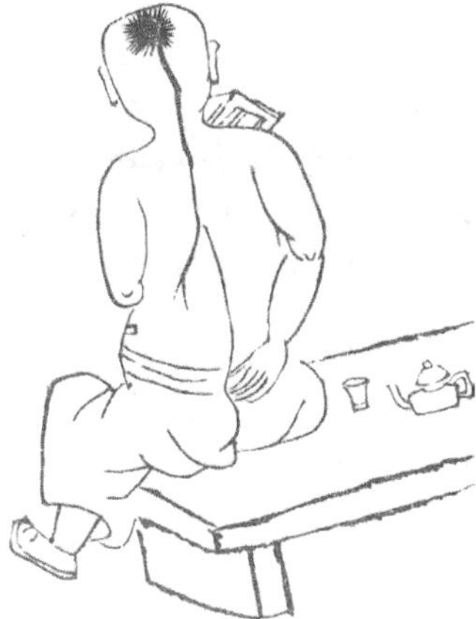

Figure 6.4. From Gu Shicheng, *Yangyi daquan* (1760).

What is wrong with this man? If this plate appeared in a nonmedical text, we probably would not suspect anything amiss—though we might be curious why the man has pulled his right hand to the base of his spine. Our eyes most likely wouldn't dwell, in any case, on the actual mark signaling pathology—the tiny rectangle in the left lower back—which looks almost accidental, like a stray ink streak, or a carver's slip. Without the accompanying text, we would never guess that this as an illustration of an ulcer in the back.

Here is a pretty young woman, contemplating her reflection in the mirror. No sooner do we chance upon her than we begin to speculate about her

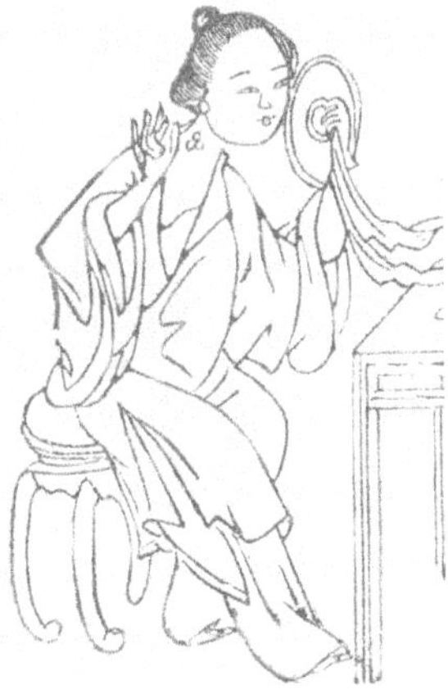

Figure 6.5. From Wang Xixin, *Waike qieyao* (1847).

thoughts, her hopes for the future, the amusements that she has planned for the day. In Europe, such a scene might be an evocation of hopeful youth, or perhaps a cautionary tale about vanity.

Once again, however, all the features that immediately catch our eye, and most engage our interest—the woman's pose and expression, and their intimations of inner life—are actually irrelevant to the announced subject of the image. This is an illustration of a kind of rash, we learn from the text of the *Waike qieyao* (外科切要)—and only then do we note the three small circles on her neck.

Waike manuals abound in such illustrations. In plate after plate of the *Yangyi daquan* we encounter intriguing characters, each of whom seems to have some tale to tell, and whose attire, accoutrements, and facial expression all lure our eyes away from the malady that is the ostensible subject of the picture.

Yes, once we read that the man on the left suffers from a malady on the chin, the one in the center from a cucumber rash on the abdomen, and the figure on the right from an eruption in the palm, we can spot the signs. But without forewarning, we are likely to miss them all, or ignore them as marks of no significance. So many other sights make more immediate, more powerful claims on out attention. Just as in daily life.

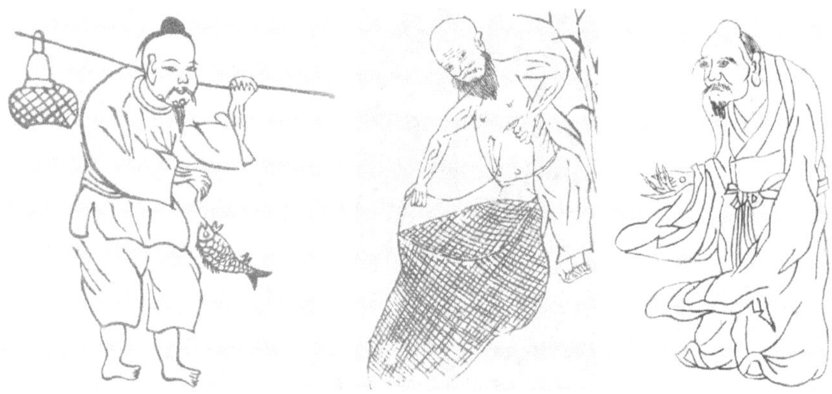

Figures 6.6, 6.7, 6.8. From Gu Shicheng, *Yangyi daquan* (1760).

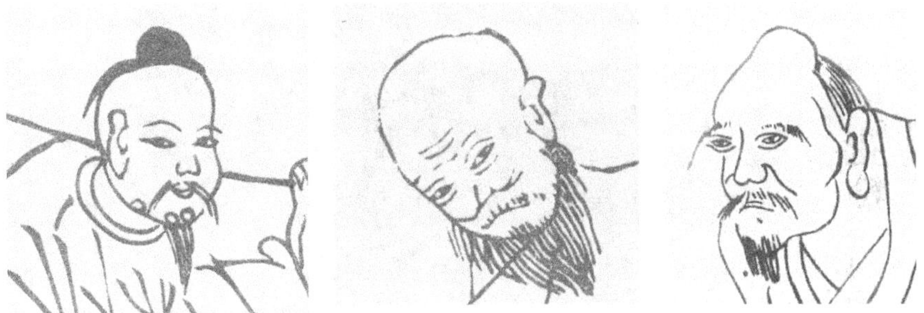

Figures 6.9, 6.10, 6.11. From Gu Shicheng, *Yangyi daquan* (1760).

We pass a stranger on the road, and we find ourselves silently assessing the person's age and station in life, his or her character and current mood. Our eyes meet, and we are instantly engaged in a mutual reading of souls. And so it is when we come upon these illustrations. We are intrigued, first and foremost, by the depicted characters as people, and curious about the thoughts behind the eyes.

We do not notice any sickness. And that is the expected response. These images educate viewers about the demands of the expert gaze by demonstrating how easily attention is led astray. Instead of highlighting pathologies and portraying them in enlarged, close-up detail, these plates purposely minimize their presence, slipping them in amid a wealth of more-intriguing, irrelevant sights. The pictures are designed deliberately to mislead, to hide by distraction. But this hiding is itself a form of showing: the figures distract to warn against distraction. They teach aspiring doctors of the need to discipline the gaze, to scrutinize details that untutored eyes habitually overlook.

Place, especially. Premodern *waike* illustrations convey almost nothing of the color, shape, or texture of the various ulcers and eruptions that disfigure the skin. Mainly, they just inscribe tiny circles to mark where the pathologies appear. But in Chinese medicine, this *where* was crucial: for doctors in China, the secret patterns governing the body were above all patterns framed by place. A rash on the left cheek signaled a different disease from a rash on the chest, even if the two rashes looked identical. A certain pulse on the left wrist might warn of an agitated liver, while the same pulse on the right wrist could mean a faltering spleen. The displacement of even a few fingerbreadths could separate a marvelous acupuncture cure from meaningless pricking.

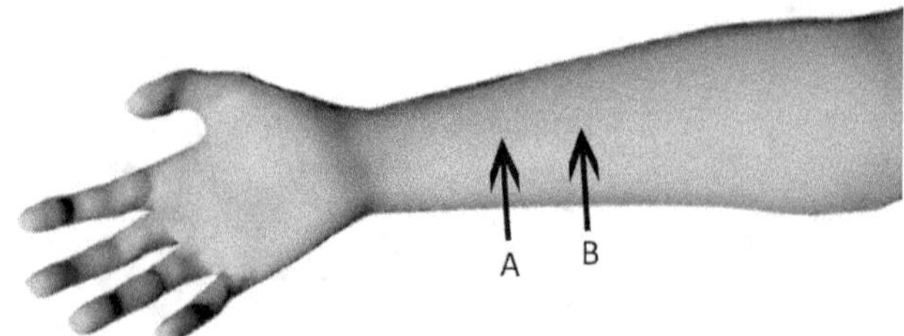

These are all meanings that elude untutored observers. A doctor says A is a potent acupuncture point, while B is a place of no significance. But the skin of my forearm at the two sites looks the same. To the layman, they are merely two featureless spots on a surface of countless featureless spots. Completely visible and yet invisible, places are the purest example of sights hidden in plain view.

Only the trained eye will seek them out.

Still, after viewing a few images like those from the *Yangyi daquan* and *Waike qieyao*, we start to catch on, appreciating the idea of place in the expert gaze. Soon, we begin to reflexively scan each plate with "Where's-Waldo" eyes, searching for some discreet mark of sickness or site of cure slipped in amid a crowd of more interesting sights. Our way of looking evolves, refashioned by pictures. The process may be unconscious, but the effect is potent: pictures inculcate viewers with a way of relating to the viewed. By pointing out what to see, they also teach us how to look.

8

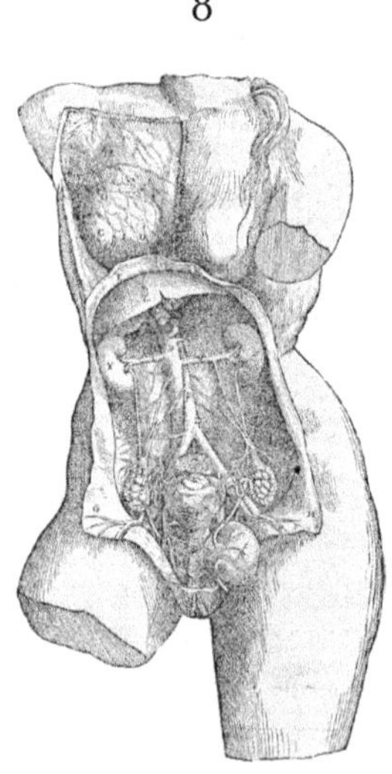

Figure 6.12. From Andreas Vesalius, *De fabrica corporis humanis* (1543).

The earnest realism of anatomical illustrations, we've noted, nurtures an objectifying gaze. Its stress on the body's solid materiality prompts us to envisage it as a *res*, a thing, an impersonal object—a perspective reinforced in this Vesalian image by the absence of a head, and by the realization, when we examine the stumps of this torso, that we are not even studying a human cadaver, but are peering, bizarrely, into a dissected stone statue.

In *Understanding Comics*, Scott McCloud observes that the more realistically a face is portrayed, the more we eye it objectively, as the face of an opposing other. He then advances an intriguing hypothesis: the more schematic the figure, he suggests, the more readily we identify with it, and experience its world as our own.[19]

Looking at a George Washington painted with near-photographic detail, we see a resolute stranger, a man who is distinctly *not us*. By contrast, when we contemplate a comic sketch, where the eyes are mere dots and the mouth a dash, we somehow glimpse ourselves. For it is our engagement that fills the empty spaces of the face. It is we who transform these spare specks into a reflective, animate being. This subtle identification, McCloud says, is central to the experience of reading comics. Their allure is above all the allure of participation.

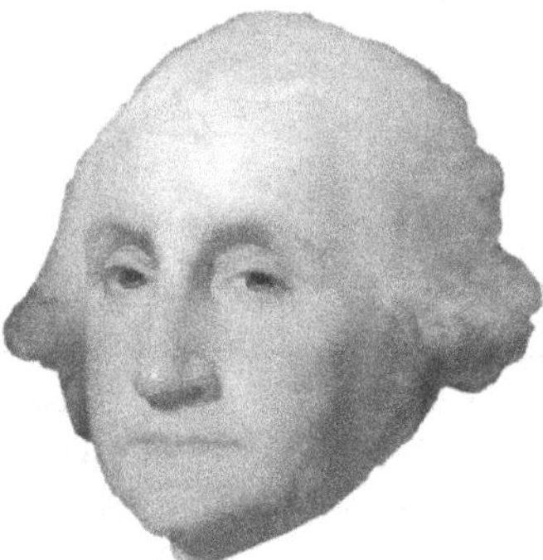

Figure 6.13. From Gilbert Stuart, *George Washington* (1796).

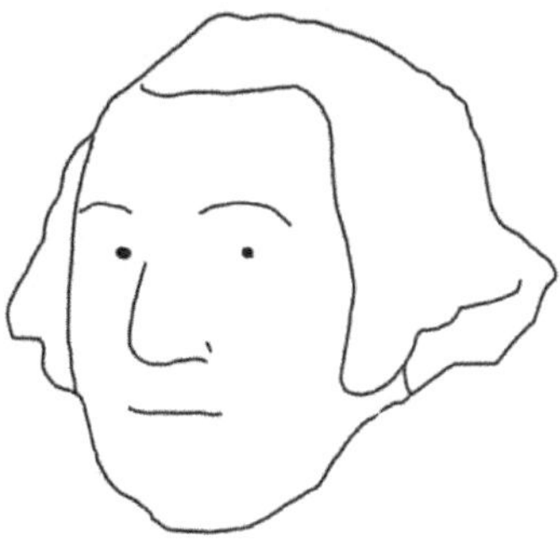

Figure 6.14. Created by Kuriyama.

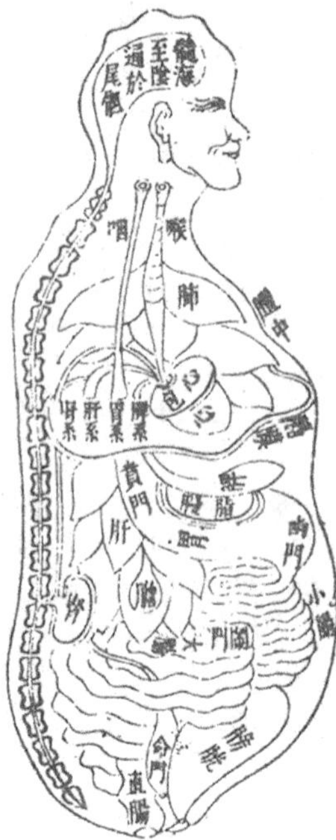

Figure 6.15. From Zhang Jiebin, *Leijing tushuo* (1624).

This tie between schematic emptiness and participation is key to understanding Chinese views of the viscera. The plate above is not a failed attempt at anatomical representation, a clumsy effort to portray an impersonal body-object. It is, instead, a mirror of the embodied self, imagined from within. Its sketchiness is indispensable: the image must leave room for viewers to slip into themselves. The message implicit in its style is: this is *you*.

Close your eyes, try to peer into your own body, and you probably see nothing. Our interior is hidden to introspection—but hidden with the obscurity of a moonless night, rather than with the hiddenness of things secreted in boxes. The inward gaze encounters no solids, no opaque, resistant surfaces, no layered depths. Everything is dark, and that is all.

Views of the viscera allow us to navigate this darkness. Just as acupuncture charts lay out the secret skein of needling points and conduits concealed in the bland sameness of the skin, so plates like these map the variegated landscape of organs—depots of distinct and varying potencies—hidden in the uniform obscurity within us. With the help of such maps, we can learn to feel and direct the circulation of life forces, guide them to this or that vital site.[20] With the help of such maps, we can more fully experience ourselves.

9

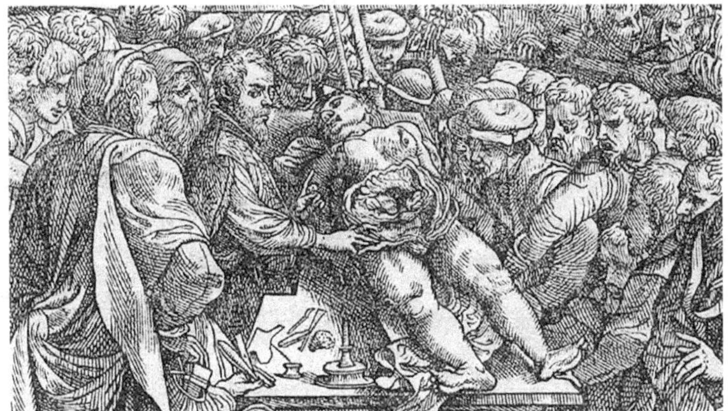

Figure 6.16. From Andreas Vesalius, *De fabrica corporis humanis* (1543).

Textbooks repeat how, for more than a thousand years, doctors had been content just to parrot the doctrines of the ancients, without bothering to study the body directly, to dissect. Andreas Vesalius's treatise on the *Fabric of the Human Body* (1543), we are told, heralded the advent of a new spirit of observation, the birth of modern science. So it seems perfectly apt that its frontispiece should show a crowd of eager observers pressing forward for a glimpse of the exposed corpse. And yet that is not all it shows.

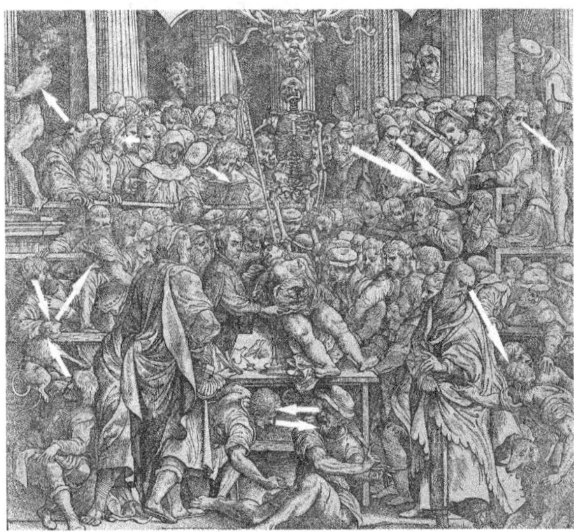

Figure 6.17. From Andreas Vesalius, *De fabrica corporis humanis* (1543).

Step back and survey the entire anatomical theater, and you discover that the spectators are actually looking in wildly diverging directions. On the lower left, a standing figure looks down toward a seated man, who peers up at a monkey, who in turn watches a young spectator perched on the back of another. On the upper left, one man puzzles over the sudden appearance of a naked interloper. On the lower right, someone turns to see who is pulling at his elbow. Higher up, another figure eyes the sleeve of the youth next to him, struck perhaps by the eerie resemblance between the latest sartorial fashion and a dissected arm. A youth is absorbed in his book; here and there companions face each other and converse.

In a work heralded as the pioneering treatise of modern anatomy, we expect a portrait of focused inspection. But its frontispiece instead presents a scene of distraction.

And Vesalius? Curiously, the gaze of even the dissector strays from the corpse. He turns toward us, the readers. Do you see? he asks, and points with his left hand.

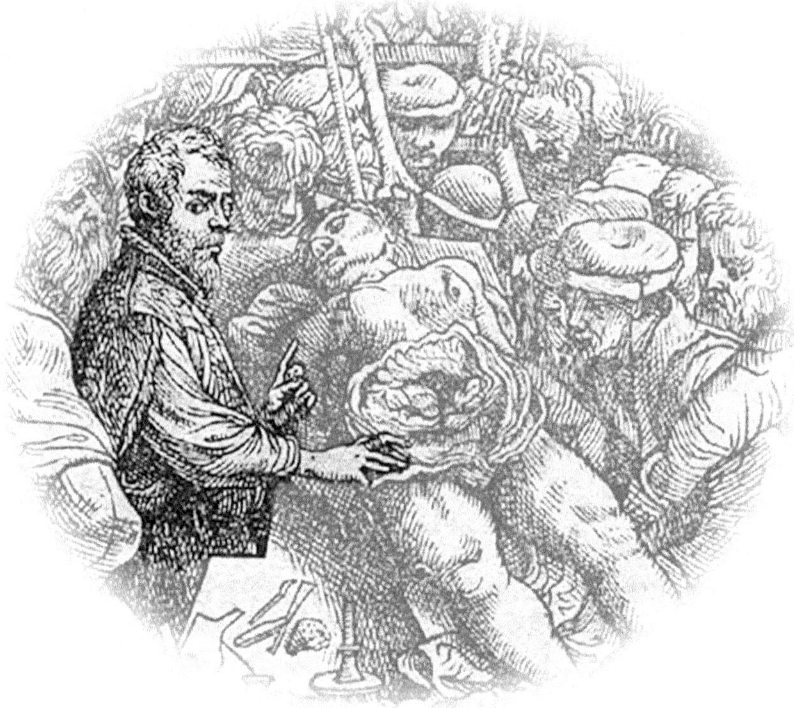

Figure 6.18. From Andreas Vesalius, *De fabrica corporis humanis* (1543).

Here is what you must observe, his glance and gesture tell us. This is what matters most. Not naked bodies or fashionable clothes, not books or climbing monkeys. Not even the dissected corpse. No, true insight must attend to the one phenomenon that everyone ignores: a skeleton rising out of the dissected womb. The irony is acute. Although it occupies the very heart of the scene, no one pays any heed to this emblem of transience and mortality, this reminder that all who are born must die.

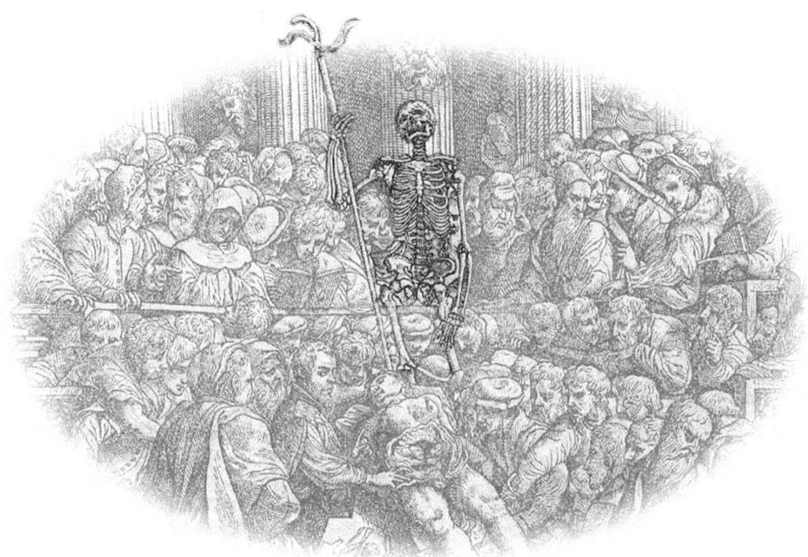

Figure 6.19. From Andreas Vesalius, *De fabrica corporis humanis* (1543).

Hans Holbein's portrait of the *Ambassadors* (1533), completed ten years earlier, conveys a similar lesson—though in this famous painting it is not the figures *in* the picture, but rather we, the viewers *of* the picture, who suffer from distraction. Beguiled by the confident aura of the ambassadors, the radiant opulence of their robes, the lush and intricate fabrics, and a wealth of exquisitely crafted instruments, we only dimly register the skull right below them—even though it is far more massive than the heads of the two living men combined.

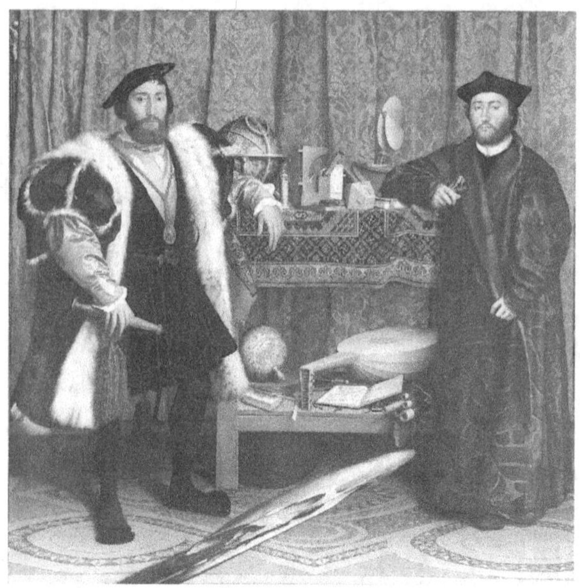

Figure 6.20. From Hans Holbein, *The Ambassadors* (1533).

We are blinded by the vanities. Confronted straight on, the wonders of life are so entrancing and absorbing that we lose sight of our mortality. To achieve clarity we thus must cultivate a special, oblique gaze. Which perhaps is why the skull is anamorphic: only when viewed from a skewed angle, contemplating the painting from the side, does death's face appear in focus.

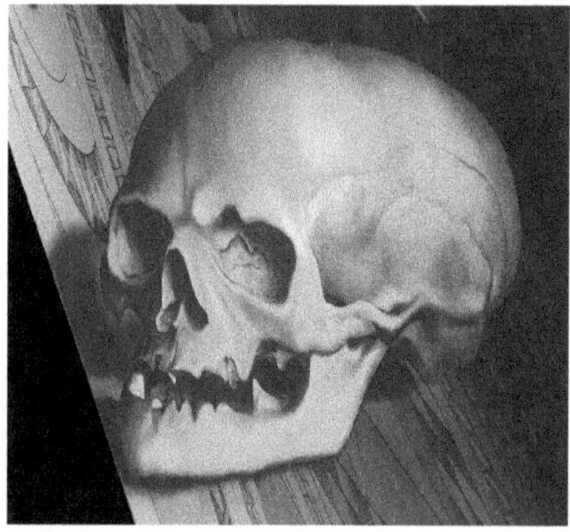

Figure 6.21. From Hans Holbein, *The Ambassadors* (1533).

The spectators in Vesalius's amphitheater who gawk at the corpse while ignoring the skeleton reprise an ancient critique. They look, but do not see. Scientific anatomy, Aristotle insisted long ago, is not about just cutting open the body and staring at grisly gore. Its aim, rather, is to envisage the eternal forms latent in perishable flesh, to apprehend the divine design that explains why each structure is shaped exactly as it is. But this design is deeply hidden, concealed not only by the layers of skin and fat, which cover the organs inside, but also by the uncovered organs themselves, whose material fascinations make us forget about the Creator's immaterial intent.[21]

Vesalius's simple gawkers are captivated by the guts. They do not understand how to see. They are looking *at* the corpse as the final object of knowledge, when they should be gazing *through* the mortal body to apprehend its immortal design—gazing, that is, in the way that we look to discern the lurking shark.

If you were earlier unable to make out the shark, here is what you must do. First bring the face right up against the page or screen, so that the left and right eyes each fix on the area directly in front of it, and then gradually pull away while keeping each eye looking straight ahead. The trick is to suppress your usual habit of looking at objects—the impulse to fix on *things* as the end of sight—and to approach the speckled field instead as a window, as a surface to be looked through. Stared at as simply objects, as the endpoint of converging sightlines, the specks of an autostereogram present only a meaningless haze. But when they are peered through, as an opening into another world, they magically coalesce into floating forms in a space of startling depth.

*looking **at** the autostereogram as an object*

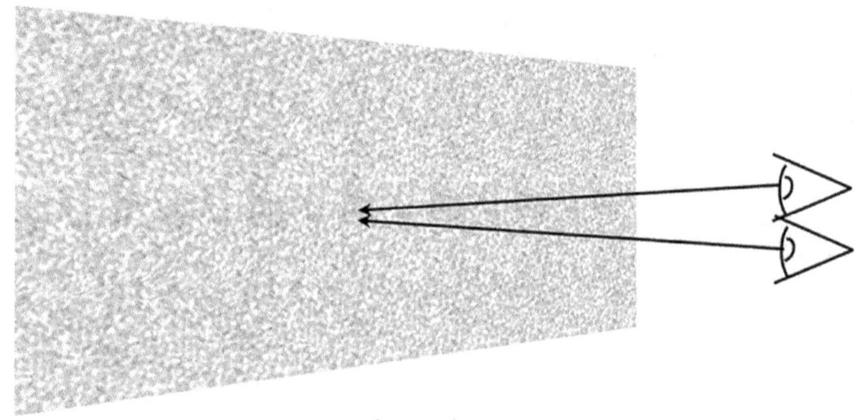

Figure 6.22. Created by Kuriyama.

*seeing **through** the surface appearance to the underlying form*

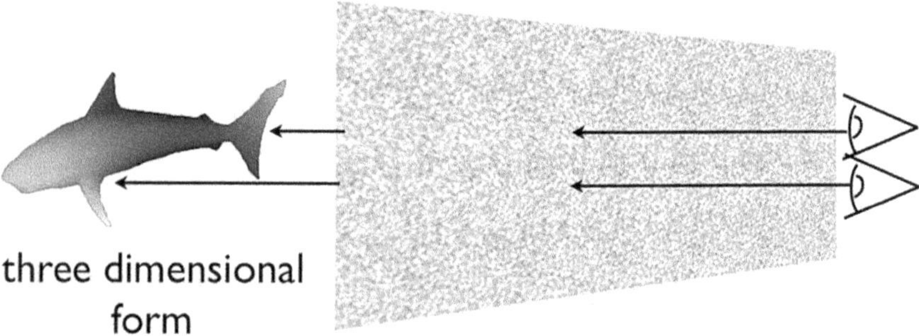

Figure 6.23. Created by Kuriyama.

There is always more than meets the eye. Surprisingly, the same autostereogram to which we turned earlier to illustrate Chinese clairvoyance now elucidates the dissector's gaze. But on reflection, this convergence makes sense. I have underscored a fundamental contrast between the transparent emptiness of Chinese views of the viscera and European anatomical efforts to uncover an opaque and solid body. But I've also pointed out how sophisticated anatomists knew that physical uncovering was just a start—how they saw the fleshly body as just the inconstant shadow of more constant designs, how the dissector's vision, like that of the acupuncturist, was shaped by a sense of mutability.

In a world ruled by change, doctors in both China and Europe agreed, things are never quite as they seem, but are ceaselessly becoming something other. Clairvoyance thus turns on a peculiar double vision, a simultaneous looking at and peering through. In a world ruled by change, all things are ultimately hidden in time, and achieving insight depends on a sort of reading.[22]

Notes

1. We may recall here how the German *Haut*, skin, is cognate with the English "hide," and the two senses of this English term.

2. "Biography of Guan Lu," in the *Records of the Three Kingdoms.* See Fang Beichen 方北辰, *Sanguozhi zhuyi* 三國志注譯 (Xian: Shanxi renmin chubanshe, 1995), 1468–1495. Translated in Kenneth J. DeWoskin, *Doctors, Diviners, and Magicians of Ancient China: Biographies of* fang-shi (New York: Columbia University Press, 1983), 91–134; see esp. 104–5.

3. DeWoskin, *Doctors*, 121. Another version of this anecdote (DeWoskin, *Doctors*, 124) reports Guan Lu guessing all thirteen items correctly; Fang, *Sanguozhi*, 1483, 1484.

4. "Biography of Tung-fang Shuo," in *History of the Former Han*. See Ban Gu 班固 (32–92), *Hanshu quanyi* 漢書全譯, eds. Liu Huaqing 劉華清 et al. 5 vols. (Guiyang: Guizhou renmin chubanshe, 1995), 3:65.2973. Translated in Burton Watson, *Courtier and Commoner in Ancient China: Selections from the* History of the Former Han *by Pan Ku* (New York: Columbia University Press, 1974), 81.

5. DeWoskin, *Doctors*, 117; Fang, *Sanguozhi*, 1481.

6. Carlo Ginzburg offers a wonderfully imaginative account of this clue-reading model in "Clues: Roots of an Evidential Paradigm," collected in Ginzburg, *Clues, Myths, and the Historical Method*, trans. John Tedeschi (Baltimore: Johns Hopkins University Press, 1992), 96–125.

7. We might recall here how the aura of occult powers surrounding written signs in a largely preliterate age led to the derivation of the word "glamour" (magic, enchantment) from "grammar."

8. Autostereograms are now also called "stereograms," but the latter term originally referred to images whose depth became visible only when viewed through special devices.

9. Stefan Zweig, *Twenty-Fours Hours in the Life of a Woman*, trans. Anthea Bell (London: Pushkin Press, 2003).

10. Sima Qian, *Shiji* 史記, chapter 105. For a recent English translation of this chapter, see Elisabeth Hsu, *Pulse Diagnosis in Early Chinese Medicine: The Telling Touch* (Cambridge, UK: Cambridge University Press, 2010).

11. *Nanjing*, "Difficulty (*nan*) 8." See Hua Shou 滑壽 (fl. 1360–1370), *Nanjing benyi* 難經本義 (Taipei: Xuanfeng chubanshe, 1987), 10. For a translation and commentary of the entire text, see Paul Unschuld, *Nan-ching—The Classic of Difficult Issues* (Berkeley: University of California Press, 1986).

12. For a marvelously lucid survey of struggles with the real in the evolution of continental philosophy since Kant, see Lee Braver, *A Thing of This World: A History of Continental Anti-Realism* (Evanston, IL: Northwestern University Press, 2007).

13. An elegant exposition of these notions of propensity and configuration in Chinese thought can be found in François Jullien, *The Propensity of Things: Toward a History of Efficacy in China*, trans. Janet Lloyd (New York: ZONE Books, 1995).

14. DeWoskin, *Doctors*, 99; Fang, *Sanguozhi*, 1471.

15. Ibid., 94–95; Fang, *Sanguozhi*, 1469.

16. Ibid., 96; Fang, *Sanguozhi*, 1470.

17. Ibid., 98; Fang, *Sanguozhi*, 1471.

18. Recall, for example, Lam Qua's paintings of the diseases treated by the surgeon Peter Parker. See Larissa Heinrich, *The After-Life of Images: Translating the Pathological Body between China and the West* (Durham, NC: Duke University Press, 2008), 39–71.

19. Scott McCloud, *Understanding Comics, The Invisible Art* (New York: Harper Collins, 1994), chapter 2.

20. I discuss the ties between meditation charts and medical images of the viscera in "The Imagination of the Body and the History of Embodied Experience: The Case of Chinese Views of the Viscera," in *The Imagination of the Body and the History of Bodily Experience*, ed. S. Kuriyama (Kyoto: International Research Center for Japanese Studies, 2000), 17–29. For more on Daoist practices of visualizing the inner body, see Kristofer Schipper, *Le corps taoïste* (Paris: Fayard, 1982); Catherine Despeux, *Taoïsme et corps humain: Le* Xiuzhen tu. (Paris: Maisnie Tredaniel, 1990).

21. For a discussion of the logic of the anatomical gaze, see chapter 3 of my *Expressiveness of the Body, and the Divergence of Greek and Chinese Medicine* (New York: ZONE Books, 1999).

22. The impulse to read the body in time was also influential in Europe, particularly prior to the post-Vesalian stress on anatomical inspection. We see it most strikingly in the many zodiac men and bloodletting charts of the fourteenth and fifteenth centuries, a beautiful selection of which can be viewed online at the *Luminarium: Encyclopedia Project*: Anniina Jokinen, "Zodiac Man: Man as Microcosm," http://www.luminarium.org/encyclopedia/zodiacman.htm.

Those interested in the enigmas posed by Chinese medical images are urged to explore Gu Shicheng 顧世澄 (fl. eighteenth c.), *Yangyi daquan* 瘍醫大全 (1760; Beijing: Renmin weisheng chubanshe, 1987), from which four of the images in this article are drawn. This Qing compendium abounds in intriguing and often puzzling illustrations, whose style and meaning still await deep reading. Researchers who seek to delve further into the relationship between time and image in Chinese medicine are encouraged as well to study Zhang Jiebin 張介賓 (1563–1640), *Leijing tuyi* 類經圖翼 (1624; *SKQS* ed.), a work made especially suggestive by its combination of pictures with *charts*.

7

Worlds of Meaning and the Meaning of Worlds in Sikong Tu's *Twenty-Four Modes of Poetry*

PAULA M. VARSANO

If one were to judge solely on the basis of the many prefaces and colophons that have been written for Sikong Tu's 司空徒 (837–908) *Twenty-Four Modes of Poetry,* or *Twenty-Four Shipin* (二十四詩品 *Ershisi shipin*),[1] it would seem that to read that elusive constellation of poems is, primarily, to confront the workings of one's own mind. Instead of elucidating the meaning of the *Shipin* and articulating its contribution, as one expects from writings in these genres, the authors of these texts choose to recount their own experience of reading it. Almost without exception the tale they tell is one of delayed recognition: a brief dramatic narration of a shift, either gradual or sudden, from a state of incomprehension to one of understanding. As if in belated response to Su Dongpo's 蘇東坡 (1037–1101) oft-quoted "I lament that those of [Sikong Tu's] time did not recognize the genius [of this work]" 恨當時不識其妙,[2] there begins to emerge in the Qing Dynasty a number of proclamations celebrating the discovery of the true value of the *Modes.*[3]

There is, for example, the tale of one scholar's admiration for another's perspicacity in recognizing the value of this work, when someone named Qin Xijiu extravagantly praises the interpretations offered by his acquaintance, Yang Tingzhi;[4] and we have Yang Tingzhi's recounting of his own process of recognition:

When I was young, I read Sikong Tu's *Shipin*. I loved its numinous flavor, but did not grasp its meaning. I presented it to my peers, and they said that it can be apprehended through one's sense of things, but that it is difficult to transmit it in words. I had never been one to think deeply about things, and also suspected that [the *Shipin*] did not lend itself to verbal explanation; but in my mind, I was never able to let it go. Later, I read all of its pieces as a whole, and mutely grasped its meaning.[5]

芝少讀司空詩品，愛其神味，未獲其意旨，參之同人，輒曰可以意會，難以言傳。芝未嘗深思，亦疑以為不落言詮，而於心終未釋然。及後總閱諸章，默會其意。

From Su Dongpo's sadness over the belated (and limited) recognition of this work's hidden genius, to Yang Tingzhi's celebrations of having at long last come to grasp its meaning, a common theme prevails: the theme of recognition, of a change of state from ignorance to knowledge, from incomprehension to understanding. Reminiscent of Aristotle's description of the dramatic mechanism of *anagnorisis*, all of these writers tell of arriving at a point from which they could perceive a heretofore hidden reality, the true identity or value of some object—in this case, the twenty-four poems that comprise the *Modes*. While the path to recognition varies from reader to reader, it always involves the passage of time: a shift in historical context, the accumulation of experience, or the maturation and training of the individual mind. In addition, all of these narratives tacitly point to the existence of some dissimulating surface under which the recognized object has been contained—a surface that, for all its effectiveness in its role of concealment, is even more effective at signaling that it conceals something.

If these readers of the *Twenty-Four Modes of Poetry* found it worthwhile to tell their tales of recognition, it is only because they wished to convey that hidden within it lies something worth recognizing. Most, though not all, modern scholars[6] seem to concur. Some, out of respect for the fundamental "suggestiveness" of its language,[7] refrain from systematically attempting to lift up the rhetorical surface of the text to reveal a hidden meaning, preferring instead to demonstrate how the elusiveness of the *Twenty-Four Modes*' discourse performs the aesthetic of elusiveness that the text upholds as a poetic value.[8] Others, perhaps motivated by a perceived need to bring the text into the canonical fold of commentarial tradition, allow themselves to go against the spirit of the poems and "translate" them into discursive, modern language: a practice that, while not without its benefits, predictably results in readings that can feel somehow reductive, beside the point, or at odds with one's own understanding.[9] Either way, we end up deferring (if not abandoning) our own encounter with the tantalizingly hidden significance of the *Shipin*.

There seems to be no denying that this is indeed a text designed to provoke a respectful search for something hidden. To draw on one of Roland Barthes's discussions of Proust (without, I hope, seeming to elevate the *Modes* beyond its relatively circumscribed status in the tradition), it presents itself as "an energy of decipherment, a search for essences,"[10] which, in turn, exhorts its reader to approach it with an eye that deciphers without delimiting. In what follows, I will analyze some of the rhetorical features of this work not only to confirm the observation of traditional readers that the primary contribution of the *Twenty-Four Modes of Poetry* lies with its genius for eliciting a particular mode of recognition, but also to show how it does so. This mode of recognition is neither teleological nor performative, but rather, indeterminate and formative. That is, rather than leading to an apprehensible revealed truth, and more than merely performing the unparaphrasable language of poetry, it is designed to act on the mind in such a way as to change its way of thinking.

The Teleological Model of Recognition

What constitutes the "teleological model of recognition" against which the *Shipin* might be more clearly evaluated? It is one that, first, assumes and is productive of a stable relationship between the recognizer and the thing recognized, and second, posits a temporal arc, promising an eventual outcome that makes the recognized object manifest to the recognizing subject, dispelling the veil of hiddenness that had divided them.

Terence Cave, in his magisterial study of what he calls the "scandal" of recognition in the Western tradition, traces (among other things) a change over the course of literary history in the attributive cause of hiddenness—the condition on which the experience of recognition depends. Throughout this history, he argues, the trope of recognition remains nothing less than an epistemological "scandal": recognition, though central to a plot, is always occasioned by something irrational, beyond articulation, and thus more than a little damaging to Platonic assertions of man's superior cognitive powers.

To focus on just one thread of his rich and nuanced study, he argues that as we move from Aristotelian to modern times, the locus of hiddenness—the precondition for the experience of recognition—shifts from the circumstantial, through the inherently structural, to the purely subjective. That is, whereas, for example, classical and Renaissance narratives might center on the recovering of a reality (usually a person's identity) that had remained unknown because of circumstances, twentieth-century stories tend to attribute ignorance of a reality to the psychological or spiritual blindness of the beholders. And, as Cave shows, the scheme can get more complicated, such that the play of withholding and revealing different sides of a hidden reality from different observers (both within and without the confines of the narrative) can become as absorbing as the hidden object itself. In all of these cases—including, by Cave's own admission, his own "recognition" of recognition—there is a teleology of some sort, a change over time and a posited resolution.[11]

The mode of resolution, however, can take different forms. Most of the examples that Cave summons for his study consist of narratives that both incite and fulfill the expectation of a reachable end within the confines of the plot. This type of resolution might be characterized as "finite." In addition, there are also texts that, themselves, become the objects of such tales; the texts are what must be revealed and recognized. When those texts are deemed sacred, endowed with elusive spiritual significance, the mode of recognition can be "infinite." In his essay, "The Plain Sense of Things," Frank Kermode demonstrates, for example, that the Hebrew exegetical tradition, the interpretative practice of midrash, enacts what is, in effect, just such an open-ended teleology. The tradition of continuously rewriting the original text in order to clarify, fulfill, or make whole its implied meaning produces, in effect, an infinite deferral of that meaning. Far from indicating the absence of meaning, this infinite deferral leads the reader on an endless path that helps establish the absolute value of that ever-receding text: in this case, the Hebrew Law.[12] In this model, each appended commentary, each rewriting, ideally brings one closer to an imagined, but unreachable end when some brilliant mind, standing on the shoulders of all the rewritings that came before it, will be able to offer a final elucidation.[13]

Both of these models of recognition, the finite and the infinite, project a change from ignorance to (or toward) knowledge, and simultaneously presuppose and sustain a distinction between the object that is known and the subject that does the knowing. Teleological models of finite recognition are also plentiful in the Chinese literary tradition. Taking due note of David Keightley's insightful observation that Chinese narrative is characterized by "representational optimism,"[14] it is still possible to point to a wide range of poems whose raison d'être is the marking of the endpoint of an invisible-but-implied path leading to the apprehension of a previously unrecognized reality: Tao Yuanming's 陶淵明 (372?–427) apprehension of that ineffable something in the return of the birds at sunset, and his recognition of his own inability to function as an official[15]; Wang Wei's 王維 (701–761) encounters with the Dao on the grounds of his Wang Stream estate[16]; Wei Yingwu's 韋應物 (737–ca. 792) apparently futile search for an absent recluse, which leads unexpectedly to the realization of a truth that they had not previously recognized[17]; and Liu Zongyuan's 柳宗原 (773–819) revelation of the unparalleled beauty of his found lands in Yongzhou—and the hints of spiritual enlightenment that this entails.[18]

In all such poems, a teleological mode of recognition is present. Yet they differ in significant ways from those considered in Cave's study. In these Chinese poems, the recognizing subject's spiritual and psychological state (which in all of these cases constitutes the locus of hiddenness) has already undergone its transformation by the time he formulates the moment in words; and, that formulation represents his transformation as having been instantaneous. The reader senses a sequence of events, to be sure. Certain conditions naturally fell into place and then the moment of recognition happened, but it is hard to identify any process, let alone any traceable chain of cause and effect.

While it is well beyond the scope of this essay to investigate the question of why the presentation of instantaneous recognition seems more prevalent than that of a gradual acquisition of understanding, and why nothing scandalous has ever been noted in these works, it is possible to point to certain contributing factors. The evolving aesthetics of their shared genre of lyric poetry[19]; the ecumenical understanding of a Dao that is always present, waiting to be apprehended in nature's unimpeded manifestations of its pattern; and the Chan Buddhist notion of sudden enlightenment are all consistent with the experience of instantaneous recognition. These aspects of middle-period Chinese intellectual life support an aesthetic and epistemological model whereby the seemingly opaque veil of mundane experience turns out—suddenly, somehow—to be the opposite: the direct manifestation of something that had heretofore always been beyond our ken.[20]

In the works of the poets mentioned above, then, it is not that a teleological model is absent; rather, there is something in their retrospective, elliptical presentations of recognition that undoes teleology even as it depends on it. The story, as told, is over before it begins; and the narrative arc that embodies the subject's transformation is only implied, never articulated. There is a kind of stubborn, evocative looseness in the narrative link between possible cause and verifiable effect, between the moments that lead up to the recognition of a hidden reality, and the moment of recognition. Often, it seems, all that can really be said is that there was a sequence of events and it ended in an experience of recognition; the effect of the sequence on the outcome is unclear.

One salient example is the traditional poetic theme, mentioned above, which is known by the self-explanatory title of "looking for the recluse and not finding him in." In the early, pre-Tang treatments of this theme, a physical journey into the mountains would at least be alluded to, providing a useful homology for the search for enlightenment that seeking a recluse implies. But by the Tang Dynasty, as the theme acquires the status of convention, the representation of the journey is eventually suppressed.[21] In Wei Yingwu's famous composition, "To a Daoist Adept on Quanjiao Mountain," all that remains of that journey is the bare-bones silhouette of a man absorbedly viewing a landscape: a silhouette not unlike that projected by the Qing critic Yang Tingzhi, beholding the *Twenty-Four Shipin*, having "mutely grasped its meaning" at last.[22]

The "Worlds" of the *Twenty-Four Modes of Poetry*

To thus draw an analogy between uncovering the significance of a landscape and recognizing the meaning of a written work is to partake of a deeply rooted tradition. As far back as the "Rhapsody on Literary Writing" (*Wenfu* 文賦) by Lu Ji 陸機 (261–303), Chinese poets have asserted a particular relationship between the world of nature and the world of texts. This relationship is both contiguous and analogous: contiguous in that landscape and literature have been presented as an uninterrupted "space" across which "wandering" can take place;[23] and analogous in that both act as vehicles through which the poet can project his subjectivity beyond the limits of his corporeal situation.[24]

At a much deeper and enduring level, the interconnectedness of topography and literary writing can also be traced to a semantic source: the word, *jing* 境, (commonly translated as "world"), which gradually became formalized as a key term in Chinese literary discourse, in modern times most commonly appearing in the compound terms *jingjie* 境界 and *yijing* 意境.[25] As I hope to show, even as the *Modes* ostensibly proposes to divide poetic rhetoric into twenty-four distinct categories, its elusive discourse reflexively presents itself as a literary rendering of one ever-fluctuating *jing* writ large, overriding—perhaps with ironic intent—the analytic façade it presents.

The term *jing* progressed from its earliest appearance as an unambiguously concrete word that denoted the "ending" or "boundary" of a piece of land, to one that meant the territories demarcated by those limits, and ultimately, to a conceptual word whose meaning could (and did) slip easily between the apparently mutually exclusive ideas of undifferentiated wholeness and clearly demarcated distinctions, of absolute space and relative place, of the universal and the particular. The Taiwanese scholar, Huang Jingjin, has recently published a remarkable study tracing this trajectory. Huang's book examines how the semantic range of *jing* grew over time, gradually broadening to accommodate, and even exploit, the uneasy aesthetic, spiritual, and philosophical alliance of the poles of differentiation and unity, boundary and body—and of familiar things and the latent conjoined patterns that they manifest in the world.[26]

Huang argues that the term *jing* underwent one of its more significant shifts in the Tang, and he attributes this first to Wang Changling 王昌齡 (698–757) and then to the innovations of Sikong Tu. Huang argues that Wang Changling, the first to apply the term in discussions of literature,[27] had benefited from the cross-pollination of the term as it appears in Confucian, Daoist, and Buddhist writings, as well as from the syncretic tendency of the times. Wang, he argues, was thus able to use *jing* to tighten the link (or, more accurately, blur the boundary) joining the poet's inner reflections (*si* 思) and the contingent world (*jing*), thereby bringing critical discourse one step closer to Wang Fuzhi's 王夫之 (1619–1692) and Wang Guowei's 王國維 (1877–1927) more thoroughgoing and synthetic formulations of what is commonly called "the blending of feeling and scene" (*qingjing jiaorong* 情景交融).

Huang then shows that Sikong Tu further deepened the term, invoking it in ways that enrich and complicate our understanding of the interaction between perceived objects and inner response, and between images and meaning during the creation and the reading of a poem.[28] Specifically, Sikong Tu "blended" the semantic fields of *jing* to embrace *both* borderline and territory. As a result, in his usage, *jing* does not merely traverse the boundary between the inner and outer worlds of the poet; it marks, and thereby enhances our awareness of, that otherwise indefinable place where the bounded world gives rise to—or even gives way to—the boundless: where form triggers the recognition of what lies beyond form.[29] Although Huang Jingjin did not put it in precisely these terms, his analysis suggests that Sikong Tu effectively harnessed, rather than circumvented, the contradictory connotations that had been accruing to this word since its earliest uses as a conceptual term.

For all the acuity of Huang's argument, and for all its obvious applicability to the *Shipin*, he nevertheless refrains from including the *Shipin* in his discussion, presumably because of the controversy surrounding its attribution to Sikong Tu.[30] Instead, his analysis focuses exclusively on two famous letters in which Sikong Tu explicitly, even systematically, discusses his approach to poetry: the "Letter to Master Li, On Poetry" 與李生論詩書 and the "Letter to Wang Jia, Critiquing Poetry" 與王駕評詩書. Huang's conservative stance is reasonable, to be sure. But, the issue of the (most likely contemporaneous) *Twenty-Four Modes*' authorship aside, the ninth-century transformation of *jing* as revealed in those letters opens up the possibility of a new and different strategy for reading it: one that does not necessarily equate the acquisition of knowledge with the unearthing of a stable, core meaning.

Indeed, reading the remarks of the *Modes'* first annotators and commentators, one senses that the notion of "worlds" hovers about the work like an aura, even though the term itself is rarely used. One discerns it in the recurring refrain that the text cannot be understood through cognitive means, but must be met with, and joined by, one's very spirit; again and again we are assured that paraphrase and analysis can never capture its essence.[31] In the brief explanatory preface written by the Qing poet Yuan Mei 袁枚 (1716–1798) for his own work, *Shipin xu* 續詩品 (*Shipin*, continued), this term appears as a succinct one-word summation of this common observation. He writes: "I love Sikong Biaosheng's *Shipin*, and cherish its reverent rendering of marvelous worlds (*miaojing*)" 余愛司空表聖《詩品》, 而惜其祗標妙境.[32]

In modern times, the practice of associating *jing* with the *Twenty–Four Shipin* is established in the preface and annotations composed by Guo Shaoyu (1893–1984), the scholar responsible for the most frequently cited modern edition, *Shipin jijie* 詩品集解 (Collected explanations of the *Shipin*).[33] In Guo's extended, surprisingly laudatory comments, he frequently draws a tacit equation between the word *pin* (of the title) and *jing*.[34] At first glance, it is reasonable to surmise that the *Shipin*'s reliance on visual imagery inspired Guo to draw this equation naturally and without any attempt to justify it.[35] Furthermore, we have already seen, *jing*, like *pin*, is etymologically rooted in the drawing of boundaries, the making of distinctions. Yet the pairing also resembles, if inadvertently, one of the *Shipin*'s central rhetorical features (most obviously, but not uniquely, in the titles of the poems): the combining of sometimes quite unrelated terms to provoke a moment of spontaneous, ineffable comprehension. As with so many assumptions or proposals of equivalency, this one reveals a stark difference as well: that between *pin*'s original connotations of objectivity (connotations that would persist in the word's continued association with the powers of lucid discernment), and *jing*'s gradually but unmistakably acquired connotations of subjectivity.

The earliest use of the term *pin* in reference to poetry occurs in the preface to the first (and only other) work to be called *Shipin*,[36] written by Zhong Rong 鍾嶸 (fl. 502–519) in the Liang Dynasty (502–557). Its most salient meaning is "grade" or "rank," consistent with its earliest denotation of rank in the court bureaucracy; this connection is confirmed when Zhong Rong helpfully states in his preface that he has in mind the ancient practice of "evaluating men" 品人. But, if Guo Shaoyu picked up on the subjective connotations of the term in its ninth-century incarnation, a contemporary scholar, Zu Baoquan, who has written extensively on this work, concurs and goes further. Explicitly contrasting the *Twenty-Four Shipin* with Zhong Rong's *Shipin*, he states:

> 司空圖的《詩品》，則是著重描繪他所想像到的各種意境，讓讀者來領悟詩的各種風格。。。這裡的“品”字 是“品味” 的意思， 因為讀者對詩的風格的領悟是建立在對詩的“品味”的基礎上。
>
> Sikong Tu's *Shipin* placed an emphasis on depicting each "lyrical world" (*yijing*) that he imagined, in order to awaken the reader to the various styles of poetry. . . . Here, *pin* carries the meaning of *pinwei*, or "tasting," because the reader's awakening to the styles of poetry is founded on the basis of tasting.[37]

If Zu is right, the subjective nature of *pin* as used in this text is a far cry from the objectivity implicit in the "ranking" or even the "styles" that *pin* denoted in earlier works; it is this new subjective quality that Guo Shaoyu is recognizing when he unapologetically glosses the word *pin* as *jing*. Perhaps this shift in connotation amounts to a tacit critique or, less polemically, a revamping of the quasirationalist reading Zhong Rong's *Shipin* seems to promote. But even the word "critique" betrays the spirit of this text, and so, instead, I propose following Zu Baoquan's lead and considering that the very invocation of *pin* in this way itself aims to viscerally "awaken" the reader to the broad, movable semantic boundaries of the term and, more to the point, of the evaluative acts with which it is associated. The title's re-use of *pin* suggests a lineage of some kind, but by the time the reader has completed the work it names, what she has actually acquired is a full appreciation of what that title no longer means.

It is consistent with the work's overall rhetorical mode that only in retrospect can one recognize that the seemingly straightforward title, "*Twenty-Four Shipin*," actually provides a foretaste of the experience of recognition it inspires. It embodies but the first of many *jing*, where *jing* is a figure that acts on the mind of the reader, presenting a shifting world that simultaneously—and unceasingly—draws and erases its own boundaries. Advancing slowly through the twenty-four poems, one discovers the multiple ways in which they suggest a space, a "world" in flux: one that sustains rather than fixes the process of constant transformation.

As I hope to show in what follows, the rhetorical patterning of the *Twenty-Four Shipin* is designed to defy both the stability of the subject-object relationship on which understanding depends, and the logic of sequential events that promises dependability. It can be likened to a constellation, not just because the identity of each element depends on its relationship with each of the others, but also because it makes us aware of our own impulse to structure and define those relationships, including that between ourselves and the text. As readers, we discover the meaning-making mechanism of our own minds, as we are made to experience the competing pulls of the text's peculiar blend of arbitrariness and inevitability.

Decoy Signposts: Mapping the Unmappable

The unifying rhetorical feature most responsible for creating this experience in the reader is what I will call the "decoy" signpost: the signpost that first stimulates the reader to build links among signs both intrinsic and extrinsic to the text, and then slips away, revealing the constructed nature of those links and the habits of mind that constructed them. The first example has already been discussed: the use of the word *pin* in the title. But that was merely introductory, and many more lie in store:

Enumeration. The author qualifies the recycled term, *Shipin*, with the number twenty-four: which is appropriate, as there are twenty-four discrete poems in this work. But the specificity of the number sets up a new expectation. That is, the twenty-four poems should constitute either a whole, complete set of *pin* (corresponding, perhaps, to some symbolic order) or a reasoned subset of an implied greater set. Several scholars have labored to bring to light some submerged pattern, some logical structure, that would give this number meaning. Yang Tingzhi argues that the internal logic of the work leads one to divide the book into two even parts, the first dealing with the experience of the "here and now" (*gezhong* 箇中), and the second with the "spirit's journey beyond images" (*shenyou xiangwai* 神遊象外).[38] More ingenious is the Qing dynasty commentator, Yang Zhenwang 楊振綱, who focuses on the organic wholeness the number would seem to imply. In each of his commentaries on the individual chapters, he proposes what amounts to an open-ended, but rational sequential structure. He systematically argues that the "world" represented in one poem acts as a kind of check, a delimiting force, on the danger of an extreme manifestation of the "world" presented in the poem preceding it.[39] Yang's scheme, like others, is convincing in its way, but, perhaps because all arguments seem convincing, no single one can succeed in settling the text into a definitive, signifying pattern, and so, enumeration emerges as a decoy signpost.[40]

Classification. If the numerical specificity of the title reassures with a promise of finiteness and rationality, the sequential structure of the work sets up an expectation that, whatever these twenty-four *pin* are, their lucid classification will yield a harmonious whole composed of distinct parts. But this signpost, too, falls by the wayside on close scrutiny. The title of the very first poem,

"Virile and Whole," might at least give the reader pause, as it establishes the aesthetic value of wholeness, of nondifferentiation, in the place of honor. The primacy of this value is borne out in the poems themselves, for, from this point on, a host of images and phrases suggesting precisely that appear repeatedly. Wind, clouds, shadow, and moon infuse the poems' evocative landscapes; a palette of predominantly translucent, liquid shades such as white (both *bai* 白 and *su* 素) and clear (*qing* 清) contribute, too, to the sense of uniformity; the reduplicative descriptive, *youyou* 悠悠—with its evocations of both boundless space and melancholy emptiness—occurs frequently; and the circular movement described by verbs meaning "to return" or "to turn back," such as *fan* 反, *fan* 返, and *hui* 迴 dominates the depiction of motion. Conversely, words that denote limitations and definition are regularly negated: *wuqiong* 無窮 (in-exhaustible), *bujin* 不盡 (un-limited), *wuyan* 無言 (in-expressible), *bubian* 不辨 (in-definable), and *feijin* 匪禁 (un-containable). And, of course, there is the tension between the apparent "finality" of the final chapter and the connotations of its title, "Flowing and Shifting" (*liudong* 流動).

A stream of semantic assertions of uniformity and boundlessness, then, creates an intriguing tension with signposts promising sequentiality, definition, and orientation. It is not easy to dismiss this apparent contradiction as an unintended inconsistency; instead, the attentive reader may well feel compelled to attend to his own strategies of reading and comprehension. The regular appearance of the word, *you* 幽 ("hidden," "retiring," "obscure"), too, functions as an insistent reminder that something—we know not what—is to be gained by a careful reconsideration of the signs at hand.

Genre. One of the most compelling and potentially meaningful signposts in Chinese poetry is that of genre; and *The Twenty-Four Shipin* makes no bones about belonging to the generic category of "poems on poetry."[41] Its best-known precedents include Lu Ji's "Rhapsody on Literary Writing" and, more immediately, Du Fu's "Six Quatrains Playfully Composed" 戲為六絕句. Both of those works, distinct as they are, are recognizable as poems and, as such, share the obvious formalistic traits of rhyme and meter. Beyond that, and for our purposes, more importantly, they also share the lyric voice, the perspective derived from these individuals' experiences as both readers and writers. In the case of the *Twenty-Four Shipin*, however, while an atmosphere, a tone, undoubtedly imbues the whole work, a lyric voice, an identifiable perspective—a "body," to borrow Wang Changling's expression—is absent.

All of the above signposts point to territories or frames of reference that are extrinsic to the twenty-four poems; but the slippage of those signposts is ultimately only realized in the reading of the poems in detail. Consider chapter 12, "Real Worlds" 實境:[42]

The chosen words are straight as can be;
Calculated reflection yields no depth.
A chance encounter with the reclusive one—
Like catching a glimpse of the heart of Dao.
A bend in a limpid ravine,
The shade of an emerald pine.
One traveler shoulders his firewood,
One traveler listens to the lute.
The ultimate of feelings and human nature—
Subtle it is, and cannot be sought.
To meet up with it is something from Heaven—
Its tone, limpid, and just beyond listening.

取語甚直 計思匪深
忽逢幽人 如見道心
清澗之曲 碧松之陰
一客荷樵 一客聽琴
情性所至 妙不自尋
遇之自天 泠然希音

When reading through the titles of the *Shipin*, this is one title that stands out, if only because the term *jing* had already accumulated so much richness of meaning, so great a theoretical and spiritual weight. For all the hidden potential harbored in the word *jing*, though, the poem as a whole is not hard to paraphrase succinctly. It describes a poem, or a passage in a poem, that spontaneously captures and conveys something that both rings true and is transcendent. This reading resonates with the aesthetic values that Sikong Tu upholds in his letters on poetry: naturalness in both imagery and language, and "meaning beyond words," "flavor beyond flavor." And so it is not surprising that the very same paraphrase applies nicely to other poems in the series, including, for example, "Self-so-ness" (*ziran* 自然), "Expansive and Unencumbered" (*haofang* 豪放), "Sparse and Untamed" (*shuye* 疎野), "Virile and Whole" (*xionghun* 雄渾).

But once you move more deeply into the world of the poem, fragmentation and internal tension take over.[43] To begin once again with titles, this one puts forward *shi*, the "real," "solid," or "substantive," as being of particular value. Commentators gloss the term in this context as meaning "whatever meets the eyes,"[44] or "to accurately and directly write down the world (*jingjie* 境界) that has been reached by way of sight and sense" 真切地直寫所見所感而達到的.[45] True, on one level, the "real," *shi*, stands in opposition to meaningless, contrived ornamentation. But, we also know that *shi*—at least, in the sense of empirical experience, of what meets the eyes—is not an unmitigated value in the *Shipin*. It sits somewhat uneasily alongside the term "emptiness" or *xu*: its conventional opposite and a term that represents an important value in these poems. Poem number one, "Virile and Whole," which is often taken (convincingly or not) as setting the stage for all that is to come, identifies *xu* as a source, an origin, the return to which brings about an ideal state of undifferentiated wholeness:

> It turns back toward Emptiness (*xu*) to enter wholeness,
> And gathers force to become virile.[46]

> 返虛入渾，積健為雄。

Poem #5, "Lofty and Ancient" (*gaogu* 高古) confirms the value of emptiness by associating it with this same lack of differentiation and effacement of boundaries when, in a transformation of Lu Ji's "Wenfu," it says:

> He stands in emptiness, spirit unblemished,
> Far beyond boundaries and distinctions.

> 虛佇神素，脫然畦封。

Less directly, perhaps, but equally clearly, several poems, most notably #4 and #20, "Weighty and Salient" (*chenzhu* 沈著) and "Description" (*xingrong* 形容) respectively, undercut the very notion of the reliable, solid "reality" of the perceptible world. In all cases, what lasts and what merits attention is the transformation of that world.[47]

So, how does this poem illustrate the ideal of "real worlds"? We find here the shifting boundaries and overlapping territories that we would expect to characterize a description of *jing*. The poem itself follows a sequence, even as it undermines the significance of sequentiality; it suggests the inevitability of recognizable images and actions, even as it conjures their arbitrariness; it tacitly upholds the importance of unmediated response to the world, even as it refrains from establishing the stability of a point of view in that world. One might argue that this blend of fragmentation, arbitrariness, and impersonality is perfectly appropriate to the pedagogic project of the work as a whole; the poem functions as a model of sorts, and as such, not only does not need context, it must transcend such contingencies. But this ungrounded quality works against the expectations set up by the decision to present these as *poems* on poetry;

and each shift of category compels the readers to reflect on the promises put forth by the title or, more importantly, on their belief in those promises.

First, let us consider the sequential structure of the poem. In general terms, it begins with a definition of the title (lines 1–2); it continues with an elucidating example that just hovers on the borderline between the substantive and the insubstantial (3–4); it moves into what would appear to be full "substantive" mode, listing four exemplary concrete images and scenes in four consecutive lines (5–8); and then it offers a reiterative summary. This pattern—definition, illustration, summary—appears in several of these poems. Such structure can function as a signpost of reason and regularity, connoting the solidity of the "real world." But this solidity dissolves precisely when we concentrate on the very lines that are intended to reflect the substance of the real world:

> A bend in a limpid ravine,
> The shade of an emerald pine.
> One traveler shoulders his firewood,
> One traveler listens to the lute.

The fragmented presentation of this sequence of images, their resistance to being situated together in what we might have thought of as a scene from the real world, suggest that either "real" or "world"—or both—do not have the solidity we thought they did. In a practical way, what these lines present is an enumeration. But there is just enough order in their parallel structure to trigger a more "lyrical" response. Some critics, uncomfortable with a simple list, hasten to point out that lines 5 and 6 are images taken from nature, while lines 7 and 8 are scenes of human activity. Read with this structure in mind, these two couplets are revealed to conform to the structure of a *xing* 興, and thus have the power to rekindle lyrical expectations. But this does not quite work either, and readers who pick up on that structure will only be compelled to let go of yet another expectation.

If we turn to the implicit "naturalness" of this grouping of images, the customary pairing of bend with ravine, shade with pine, and the anonymous forest-dweller with firewood and lute suggests just that. These lines are presented as unadorned examples of sights we might come upon, or rather, sights we hope to come upon because they exemplify (again, in a conventional way) things pure and untouched by the grime and pettiness of life in human society. It is in this sense that the second couplet makes the most sense: "A chance encounter with the reclusive one—Like catching a glimpse of the heart of Dao." But the same random order, lack of "scene" in which to place these images is what plays against the very naturalness they are meant to exemplify. The tension between the randomness of their presentation, and their familiarity and apparent inevitability, produces a kind of aphasia and requires that the reader rethink her categories once again. Images that had been thought of as unquestionably real become drained of that reality, and become part of a larger, shifting world in which context and relationships are revealed as both ephemeral *and* essential.

Finally, there is the lack of particular perspective—a striking lacuna in a statement that attempts to emphasize the poet's experience of the real world. The impression of impersonality grows primarily out of the two discordant notes just mentioned: the random order and arbitrariness of the images. Again, there is the voice of the pedagogue that undeniably holds the entire poem cycle together. But, on the level of the individual poems, there is a disorienting feeling of subjectless modality that promotes a more intense awareness of one's own subjective response to the language at hand.

Still, keeping its pact with the overall structure of this poem, it is the conclusion of "Real Worlds" that produces the key to what a real world truly means: "To meet up with it is something from Heaven— / Its tone, limpid, and just beyond listening."[48] This is an evocation, not of solidity, but of emptiness or, more to the point, of *jing*: precisely that unnamable place that is both boundary and territory, where substance triggers an awareness of what lies beyond. In effect, the poem seems to have followed the instructions laid out in the first poem, "Virility and Wholeness," by "returning to Emptiness to enter a state of undifferentiated wholeness." Here is a tension between the implied solidity and substance of *shi*, clearly presented in the title as a desirable quality, and the final line's subversion of the very solidity and substance of *shi*, presented as a quality at least as desirable, if not more so. Again, the reader experiences the dizzying need to rationalize it; or, he just learns to let it go.

By now, we recognize this as a familiar move, for it echoes Sikong Tu's choice of his title for the whole: the *Twenty-Four Shipin*. Like that title, the particular title of Poem #18, "Real Worlds," provokes a visceral awakening—that is, once the poem itself has been read. We realize that a more accurate understanding of this title, the poem it describes, and ultimately the work as a whole, may not be arrived at by focusing on what may or may not be "real," but by allowing the mind to comprehend—in the sense of encompassing—its beckoning, mutable, and ineffable "worlds."[49]

Conclusion: An Invitation to the Infinite

The teleological model of recognition is not the only way to unearth hidden meaning. The *Twenty-Four Shipin* is one text where both the temporal arc of discovery and the subject-object divide, which are essential components of that model, do not hold. Instead of "meaning" something in the world, this work produces meaning by working on the mind of the reader. Structure is illusory; images are presented, not as signifying in the world, but as belonging to a finite repertory of objects that can be removed from their habitual setting and exploited as triggers for an unaccustomed mental dynamic. Theoretical terms, too, drawn from a tradition of poetic criticism, can be shifted to reverse or skew accustomed structures of understanding. Rather than a subject-object structuring of the acquisition of hidden value, perhaps what we have here is something more akin to a kind of mirror structure or, better yet, to coin a new phrase, a "blending of language and mind" (*wen xin jiaorong* 文心交融).

This creates a strain on the usual process of interpretation and, in particular, on the commentary and paraphrase that later readers rely on to discover the latent meaning of a text. Even the "infinite" resolution of the teleological model, as practiced by midrashic scholars, would not work well here. The paratactic structure of the whole frustrates the kind of rewriting that midrashic scholars practiced. However, this text did enable—indeed, it inspired—another kind of rewriting: that of imitation. There were, as we know, many imitators of the *Twenty-Four Shipin*, among them the illustrious Yuan Mei. But, for now, we might think of the unbounded form and moveable content of the *Twenty-Four Shipin* as an invitation, if not to rewriting in the form of elucidation, then to rewriting as infinite extension, much as it invites the mind into a state of unbounded suppleness and nonattachment.

Notes

1. In recent years, there has been considerable debate regarding the reliability of this attribution. A comprehensive list of discussions up through 1998 is provided in Kadowaki Hirofumi 門脇廣文, *Nijushi shihin* 二十四詩品 (Tokyo: Meitoku Shuppansha, 2000), 60–64. Kadowaki himself does not feel that the arguments against attribution are persuasive enough to warrant retraction. For an argument that summarizes current reasons for casting serious doubt on the attribution, see Wang Yunxi's 王運熙 justification of his own reversal of opinion in his short essay, "*Ershisi shipin* zhenwei wenti wo jian" 二十四詩品真偽問題我見, originally published in 1997 in *Zhongguo shixue* 中國詩學, conveniently anthologized in a supplementary volume to his collected essays, *Zhongguo gudai wenlun guankui* 中國古代文論管窺 (Shanghai: Shanghai guji, 2006), 432–35. For a strong dissenting argument, see Zhang Shaokang 張少康, "Qingren lun Sikong Tu 'Ershisi shipin'" 清人論司空圖《二十四詩品》, *Nanyang shifandaxueyuan xuebao-Shehui kexue ban* 南陽師範大學學報（社會科學版）, vol. 1, no. 5 (October 2002): 32–37.

2. Quoted by Zhen Man 鄭鄤, "An Inscription for the *Shipin*" 題詩品. In Guo Shaoyu 郭紹虞, ed., *Shipin jijie/Xu Shipin zhu* 詩品集解／續詩品注 (Beijing: Renmin wenxue chubanshe, 1963; reprint 2005) [Hereafter, Guo Shaoyu], 57. It should be noted that some scholars argue that Su Shi actually made this remark regarding Sikong Tu's letters, and not the *Shipin*. For both the basis of this argument and a retort, see the articles by Wang Yunxi and Zhang Shaokang, respectively, in the preceding footnote.

3. Not all Qing scholars were so positively disposed. Jiao Xun 焦循, for example, defends the continued reproduction of the work (as opposed to its eradication) by asserting that the best way to neutralize its malevolent influence is through exposure. "Ke *Shipin* xu" 刻詩品敘 (Upon the engraving of the *Shipin*). In Guo Shaoyu, 58–59.

4. Qin Xijiu 秦錫九, "*Shipin* qianjie xu" 詩品淺解序 (Preface to *A Superficial Explanation of the* Shipin). In Guo Shaoyu, 59–60.

5. Yang Tingzhi 楊廷芝, "*Shipin* qianjie ba" 詩品淺解跋 (Postface to *A Superficial Explanation of the* Shipin). In Guo Shaoyu, 61.

6. One notable exception is Stephen Owen, who expresses a fair amount of skepticism concerning the depth of the *Twenty-Four Shipin*'s meaning. Noting that Sikong Tu was "immensely attracted" to the false profundity of Daoist discourse, Owen states that this tendency "compromises all the best aspects of his work: at its worst it is the 'poetics of Oz.'" See his *Readings in Chinese Literary Thought* (Cambridge, MA: Harvard University Asia Center, 1992), 301.

7. Gu Mingdong, "Aesthetic Suggestiveness in Chinese Thought: A Symphony of Metaphysics and Aesthetics," *Philosophy East and West* 53, no. 4 (Oct., 2003): 490–513.

8. Pauline Yu, "Ssu-k'ung T'u's *Shih-p'in*: Poetic Theory in Poetic Form," in *Studies in Chinese Poetry and Poetics*, vol. 1, ed. Ronald C. Miao (San Francisco: Chinese Materials Center, 1978).

9. Guo Shaoyu, throughout.

10. Roland Barthes, *The Rustle of Language*, trans. Richard Howard (Berkeley: University of California Press, 1989), 272.

11. Terence Cave, *Recognitions: A Study in Poetics* (Oxford, UK: Clarendon Press, 1988). See especially chapter 5, "Plots of the Psyche," 144–80, and chapter 6, "Modern Commentary and Criticism," 181–219.

12. The same might be said of certain examples of modernist fiction, most notably Proust's *À la recherche du temps perdu*. For an analysis of that work that approaches it in terms that seem quite similar, see Gérard Genette, "Proust Palimpseste" in *Figures I* (Paris: Éditions du Seuil, 1966), 39–67.

13. Frank Kermode, "The Plain Sense of Things" in *An Appetite for Poetry* (Cambridge, MA: Harvard University Press, 1989), 172–88.

14. It is not possible to do justice to Keightley's discussion here, but he argues that the lack of the use of disguise in early Chinese narrative is an expression of the culture's general "representational and epistemological optimism." See David N. Keightley, "Epistemology in Cultural Context: Disguise and Deception in Early China and Early Greece," in *Early China/Ancient Greece: Thinking Through Comparisons*, eds. Steven Shankman and Stephen W. Durrant (Albany: SUNY Press, 2002), 119–53.

15. Tao Yuanming, "Drinking Wine, no. 5" 飲酒其五. In *Tao Yuanming ji jianzhu* 陶淵明集箋注, ed. Yuan Xingpei 袁行霈 (Beijing: Zhonghua shuju, 2003), 247.

16. Wang Wei, "Wang Stream Collection" 王川集. In *Wang Youcheng ji jianzhu* 王右丞集箋注, comp. and ann. Zhao Diancheng 趙殿成 (Shanghai: Shanghai guji chubanshe, 1998), 241–50.

17. Wei Yingwu, "To a Daoist Adept on Quanjiao Mountain" 寄全椒山中道士. In *Wei Yingwu ji jiaozhu* 韋應物集校注, comps. and anns. Tao Min 陶敏 and Wang Yousheng 王友勝 (Shanghai: Shanghai guji chubanshe, 1998), 173.

18. Liu Zongyuan, "Travel Notes of Yongzhou" 永州八遊記. In *Liu Zongyuan Yongzhou youji jiaoping* 柳宗元永州遊記校評, ed. Xu Shantong 徐善同 (Yangming shan: Huagang chuban bu, 1974).

19. As summarized by Yu-kung Kao, the lyric *shi* poem developed in response to the widely and long-held conviction that only a particular type of language, "artistic" language, can fulfill the recognized social and personal need to communicate one's inner state. Simply put, this special, poetic language eschewed both direct description and narration, and relied instead on the positing of deep personal meaning in the objects of the perceptual world. See his essay, "The Aesthetics of Regulated Poetry," in *The Vitality of the Lyric Voice*, eds. Shuen-fu Lin and Stephen Owen (Princeton, NJ: Princeton University Press, 1986), 332–85.

20. For a full appreciation of how the aesthetic rendering of recognition, under consideration here, complements the politico-moral treatment of recognition in non-poetic Chinese texts, see Eric Henry, "The Motif of Recognition," *Harvard Journal of Asiatic Studies* 47, no. 1 (June 1987): 5–30.

21. Paula Varsano, "Looking for the Recluse and Not Finding Him In: The Rhetoric of Silence in Early Chinese Poetry," *Asia Major*, vol. XII, part 2 (1999): 39–70.

22. One scholar, Xiao Shuishun 蕭水順, makes a point of saying that the *Twenty-Four Modes of Poetry* is not a description of how poems should be written, but a rendering of what the finished product should be like. Indeed, in a remark that would later be echoed by Huang Jingjin, he notes that this text really concerns itself with the point of view of the reader, rather than that of the writer. He calls this a "discourse of ends" (目的論) rather than of means; and then goes on to compare its role in the overall body of traditional Chinese theory as the "woof" interwoven with "warp" of the rest of the theoretical works. See his *Cong Zhong Rong Shipin dao Sikong Tu Shipin* 從鍾嶸詩品到司空圖詩品 (From Zhong Rong's *Shipin* to Sikong Tu's *Shipin*) (Taipei: Wenshizhe, 1993), 91, 148.

23. Lu Ji, for example, in the first section of his *Wenfu*, seamlessly depicts the writer's mind wandering, unimpeded, through the seemingly adjacent expanses of the cosmos and the "forests" of literary writing.

24. For a thorough study of one particular subgenre—climbing high and looking afar—that exemplifies this practice, see Wang Longsheng 王龍升, *Tangdai denglinshi yanjiu* 唐代登臨詩研究 (A study of Tang Dynasty poems on climbing high) (Taipei: Wenjin chubanshe, 1998).

25. The translation of this term is as challenging as any of the chapter titles of the *Twenty-Four Modes of Poetry*, at least partly because it is a compound that can

be read as both a binomial conjoining of contrastive nouns (i.e., [internal] meaning-[external] world) or as a modifier-modified phrase (i.e., affective world). In the first case, it suggests, accurately, that the poem occupies a conceptual space in which the inner and outer world of the poet become one; in the second, it suggests that the "world" bodied forth by the poem is indelibly marked by the feeling of the poet.

26. Huang Jingjin 黃景進, *Yijinglun de xingcheng: Tangdai yijinglun yanjiu* 意境論的形成- - 唐代意境論研究 (The formation of the discourse on "worlds": A study of Tang "conceptual worlds" discourse) (Taipei: Taiwan xuesheng shuju, 2004).

27. He is referring to the essay, traditionally attributed to Wang Changling, entitled "Lun wenyi" 論文意 (On literary meaning), which survives in the ninth-century anthology of Tang Dynasty writings on literature, *Bunkyô hifuron* 文鏡秘府論 compiled by the Japanese monk, Kûkai 空海 (774–835). For a translation into English, see Richard Wainwright Bodman, *Poetics and Prosody in Medieval China: A Study and Translation of Kûkai's* Bunkyô hifuron (Ann Arbor: University Microfilms International, 1978).

28. Ibid., 210–20.

29. This brings us close to a concept he developed in his "Letter to Jipu" 與極浦書: "meaning beyond flavor" 味外之旨 and "the image beyond image" 象外之象, harking back to ideas formulated by the poet-monk Jiaoran 皎然 (730–799) in his discussions of "meaning beyond the text" 文外之旨 in his work, *Shishi* 詩式.

30. See my discussion in note 1.

31. Perhaps the pithiest version of this observation is by Zhao Jianyan 趙健奄, as quoted by Wang Fei'e 王飛鶚, in his "Shipin xujie xu" 詩品續解序: "The *Shipin* prizes sudden realization, and not analytical comprehension" 詩品貴悟不貴解. Cited in Guo Shaoyu, 66.

32. As cited in Guo Shaoyu, 145.

33. Two recent articles that demonstrate (but never explicitly justify) the utility of the concept of *jing* in understanding the fluidity of the *Shipin* categories are: Ding Jimao 丁吉茂, "Sikong Tu 'liudong' shijing shixi" 司空圖流動詩境試析 (Towards an analysis of Sikong Tu's "flowing" poetic worlds), *Mingdao tongshi luncong* 明道通識論叢 6 (May 2009): 147–75; and Xiao Chi 蕭馳, "Xuan, Chan guannian zhi jiaojie yu 'Ershisi shipin'" 玄，禪觀念之交接與《二十四詩品》(The interconnectedness of Xuan and Ch'an [thought] in the *Twenty-Four Shipin*), in *Zhongguo wenzhe yanjiu jikan* 中國文哲研究集刊 24 (March 2004): 1–37.

34. See his comments on chapters 1, 2, 3, 6, 12, 16, 18 (to be discussed in detail below), 19, 21, and 23. In certain instances, where visual perception is brought most strongly into play (as in his comments on chapter 3, "Intricate and Richly Colored" (*Xiannong* 纖穠), and on chapter 9, "Ornate and Radiant" (*Qili* 綺麗), he also uses the word *jing* 景 or "scene."

35. For a discussion of the connection between the development of imagistic criticism and the history of the word *pin*, see Zhang Bowei 張伯偉, *Zhongguo gudai wenxue piping fangfa yanjiu* 中國古代文學批評方法研究 (Study of the methods of ancient Chinese literary criticism) (Beijing: Zhonghua shuju, 2002), 242–44.

36. In fact, in the earliest references, such as the *Liangshu*, Zhong Rong's work was referred to as *Shiping* 詩評 (Poetry criticism); but by the time of the writing of the *Suishu*, there is already mention of its alternate title, *Shipin*. See Zhang Bowei 張伯偉, *Zhong Rong Shipin yanjiu* (A study of Zhong Rong's *Shipin*) (Nanjing: Nanjing daxue chubanshe, 1993), 18–20.

37. Zu Baoquan 祖保泉, *Sikong Tu de shige lilun* 司空圖的詩歌理論 (Sikong Tu's poetic theory) (Shanghai: Shanghai guji, 1984), 32.

38. Cited in Guo Shaoyu, 62.

39. Yang explicitly states that, although readers have previously assumed that the chapters are arranged in no particular order, it is "nevertheless possible to trace a clear line of thought" (卻有脈絡可尋) throughout the whole. See Yang's "Two Trivial Remarks" (*Suoyan erze* 瑣言二則), cited in Guo Shaoyu, 68; and his chapter commentaries in Guo, throughout.

40. Zu Baoquan is one who mocks the whole idea of trying to establish an underlying structure to the whole. See his *Sikong Tu de shige lilun*, 39–41.

41. See Zhang Bowei, *Zhong Rong Shipin yanjiu*, 387–422.

42. Guo Shaoyu, 33–34.

43. We are reminded here of Stephen Owen's observation that "The parts are incomprehensible, but the impression of the whole is clear." See his *Readings*, 301.

44. Sun Liankui 孫聯奎, *Shipin yishuo* 詩品臆說, in *Sikong Tu Shipin jieshuo erzhong* 司空圖《詩品》解說二種 eds. Sun Changxi 孫昌熙 and Liu Gan 劉淦 (Jinan: Qi Lu shushe, 1980), 37. In the full text of Sun's opening annotation to this poem, he is actually commenting on the relevant line in a series of six quatrains composed by another Qing dynasty scholar, Jiang Dounan 將斗南, titled "*Shipin* mulu jueju"《詩品目錄絕句》. Each line of these six quatrains is dedicated to summarizing each of the *Shipin*. Sun's full comment reads, "Dounan wrote, '"Real Worlds" describes true events.' I would say, 'In the poetry of the ancients, whatever met their eyes, whatever activities they were engaged in, were all "real worlds."'" 斗南云：古人詩, 即目即事, 皆實境也.

45. Du Liqun 杜黎均, *Ershisi shipin yizhu pingxi* 二十四詩品譯注評析 (Beijing: Beijing chubanshe, 1988), 153.

46. Guo Shaoyu, 3.

47. In "Weighty and Salient," we note a gradual transformation through the poem wherein light gives way to dark, vision is replaced by hearing, reality triggers and is replaced by imagination, and language gives rise to vision: "If there are fine words, the great river courses before him" 如有佳語, 大河前橫. (Guo Shaoyu, 9). In "Description," one of the poems that seems to rely most heavily on paradox, the attainment of likeness is praised—but mostly because of the impossibility of fixing in a stable form that which is inherently in flux. What is valued here, then, is not so much the end product as the process that enables one to catch the essence of flux itself. As Yang Tingzhi put it in his opening comment to this poem, "In my opinion, description originally is a term of stasis; here it has become a term of dynamism" 按形容本是靜字, 而此則動字也. As cited in Guo Shaoyu, 36.

48. Qing commentators have noted that the term *xiyin* 希音 (rarefied tones) can be elucidated by this line from the *Laozi*, "Listening and not hearing: this is called 'rarefied' " 聽之不聞名曰希; my translation attempts to integrate this reference.

49. Kadowaki Hirofumi suggests something similar when he argues that the focus is not on the "real" but on the nature of *jing*, concluding that it is to be understood here as the natural, unforced blend of the objective scene before one's eyes and the emotional response of the viewer who composes the poem. In this, he represents the view of many contemporary scholars. However, this view does not fully account for the degree and nature of the subjective view that are implied by the text as a whole. See Kadowaki, *Nijushi shihin*, 144–46.

On Blind Spots

8

Hidden in Plain View

Concealed Contents, Secluded Statues, and Revealed Religion

JAMES ROBSON

> What can be seen on earth indicates neither the total absence, nor the manifest presence of divinity but the presence of a hidden God. . . . God being thus hidden, any religion that does not say that God is hidden is not true, and any religion which does not explain why does not instruct.
>
> —Blaise Pascal, *Pensées*

> Hide and Seek is not a game you can play successfully by yourself.
>
> —Malcolm Bull, *Seeing Things Hidden*

Introductory Remarks: Hidden Theory

In a short philosophical meditation on the topic of "hiddenness" (where we sense something but do not perceive it, or perceive something but cannot sense it), Malcolm Bull recently suggested that "we look for what is hidden, anxious about what we might find—in the small print, under the bed—or else driven by fantasies about what may be concealed—buried treasure, unexpressed emotion. And yet the two hardly seem distinct. Our anxieties are fuelled by the play of imagination, our fantasies by the numbing fear that there may be nothing hidden, that what we already know is all there is."[1] Inspired by similar fantasies and anxieties alluded to in Bull's analysis of hiddenness, I set out in this paper to attend to a particular instance of things that are hidden (statues with hidden contents inside them), but as this study developed I was forced to ask questions about the reasons why certain methodological blind spots persist within our discipline and why particular things (and topics) are systematically concealed from scholarly attention. Before zeroing in on the Chinese material, it is pertinent to reflect for a moment on some methodological issues related to a consideration of hiddenness and to point out that many different disciplines in the humanities claim a privileged ability to uncover hidden meanings. In some cases, however, those same disciplines—either explicitly or implicitly—hide or conceal aspects of precisely that which they are ostensibly supposed to reveal.

In the tradition of anthropology and sociology, for example, it was long assumed (at least since Emile Durkheim, and up through Victor Turner, Marcel Griaule, Claude Levi-Strauss, and Clifford Geertz) that there was a hidden layer of meaning beneath the superficial surface layer of culture that had to be uncovered.[2] It was the task of the researcher to "reach beneath the symbol to grasp the reality it represents and that gives the symbol its true meaning." "The most bizarre or barbarous rites and the strangest myths," Durkheim averred, "translate some human need and some aspect of life, whether social or individual. The reasons the faithful settle for in justifying those rites and myths may be mistaken, and most often are; but the true reasons exist nonetheless, and it is the business of science to uncover them."[3] The anthropological drive to reveal the hidden aspects of culture is a classic example of a type of crypto-analytic approach that involved the decoding of covert symbols.[4]

Similar instances of the rhetoric of hiddenness are also found at the heart of recent (and not so recent) developments in the study of literature, history, psychology, and art history. It is found, for instance, in the hermeneutic method that Arthur Danto called "deep interpretation" (which, incidentally, he introduced with a quote from the *Zhuangzi*) and in the quasi-theological methodologies employed by the New Critics.[5] It is found within history, especially in the subfield known as microhistory, where there has been much concern with retrieving the lost or hidden peoples (primarily of Europe) who had fallen into the dark realm of unwritten histories.[6] The rhetoric of hiddenness is also, of course, present in psychological theories forwarded by Sigmund Freud, who not only posited a deep hidden recess of the mind (the unconscious), but also a technique that claimed to access that realm (psychoanalysis).[7] Finally, within the history of art, the rhetoric of hiddenness is most closely associated with the work of Erwin Panofsky, who posited different levels (from deeper to deepest) of hidden meaning in works of art that had to be unpacked by the investigator.[8]

If there is one field, however, where there has been a particular flurry of recent work explicitly focused on the nature of hiddenness and secrecy, it is religious studies.[9] In the introductory essay to *Rending the Veil: Concealment and Secrecy in the History of Religions*, Elliot R. Wolfson began by pointing out the conundrum at the heart of religion's engagement with the hidden or secret: "Is it not the case that secrecy imposes seclusion and encirclement that cuts one off from the greater society of practitioners? In that respect, secrecy would appear to be at odds with the teleology of a religious culture, which seeks through its institutions to disseminate what it considers to be true doctrines and right actions."[10] Yet Wolfson's statement is perhaps too limiting, since from a different perspective, it is precisely this direct engagement with the hidden or the secret that provides the motor for much religious thought and practice. Doesn't religion itself depend in large part on precisely the tension between elements of the hidden (a mystery) and access to it (which different religions each claim to be privy to)? Isn't the notion of hiddenness essential to conceptions of transcendence and metaphysics?

Much of the recent theoretical work on religion and secrecy has, however, also pointed out how "hiding" is in fact a form of "revelation" and that the "revealing" is merely another form of "hiding." Wolfson offers this formulation: "The secret, therefore, retains its secretive character if it is hidden in its exposure only if it is exposed in its hiddenness."[11] The taking off of the veil, in other words, gives the pretense of revealing, but may in fact be an even more pernicious form of hiding. Once that philosophical limit was hit on, new approaches inevitably emerged and we now find an explicit turn, represented in the work of Hugh Urban, to how issues of social power and authority condition the functioning of secrecy and esotericism within different religious traditions.[12]

Given the seemingly ubiquitous presence of the notion of hiddenness in a variety of humanistic disciplines, it is rather surprising that the conference that generated the papers collected in this volume was the first (as far as I know) collective engagement with the theme of hiddenness as it relates to the study of China. As noted by Paula Varsano in her introductory comments for the conference, however, the notions of hiddenness and secrecy provide sharp hermeneutical tools for thinking about various aspects of Chinese thought and practice. In a recent article on secrecy and transcendence in early China, Robert Campany demonstrated some of these possibilities by bringing Chinese material on secrecy and display into dialogue with work on other cultures. He highlighted how, for example, "In the case of Chinese masters of esoterica, at least, we find something more complex: a set of discursive strategies and patterns of depicted behavior that worked to create a tension between secrecy regarding methods and texts, on the one hand, and a sometimes eager and insistent display of wondrous results, on the other. Furthermore, not only the dramatic, visual display of arts' results but also the carefully maintained aura of secrecy surrounding their contents had the same effect: the enhancement of practitioners' prestige in the eyes of many non-arts-practicing but nevertheless interested and involved witnesses."[13] What Campany noted in regard to early esoteric masters could apply equally well to the later Chinese Buddhist tradition, where figures such as Huineng 慧能 (638–713) seem to have had privileged access to all the secrets of self-cultivation, but the main text that displays his wondrous achievements—the *Platform Sūtra of the Sixth Patriarch* (Liuzu tanjing 六祖壇經)—is notable for its reluctance to reveal the secrets about how to attain what he has or become who he is.[14]

In short, a tension between hiding and revealing thoroughly permeates the different realms of Chinese philosophy, art, literature, and religion, as recent scholarship and many of the papers in this volume reveal. While a detailed study of any one of those areas could no doubt yield rich results for thinking about the topic and rhetoric of hiddenness within Chinese history and culture, the particular instance of hiddenness that is focused on here is a consideration of a curious collection of Chinese religious statues and their contents. In addition to describing those statues, my approach in this paper is to address two different senses of the term "hidden." The first part of the paper involves a discussion of deity statues that contain cavities where objects and documents are hidden away. The second part of the paper involves a critical engagement with some of the possible reasons why these statues remained hidden in storerooms of museums and have been systematically ignored by contemporary scholars. As I hope to demonstrate below, at least one of the reasons they have been overlooked or sequestered away is the dual issue of idolatry and iconoclasm, since the objects put inside the statues were perceived to instill life into those objects. As Carlos Eire notes, "wherever there are idolaters, there, too, lurk some iconoclasts."[15]

Visible and Invisible Statues: Storage Rooms (*kufang* 庫房), Private Collections, and the Marketplace

During his protracted stay in China from 1583–1610, the Jesuit missionary Matteo Ricci (1552–1610) wrote that "the number of idols in evidence throughout the kingdom of China is simply incredible. Yet, it is quite certain that comparatively few of these people have any faith in this unnatural and hideous fiction of idol worship."[16] Ricci's journal entry provides us with an intimate—if overly general and acerbic—look at the abundance of images that populated the public and private spheres in China during the Ming Dynasty.

More recently, the writer Shen Congwen published a number of evocative essays that depict the ubiquitous presence of Chinese religious statuary in the local culture of west-central Hunan province. He wrote in 1930 that "none of the households had fixed religious beliefs. On the altar in the middle of the hall were offerings to Heaven and Earth and the ancestral tablets. They also sacrificed there to the Year God and the Tutelary God. In the kitchen was the God of the Hearth, while the pigsty, cowshed and barns had their deities too."[17] Shen Congwen's essays on Hunan depict a world populated with deity statues—a sketch of local culture that differs little from the journal notes penned by Ricci some three hundred years earlier.

The ubiquity and visibility of deity statues in public spaces as well as in private homes that was so apparent in the writings of Ricci and Shen Congwen underwent a rather drastic change in the mid–twentieth century. With the rise of the People's Republic of China in 1949, traditional forms of local religious practice became labeled as "feudal superstitions" unworthy of being recognized as "true" religions, and they were summarily repressed and destroyed. The intensity of attacks on traditional forms of Chinese religious practice escalated during the Cultural Revolution, when government policies were directed at the destruction of old social and religious traditions. Thus, from about 1949 until the early 1980s, the deity statues that had been so much a part of the Chinese religious and social landscape just a few decades earlier, largely became hidden from view. Religious practices ceased or went underground, ritual manuals were burned, and religious statues were removed from local shrines and domestic altars.

Therefore, the types of statues under discussion here have had a particularly intriguing history of visibility and concealment. In their native historical context—at least through the 1940s—they would have been found inside of the private realm of people's homes or in the public realm of temples and shrines. Despite their embattled history of suppression and neglect, popular religious statues have survived, and began to emerge from hiding in the early 1980s. Over the past twenty or so years, these small images also found their way into the very public settings of outdoor antiquities markets in Hunan, Beijing, and Shanghai, but at the same time they were also being relegated to the dark recesses of museum storerooms and into the closed domain of private collections. The paradox of visibility and concealment associated with these statues has resulted in an almost complete neglect, until very recently, of these statues by scholars of Chinese art and religion.

In 1984 Chinese customs officials in the regional capital of Changsha intercepted a container filled with nearly 1,000 small wooden images bound for the antiquities markets in Hong Kong, but this customs seizure did not attract the attention of the news media or scholars, since the images in question were wooden statues judged to be of a rather poor aesthetic quality, not very old, not well preserved, and of an unknown provenance. The images were eventually deposited in the Hunan Provincial Museum in the regional capital of Changsha. Museum officials placed them on shelves in a storage room, where they remain today. In 2002, Professor Alain Arrault of the École Francaise d'Extrême-Orient began directing a collaborative research project cataloging the Hunan Provincial Museum statue collection, along with the over 1,000 statues in a private collection in Beijing. Later, the same research project expanded to include the cataloging of over 1,000 statues held by a private collector in Changsha.[18] More recently, two other collections have been identified, including the Artasia Gallery collection in Milwaukee and another privately held collection in Taiwan. The latter two collections are presently being cataloged.

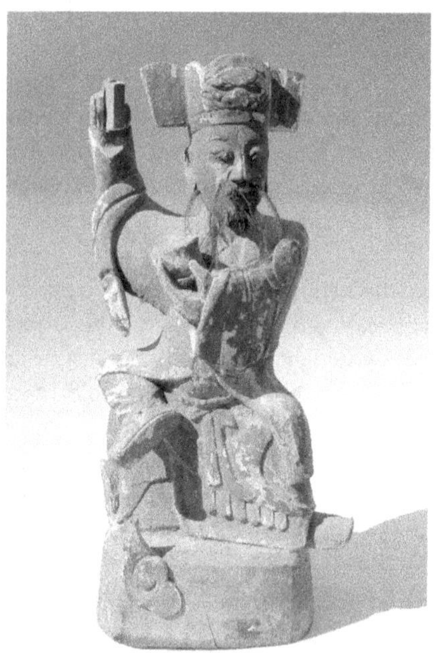

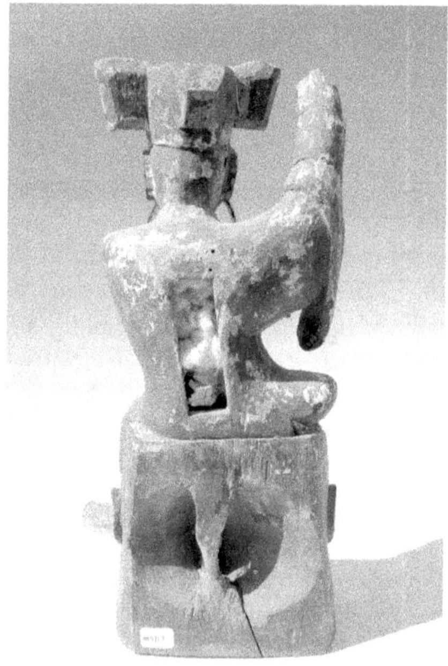

Figure 8.1a, b. Front and back of Hunan statue, photograph by Robson.

Figure 8.1, above, presents one example of a Hunan statue. Other types of Chinese deity statues have been known to the Western world from at least the sixteenth century (as the writings of Matteo Ricci attest). Those types of statues are best known from the well-known de Groot collection.[19] The establishment of the de Groot collection was modeled on the example of Emile Guimet, who had commissioned a set of Japanese esoteric figures that constituted a complete mandala. It seems that de Groot was a great admirer of Guimet, and it was when he returned to Fujian that he commissioned an artisan to carve a complete set of divinities. Those images were sent back to Guimet in Paris, and they were ultimately relocated to Lyon in 1913. Lyon was deemed the place where ethnographic materials would be housed, rather than in Paris (where the high art was to be kept). The wooden statues in de Groot's collection are presently held by the Muséum naturelle in Lyon, although some of the statues from the original collection are now also kept in Leiden.[20]

The statues from Fujian in de Groot's collection, with their bright paint and clean surfaces, were not ritual objects—they were never consecrated (*kaiguang* 開光)—but unlike the statues from Hunan they entered Western discourse as commissioned works of art. The plethora of other deity statues, such as those from Hunan, that are encrusted with dirt and blackened by decades of exposure to thick incense smoke or the flames fanned by the Cultural Revolution, were ignored.[21] While the statues under discussion here attracted the attention of a handful of collectors, they seem to have been almost entirely scamped by historians of Chinese art and religion.[22] What, we might ask, can be learned by bringing these statues out of hiding and back into the light of day for scholarly analysis?

The Hidden Cache: Revealing and Concealing Contents

The statuettes from Hunan are distinguished from similar religious images in other regions of China, such as those in the de Groot collection from Fujian and deity statues in Taiwan, by the nature of the contents in a small niche carved into their back. On the backside of these statues there is a small piece of wood that conceals a cavity. When that piece of wood is removed it is possible to see that the statue is filled with a variety of objects, including a medicinal packet (*yaobao* 藥包), coins or paper money, desiccated animals (sea horses and spiders), rice grains, small pieces of lead or jewelry, talismans (*fu* 符, *lu* 錄, and *hui* 諱) written on paper, and a consecration certificate (*yizhi* 意旨) (see figure 8.2).[23] All of these items are placed inside the statue during an elaborate consecration ritual (*kaiguang*) that brings life to the image. Interestingly, it is

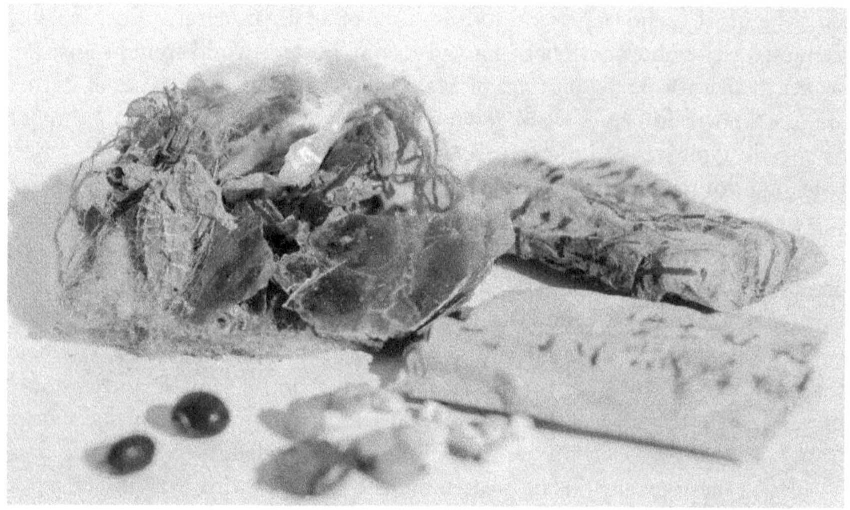

Figure 8.2. Contents of a Hunan statue, photograph by Robson.

the hiding of things in the dark inner recess of the statue that helps to bring forth the light and give the statue life.

The medicinal packet contains a variety of seeds, herbs, tea leaves, and minerals (such as mica flakes). The identification of the precise contents of these medicinal packets is difficult and not entirely understood at this point. It is possible to say, however, that the identifiable contents are all well attested in early Chinese medicinal recipes.[24] It is also not entirely clear what function these small packets of medicine were perceived to have served inside of the statues, and different explanations have been offered by contemporary carvers. Some of the consecration certificates mention the efficacious healing properties of the medicines contained inside of a statue, but were they there to heal the statue from the carving process or to somehow benefit the afflicted? In addition to their medicinal properties, many of the specific objects found in the medicine packet also seem to have symbolic meanings. The abundance of seeds, for example, is sometimes explained as representing fertility, and the seahorses were considered to be auspicious dragons or "vehicles to cross over the sea of suffering." The medicine packet itself, though often deteriorated or eaten by bugs, can be as simple as a paper envelope, or it can be comprised of a pouch tied with five strings of different colors. The different-colored strings may symbolize the five viscera, though Lin Wei-Ping has also shown that in Taiwan the five colored threads represent the five spirit-soldier camps, each of which has a symbolic color and is located in one of the cardinal points.[25]

For scholars of Chinese religion, anthropology, and social history, perhaps the most significant object hidden in the cache is the consecration certificate, which is a hand-written document (though in more recent statues we find the introduction of printed texts) providing an unprecedented amount of information about the statue and its provenance.[26] Indeed, it is this document placed inside the statues that sets the Hunan statues off from those found in other regions. The consecration certificates tend to have a rather standardized form, though the content of the certificate can vary dramatically in length. The consecration certificate usually begins with the precise address of the home or shrine were the statue was installed, indicating the district, town, village, and name of the temple or shrine (such as City God Temple [*chenghuang miao* 城隍廟], Temple Deity [*miaowang* 廟王], and Earth God Shrine [*tudi ci* 土地祠]).

Following the address on the *yizhi* is a section that includes the names of the patrons who commissioned the statue. These names are usually members of a family (or extended family) or of the disciples of a particular master. Due to the ambiguous language used in the consecration certificates it is not explicitly clear if one is dealing with a familial lineage or a religious initiation lineage. It is clear in the context of the Hunan statues, however, that some designations indicate successive religious ordination names (given by Daoist priests or ritual masters in the shigong 師公 or other local religious traditions), much as they do for the names found in Hakka genealogies that have been studied by Chan Wing-Hoi and among the Yao peoples studied by Jacques Lemoine.[27] It is too early to tell if a similar phenomenon is at work in the Hunan statues, but there is evidence of other forms of hiding in relation to what is included on the consecration certificates.

If the names in this section of the consecration certificate are not of religious disciples, then they are usually those of members of the same family, and tend to include the name of the main patron (usually the father) and his wife, as well as their sons (and their wives) and daughters. While this may seem like a trivial point, it is actually quite significant for those interested in genealogy, since in other historical documents women are hidden away—either through neglect or because they remain nameless.

Following the names of the donors on the consecration certificate is usually the name of the figure represented by the statue. The fact that the consecration certificates provide the precise identity of the statue takes away much of the indeterminacy associated with identifications based solely on external iconographic features. Based on these names, the identities of the statues can be classified into roughly four general categories: national deities, local deities, ancestors of family members, and Daoist priests and ritual masters.[28]

The category of national deities refers to deities whose cult is spread throughout China and is not local to any particular region. Within this category we find familiar Daoist and Buddhist deities, as well as deities of Chinese popular religion. One of the distinct features of the Hunan statues is the fact that many of them, as the names on the consecration certificates attest, are of either distant or proximate familial ancestors.[29] Statues dedicated to fathers are the most common, but images identified as being of grandparents, brothers, mothers, uncles, and aunts are also well attested. This is a rather striking phenomenon, since in traditional forms of Chinese ancestor veneration, anthropomorphic images of the ancestors were forbidden. During the twelfth century, for example, Zhu Xi 朱熹 (1130–1200) was rather outspoken in his disapproval of the use of portraits or statues in ancestor worship, and he carefully refrained from the use of the term "image halls" (*yingtang* 影堂).[30] The proper form of veneration was to merely set up an aniconic spirit tablet (*shenwei* 神位). Therefore, while it is exceedingly rare to find statues representing members of the family in other regions of China, they are one of the main categories of statues in central Hunan.

Now that I have laid out the range of possible figures identified by name on the consecration certificate, let me return to the next element mentioned in the document: the reason for the consecration of the statue. This section can vary dramatically in specificity of content and length. The reasons a statue was consecrated tend to fall into two main categories: (1) to express a vow or a wish for something (*xuyuan* 許愿), and (2) to express thanks for something provided by the deity (*huanyuan* 還愿). The wishes that accompany vows to animate and worship deities often have a rather general content: "Holding the incense of longevity, I implore your protection so that people may be at peace, the domestic animals fat, business good, that everything is accomplished according to our wishes, and that in a general manner all that is found under the light will be protected."[31] While these kinds of formulaic statements characterize many of the consecration certificates, others reveal more concrete motivations, such as assistance with a specific illness or a problem in the family. Since some consecration certificates include rather lengthy stories and biographies that give us an intimate glimpse of the religious motivations of those whose religious lives rarely appear in other standard historical sources, this section of the consecration certificates deserves extensive study.

The final piece of information contained on the consecration certificates is the date of the image consecration, the name of the statue carver, and often a litany of talismans. The date on which the statue was consecrated is obviously essential for dating, but the seemingly trivial mention of the carver's name turns out to be quite useful as well, since it is already evident from other research that statue carvers were not merely part of a trade, but were in fact religious figures themselves who could don religious vestments and perform the consecration ritual. Statue carvers are connected with a guild of woodworkers who venerate the deity Lu Ban 魯班. Their initiation into carving is not just about acquiring the technical skills necessary to practice the trade, but is also akin to initiation into a religious lineage.[32] As Alain Arrault has put it,

> Lu Ban, protector of all the guilds relating to construction (carpenters, cabinetmakers, roofers, bridge and boat builders, etc.) and for this reason also designated by the name Great Divinity of the Ink-Cup Marker and the Five-Foot Ruler (*Wuchi modou dashen* 五尺墨斗大神), is said to have been born in 587 BC (T0305). One asks him to ensure that the craft (*shouyi* 手藝) be profitable; one presents oneself as a woodworker (*mujiang* 木匠) or a journeyman (*gongshi* 工師), but this would be to forget that these guilds equally imply a religious formation. The disciples studied the orthodox doctrine of Lu Ban (Lu Ban zhengjiao 魯班正教), the secret formulas (*fajue* 法訣), talismans (*fufa* 符法), and the use of lustrous water; they were accepted and initiated by the masters to whom they paid homage. To enter into the guild was also to enter into a religious lineage.

Guilds related to trades or occupations are of course not unique to the Hunan region, but the study of the religious nature of Chinese guilds is in dire need of further study.[33]

Talismans (*fu*, *lu*, *hui*)—diagrams written in a strange or esoteric script—are found at the end of the certificates or on a separate sheet of paper in the cache. Some of these talismans are well known from standard Daoist canonical sources, but others are difficult to study since they belong to the preserve of esoteric ritual knowledge, and information about them is usually transmitted secretively.[34] Thus, there is a secondary level of "hiddenness" found in the documents that can be extricated from the statue's cache. Some of the talismans are quite simple, usually consisting of imbricated graphs with a legible command. Other talismans include the secret names of the deities. (In China, to know the name of a deity was to ensure control over it.) Others of the esoteric diagrams are in fact "registers" that include the names of celestial warriors or soldiers who serve the deceased and form a kind of procession. These spirit warriors are sometimes depicted as lined up in a row, and it is this pantheon of figures that constitute a hidden presence at the altar during the time of ritual. Ultimately, however, the second level of "hiddenness" represented by these talismans is only interpretable if one has recourse to the oral explanation of a ritual master or if one can access the handwritten esoteric ritual manuals that explain them.

Hidden Within: Statues Inside Out

The most distinctive feature of the Hunan statues is no doubt their cache and the nature of the objects that are hidden therein. How are we to account for the development of this phenomenon? Why were things interred inside of statues? While I have to a large extent discussed the Hunan statues in isolation, when put within a larger comparative perspective it is clear that the interring of things inside of statues was not unique to the Hunan region—or to East Asia. Cyril Mango long ago directed the attention of art historians to the comments of the Byzantine intellectual Michel Psellus, who had reported on the ways that icons received talismanic powers through a ritual, referred to as *stoicheiosis*, in which different substances were inserted into the cavity of a statue to activate it.[35] The *Greek Magical Papyri* also contain many examples of statues with cavities that were filled with all manner of things as well as a piece of papyrus with magical incantations, the names of gods, and what one wants to be accomplished.[36] Sarah Iles Johnston has also recently discussed the development of icon animation practices and the important shift that is discernible from the Greco-Roman period into late antiquity connected with the Theurgists.[37]

I have already mentioned above the comparable type of statues found in Taiwan and other regions of southern China, but efforts to trace the history of this practice primarily led back to Buddhist examples.[38] Scholars are already quite familiar with the fact that early Buddhists consecrated images and stūpas by interring a small relic fragment.[39] We also find images and icons with inscriptions or other forms of writing inside, including a vast number of Buddhist images with what are called *dharma sarîra*, or texts that are taken as instilling the presence of the living Buddha in the image.[40] A short text from Gilgit states that "images of the Buddha should be made either tall or short and with either a relic or with the *pratityasamutpada gatha* inside" and a later Indian text states that "you should at the time of making an image leave the head or back hollow. When completed you should write a *dharani* on birch bark with saffron or bezoar and wrap them around the relic which has been purified through the bathing ritual and then place them in the hollow space."[41]

In the case of East Asian religious icons, these contents can range from minuscule fragments of relics all the way to the famous example of a Buddha image that had a full body mummy inside: the spectacular Seiryoji image in Japan—replete with a full set of brocade inner organs, consecration documents, coins, and cloth fragments. Ever since its discovery in 1954, historians of Asian art and religion have become more attuned to the possible rewards of looking inside religious images.[42] The material record of Korean statues with contents appears to be equally rich.[43]

It is not entirely clear how many statues with interred objects have survived to the present, but many examples are preserved in museums throughout the world. The statues that contain symbolic viscera seem to date primarily to the Northern Song at the earliest. There are, for example, statues of two Arhats from the Lingyan Temple in Shandong that have full viscera—and mirrors—dated to the eleventh century, and there is a Guanyin image at the Kanagawa Prefectural Museum of History in Yokohama, which we are told had incense and cloth viscera. In a study of a Guanyin image at the Princeton University Art Museum, Robert Hawkins noted the importance of the practice of "making cavities in the back of [statues], in which magic or symbolic materials were placed" and how it was useful in assigning precise dates to the images. "The contents of these cavities," he continues, "might include a record of the making or repairing of the image, or an inscription might be written on the plug of wood which sealed the cavity."[44] Hawkins identified other such examples, including a standing bodhisattva in Toronto dated to 1195; two images at the Metropolitan Museum of Art in New York, including a standing bodhisattva dated to 1282 and a seated Guanyin dated to 1385; and finally a seated Guanyin at the Victoria and Albert Museum in London, dated to 1374.[45] He further noted that "these openings were originally concealed under the layers of gesso" and that he has not yet been able to ascertain how many other examples of wood sculpture have been examined for such cavities.

A recent archaeological report from Xiabali Village in Hebei province discusses the discovery between 1972 and 1993 of a series of tombs dedicated to the Zhang family that date to the Liao (916–1125) and Jin periods.[46] When further excavations were conducted in 1998, another cemetery was discovered and eight more tombs were excavated. The tomb labeled as M1 in the new excavation report is described as that of an elite figure; it contained two life-sized wooden statues (in addition to a copper net and copious wall murals). One statue, of an old woman, was carved out of cypress and contained a large cavity in the midsection. It has been suggested that this statue was a lifelike representation of the female tomb-owner and that her own ashes were interred inside of the cavity in her statue. The second statue in the tomb is identified as a Buddha image in the excavation report.

The Seattle Art Museum collection includes a child attendant of Guanyin that is dated to the Ming Dynasty (1368–1644). When the small cavity on the back of the statue was discovered and opened in 1957, "a curious inventory of objects" was removed. "The contents included a bronze mirror, fabric in the shape of various vital organs, charms, seeds, herbs, semi-precious stones, bits of metal, and a metal pendant."[47] One wonders just how many other museums have statues with these types of contents. It is hoped that future research will help to identify precisely how many of these statues are extant in museums around the world so that we might arrive at a better sense of their ubiquity and chronology.

In addition to the occasional mention of statues with objects hidden inside of them in museum catalogs and excavation reports, we also have recourse to a rich body of ethnographic and missionary writing that helps to provide a sense of the nature and range of the practice of interring objects in statues. Consider the following extract from this report from Joseph Edkins, included in a chapter entitled "Images and Image Worship" from his book *Chinese Buddhism*, published in1879:

> The Peking custom in making large images, whether they are of brass, iron, wood or clay is to construct them with the internal organs as complete as possible. While the smaller images are filled with incense or cotton wool, the larger have the interior arranged according to Chinese notions of anatomy. The heads are always empty. The chief viscera of the chest and abdomen are always represented. . . . Embracing all like the peritoneum is a large piece of silk covered with prayers or charms. Inside are also to be found little bags containing the five kinds of grain, pearls, jade, small ingots, and gold of five candareen's weight. The larger and older idols have in many cases been rifled of these little valuables, no one knows when. . . . [T]he clay and wooden images are packed from the whole in the back and are more liable to thievish depredation.[48]

Slightly later, in 1887, we also find the following account by Hampden C. DuBose in a chapter entitled "The Idol Factory"—in his tellingly entitled book *The Dragon, Image, and Demon; Or, The Three Religions of China; Confucianism, Buddhism and Taoism, giving an account of the Mythology, Idolatry, and Demonolatry of the Chinese*:

> The manufacture of images is an important branch of trade and is generally considered a profitable industry. It is not an art, as where in Italian marble by master-hands, the body of man is chiseled in proportions so majestic, so gigantic, that men scarcely know which most to admire, the sculptor or the statue. The Chinese figures are misproportioned, grotesque, and hideous, their faces are glum, frightful, and repulsive; if sitting they are awkward and clumsy, when standing the images are both fantastic and cadaverous. Why these hideous idols? Christianity teaches of a God of love, paganism, of deities who will punish the wrong-doer. The gentler attributes of the Godhead—love, pity, compassion, gentleness, longsuffering—are little taught by heathenism. Walk into one of the shops, with several hundred images of all sizes, from three inches to ten feet high. . . . Note the hole in the back. A frog, snake, lizard or centipede is caught and put inside for the soul, and then it is a living deity.[49]

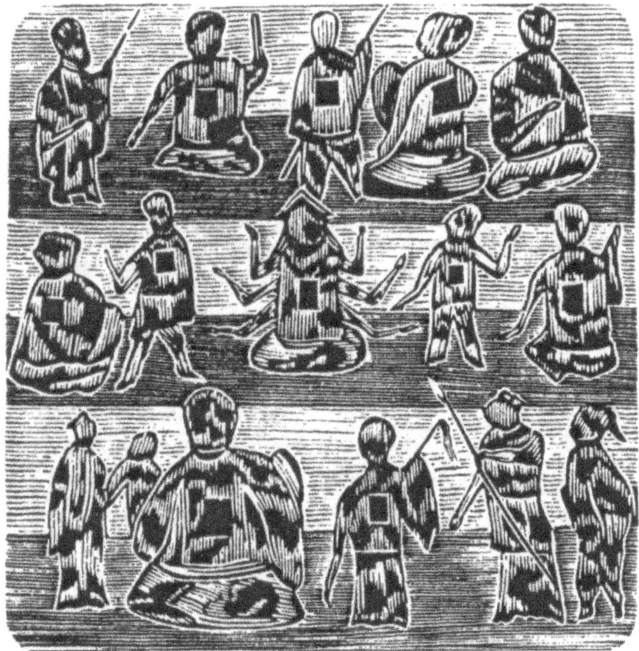

Figure 8.3. Woodcut showing the backsides of statues with cavities, from Hampden C. DuBose, *The Dragon, Image, and Demon or The Three Religions of China: Confucianism, Buddhism, and Taoism* (New York: A. C. Armstrong and Son, 1887), 257–59.

Unfortunately the authors of these accounts do not provide further details about the history and specifics of the practices they record, though we do know they were primarily writing about Beijing and the northern regions of China.

While the preponderance of evidence for the interring of objects in statues comes from Buddhist materials and Chinese popular religion, we also have recent examples of Confucian statues with internal objects. Jun Jing reports, for instance, that when an image of Confucius was fashioned in north China, they followed the custom (again suggesting how common the practice was) that "a statue's internal parts must approximate the anatomy of a real person in order to activate the deity's ability to respond to human supplications. Thus, a ruby and artificial pearls were installed in the statue of Confucius to represent his heart and intestines. The spine was a pole fashioned from a pine tree, the arteries were made of red threads, and the kidneys and liver were constructed with silk bags containing twelve traditional medicinal herbs."[50] Indeed, it was the rumor that the statue contained gold, pearls, and rare gemstones that fueled the curiosity of outsiders, who came from far away to make a pilgrimage to see the image. Wang Liang has also recounted a striking story about Red Guards storming into the Temple of Confucius in Qufu and desecrating all of the statues. According to one account of the scene, a person "noticed a hole in the belly of Old Kong, and stuck his hand in. As he used his strength to make a hollow in Old Kong's belly, others joined in. From within the hole, they pulled out a bunch of cotton, books, and the lousy guts of Old Kong (made of bronze mirrors and pieces of bronze)."[51] Therefore, it appears that at least some Confucian statues also had internal organs placed inside.

Other anecdotal evidence suggests that the interring of symbolic viscera into Chinese statues was rather widespread, and we also find accounts of the practice in disparate—and disparaging—missionary writings. The *Church Missionary Gleaner* of 1916 includes a report, for example, about something called "the soul of an idol." The report says,

> Two years ago the C.M.S (Church Missionary Society) purchased a group of monasteries and temples in the eastern suburb of Canton. The idols which were removed when the missionaries entered into possession were many and varied. Some were valuable works of art; some were quite common and ugly images. . . . Their removal cannot have failed to dispel some of the untold darkness and superstition in the minds of many thousands of people, for the event was discussed in the Canton daily papers for weeks. This particular soul of an idol was taken from one of the principal images . . . it is not hung on the outside of the image as a decoration might be,

> but in the hollow chest of the idol which is specially constructed to receive it. A religious ceremony of exceptional importance is performed by a high dignitary when the idol is consecrated and the invocation of the soul is made; and then, after all the necessary ritual has been observed, the symbol is wrapped in silk and solemnly suspended inside the newly-created god, introduced through a small hole in the back.[52]

This is a valuable description that documents a practice that is difficult to find in other types of sources. It is interesting how these iconoclastic missionaries, in their efforts to rid the Chinese of their benighted ways, also served to keep information about these practices alive through their critiques and maledictions.

Despite the existence of occasional reports and brief mentions of statues with interred objects, information about them has remained rather scattered and has largely been left unexplored. In a brief report on a wooden statue of Guan Di 關帝 housed at the Victoria and Albert Museum, John Larson and Rose Kerr put their finger on an important set of issues—which are also pertinent to the Hunan statues—when they noted that "the Victoria and Albert Museum's lacquered wood image of Guan Di has seemingly never been on public display and has languished in store for some twenty years. The decision to conserve, display, and publish the sculpture represents a concern that images of this type and period have not been seriously examined by scholars, nor have they created any interest in the international art market."[53] If there is potentially so much that can be learned from these statues and they once had such a visible presence in the premodern and modern period, then we must return to the question posed above: why have these statues remained hidden away in storerooms and why have they been invisible to scholars of Asian art and Asian religions?

Hidden from History: Idolatry, Iconoclasm, and Ideological Blind Spots

Sacred images and icons have presented problems for priests, politicians, philosophers, and academics who for various reasons have throughout history found them distasteful, attacked their validity and power, and have tried to hide them away or destroy them. Yet even in the face of critique and destruction they have proliferated. The ubiquitous presence of sacred icons and popular religious statues remains distinctly out of proportion with the paucity of scholarship on those images. At least one of the reasons for this silence is perhaps apparent in the last line of Matteo Ricci's comments quoted earlier. That final sentence suggested that the veneration of images and icons was an "abomination," or a form of idolatry—debased religious beliefs and practices that take inanimate objects such as pieces of wood and metal and impute a living presence to them. For Europeans, there was something about this particular type of veneration of these types of images that constituted incontrovertible evidence that the Chinese were benighted and idolatrous.

In their thought-provoking book entitled *Idolatry*, Moshe Halbertal and Avishai Margalit demonstrate how the notion of idolatry is linked in the West with issues of monotheism and iconoclasm.[54] In the case of Chinese deity statues, then, there is a dual problem: (1) worship of false gods, and (2) the problematic representation of God. The roots of the notion of idolatry lie in the Hebrew Bible and its condemnation of the pagan worship of other gods, of strange gods, which is to say "false gods." The notion of idolatry is also connected with a ban on certain ways of representing the right God, a ban on visual images, but, interestingly enough, not on verbal descriptions.[55] The term "idolatry" is a pejorative term, a fighting word that, like the term "magic," is always applied to someone else. In this sense, to charge someone with being an idolater is tantamount to accusing that person of being confused and ignorant (due to their perception of the icon as being alive) and ultimately immoral (due to their worship of a "false god").[56]

We should recognize that there is also a long history of iconoclasm in China that awaits a comprehensive study. Iconoclasm in China was evident as long ago as the eighth century—and much earlier evidence could no doubt be found—when the Chan monk Danxia Tianran 丹霞天然 (739–824) burned a statue of the Buddha.[57] When he was criticized for this act, he merely replied that he was looking for relics and that if there were none there, then the statue was nothing more than a piece of wood.[58] This perspective on carved wooden images resonates well with some Western thinking about icons that questioned how a divine image could be created by a mortal human out of a mundane substance, materials that might also be used to fashion ordinary objects such as bowls and furniture.[59] Like the "mighty Sejanus" of Juvenal's *Satires*, the images of Chinese deities suffered under the ideological attacks on anthropomorphic representations of a transcendent figure, while later in history the iconoclasm of the Cultural Revolution led to the wholesale cleansing of the altars, as images were destroyed or melted down to make household items.

The second issue raised above, that of the problematic representation of God, is a topic that raises other intractable questions. There is a vast literature on the ongoing debates about the anthropomorphic representation of God and the history of iconoclasm, but the main issue seems to boil down to questions about figural representations based on the logic of mimesis. The injunction against figurative representations is, of course, formulated most strongly in the Second Commandment: "Thou shalt not make unto thee any graven image of any likeness of any thing that is in heaven above, or that is on the earth beneath, or that is in the water under the earth" (Exodus 20:4). Although it is clear here that the issue of representation is not merely related to God, and any "likeness"—regardless of what it depicts—is forbidden, the question of representation arose most often with regard to God.[60] It would lead the discussion too far astray to further track the ongoing debates about figuration and mimesis here, but it is necessary to first understand the shift from the iconic to the aniconic that is at the basis of that discussion, before we can really engage with the ways that the rhetoric of iconoclasm has infected the study of Chinese art.

Isn't it possible to understand the prohibition against making images of God as implying a more general shift away from sensory perception to abstract ideas? The victory, in other words, of transcendence (the hidden) over immanence (the perceivable), of Kandinsky, and of the abstract over form and the material? One of the main issues in debates about figurative representations of God was that it "limited" God, when the proper form of representation should point beyond itself to that which is unrepresentable and hidden—yet nonetheless somehow present in the image.[61] The astute reader will no doubt realize here that if the true essence of the image is to remain hidden, then the literal enlivening of the statue by interring within it material viscera and other objects actually compounds the problematic nature of these images in the eyes of iconoclasts.

The intellectual trajectory that finds meaning beyond the material form of a work of art is what seems to have inspired Alfred Gell to write an intriguing essay that explicitly connected art and aesthetics to religion. "Aesthetics," he suggested, "is a branch of moral discourse which depends on the acceptance of the initial articles of faith; that in the aesthetically valued object there resides the principle of the True and the Good, and that the study of aesthetically valued objects constitutes a path towards transcendence." Yet, he continues, "this willingness to place ourselves under the spell of all manner of works of art, though it contributes very much to the richness of our cultural experience, is paradoxically the major stumbling-block in the path of the anthropology of art."[62] Thus, according to Gell it is a rather short journey from the church to the museum.

Even with the support implied in Gell's critiques (and the similar arguments made by Georges Didi-Huberman[63]), it is rather difficult to draw a distinct line of causality from religious devotion (and its inverse of iconoclasm) to a lack of attention to certain types of art by art historians and the failure of contemporary museums to exhibit that art (two concerns explicitly addressed in the comments by the curators of the Victoria and Albert Museum cited above); but let me attempt to make some gestures in that direction. Art historians have produced many fine-grained studies of the iconography of different kinds of deities, and they have been largely successful in pinpointing the temporal and cultural provenance of specific images based on stylistic elements, material properties, and production techniques. Therefore, we do know quite a bit about the aesthetic, iconographic, and even technical development of statuary in East Asia. Art historians have also been able to articulate the spiritual significance and symbolic meanings of different forms of iconographic elements. Yet until recently, little effort had gone into discerning the function of images, and what has been said is based on an overly thin textual record.

Perhaps the reluctance to bring together the material and textual record was due to a perceived division of academic labor. I suspect, however, that something deeper is responsible for the way that Western interpreters have traditionally been so seduced by the surfaces of unfamiliar images that they have neglected to plumb their hidden depths for other meanings and functions. It is understandable, for example, that European historians of Buddhist art would have initially ignored the function of Buddha images, given that Buddhism was initially understood by its European interpreters as an atheistic tradition that did not venerate gods, whether in iconic or aniconic forms. There is a certain irony in all of this, since at the same time that Western interpreters were touting Buddhism as a "modern" atheistic creed, something more akin to a philosophy than a religion, museums throughout the world were beginning to fill up with all kinds of Buddhist images—from Buddhas and bodhisattvas to different guardian figures. The aesthetic quality of those images was, it seems, difficult to resist.

Buddhist images were able to enter museums solely based on their aesthetic credentials, and the misplaced perception that their aesthetic representation was aimed at pointing beyond their material form to an immaterial divine presence (a different sense of hiddenness).[64] Ernest Fenollosa, who became the first curator of the Oriental collection at the Boston Museum of Fine Arts in 1890, expressed this sentiment well when he wrote about a statue of Maitreya Buddha: "The impression of this figure, as one views it for the first time, is of intense holiness. No serious, broad-minded Christian could quite free himself from the impulse to bow down before its sweet powerful smile. With all its primitive coarseness of detail . . . it dominates the whole room like an actual presence."[65] If that quasi-religious sentiment has operated as a kind of standard for entrance into the Western museum (or the museum of the Western imagination), then images such as the Hunan statues could never measure up. Their purpose is not to point beyond themselves to a transcendent entity or ideal whose presence one can enter. Rather, those statues are precisely the type of objects that are denigrated (a modern form of iconoclasm) by being classified as merely part of Chinese popular or folk religion and art. Moshe Halbertal and Avishai Margalit have perceptively noted how the criticism of idolatry is easily "transformed into the criticism of folk religion."[66] While there has been a movement toward erecting museums of folk art throughout the world, I think we would do well to also consider further the fundamental separation that has been enacted by severing "folk art" from "art"—recall the move of de Groot's collection from Paris to Lyon. Like the cleansing of religion from magic, that separation serves to protect the former from the perceived dangers of mixing with the latter.

Historians of art do not always agree with the perspectives of museum curators, and they have also begun to adopt radically different approaches to the study of religious images. This shift has contributed to the reorientation of the gaze of earlier scholars, which had been colored by Western values of aestheticization, desacralization, and secularization. No one has expressed this new scholarly agenda more clearly and forcefully than Alfred Gell. Gell advocated an anthropology of art, or what he called a *methodological philistinism*, which would consist of "taking an attitude of resolute indifference towards the aesthetic value of works of art—the aesthetic value they have, either indigenously or from the standpoint of universal aestheticism."[67] In Gell's later writings, he elaborated on what he meant by an anthropological approach to art. He states that it should focus on the "social context of art production, circulation, and reception, rather than the evaluation of particular works of art."[68] Gell was concerned with walking a fine line between the sociological perspective of Pierre Bourdieu (which he critiqued by saying it never looked at the art object itself, but only focused on its power to mark social distinctions) and the iconographic approach of Erwin Panofsky (a semiotic approach that he also critiqued due to its primary focus on symbolic meanings without consideration of the object itself). Gell suggested that the anthropology of art should pursue two lines of inquiry: (1) the study of the social relations in the vicinity of objects mediating social agency, and (2) the treatment of art objects as the equivalents of social agents. I trust that it is already clear to the reader how the Hunan statues and their rich contents provide a uniquely rich body of material for carrying out and exploring Gell's research directives.

Despite the novel new approaches to art developed in some quarters of the humanities, the types of images and icons from Hunan that are the centerpiece of this paper have heretofore remained hidden beyond the purview of scholars of Asian art and scholars of Asian religions. The reason they have been ignored is their perceived lack of aesthetic quality, and the reason they were denigrated by early missionaries was because they were perceived to be literally enlivened by the contents inside of them. For these reasons (and perhaps many others) they have fallen into the gap that separates the study of religion and the study of art. The Hunan statues may not elevate us to the rarified heights inspired by other sculpture, but that may be their most important contribution to the history of art. It is not the material form of the statue that aims to capture the presence of a hidden deity behind the statue. Rather, all of the contents hidden within the statue are aimed at bringing "life" to the statue (be it a national deity, local god, master, etc.) so that it is immediately accessible for people to call on.

Hiddenness, in other words, does not refer to a hidden god that is reflected (however imperfectly) in the image, but the hidden materials ensure the actual presence of the living god on the altar. These statues and their contents take us down into the terrain of family practice and popular village culture, itself an often hidden level of society that is difficult for historians to grasp due to a paucity of sources. In studying these statues my goal is not, therefore, to discern how the hidden and unrepresentable is presented, but to assess what is provided in concrete detail on the consecration certificates found inside the statues (while remaining aware of the possibility that some things may be hidden in what is revealed there). Thus, we should resist the seduction (or repulsion) of the surface of these statues and explore the value of the images from the inside out. I have suggested that it is necessary to turn away from issues of external aesthetics—which is not to say that we should forego the analysis of their external features, such as clothing styles, hats, mudras, and so on—and focus on what is hidden inside those statues to better understand many heretofore hidden aspects of local Chinese religious practice. At the same time, however, by tracing the reasons why these statues have remained hidden from view and beyond scholarly comment, it is possible to more clearly see how certain methodological presuppositions and classificatory schemes have conditioned what we see and do not see in the study of Chinese religions.

Notes

1. Malcolm Bull, *Seeing Things Hidden: Apocalypse, Vision and Totality* (London: Verso, 1999), 1.

2. See, for example, the work of Emile Durkheim, *The Elementary Forms of Religious Life* (New York: Free Press, 1995), and his collaboration with Marcel Mauss

on a project that included aspects of Chinese material, *Primitive Classification* (Chicago: University of Chicago Press, 1963); Victor Turner, *The Forest of Symbols: Aspects of Ndembu Ritual* (Ithaca, NY: Cornell University Press, 1967); Marcel Griaule, *Conversations with Ogotomelli: An Introduction to Dogon Religious Ideas* (London: Published for the International African Institute by Oxford University Press, 1965); and Clifford Geertz, *The Interpretation of Cultures: Selected Essays* (New York: Basic Books, 1973). See also Georg Simmel, "The Sociology of Secrecy and of Secret Societies," *American Journal of Sociology* 11, no. 4. (Jan., 1906): 441–98.

3. Durkheim, *Elementary Forms of Religious Life*, 2.

4. A classic of this genre is Alfred Gell, *Metamorphosis of the Cassowaries: Umeda Society, Language and Ritual* (London: The Athlone Press, 1975).

5. See Arthur Danto, "Deep Interpretation," in *The Philosophical Disenfranchisement of Art* (New York: Columbia University Press, 1986), 48; Frank Kermode, *The Genesis of Secrecy* (Cambridge, MA: Harvard University Press, 1979). On the New Critics see William K. Wimsatt, Jr., and Cleanth Brooks, *Literary Criticism: A Short History* (New York: Vintage Books, 1957), 147; for an analysis of what I have called their quasitheological method, see Roger Seamon, "Theocratism: The Religious Rhetoric of Academic Interpretation," in *Philosophy and Literature* 21, no. 2 (1997): 319–31. Hayden White also noted long ago the role of hiddenness in literary and philosophical inquiry, suggesting it was present "in modern Western philosophy, with its insistence that things are never what they appear to be but are manifestations of noumenal essences whose reality must be supposed but whose 'natures' can never be known" (Hayden White, *Tropics of Discourse* [Baltimore, MD: Johns Hopkins University Press, 1978], 282). It was not only theories of literary interpretation that claimed a space for hidden meanings. Authors themselves have long tried to hide meanings in their texts, as Shawn Rosenheim ably captures. Shawn Rosenheim has traced the genealogy—from Poe to Pynchon and Borges to William Gibson—of crypotographic writing that deploys different forms of ciphers and codes. See his *The Cryptographic Imagination: Secret Writing from Edgar Poe to the Internet* (Baltimore, MD: Johns Hopkins University Press, 1997).

6. Pierre Goubert, "Local History," *Daedalus* 100, no. 1 (1971): 113–27; Giovanni Levi, "On Microhistory," in *New Perspectives on Historical Writing*, ed. Peter Burke (University Park: Pennsylvania State Press, 1991) 93–113; Edward Muir and Guido Ruggiero, eds. *Microhistory and the Lost Peoples of Europe* (Baltimore, MD: Johns Hopkins University Press, 1991); Carlo Ginzburg, *The Cheese and the Worms* (Baltimore, MD: Johns Hopkins University Press, 1980); Michel-Rolph Trouillot, *Silencing the Past: Power and the Production of History* (Boston: Beacon Press, 1995).

7. While Freud was concerned with the recall of memories, other writers and philosophers from Nietzsche and Borges to Marc Augé have also pointed out the necessity of leaving some memories hidden in the unconscious or getting rid of them. Friedrich Nietzsche, *The Use and Abuse of History* (New York: Macmillan Library of Liberal Arts, 1985); Jorge Luis Borges, "Funes, His Memory," in *Collected Fictions*, trans. Andrew Hurley (New York: Viking Penguin, 1998); Marc Augé, *Oblivion* (Minneapolis: University of Minnesota Press, 2004). Interestingly, researchers at Stanford University

also claim to have demonstrated the utility, even necessity, of hiding away memories to provide space to remember new things. See Lisa Trei, "Forgetting Helps you Remember the Important Stuff, Researchers Say," in *Stanford Report* (June 6, 2007). http://news.stanford.edu/news/2007/june6/memory-060607.html.

8. See Erwin Panofsky, *Studies In Iconology: Humanistic Themes in the Art of the Renaissance* (Oxford, UK: Oxford University Press, 1939). There has been a certain amount of unease among contemporary theorists of art toward the Panofskian iconological approach that has been captured well in Svetlana Alpers's critique, which says that images in Dutch art "do not disguise meaning or hide it beneath the surface but rather show that meaning by its very nature is lodged in what the eye can take in—however deceptive that might be" (Svetlana Alpers, *The Art of Describing: Dutch Art in the Seventeenth Century* [Chicago: University of Chicago Press, 1983], xxiv).

9. See the special issue of the *Journal of the American Academy of Religion* 74, no. 2 (2006), which focused on the topic of religion and secrecy. See also Elliot R. Wolfson, ed., *Rending the Veil: Concealment and Secrecy in the History of Religions* (New York: Seven Bridges Press, 1999); Kees W. Bolle, ed., *Secrecy in Religions* (Leiden: E. J. Brill, 1987).

10. Wolfson, *Rending the Veil,* 1.

11. Wolfson, *Rending the Veil,* 3.

12. Hugh B. Urban, *Tantra: Sex, Secrecy, Politics and Power in the Study of Religion* (Berkeley: University of California Press, 2003); "The Torment of Secrecy: Ethical and Epistemological Problems in the Study of Esoteric Traditions," *History of Religions* 37, no. 3 (February 1998): 209–48; and "Elitism and Esotericism: Strategies of Secrecy and Power in South Indian Tantra and French Freemasonry," *Numen* 44 (1997): 1–38.

13. Robert Ford Campany, "Secrecy and Display in the Quest for Transcendence in China, ca. 220 BCE–350 CE," *History of Religions* 45, no. 4 (May 2006): 336.

14. *Liuzu tanjing* 六祖壇經 (Platform sūtra of the Sixth Patriarch). T. 48, #2007 and #2008. See the translation of the Dunhuang version of this text in Philip B. Yampolsky, *The Platform Sūtra of the Sixth Patriarch* (New York: Columbia University Press, 1967).

15. Carlos M. N. Eire, *War Against the Idols: The Reformation of Worship from Erasmus to Calvin* (Cambridge, UK: Cambridge University Press, 1986), 6.

16. Matthew Ricci, "Religious Sects Among the Chinese," in *China in the 16th Century: The Journals of Matthew Ricci 1583–1610*, trans. Louis J. Gallagher (New York: Random House, 1953), 105.

17. Shen Congwen, *Recollections of Western Hunan* (Beijing: Panda Books, 1982), 174.

18. Descriptions and analysis of those collections can be found in Alain Arrault, "Analytic Essay on the Domestic Statuary of Central Hunan: The Cult to Divinities, Parents, and Masters," *Journal of Chinese Religions* 36 (2008): 1–53; Alain Arrault and Michela Bussotti, "Statuettes religieuses et certificats de consécration en Chine du Sud (XVIIe–XXe siècle)," *Arts Asiatiques* 63 (2008): 36–59.

19. R. J. Zwi Werblowsky, Keith Stevens, and Roland Mourer, eds., *Dieux de Chine, le panthéon populaire du Fujian de J. J. M. de Groot* (Lyon: Muséum d'histoire naturelle de Lyon, 2003). On other popular religious statues see, among others, Keith Stevens, *Chinese Gods: The Unseen World of Spirits and Demons* (London: Collins and Brown, 1997); Museum of East Asian Art, Bath, England, *Shen: Chinese Icons of Divinity* (Bath: Museum of East Asian Art, 2008); Neal Donnelly, *Gods of Taiwan: A Collector's Account* (Taipei: Artist Publishing Company, 2006); Joe Papenfuss, *Yilan God Statue Exhibition* (Yilan, 2007); Zhang Yanping 張燕平, *Minjian mudiao yishu jianshang* 民間木雕藝術鑒賞 (An appreciation of the art of folk carving) (Changsha: Hunan renmin chubanshe, 2003); Liu Wensan 劉文三, *Taiwan shenxiang yishu* 台灣神像藝術 (Deity statues of Taiwan) (Taipei: Yishu chubanshe, 1981).

20. See also Zwi Werblowsky, "Catalogue of the Pantheon of Fujian Popular Religion," *Studies in Central and East Asian Religions* 12/13 (2001): 95–186.

21. It is pertinent to note here how in Taiwan it is precisely the dirty statues with blackened faces that are considered to be the most efficacious (ling 靈), since the residue is considered to be the tangible proof that the statue is being venerated. See Steven P. Sangren, *Chinese Sociologics: An Anthropological Account of the Role of Alienation in Social Reproduction* (London: Athlone Press, 2000), 73–75.

22. The exceptions that prove this rule include articles by Keith G. Stevens, "Altar Images from Hunan and Kiangsi," *Journal of the Hong Kong Branch of the Royal Asiatic Society* 18 (1978): 41–48. Illustrations 1–10 (end of the volume) and "Portraits and Ancestral Images on Chinese Altars," *Arts of Asia* 19, no. 1 (1989): 135–45, as well as Fu Juliang 傅聚良, "Hunan minjian mudiao shenxiang 湖南民間木雕神像," *Zhongguo wenwu shijie* 中國文物世界 150 (1998): 54–68.

23. In some areas of Taiwan, Fujian, and Jiangxi, statues are also carved with a small cache in the back, but they tend to usually just have a small insect inserted into the space. See Wei-Ping Lin, "Conceptualizing Gods through Statues: A Study of Personification and Localization in Taiwan," *Comparative Studies in Society and History* 50, no. 2 (2008): 454–77.

24. See, for example, Donald Harper, *Early Chinese Medical Literature: The Mawangdui Medical Manuscripts* (London: Kegan Paul International, 1998); Paul U. Unschuld, *Medicine in China: A History of Pharmaceutics* (Berkeley: University of California Press, 1986).

25. Lin Wei-Ping, "Conceptualizing Gods through Statues," 465, though she also notes that other sets of five may correspond to the organs.

26. See Arrault and Bussotti, "Statuettes religieuses," and James Robson, "The Archive Inside: Manuscripts Found Within Chinese Religious Statues," in *Manuscript Culture in Asia*, eds. Jörg Quencer, Michael Friedrich, Matthew Driscoll, and Jan-Ulrich Sobisch (forthcoming).

27. Chan Wing-Hoi, "Ordination Names in Hakka Genealogies: A Religious Practice and Its Decline," in *Down to Earth: The Territorial Bond in South China*, eds. David Faure and Helen F. Siu (Stanford, CA: Stanford University Press, 1995); Jacques Lemoine, *Yao Ceremonial Paintings* (Bangkok: White Lotus, 1982), 24–27. On the

use of the *langming* in the Hunan statues, see also Arrault, "The Domestic Statuary of Central Hunan," 34–35.

28. See the similar (yet more precise) rubric employed by Arrault in "The Domestic Statuary of Central Hunan."

29. See the early work of Keith Stevens, "Portraits and Ancestral Images on Chinese Altars," *Arts of Asia* 24, no. 6 (Nov.–Dec. 1994): 88–95, as well as the more recent work of Arrault, "The Domestic Statuary of Central Hunan," 39–43. See also the section on ancestors in *Shen: Chinese Icons of Divinity*, 61–68.

30. Patricia Ebrey, "Education through Ritual: Efforts to Formulate Family Rituals During the Song Period," in *Neo-Confucian Education: The Formative Stage*, eds. William Theodore de Bary and John W. Chaffee (Berkeley: University of California Press, 1989), 301–2.

31. Translation (with some minor changes) from Arrault, "The Domestic Statuary of Central Hunan," 17.

32. For information on the ritual nature of carving and woodworking see Klaas Ruitenbeek, *Carpentry and Building in Late Imperial China: A Study of the Fifteenth-Century Carpenter's Manual* Lu Ban jing (Leiden: E. J. Brill, 1993).

33. Some of the classic works on Chinese guilds that touch on their religious elements include Niida Noboru 仁井田陞, *Chûgoku no shakai to girudo* 中国の社会とギル (Tokyo: Iwanami shoten 1951); Li Qiao 李喬, *Zhongguo hangyeshen chongbai* 中國行業神崇拜 (Taibei: Yunlong, 1996); Wang Shucun 王樹村, *Zhongguo chuantong hangye zhushen* 中國傳統行業諸神 (Chinese Gods of Old Trades) (Beijing: Foreign Languages Press, 2004); Shigeshi Katô, "On the *Hang* or the Associations of Merchants in China," *Memoirs of the Research Department of the Toyo Bunko*, no. 8 (1936): 45–83.

34. On talismans in general see Christine Mollier, "Talismans," in *Divination et société dans la Chine médiévale: Étude des manuscrits de Dunhuang de la Bibliothèque nationale de France et de la British Library*, ed. Marc Kalinowski (Paris: Bibliothèque nationale de France, 2003), 405–29; James Robson, "Signs of Power: Talismanic Writing in Chinese Buddhism," *History of Religions* 48, no. 2 (2008): 130–69.

35. Cyril Mango, "Antique Statuary and the Byzantine Beholder," in *Dumbarton Oaks Papers* 17 (1963): 61. See also the very interesting material on animation presented in Christopher A. Faraone, *Talismans and Trojan Horses: Guardian Statues in Ancient Greek Myth and Ritual* (Oxford, UK: Oxford University Press, 1992).

36. Adria Haluszka, "Sacred Signified: The Semiotics of Statues in the *Greek Magical Papyri*," *Arethusa* 41, no. 3 (2008): 479–94.

37. Sarah Iles Johnston, "Animating Statues: A Case Study in Ritual," *Arethusa* 41, no. 3 (2008): 445–77.

38. I am only aware of one textual reference to interring objects inside a Daoist image. See Du Guangting 杜光庭 (850–933), *Daojiao lingyan ji* 道教靈驗記 (Evidential miracles in support of Daoism), included in *Yunji qiqian* 雲笈七籤 (Seven lots from the bookbag of the clouds), comp. Zhang Junfang 張君房 (fl. 1008–1029), *juan* 119. I would like to thank Professors Wang Yucheng and Susan Huang for sharing this reference with me.

39. See Michel Strickmann, "L'icône animée," in *Mantras et Mandarins, le bouddhisme tantrique en Chine* (Paris: Gallimard, 1996), 165–211; Daniel Boucher, "Sutra on the Merit of Bathing the Buddha," in *Buddhism in Practice*, ed. Donald S. Lopez, Jr. (Princeton, NJ: Princeton University Press, 1995) 59–68; reprinted in *An Anthology of Asian Religions in Practice*, ed. Donald S. Lopez, Jr. (Princeton, NJ: Princeton University Press, 2002), 206–15.

40. Richard Gombrich, "The Consecration of a Buddhist Image," *Journal of Asian Studies* 26, no. 1 (1966): 23–36.

41. Yael Bentor, "On the Indian Origins of the Tibetan Practice of Depositing Relics and Dhâraṇîs in Stûpas and Images," *Journal of the American Oriental Society* 115, no. 2 (Apr.–Jun. 1995): 248–61, esp. 255. Yael Bentor has written a series of very illuminating studies on the interment of objects in icons and stūpas. See, for instance, her *Consecration of Images and Stūpas in Indo-Tibetan Tantric Buddhism* (Leiden: E. J. Brill, 1996).

42. Gregory Henderson and Leon Hurvitz, "The Buddha of Seiryôji: New Finds and New Theory," *Artibus Asie* 19 (1956): 4–55.

43. Kurata Bunsaku 倉田文作, "Zōnai nōnyūhin 像内納入品" (Objects deposited inside of sculptures), in *Nihon no bijutsu* 日本の美術 (Art of Japan), vol. 86 (Tokyo: Shibundō, 1973). The literature on Japanese images with interred objects is immense and impossible to review here, but see (in addition to the references above to the work of Kurata Bunsaku) Helmut Brinker, "Facing the Unseen: On the Interior Adornment of Eizon's Iconic Body," *Archives of Asian Art* 50 (1997–98): 42–61; Roger Goepper, "A Early Work of Kōen in Cologne," *Asiatische Studien* 37, no. 2 (1983): 67–102; Paul Groner, "Icons and Relics in Eison's Religious Activities," in *Living Images: Japanese Buddhist Icons in Context*, eds. Robert H. Sharf and Elizabeth Horton Sharf (Stanford, CA: Stanford University Press, 2001), 114–51; Wu Pei-jung, "The Mañjuśrī Statues and Buddhist Practice of Saidaiji: A Study of Iconography, Interior Features of Statues, and Rituals Associated with Buddhist Icons" (PhD diss., UCLA, 2002). On the interment of objects inside of Korean images (*pokchangmul* 腹藏物), see Choi In Sun 崔仁善, "A Study of the Two Wooden Buddha Statues at Samgyeong Temple in Chunju and Those Contents That Were Found Inside of Buddha Statues" 全州三曝寺木造佛像2軀와? 腹藏物 in *Munhwa sahak* 文化史學 21 (2004): 855–73.

44. Robert B. Hawkins, "A Statue of Kuan-Yin: A Problem in Sung Sculpture," *Record of the Art Museum* (Princeton University) 12, no. 1 (1953): 2–36, see esp. 13–16.

45. On the standing Guanyin at the Metropolitan Museum of Art in New York, see Donald Jenkins, ed., *Masterworks in Wood: China and Japan* (Portland, OR: Portland Art Museum, 1977), 48–49.

46. The information discussed here derives from the following excavation report: Liu Haiwen 刘海文 ed., *Xuanhua xiabali 2 qu Liao bihua mu kaogu fajue baogao* 宣化下八里II辽壁画墓考古发掘报告 (Excavation report of the Liao Dynasty tomb with murals at the second area of the Xiabali village in Xuanhua District] (Beijing: Wenwu, 2008). I would like to thank Eugene Wang for informing me about this publication.

47. Jenkins, ed. *Masterworks in Wood: China and Japan*, 53.

48. Joseph Edkins, *Chinese Buddhism: A Volume of Sketches, Historical, Descriptive, and Critical* (London: Kegan and Paul, Trench, Trubner and Co., 1880), 251–52.

49. Hampden C. DuBose, *The Dragon, Image and Demon orr the Three Religions of China: Confucianism, Buddhism, and Taoism* (New York: A. C. Armstrong and Son, 1887), 257–59.

50. Jun Jing, *The Temple of Memories: History, Power, and Morality in a Chinese Village* (Stanford, CA: Stanford University Press, 1998), 152.

51. Wang Liang, "The Confucius Temple Tragedy of the Cultural Revolution," in *On Sacred Grounds: Culture, Society, Politics, and the Formation of the Cult of Confucius*, ed. Thomas A. Wilson (Cambridge: Harvard University Asia Center Publications, 2002), 376–98.

52. "An Idol's Soul," *The Church Missionary Gleaner* (May 1916): 68.

53. John Larson and Rose Kerr, "A Hero Restored: The Conservation of Guan Di," *Orientations* 22, no. 7 (1991): 28–34.

54. Moshe Halbertal and Avishai Margalit, *Idolatry* (Cambridge, MA: Harvard University Press, 1992).

55. Ibid., 37, 45.

56. Goody, *Representation and Contradictions*, 43.

57. The only systematic treatments of the history of Chinese iconoclasm that I am aware of are Deborah A. Sommer, "Images into Words: Ming Confucian Iconoclasm," *National Palace Museum Bulletin* XXIX, nos. 1 & 2 (1994): 1–24; and Fabio Rambelli and Eric Reinders, "What Does Iconoclasm Create? What Does Preservation Destroy? Reflections on Iconoclasm in East Asia," in *Iconoclasm: Contested Objects, Contested Terms*, eds. Stacy Boldrick and Richard Clay (Surrey, UK: Ashgate, 2007), 15–33.

58. This story is recounted in the *Song gaoseng zhuan* 宋高僧傳 (*Song biographies of eminent monks*). Completed by Zanning 贊寧. T.50.773b.

59. See Barasch, *Icon*, 19–20.

60. See Barasch, *Icon*,15.

61. On this notion see Goux, *Symbolic Economies*, 134–50.

62. Alfred Gell, "The Technology of Enchantment and the Enchantment of Technology," in *Anthropology Art and Aesthetics*, eds. Jeremy Coote and Anthony Shelton (Oxford, UK: Clarendon Press, 1992), 41. For a different critique of Western aesthetics and the distinction between "high" and "low" art, see David Morgan, *Visual Piety: A History and Theory of Popular Religious Images* (Berkeley: University of California Press, 1998).

63. Georges Didi-Huberman, *Confronting Images: Questioning the Ends of a Certain History of Art* (University Park: Pennsylvania State University Press, 2005), 3–4.

64. See Bernard Faure, "The Buddhist Icon and the Modern Gaze," *Critical Inquiry* 24, no. 3 (1998): 768–813; Stanley K. Abe, "Inside the Wonder House: Buddhist Art and the West," in *Curators of the Buddha: The Study of Buddhism Under Colonialism*, ed. Donald S. Lopez, Jr. (Chicago: University of Chicago Press, 1995).

65. Ernest F. Fenollosa, *Epochs of Chinese and Japanese Art: An Outline History of East Asiatic Design*. 2 vols. (New York, 1913), 1:xxiv.

66. Halbertal and Margalit, *Idolatry*, 3.

67. Gell, "The Technology of Enchantment and the Enchantment of Technology," 42.

68. Alfred Gell, *Art and Agency: An Anthropological Theory* (Oxford, UK: Clarendon Press 1998), 3.

9

The Vernacular Story and the Hiddenness of Value

SOPHIE VOLPP

The Chinese vernacular story is probably the genre one would least associate with the term "hiddenness." Notoriously garrulous, unabashedly interested in the prosaic, *huaben* 話本 almost seem to tell too much. Terms such as *yin* 陰, *mi* 密, and *nei* 内 are more likely to refer to the physical location of objects in the vernacular short story than to be thought of as an apt description of its aesthetics. Indeed, we rarely link the words "vernacular" and "aesthetic," and this is perhaps in part because we believe that vernacular fiction lays itself bare, that it contains few of the hidden recesses or productive ellipses of the classical tale. Yet even as the loquaciousness of the vernacular seems to suggest an aesthetic of "what you see is what you get," many of these stories find ways to let us know that what you see is not what you get, that perception in fact falls short of full knowing or possession.

The hidden aesthetic question in the vernacular tale, then, is the relation between exposition and enigma. The concern of these stories with the limits of semantic intelligibility becomes particularly clear if we consider the question of hiddenness with regard to the materiality of the objects featured in these tales. In Feng Menglong's 馮夢龍 (1574–1645) most famous tale, "Du Shiniang Sinks the Jewel Box in Anger" (Du Shiniang nu chen baibaoxiang 杜十娘怒沉百宝箱), a plethora of terms describe the protagonist's jewel box (*xiangzi* 箱子, chest; *xiaer* 匣兒, box; *zhuangtai* 妝台, dressing case; and *miaojin wenju* 描金文具, casket speckled with gold).[1] The very abundance of these terms both conceals the difficulty of describing the mysterious box and suggests that the materiality of the box eludes semantic intelligibility. It is precisely because of this failure of semantic possession that the box seems a locus of hidden value with endless and unknowable depths, depths that are only partially manifested when the heroine Du Shiniang reveals that the recesses of the box contain emeralds, pearls, and other precious jewels.

Ling Mengchu's 凌濛初 (1580–1644) story, "A Man, Whose Fortune Has Turned Coincidentally, Happens Across Oranges from Dongting" (Zhuanyun han qiaoyu dongting hong 轉運漢巧遇洞庭紅), which opens his first collection of vernacular tales, similarly features a locus of hidden value, a seemingly useless tortoise shell that conceals several dozen fabled pearls. As Patrick Hanan has observed, the tale incarnates a perennial theme of Ling Mengchu's: fate controls the workings of fortune.[2] The tale features a young educated man who tries his hand at business, attempting to sell fans on which he has inscribed plagiarized calligraphy and paintings, but is punished by fate for his overly strategic thinking. It is only when he no longer attempts to think strategically that he gains wealth beyond conception. The tale features a long sea voyage to foreign lands, and the exposure to other cultures furnishes a premise for thinking about contrasting systems of valuation. The story's concern with the hiddenness of value allows us to reconsider the relation between materiality and semantic intelligibility in the vernacular story, and to think about the relevance of such concerns for the vernacular tale's interest in the question of literary verisimilitude.

Critics who discuss this tale often omit mention of the prologue story, but it is worth beginning with the prologue, for it addresses the question of hidden value in terms so concrete as to be almost cartoonish. Set in the Song, the prologue seemingly presents the thinking of an older, simpler time with regard to the relation between materiality and value. It tells us that capital literally has a life of its own—that it cannot be controlled by human actions and decisions. These are conclusions that Wen, the protagonist of the main tale, will reach in the course of his adventures in overseas trade, conclusions that will be mocked by his friends until they see the rewards such thinking brings. In the prologue tale, silver is fetishized as a sensuous object as well as a currency. Silver literally has the capacity to hide itself, so that it has a mercurial presence; it is animate and controls its own fate.

The prologue tale features a miser whose name, Jin Weihou 金維厚, puns quite transparently if not univocally; his name sounds as though it means "one who values gold," or "one who amasses gold." Jin is a professional middleman (*jing ji hang zhong ren* 經紀行中人), a precursor to the Persian middleman we will encounter in the main tale. He conceives of a strategy for long-term stability for his family: he reserves the bits of silver of good quality that come his way and melts them into large ingots, tying their waists with red thread. The ingots are kept by his pillow, where he fondles and plays with them before falling asleep each night. By his seventieth birthday he has accumulated eight ingots, tied in four pairs of two. He tell his sons he intends to present them with these ingots, which, he states proudly, have never been used, but simply kept by his pillow, never once used nor even touched (*yong bu dong yong de* 用不動用的).

That night Jin goes to bed a bit tipsy, and in his drunkenness gazes at the ingots gleaming by his pillow, caressing them as he chuckles to himself. He is half-asleep when he hears the sound of footsteps by his bed. When he lifts the bed curtain, he sees eight stalwart men (大漢) by his bedside wearing white robes, their waists tied with red sashes. The transformed former ingots bow and advance, telling him that they were given human shape thanks to his excessive love. Now, however, their allotted time with him has reached its end; they have no karmic affinity with his sons. They will "seek refuge with a man surnamed Wang in a certain village of a certain province" 往某縣某村王姓某招投托, and promise that if their karmic affinity with him is not exhausted, they will meet again.[3]

Jin wakes to find that this was all a dream—and yet the ingots are gone. Tremendously distressed, he travels to the home of the man they identified, where indeed he finds the ingots. Although he bemoans his loss, he states that he has no resentment because it is clear that this is the working of fate. He asks "only to look at the ingots one more time, to end this old man's affair of the heart" 但只求取出一看，也完了老漢心事.[4]

As a professional middleman, the aptly surnamed Jin (gold) inhabits a world in which objects are abstracted and fungible. Yet the ingots have an auratic particularity that is evident in their personification. Jin's relation to his eight ingots is clearly eroticized, even homoerotic; as the ingots themselves tell him, his loving caresses have given them human form.[5] Oddly, given that their defining characteristic as material objects is uniformity, they seem the sort of object that should least elicit this qualitative fascination. The materiality of the ingots should be subsumed into abstraction, but there is a residue that resists.

The ingots, then, encapsulate a contradiction that is almost a joke. They bodily incarnate a form of capital whose standardization has been hard won (as Jin's efforts to save the best bits of silver he receives in the context of his everyday commercial exchanges suggest).[6] Yet as they take human form and speak of their own fates, they seem to recall a potentially animate world of things reminiscent of precapitalist exchange.[7] Here capital, the *ur* incarnation of the commodity fetish, has become a fetish in the eighteenth-century European sense of the word: the ingots are material objects personified by the superstitious mind.[8] The story of the ingots graphically illustrates how an earlier notion of fetishism might adhere within commodity fetishism and even enable it.

The ingots, as the anthropomorphized incarnation of value, have the ability to hide themselves. It is this capacity that gives them a value beyond their evident exchange value. It is not that value is obscured only to be detected by the discerning observer, but rather that value incarnate has a mercurial presence—it appears and disappears of its own volition. Otherwise put, it is because the ingots can make themselves disappear that they control the possessor's relation to them, and this is what grants them animacy.

Prior to Jin's caresses, the ingots had the characteristic properties of the commodity fetish: their material specificity was of little interest, their fungibility their relevant feature. As the ultimate object of transaction, the silver was presumed to have no agency. The anthropomorphized ingots have desire and purpose, know themselves to have their own fates (*ming* 命), and are absolutely clear that humans do not control the conditions of their exchange. They literally disappear when Jin attempts to pass them on; they were his only if he did not use them. By controlling the conditions under which their valuation becomes possible, they ensure that they will not be reduced to their exchange value. In other words, by refusing to enter circulation on any terms but their own, they refuse to be reduced to an abstraction, to be dulled or diminished by becoming capital.

Set during the Song, the prologue story initially appears to propose an older way of thinking about capital. But the productive contradiction in which elusiveness gives capital a value beyond its exchange value suggests that this notion has achieved significance and gained currency in part because of the symbolic pressures exerted by money and the mercantile during the seventeenth century.[9] Rather than describing a vanished mode of thought, the prologue story proposes a way of thinking about things that adheres even within the relentless world of commodity exchange.[10] The prologue story, then, seems to be a parable in which the conceptualization of the ingots in terms of their exchange value is trumped by an insistence that they have something ineffable in excess of exchange value that controls valuation itself.

We might recall here the Americanist Bill Brown's efforts to delineate a way of thinking about materiality that acknowledges its elusiveness. Drawing on Heidegger's generative essay "The Thing," he describes the "thing" as a material entity that escapes semantic intelligibility:

> *[T]hing* is a word that tends . . . to index a certain limit or liminality, to hover over the threshold between the nameable and unnameable,

> the figurable and unfigurable. . . . You could imagine things . . . as what is excessive in objects, as what exceeds their mere materialization as objects or their mere utilization as objects—their force as a sensuous presence or a metaphysical presence, the magic by which objects become values, fetishes, idols and totems . . . thingness amounts to a latency (the not yet formed or the not yet formable) and to an excess (what remains physically or metaphysically irreducible to objects).[11]

The hidden recesses of the "thing" create an indefinable excess, which can be felt and intuited but not known and therefore not possessed. This excess marks the distance between "object" and "thing," and this distance gives the thing an almost hydraulic power.

What we might note, however, is that "thing theory" has concerned itself with the definition of the "thing," leaving the term "object" presumably transparent and relatively uninterrogated. The ostensibly intelligible object, intelligible precisely because it is subsumed in a subject-object dynamic that presumes the openness of the object to interpretation, thus has a synecdochal relation to the unintelligible thing. The assumed transparency of the object comes to serve as a baseline that is actually a false bottom, a necessary fiction that permits the romanticization of the more elusive "thing."

Brown's distinction between "object" and "thing" provides an entry into considering the configuration of the question of hiddenness of value in both the prologue and the main tale. At the same time, Ling Mengchu's story illuminates certain aspects of Brown's pairing of object and thing. The main tale draws the readers' attention to a venerable dyad, "shi" 實 (concrete, actual, factual) and "xu" 虛 (insubstantial, empty, imagined). It uses this traditional pairing of a seemingly transparent term with one that is romantically elusive to explore the complex relation between materiality, semantic intelligibility, and the hiddenness of value. The structural relationship between the two terms, which is characteristic of similar foundational pairings in the early Daoist thought of Laozi and Zhuangzi, is such that each term not only produces the other but can be found within the other.[12] They complement and complete each other; together, they constitute a totality.

❧

The nature of such terms as *xu* and *shi* is such that they seem to resist encapsulation; *xu* in particular is a term that almost exaggerates its own capaciousness. *Xu*, because it connotes insubstantiality and emptiness, embodies the principle of constant mutation, and so seems to embody a wider range of meanings than *shi*.[13] It is precisely because the significance of *shi* seems readily available that *xu* gains importance as an indefinable quality. However, although the significance of *shi* seems transparent, it is likewise capacious; it is perhaps only because it signals solidity, actuality, and concreteness that it appears more readily grasped. As is the case with other dyads in traditional Chinese thought, in particular the pairing of *you* 有 (being) and *wu* 無 (nothingness), *xu* and *shi* are thought to be generated from each other, so that *shi* takes form in the extremes of *xu*. In the words of Ye Xie 葉燮 (1627–1703), as *xu* and *shi* mutually take shape, presence and absence are mutually established (*xu shi xiang cheng, you wu hu li* 虛實相成, 有無互立).[14]

It may seem an odd gesture to employ structures of thought fundamental to Daoist philosophy, and in particular, the opposition between emptiness and actuality, to discuss the weaknesses in Brown's conceptualization of the distinction between object and thing. The desirability of introducing Daoist philosophy at this point may become clearer, however, when we consider that Brown's conception of the opacity of "thingness" is very much derived from Heidegger's essay on "The Thing," which in turn was indebted to Heidegger's interest in the philosophy of the *Laozi* and *Zhuangzi*. The influence of the *Laozi* and *Zhuangzi* on Heidegger has been acknowledged since shortly after Heidegger's death in 1976, when it was revealed that Heidegger had asked the Chinese scholar Paul Shih-yi Hsiao to work with him on a translation of the *Laozi* in 1946 that was later abandoned.[15] Heidegger's emblematic example of a thing, the jug that is defined by a void in its center, seems in particular to be indebted to early Daoist thought.[16]

Thus to think of "the thing" in terms of the opposition of *shi* and *xu* is to recover a deep background that has been lost as Heidegger's essay has been transformed into contemporary thing theory. Restoring that background sheds light on the weakness of contemporary conceptualizations of the relation between object and thing. Rather than opposing thing and object, we might see the opacity of the thing as already seeded in the object. The object inevitably yields to thingness and vice versa.[17] Thus the two terms should not be conceived of as entirely oppositional; rather they are a complementary bipolarity. Neither is conceptually self-sufficient; the shadow of the thing is integral to our conception of the object, and vice versa.[18]

The terms *shi* and *xu* have significances in literary criticism that will allow us to link such concerns regarding the elusive intelligibility of the thing to conceptions of fictional verisimilitude. In Chinese poetics, *shi* designates couplets that describe a scene that is something actual and concrete; this usage in fact predates the usage in fiction. *Xu*, by contrast, is used to describe the space of subjective coloring with feeling or opinion; *xu* couplets express emotion and longing directly. In critical writings on Chinese fiction, the terms *xu* and *shi* have quite specific meanings. The terms may speak to the degree to which the narrative is based on historical events: *shi* refers to the historical events that undergird the story, whereas *xu* refers to the imaginative component.[19] They also may refer to the directness of presentation; elements that are directly presented are described as *shi*, whereas elements that are indirectly presented are characterized as *xu*.[20] The notion that fiction and drama ideally are formed from an admixture of *xu* and *shi* was developed around the time of Ling Mengchu's writing. Jin Shengtan 金聖嘆 (?1610–1661), in his commentary on the *Water Margin* (*Shuihu zhuan* 水滸傳), used as praise the phrase "*shi* within xu, and *xu within shi*" (*xu zhong you shi, shi zhong you xu* 虛中有實, 實中有虛), which later became a commonplace.[21] The notion that each quality should contain and become the other became an ideal, as encapsulated by the phrase "render the *xu* more *shi*, and the *shi* more *xu*" (*xuzhe shi zhi, shi zhe xu zhi* 虛者實之, 實者虛之).[22]

❧

Ling Mengchu's story employs the range of meaning we have discussed in the terms *xu* and *shi* to make the assertion that the opacity of the thing forms a kind of false bottom. The story then links this concern to the notion that a certain sleight-of-hand underwrites the notion of fictional verisimilitude. The main story, set in the Chenghua reign period (1465–1487) several hundred years after the prologue, furthers the concern incipient in the prologue regarding the intelligibility of things in a mercantile culture that is more comfortable with commodities, whose exchange value is perceived as readily apparent. As the pairing of the protagonist's given name (Wen Shi 文實 "Literary culture actualized") and literary name (*zi* Ruoxu 若虛 "[but] as though insubstantial") might suggest, he is a failed literatus who has tried his luck as a resident tutor to gentry families only to be disdained for his shallow learning. But rather than merely making much of the way in which Wen's literary learning is actually not substantive, the text uses the play on words inherent in his paired given and literary names to introduce the notion that *wen* (writing or marking) that seems *shi* 實 (substantive, concrete, factual) may become *xu* 虛 (unsubstantive, indeterminate, imagined) in the context of commercial exchange. The story plays with various perspectives regarding the combination of *xu* and *shi*; it's not just that the unsubstantial seems substantive (*xu ruo shi* 虛若實) but that the substantive seems unsubstantial (*shi ruo xu* 實若虛), so that which is unsubstantial but seemingly substantive (*xu ruo shi* 虛若實) comes to seem substantive but seemingly unsubstantial (*shi ruo xu* 實若虛). These two processes are linked in such a way as to create an elaborate con game in which values seem evident, but then become problematized. The tale uses the playful juxtaposition of *shi* and *xu* in Wen's given and literary names to show us how the substantive and insubstantial not only contain each other but are seeded in each other, as we see in an episode in which Wen attempts to make money by counterfeiting the work of famed painters and calligraphers. An incorrigible failure in business, Wen hears that fans from his native Suzhou sell well in Beijing. He hits on the idea of having well-known artists inscribe calligraphy on some fans of high quality. A few strokes of the brush from celebrities such as Wen Zhenheng and Shen Zhou instantly make his fans several times more valuable. Wen then takes fans of middling value and plagiarizes the calligraphy. However, both the originals and the counterfeits are ruined by the unusual humidity of Beijing that year, and Wen finds that "all those that had calligraphy or painting, the ones that were worth money, were completely useless."[23] By a strange coincidence, the only fans that are not ruined by the humidity are the ones that were originally so cheaply made that he left them blank (*xu* 虛). He sells these blank fans, but is only able to pay his return trip home with the proceeds. He has made no profit and lost his capital to boot.

That the blank fans survive and bring Wen enough money to make the journey home enables the text to engage in a bit of sleight-of-hand. The addition of patterning or marking (*wen*) to the fans focuses our attention on the valuation of calligraphy (*wen*), allowing the valuation of the blank fans to remain relatively uninterrogated. Thus, we witness an apparent reversal of value whereby the uninscribed fans serve as a term that is presumed to be transparent in contrast to the excitingly unpredictable valuation of the inscribed fans. The unembellished fans furnish a kind of false bottom, in a dynamic reminiscent of the tension in Bill Brown's dichotomy between the unintelligible thing and the presumably intelligible object.

This dynamic will become more marked in the next episode, in which Wen embarks as a lark on an overseas voyage with a group of friends who are merchants. He is entirely cured after years of business failures of the notion that he might make a profit. He has no capital, just a bit of silver that his friend Zhang Shihuo has lent him to buy some fruit for the voyage. Directly before he boards ship, he sees some oranges from Lake Dongting for sale, and hits on the idea of buying some of this fruit, famous for its fragrance, to treat his companions on board. When he brings the oranges on board the ship, however, his shipmates exclaim sarcastically, "Mr. Wen's precious merchandise has arrived."[24] He hangs his head in shame and leaves the oranges buried in their baskets until the boat arrives at its destination. When the ship docks at a foreign country named Jiling (*Jiling guo* 吉靈國), his shipmates depart to sell their wares, and Wen is left alone on board.[25] He takes out the oranges to check for mold, and a crowd of natives assembles, attracted by the brilliance of the fruit, which they have never before seen. A man in the crowd ventures to ask the price. Wen cannot understand the language of this country, but a sailor raises one finger as a joke: "This much." Wen has no idea how much the coins he receives are worth, nor has he any way of weighing the oranges. He has no way of estimating or calculating during these transactions at all. He simply accepts the cheapest coinage of the country, which is silver marked with pictures of seaweed, one coin per orange.

As he begins to run out of oranges, Wen raises the price, pretending that he'd rather keep the remainder for himself. A customer claims that he will buy all the remaining oranges to present in tribute to the Khan, and offers him a different sort of coinage, silver marked with trees. Wen refuses, saying he wants only the kind he'd received before. The stranger then offers a coin with dragon and phoenix markings. When Wen refuses again, the stranger laughs sardonically, saying that these coins are worth many times the coins with depictions of seaweed. Wen sticks to his guns: for each orange, he wants three of the coins embossed with seaweed.

When the transaction is finished, he weighs the silver. He has gained many times more silver by accepting the least valuable coins. Since the markings on the coin are meaningless to the Chinese, he is trading as though there were no such thing as specie value, accepting only the substance value of the silver.[26] It is not that he does not strategize or bargain at all—he raises the price when the oranges become more scarce—but that he refuses to treat silver as currency. It is as though his failed attempt to create capital in the episode of the fans had shocked him from the mercantile age back to an earlier age perhaps reminiscent of that of the prologue.

The markings on the coins, which distinguish specie value from substance value, are as if insubstantial (*ruo xu* 若虛) to Wen, and this has the effect of making the substance value of silver appear to be truly substantive. Like the blank fans, the silver furnishes a sort of false bottom. It seems to have a concrete, actual value. But that the valuation of silver is culturally specific becomes clear as we are told that the people of Jiling in fact do not pay for cloth with silver, but only with other goods. Even the value of silver, then, is a cultural fiction; it too is *ruo xu*. In this regard, the text seems now to suggest that the opposition of systems of signification and materiality is a false dichotomy.

As Patrick Hanan has observed, it is Ling Mengchu's stock advice that it is useless to try to control one's destiny.[27] In this story, that concern takes shape precisely because *wen* that seems *shi* becomes *ruoxu* once it enters a new geographical context. In the episode of the fans, Wen's efforts to engage in a con come to naught because all the fans that had *wen*—calligraphy—on them were destroyed by mold in the unexpected humidity of Beijing. In the episode of the oranges, Wen soon realizes that he might bargain all he likes, but because he does not know the significance of the markings on the coins of Jiling, it is pointless. It is the relativity of value that makes strategizing unprofitable; there is no way to appreciate the degree to which value is relative because the units of valuation are inaccessible. Thus an encounter with another culture renders the claim of specie value to be substantive (*shi*) as though insubstantial *(ruo xu)*.

The story's interest in exploring the significance of ethnographic encounter to the relation between materiality and the hiddenness of value reaches an apogee in the final episode of the story, in which Wen Ruoxu finds an enormous shell on a deserted island and drags it on board ship to keep as a souvenir. Unbeknown to him and the other Chinese merchants, hidden in its recesses are twenty-four rare pearls with a marvelous capacity to emit light. Once the ship docks in Fujian, a Persian merchant comes on board to evaluate the merchandise of Wen's companions, and happens to see the shell. He purchases it from Wen for 50,000 taels, a windfall that means a lifetime of ease for Wen, but a trivial amount for the Persian given that each pearl is worth 50,000 taels in his home country. Wen is ultimately rewarded with an incalculable windfall for his affection for this object with no obvious use, in what is clearly a reproach to mercantile values. As in the episode of the oranges, Wen is mocked by the other merchants for bringing such laughable merchandise on board, but is then rewarded for his lack of calculation as he encounters the alternative system of valuation or proprietary knowledge of another culture.[28]

Wen seems to happen on the shell as a prize for truly understanding that things have their own destinies, that humans do not control their trajectories. Sitting alone on the highest point of a desert island, mournfully meditating on his fate, it occurs to him that "even though I am fortunate to have over a thousand silver coins in my purse, how do I know if it is in their fates to be mine or not?"[29] Wen's thoughts recall the sentiments of the prologue. The episode of the fans has taught him what the miser Jin did not realize: capital has a predestined fate (*ming* 命) of its own. Just as Wen is lamenting that he has no control over his fate or that of the silver, he spies the empty shell—his prize for realizing that life is not a game of skill but of chance.

The shell seems to have neither use value nor exchange value, and this seems central to Wen's affection for it. Wen's liking for the shell reactivates his shipmates' jibes about his inability to evaluate merchandise. As he drags it on board, he jokes, "I want to inform you all that this is my merchandise from abroad!" His companions retort, "You did not want a single piece of good merchandise; why would you want this?" The crowd of merchants laughingly speculate on the possible uses of the shell—in divination, or making elixirs—but Wen simply enjoys it because it is a rarity—"it doesn't matter whether it's useful or not; it's just that it's rare."[30] Wen then washes the shell out and makes it into a suitcase, keeping his valuables in it. His shipmates joke, "What a great strategy (*suanji* 算計). Mr. Wen is quite clever after all." The narrative ironizes the impoverishment of mercantile valuation, revealing the narrowness of understanding that bankrupts the mercantile mentality.

If we were to return to the distinction that Brown makes between object and thing, the dragon shell clearly appeals to Wen because of its "thing-like" qualities. The island on which the shell is found looks as though it has never been inhabited, and this ensures that the shell has no cultural context, making it possible for the shell's significance to be completely opaque. The island is explicitly described as a space that is not "solid ground" (*shidi* 實地). By implication, it is a vacuous space of potential (*xu* 虛). Although on the high seas, the dragon shell's significance is stubbornly enigmatic, once Wen's ship docks in Fujian, the dragon shell enters an economy in which the trade in rarities stretches all the way to the Middle East, and within the context of this global trade, the shell's significance is easily legible. To the Persian, the dragon shell has a manifest rather than a latent meaning. If, for Wen, the shell had the sensuous, numinous presence of the "thing," once it is absorbed into global exchange, it is so easily read as to be transparent. Indeed, when the pearls are extracted from it, the shell is discarded as mere casing.

In quick succession the shell is described as a thing (using both the vernacular *dongxi* 東西 and the more classical *wu* 物), as precious merchandise (*baohuo* 寶货), and as a precious instrument (*baoju* 寶具). With each shift, the shell's preciousness is more precisely indicated, but—as in the case of Du Shiniang's box—the multiplicity of terms that describe the shell do not aid our ability to visualize it.[31] Like Du Shiniang's box (and Du Shiniang herself), the shell is an enigma that conceals endless riches within its depths.

The Persian initially believes that the Chinese traders have deliberately concealed the shell from him. In fact it was not hidden; it simply wasn't deemed worthy of note. Its value emerges only in the context that the Persian provides for it, that is, as a container for the pearls.

In describing the Persian, the narrator assumes an ethnographic tone, relating that (seemingly unlike the Chinese) the Persian "cares only for profit" (*yi li wei zhong* 以利爲重), and has everyone sit at the banquet table according to the value of their goods, ignoring both age and social status.[32] As a professional middleman, he incarnates a purely mercantile sensibility, and in that sense seems uninfluenced by the potential animacy of things—he is interested in acquiring them only to exchange them. In this, he is the opposite of the poor Jin Weihou, the middleman of an earlier time who fell in love with his ingots and lost them when he believed he could control their fates. The Persian's quickness to cast the shell aside stands in stark contrast to Wen's affection for it; for Wen, the dragon shell has no exchange value, but rather has a singularity that allows him to have a specific but unspecifiable relation to it.

Ultimately, the tale relates this episode of the dragon shell to the question of the relationship between the literary and the factual. If we were to return to the significance of *xu* and *shi* in seventeenth-century fictional and dramatic criticism, the world of historical event, which presumably exists beyond the text and inspires the text, is the *shi* to the *xu* of the literary. As we have seen in this tale of false bottoms, however, the actuality of that which is considered substantive often proves to be a cultural fiction. How would one extend that insight to the tale's treatment of the question of literary verisimilitude? The latter part of the tale examines this question, ultimately suggesting that the fictional text is not so much an approximation of the "real" as that the "real" is a fiction created by the literary text.

The signing of the contract regarding the transfer of the dragon shell offers a momentary crack in the text's relation to verisimilitude that allows us to pursue this question further. The contract is copied into the text with an exactitude that is customary to the genre:

> Zhang Da pointed to one of the men who had come with them and said, "This traveler, Zhu Zhongying, has good calligraphy," and ceded paper and brush to him. Zhu ground the ink till it was thick. He folded the paper, raised his brush and wrote: "A contract established by Zhang Chengyun and his friends:
>
> "At present there is a traveler from Suzhou named Wen Shi, who has brought a large dragon drum shell from abroad; he presents it to the store of the Persian Ma Baoha, who is willing to offer 50,000 taels of silver; once the agreement is completed, one party will pass over the goods, the other the silver, and neither go back on the contract. If either party does so, the penalty will be the amount plus 10 percent. The contract is the proof."

Two copies were made, and at the end of the paper the year, month, and date were inscribed, and beneath this Zhang Chengyun signed his name, as well as the names of the ten from their group who had accompanied them. Zhu Zhongying took the brush himself, and wrote his name last. Before the year and month, where there was a blank line, they placed the two contracts side by side, and wrote the words "contractual agreement" with the names of seller Wen Shi and buyer Ma Baoha across the flap.[33]

With the replication of the contract, the texture of the text feels different. The reader no longer has the sense of an approximation; the aesthetic has shifted from "*ruo xu*" to "*shi*." The use of Wen's given name, Wen Shi, in the contract is striking in that, up to this point, he has been identified primarily as Ruoxu. It reminds us that the written language (*wen*) of the contract presumes itself to be *shi*—historically factual—and must make explicit that it is not indeed *ruo xu* (as if insubstantial).

Silver here is the standard that backs language, that renders language *shi*. It becomes clear that the language of the contract is not in itself *shi* when the Persian brings out silver to seal the deal. "Now that they saw the dazzling white silver coming to serve as a deposit, they knew for the first time that it [the deal] was for real (*fang zhi shi shi* 方知是實)." We recall the dichotomy between substance value and specie value in the coins of Jiling, and remember that in fact the inscription of specie value made substance value seem substantive. In this instance, the language of the contract serves a function similar to the inscription of specie value; it allows silver to *act* as a standard.

There is a fissure in the texture of the text after the replication of the words of the contract; for a brief moment, as the contract was being written, the words of the literary text had followed Zhu Zhongying's brush. With the next words, "Two copies were made," there is a rupture; suddenly the words in the world beyond the text have multiplied beyond the words on the page, so that another contract has been generated in the space of four words. In this instant, we become aware of the impossible demand on the text to provide a sense of verisimilitude. The "false bottom" of the fictional—the equivalent of the *shi* of the blank fans or the substance value of silver—is the presumption that it describes a world that exists beyond the boundaries of the fictional text in a fuller, more realized state. But as I will suggest below, the tale suggests that the "real" world exists within rather than beyond the tale, hidden in its recesses like the pearls of the dragon drum shell. It suggests that the substantive quality of the real is a fiction created by the literary.

As we have seen, the presumed transparency and assumed accessibility of that which is considered *shi* renders that which is *xu* mysterious and evocative, as our attention is arrested by the hidden recesses of the dense and elliptical. The use of the character "*mou*" 某 ("a certain") in the prologue provided an instance in which the literary text created a sense of a mysterious "real" that exists within its own confines and is inaccessible to the reader.[34] We recall that in the prologue, the ingots told the miser Jin that they were moving to "seek refuge with a man surnamed Wang in a certain village of a certain province"

(往某縣某村王姓某招投托). The address was disclosed to Jin (the proof being that he tracked them down), but not to the reader. The address is in fact stated in the classical tale on which Ling Mengchu based the vernacular prologue; Ling Mengchu removed this detail in his retelling.

This use of the character *mou* 某 is a naturalized convention in the vernacular, but becomes interesting in the context of our concern regarding the limits of verisimilitude. When a date ought to appear on a bill of divorce or on a contract, the convention is to insert the character *mou* 某, so that the text reads "a certain year, a certain month, a certain date" (*mou nian mou yue mou ri* 某年某月某日). It is as though the narrative telegraphs the fact that its verisimilitude is an approximation.

There is a limit to what the readers of the narrative, rather than the characters, can be told, so that the true "real" remains inside the story, in the world of the characters, and the approximation is left on the page for the reader. Jin knows the address to which the ingots remove themselves; the reader does not. At these moments, the literary text is telling us that it is not a failed or studied approximation of the "real." Rather, the literary creates the "real" by a sleight of hand in which it suggests that the action has moved beyond the field of vision afforded by the literary. The text creates the sense that perception falls short of possession, that there is a reality interior to the text that can only be partially apprehended. This, in part, is how the vernacular story mimics a lived experience of the real—in this inscription of a falling-short.

It is axiomatic that vernacular fiction has a different relation to verisimilitude than does the classical tale, that it is less evocative and more explicit. The garrulousness of vernacular fiction often is spoken of almost as though it were a quality or function of the vernacular language. Ling Mengchu's tale shows us that the aesthetic of the vernacular story is in fact predicated on a hidden tension between loquaciousness and semantic unintelligibility. Repeatedly, this story opposes writing or design (*wen*) that has become "as if empty" (*ruoxu*)—plagiarized calligraphy, embossed images on coins, the language of a contract—to the apparently substantive (*shi*)—a blank fan, the silver in coins, the silver that backs a contract. Yet as we have seen, this was just a bit of sleight-of-hand that allowed *shi* to seem substantive. This, ultimately, may be the story's comment on the relation of the literary and the "real," that it is through a similar sleight of hand that the literary makes the "real" seem real. It is not that the literary is deficient in not being able to entirely encapsulate the real; it's that the substantive quality of the real is a fiction created by the literary itself.

In closing, I would like to suggest that there is a similar fiction of substance that is created in the conventional gesture that we make as we juxtapose premodern Chinese literature and contemporary theoretical texts, as we did in taking Bill Brown's conceptualization of the "thing" as a point of departure in a reading of Ling Mengchu's story. Part of the presumed necessity of the almost ritual gesture with which, after considering a literary text in light of a theoretical text, we turn and invert the presumed relations between theoretical and literary text, asking how the literary text exceeds the theoretical text and thus comments on its limitations, is that this is the critic's way of making the literary text appear to have a fate of its own. The literary text is enlivened, becoming the site of unintelligible excess. Suggesting that the literary exceeds the theoretical becomes a way of granting the literary a sensuous animacy. Ultimately, however, this gesture is nothing more than an act of fetishism—in the eighteenth-century sense of the word.

Notes

1. Feng Menglong, "Du Shiniang Sinks the Jewel Box in Anger" (Du Shinang nuchen baibao xiang), in Feng Menglong, *Jingshi tongyan* 警世通言, ed. Yan Dunyi 嚴敦易 (Beijing: Renmin wenxue chubanshe, 1995).

2. Patrick Hanan, *The Chinese Vernacular Story* (Cambridge, MA: Harvard University Press, 1981), 153.

3. Ling Mengchu, *Chuke pai'an jingqi* 初刻拍案驚奇, ed. Wang Gulu 王古魯 (Shanghai: Shanghai gudian wenxue chubanshe, 1957), 4.

4. Ling Mengchu, *Chuke pai'an jingqi*, 4.

5. The contrast between the prologue tale and its classical antecedent is particularly instructive. Jin Weihou's attachment to the ingots is far more eroticized than in the original. In the classical anecdote, the miser Jin's place is taken by a couple surnamed Chen, who have worked all their lives to save twenty-four ingots of silver. They wrap and seal the ingots multiple times, then sew them into their pillow. One night they both share the same dream, that twenty-four licentiates (*xiucai* 秀才) wearing white clothes bow to them from the foot of the bed, saying "We are leaving you to go to the Ju family of Sanpai lou." They wake with a start, find they have shared the same dream, open the pillow, and find the silver gone; when they locate the Ju family, Ju confirms that he did obtain twenty-four ingots. The prologue tale was collected in a collection of anecdotes roughly contemporary to Ling Mengchu's story. See Zhou Hui 周暉, *Jinling suoshi* 金陵瑣事, *juan* 3, "Yin zou" 銀, in Tan Zhengbi 譚正璧, *Sanyan liangpai ziliao* 三言兩拍資料 (Shanghai: Shanghai guji chubanshe, 1985), 573.

6. The weight of a tael of silver was different in various geographical regions, but this was known, and conversion rates were established. Moreover, all ingots were not of the same quality; the patterns of markings on the silver after it was cast indicated the purity. Thus Jin needs to save the best bits of silver to cast the taels.

7. We might also view the animated ingots as transitional objects in the psychologist D. W. Winnicott's sense of the word; in this case they would speak to Jin's

personification of the objects as a means of coping with the anxieties caused by a purely symbolic conception of capital. See D. W. Winnicott, *Playing and Reality* (London: Tavistock Publications, 1971), 1–25.

8. For more on eighteenth-century notions of the fetish, see William Pietz, "The Problem of the Fetish, IIIa, Bosman's Guinea and the Enlightenment Theory of Fetishism" in *RES: Anthropology and Aesthetics* 16 (Autumn, 1988): 105–24. This adhesion of an older notion of fetishism within commodity fetishism itself could be read into Marx's paradigmatic example of the commodity fetish, his talking table that "so soon as it steps forth as a commodity . . . is changed into something transcendent . . . in relation to all other commodities, it stands on its head, and evolves out of its wooden brain grotesque ideas, far more wonderful than 'table-turning' ever was." Karl Marx, "The Fetishism of the Commodity and Its Secret," in *Capital*, trans. Ben Fowkes (New York, 1976), 1: 163–77. Peter Stallybrass has observed that the paradoxical relation of the two conceptions of fetishism is one of Marx's least understood, or least recognized, jokes. Peter Stallybrass, "Marx's Coat," in *Border Fetishisms*, ed. Patricia Spyer (London: Routledge, 1998), 184. For relevant readings of this passage in Marx, see Bill Brown, *A Sense of Things: The Object Matter of American Literature* (Chicago: University of Chicago Press, 2003), 29; Barbara Johnson, *Persons and Things* (Cambridge, MA: Harvard University Press, 2008), 141.

9. Richard von Glahn has written that at no point in Chinese history did money have a greater symbolic import than in the late Ming. See his "The Enchantment of Wealth: The God Wutong in the Social History of Jiangnan," *Harvard Journal of Asiatic Studies* 51, no. 2 (Dec. 1991): 651–714.

10. Eileen Freedgood makes a related point as she emphasizes that the mid-Victorian period is one in which "thing culture" does not give way to commodity culture "but persists within it, however vestigially or invisibly." Elaine Freedgood, *The Ideas in Things: Fugitive Meaning in the Victorian Novel* (Chicago: University of Chicago Press, 2006), 142.

11. Bill Brown, "Thing Theory," in *Things*, ed. Bill Brown (Chicago: University of Chicago Press, 2004), 5. Brown draws on Heidegger, Lacan, and Ponge for his conceptualization of "the thing" in this essay; see also Martin Heidegger, *Poetry, Language, Thought*, trans. Albert Hofstadter (New York: Harper and Row, 1971); Jacques Lacan, *The Seminar of Jacques Lacan*, Book VII: *The Ethics of Psychoanalysis, 1959–1960*, ed. Jacques-Alain Miller, trans. Dennis Porter (New York: Norton, 1992), 119; Francis Ponge, *Things: Selected Writings*, trans. Cid Corman (New York: White Pine Press, 1986).

12. See for example, the second chapter of the *Laozi* 老子: "Being and non-being produce each other; difficult and easy complete each other; long and short contrast each other; high and low distinguish each other; sound and voice harmonize with each other; front and back follow each other" 有無相生、難易相成、長短相形、高下相傾、音聲相和、前後相隨. In *Laozi jiaoshi* 老子校釋, ed. Zhu Qianzhi 朱謙之 (Beijing: Zhonghua shuju), 9–10. Trans. and comp. Wing-tsit Chan, "The Natural Way of Lao tzu," in *A Sourcebook in Chinese Philosophy* (Princeton, NJ: Princeton University Press, 1963), 140.

13. A word is considered *xu* if its meaning cannot be fully defined or pinned down (the term *qing* 情 is an excellent case in point), and for this reason words that have an emotive, subjective context are considered *xu*. As a linguistic term, "*xu* characters" (*xuzi* 虛字) are those that impart modality or indicate sentiment. See Stephen Owen, *Readings in Chinese Literary Thought* (Cambridge, MA: Harvard Council on East Asian Studies, 1996), 425.

14. Ye Xie, *Yuan shi* 原詩, cited in Owen, *Readings*, 532.

15. Paul Shih-yi Hsiao, "Heidegger and Our Translation of the Tao Te Ching," in *Heidegger and Asian Thought*, ed. Graham Parkes (Honolulu: University of Hawaii Press, 1987), 93–104. See also Otto Pöggeler, "West-East Dialogue: Heidegger and Lao-Tzu," in Parkes, ed., *Heidegger and Asian Thought*, 47–48.

16. See Graham Parkes, "Thoughts on the Way: Being and Time via Lao-Chuang," in Parkes, *Heidegger and Asian Thought*, 121; Reinhard May, *Heidegger's Hidden Sources: East-Asian Influences on His Work*, trans. Graham Parkes (New York: Routledge, 1996); Bryan Van Norden and Taylor Carman, "Being-in-the-Way: A Review of Heidegger and Asian Thought." http://evansexperientialism.freewebspace.com/parkes.html.

17. Brown may be referring to a similar dynamic in a passage that is difficult to parse: "Temporalized as the before and after of the object, thingness amounts to a latency (the not yet formed or the not yet formal) and to an excess (what remains physically or metaphysically irreducible to objects). But this temporality obscures the all-at-onceness, the simultaneity, of the object/thing dialectic and the fact that, all at once, the thing seems to name the object, just as it is, even as it names some thing else." Bill Brown, ed. *Things* (Chicago: University of Chicago Press, 2008), 53.

18. In his criticism of literary texts, Brown does not adhere to the rigid distinction between object and thing that he makes in "Thing Theory"; the difficulty of consistently maintaining such distinctions in itself points to the impossibility of conceiving of "object" and "thing" as mutually exclusive.

19. See, for example, Wang Jide's 王驥德 (d. 1623) dramatic criticism. Wang wrote: "In choosing a subject one prizes *shi* [historical validity]; in treating it one prizes *xu* [the creative additions of the author]." (Wang Jide, *Qulü* 曲律, in *Zhongguo gudian xiqu lunzhu jicheng* 中國古典戲曲論著集成 [Beijing: Zhongguo xiju chubanshe, 1959], 4: 154).

20. David Rolston notes that events characterized as *xu* may also be factual in nature, but "are merely told indirectly; they happen offstage, as it were," and that in criticism of the essay, arguments thought to be *shi* are presented directly, whereas arguments characterized as *xu* are presented indirectly. Similarly, in painting, detailed depiction is labeled *shi*; washes are considered *xu*. David Rolston, *Traditional Chinese Fiction and Fiction Commentary: Reading and Writing Between the Lines* (Stanford, CA: Stanford University Press, 1997), 182.

21. It is not known when Jin Shengtan began writing the commentary on *The Water Margin* (*Shuihu zhuan*), but the third preface to his commentary is dated 1641, thirteen years after Ling Mengchu published this story.

22. See Rolston, *Traditional Chinese Fiction and Fiction Commentary*, 183; Rolston quotes Li Rihua 李日華 (1565–1635), "Guang Xieshi xu" 廣寫實序 (*Preface to the*

expanded Xieshi), dated 1615, in *Zhongguo lidai xiaoshuo xuba xuanzhu* 中國歷代小說序跋選注, eds. Zeng Zuyin 曾祖陰 et al. (Xianning: Changjiang wenyi, 1982), 76.

23. Ling Mengchu, *Chuke Pai'an jingqi*, 5.

24. Ibid., 7.

25. In Feng Menglong's *Zhi nang* 智囊 (Bag of wisdom), Jiling 吉靈 refers to Darjeeling. However, Darjeeling is transliterated as "De jiling" 德吉靈 in the *Ming shi* 明史 (Ming history). It would make little sense for Wen Ruoxu's ship to sail for Darjeeling, unless it was not known in late Ming Suzhou that Darjeeling is landlocked and mountainous. As Tina Lu has remarked, Jiling is unmappable, and it is precisely the fictive, unmappable quality of Jiling that is key to Wen Shi's fabulous acquisition of wealth. Tina Lu, *Accidental Incest, Filial Cannibalism and Other Peculiar Encounters in Late Imperial Chinese Literature* (Cambridge, MA: Harvard University Asia Center, 2008), 37.

26. Ling Mengchu based the episode of the oranges from Lake Dongting on a classical anecdote, and the contrast between the original version and his illuminates Ling Mengchu's concern to illustrate the limitations of strategic thinking in business. In the original version, recorded in Zhou Yuanwei's 周元暐 (*jinshi* 1585) *Jinglin xuji* 涇林續記, a merchant buys oranges in Fujian to sell abroad precisely because this requires little capital. When he reaches his foreign destination (identified only as an area that is foreign (*fan* 番), he deliberately displays the oranges on dozens of plates, in an attempt to attract the barbarians (*yi* 夷) of this region. He haggles with the natives, ultimately reaping 1000 taels. The classical anecdote contains none of the moralizing against strategic thinking that is the primary concern of the vernacular; Ling Mengchu rewrote the anecdote to emphasize that Wen reaps a windfall precisely because he is not interested in trade. See Tan Zhengbi, *Sanyan liangpai*, 573. As Chen Yongzheng points out, Ling Mengchu also revises the original to praise the spirit of risk in engaging in overseas trade; Zhou Yuanwei had spoken of the merchants of Fujian and Guangdong who engaged in trade with the "barbarians" as "merchant traitors" (*jian shang* 姦商). Chen Yongzheng 陳永正, *Shijing fengqing: Sanyan er pai de shi jie* 市井風情：三言二拍的世界 (Hong Kong: Zhonghua shuju, 1988), 29.

27. Patrick Hanan, *The Chinese Vernacular Story* (Cambridge, MA: Harvard University Press, 1981), 153.

28. When the Persian first catches sight of the shell, it is described as a "thing" (*dongxi* 東西). The vernacular term *dongxi* has a very different genealogy than does the English word "thing;" the various traditions concerning its etymology all suggest that it has its origins in the marketplace—in the need to come up with an abstraction that could simultaneously describe disparate classes of goods. The term first appears in the Ming, although, as is characteristic, Ming anecdotes date the origin of the term to the Song.

29. Ling Mengchu, *Chuke Pai'an jingqi*, 12.

30. Ibid., 12.

31. Ibid., 14–15.

32. The narrator observes that the Persian has an eccentric last name: his surname is Ma with a jade radical, as in *manao* 瑪瑙 (agate). As a Muslim, one would expect

him to have the surname Ma—the same character without the jade radical. This is a pun that one cannot hear, detectable only to the observer of the written word. The doubling of characters here is not a productive juxtaposition. Rather, punning seems a way of indicating excess of significance and controlling it—the pun is, after all, a one-liner, so that excess is circumscribed as soon as it is indicated. Both middlemen, the Persian and the miser, have names that signify doubly, and this perhaps points to their function as translators, as mediators of value.

33. Ling Mengchu, *Chuke Pai'an jingqi*, 16.

34. A related phenomenon occurs in vernacular stories that feature crimes; key information is obscured, seemingly with the primary purpose of alerting the reader to the fact that he or she has impartial information and does not understand fully the internal conditions operating inside the tale. Almost as if to tease the reader, the text will state "the magistrate told the jailers to do such and such." It is not that the literary approximation of the "real" is imperfect, but that the literary text will not divulge the information. The magistrate, whose position is analogous to that of the detective in a Western crime novel, typically has a complete understanding of the situation that the text does not divulge. The reader then plays the role that the detective plays in the West, learning only at the close of the tale the information that the magistrate has long possessed.

10

Absence and Presence

The Great Wall in Chinese Art

LILLIAN LAN-YING TSENG

The Great Wall, winding over the hills and mountains in north China for more than 4,000 miles, dwarfs the seven wonders of the ancient Western world.[1] Built and rebuilt many times since the third century BCE, when the First Emperor of the Qin erected it to defend against nomads' attacks from the northern steppe, the Great Wall has remained culturally significant and monumental from the beginning, so it is striking that, from the Qin Dynasty up to the twentieth century, it never appeared as an artistic motif. When it finally did become an object of pictorial representation, it was in the twentieth century, arguably when the defensive capabilities of the Wall were definitively and irreversibly proven defunct.

An examination of the apparent inverse correlation between the wall's overwhelming presence in the Chinese cultural and historical landscape and its stark absence in pictorial art promises to shed light on the representational uses and significance of hiddenness in traditional Chinese art. To best demonstrate what transpires, I move backward in time, first investigating how one major artist in the contemporary avant-garde movement has recently treated this ancient legacy, then how modern artists in the first half of the twentieth century had become fascinated with it, transforming it from a spectacular landmark into a national icon.[2] Finally, I examine the art of the Han Dynasty, 2,000 years earlier, when the physical Great Wall was at its most effective, and—counterintuitively—when its pictorial representation is perhaps best qualified as being "hidden." In the process, I hope to draw attention to the intriguing inverse relationship between the Wall's diminishing real-world usefulness and its increasingly explicit manifestation in the visual arts. Is this phenomenon an example of the predictable process by which power is transferred from the effective to the symbolic, from the real to the remembered? How does the advent of new artistic media, and the self-consciousness they bring to how we see, complicate the Great Wall's progression from a universally acknowledged-but-hidden entity to a monumental-but-impotent reproduction?

Authenticity

Representing a gigantic object is always a challenge, and the Great Wall is among the most gigantic of gigantic objects. Photography has been a major medium for recording it ever since the introduction of the camera to China in the 1840s. The American chemist who wrote and lectured about his travels in China in Japan, Romyn Hitchcock (1851–1923), was among the first to capture the Great Wall with his camera, although what he chose to publish instead were five drawings based on the photographs he brought back in 1893.[3] Whether in terms of scope or attention garnered, Hitchcock's short magazine article and its accompanying drawings would prove no match for *The Great Wall of China* of William Edgar Geil (1865–1925), published in 1909. Geil, another avid traveler to China, and noted in at least one source as very likely the first person to traverse the full length of the Great Wall, incorporated into his book more than 100 photographs, which he and some of his friends took at various points along the wall. A note from the publishers emphasized their centrality: "The illustrations are inserted not only to substantiate the text but to make material additions to it. . . . The illustrations should be carefully studied during the reading of the book."[4]

In portraying the Great Wall, the challenge posed by its scale is primary. Photographers, perhaps following the practices put in place by early illustrators (whom I will discuss below), usually indicate its size by comparing it to nearby hills or people on its walkway (See Figure 10.1). Viewers, then, have been able to rely on photographs to *perceive* the scale of the Great Wall, but not to *experience* it in any physical sense. This would change in 1991, when the contemporary artist Xu Bing (b. 1955), in his monumental installation *Ghosts Pounding the Wall*, represented the Great Wall, not in photographs or even in drawings, but in a traditional Chinese medium that can only reproduce an object true to its size: the ink rubbing.

The Chinese developed the technique of ink rubbing no later than the fifth century to copy inscriptions engraved on stone steles.[5] Paper and ink

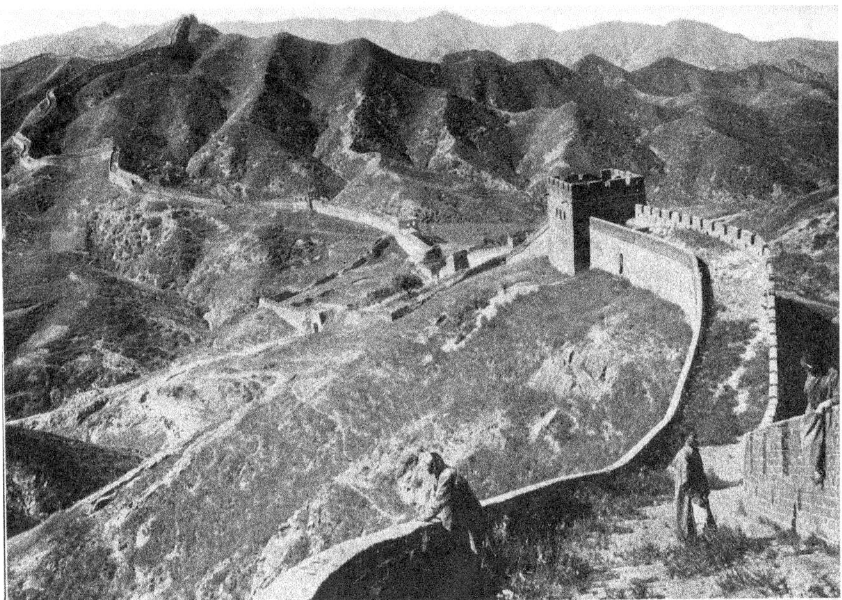

Figure 10.1. *The Great Wall as Seen at the Nankou, Showing the Badaling Gate.* Photo by H. G. Ponting. From William Edgar Geil, *The Great Wall of China* (1909), 170–71.

were essential for the task. As an impression made directly from a surface, a rubbing necessarily matched in size the surface against which the paper had been pressed. However, since it was so difficult to appreciate rubbings of massive steles in domestic spaces, many large rubbings were cut into pieces and remounted in handscrolls or placed in albums.[6]

Using the same basic technique, Xu Bing and his team produced ink rubbings of a section of the Great Wall at Jinshanling, including a tower and a nearby walkway. Unlike the ancient Chinese, however, Xu did not shy away from the massiveness that the rubbings reflected; instead, he dramatized it. When the installation first appeared in the United States in 1991, the rubbings of the watchtower, mounted as hanging scrolls, covered the two long walls of the Paige Court in the Elvehjem Museum of Art at the University of Wisconsin–Madison (Figure 10.2).[7]

The rubbings of the walkway, in the center of the space, hung from the ceiling and extended across the floor. The two-story-high rubbings easily overwhelmed viewers, and the cramped, rectangular space added to their towering impact. Moving in the narrow strip between the rubbings on the walls and those draped in the center, viewers had no choice but to experience the

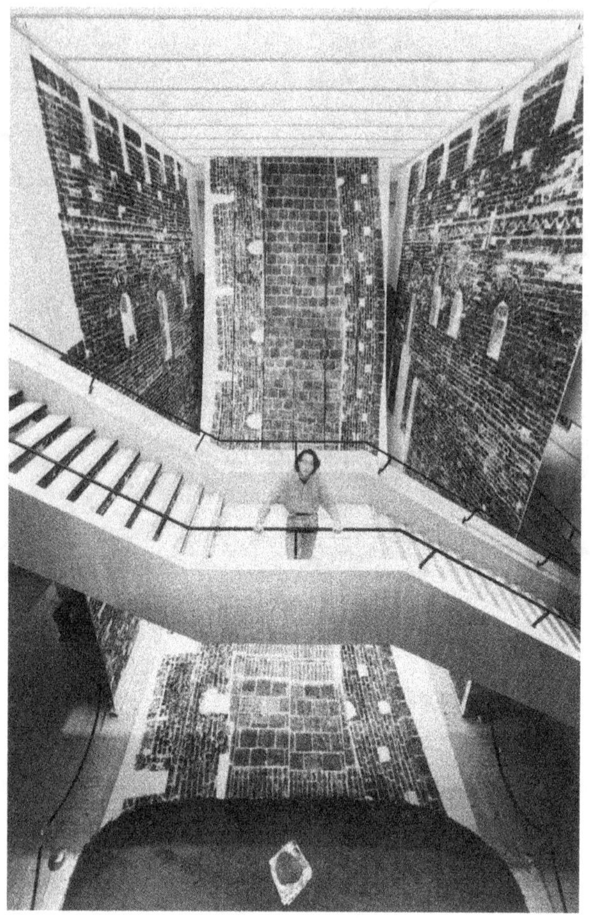

Figure 10.2. Xu Bing, *Ghosts Pounding the Wall*, 1991. Mixed-media installation. From Britta Erickson, *Three Installations by Xu Bing*, 26. Chazen Museum of Art, University of Wisconsin–Madison (formerly the Elvehjem). Photograph, 2014, courtesy of the David and Alfred Smart Museum of Art, University of Chicago.

Great Wall in proportion to their own bodies (Figure 10.3). The scale of the installation invited viewers to imagine the immensity of the Great Wall in its 4,000-mile entirety.

A photographer may need only a fraction of a second to press a camera button, and, if working before the prevalence of digital cameras, several hours to develop the film; Xu Bing spent five months preparing for the installation.

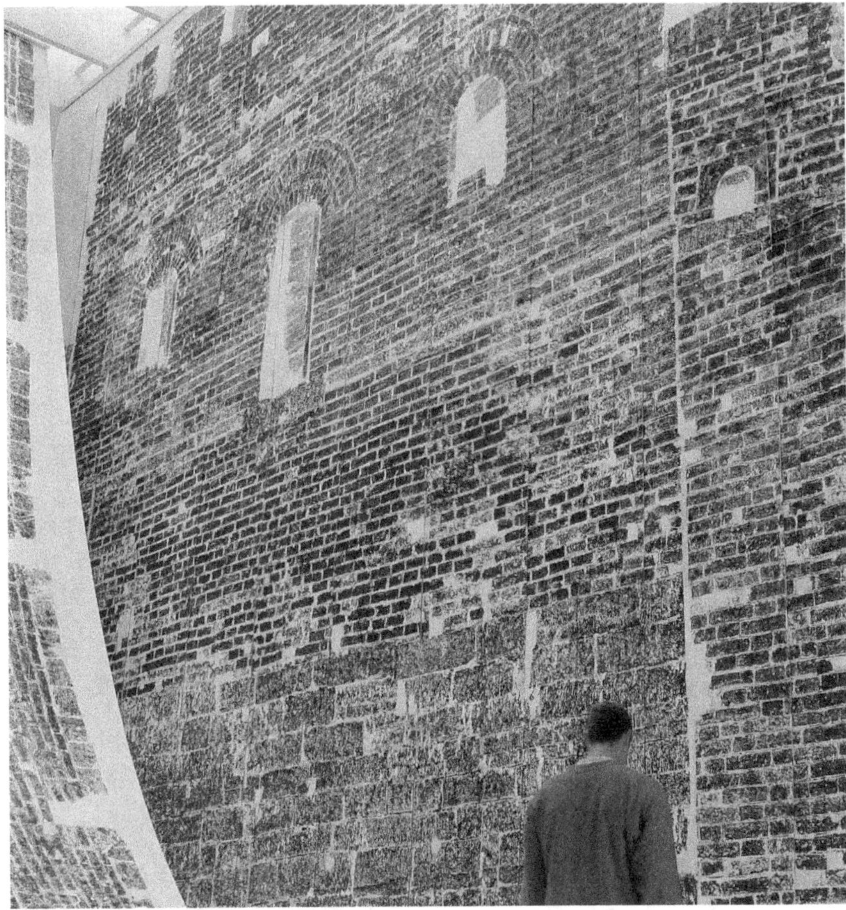

Figure 10.3. Xu Bing, *Ghosts Pounding the Wall,* 1991. From Wu Hung, *Transience,* pl. 1.

In the first stage, he hired seven art students and eight local residents to make rubbings in situ. Working from sunrise to sunset for twenty-four days, they used 1,300 sheets of paper and three hundred bottles of ink to make the rubbings. In the second stage, Xu and his assistants repaired the rubbings, arranged them in order, and mounted them on backing paper. They toiled away in the studio for four months to finish the task, using another 7,000 sheets of paper.[8] Even a museumgoer not aware of the laborious process of making the rubbings must have realized at some level that a great deal of work had been done to create them, work that in turn alluded to the even more strenuous labor of building the Great Wall itself.

When a photographer has to represent the Great Wall in one shot, in a single frame, the usual choice is to show a stretch of the wall from a certain distance, curving along the mountain ridges. The shot is necessarily made at the expense of near-distance details. When a photographer chooses to amplify that panoramic impression with more photographs, as did Geil, the lens tends to turn to the surface of the wall; only then can the focus be solely on its stones or bricks (Figure 10.4).

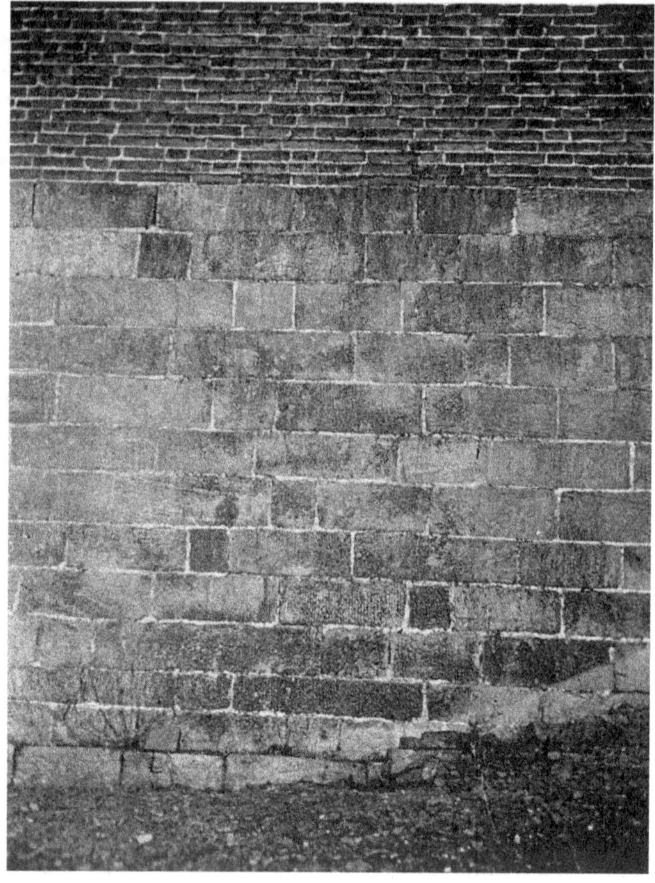

Figure 10.4. *Section of a Tower.* Photo by William Edgar Geil. From Geil, *The Great Wall of China*, 162–63.

But, even here, the glossy photographic paper smoothes out the rough surface that the photographer intends to capture. In a rubbing, by contrast, nothing on the surface of the wall escapes reproduction. The person making the rubbing pounds hard, again and again, on the rice paper attached to the wall. If the surface is not level, the rubbing bears uneven wrinkles. The ink rubbings in Xu Bing's installation vividly show the texture of the tower, including the rugged stone blocks at the bottom, the smoother bricks at the top, and the concave mortar fillings (see Fig. 10.3). The ink rubbings also faithfully reveal the passage of time: bricks and stones have been eroded, damaged, and repaired, and some are missing. In short, the uneven surface of the ink rubbings makes the represented Great Wall tangible.

In both scale and detail, then, Xu Bing's installation defies the materiality of photography by challenging its glossy surface. The installation also addresses modes of reproduction. Photography as a modern mode of production celebrates the triumph of science and machinery, boasting of objectivity, precision, and efficiency. The photographic mode of reproduction, after all, excels in reducing labor and minimizes the potential for error inherent in human participation. But Xu Bing's work casts grave doubts on the modern myth of optical realism—or, perhaps, it recasts that particular notion of realism by bringing the human element back into the process of (re)production. It was, after all, through direct human contact, the work of human hands, that the Great Wall itself was constructed, a process echoed when Xu and his assistants transformed it into ink rubbings. Clearly, the life-size installation was designed to compel viewers both to experience the scale of the wall and to apprehend its minutest details. The project posed controversial, fundamental questions about replication: Which mode of reproduction is more reliable—modern photography or traditional ink rubbing? In evaluating the relative authenticity of these modes of reproduction, what should be the criterion—scientific measurement or human judgment?

The ink rubbings in Xu Bing's installation may seem traditionally Chinese, but they are far from conventional.[9] In particular, Xu's rubbings have two features that would probably have astonished early artisans. First, they are huge. Early practitioners seldom dealt with a surface larger than fifty square feet. Xu's project, based on hundreds of rubbings, covered more than five thousand square feet of the Great Wall, a scale beyond their imagination. Second, Xu's rubbings are completely devoid of writing. Historically, large-scale rubbings were always undertaken specifically with the primary goal of obtaining and preserving precious texts on steles, walls, and cliffs. It would never have been considered worthwhile to take a rubbing of the surface of a structure that bore no inscription. In apparent defiance of this practice, Xu

Bing's rubbings betray his distrust of texts as a form of human communication, an attitude he had already articulated in his 1988 installation, *Book from the Sky*.[10] Expending labor and materials for no apparent gain normally dampens any incentive to repeat an endeavor; and without repetition, rubbings as such cannot exist. *Ghosts Pounding the Wall* is thus a unique work unlikely to be replicated—even as, just as in the case of photographs, multiple replication is an essential feature of its own medium.

In his installation Xu Bing revived and refashioned the art of ink rubbing to deconstruct the myth of photography. He exposed the inadequate materiality of photography by producing a work based entirely on individually executed measurement, physical labor, and handcrafted detail. Yet Xu Bing knows well that, for all this, his ink rubbings are every bit as two-dimensional as photographs, which, like paintings, rely on linear or vanishing-point perspective to create the illusion of depth on a plane. Xu Bing used the installation space in such a way as to lend his ink rubbings a sense of space, but he also ensured that their spatiality remained bizarre and ambiguous. At first glance, the installation seemed to portray a walkway passing through a watchtower. But the walkway should have been outside a tower, not within it (see Figure 10.1). Furthermore, viewers who knew that the rubbings of the tower were produced from its exterior walls would have realized that the spatial arrangement—making two exterior walls face each other—turned the tower outside in.

In pondering the confusions of inside and outside, viewers would have come to understand that the installation went further than photography ever could in showing both the presence and the absence of the Great Wall. It meticulously translated the exterior texture of the Great Wall but completely omitted all features from the inner core, its presumed source of strength. Only a stone and a pile of dirt on the floor at the end of the walkway rubbings might be construed as referring to the massive and enduring center of pounded earth concealed by the bricks and stones (Figure 10.5). But, rather than serving as a reminder of its impregnability, the combined presence of a fragile exterior (rubbings) and a soft interior (a pile of dirt) seems to mock the legendary impression of the Great Wall as firm, solid, unshakable, and immovable. Indeed, it dramatizes one of the great hidden truths about the historical Great Wall: its disturbing—ultimately even fatal—inefficacy.

The installation thus became a farce: on the one hand, the "authentic" surface mocks the absurd, illegible space it delineates; on the other, the time-consuming labor draws attention to pointlessness of its own goal. By pushing the frontiers of visual reproduction, Xu Bing reiterates the undeniable fact that the Great Wall, promoted as a national icon under the Communist regime, has not succeeded in defending China at least since its reconstruction in the sixteenth century.

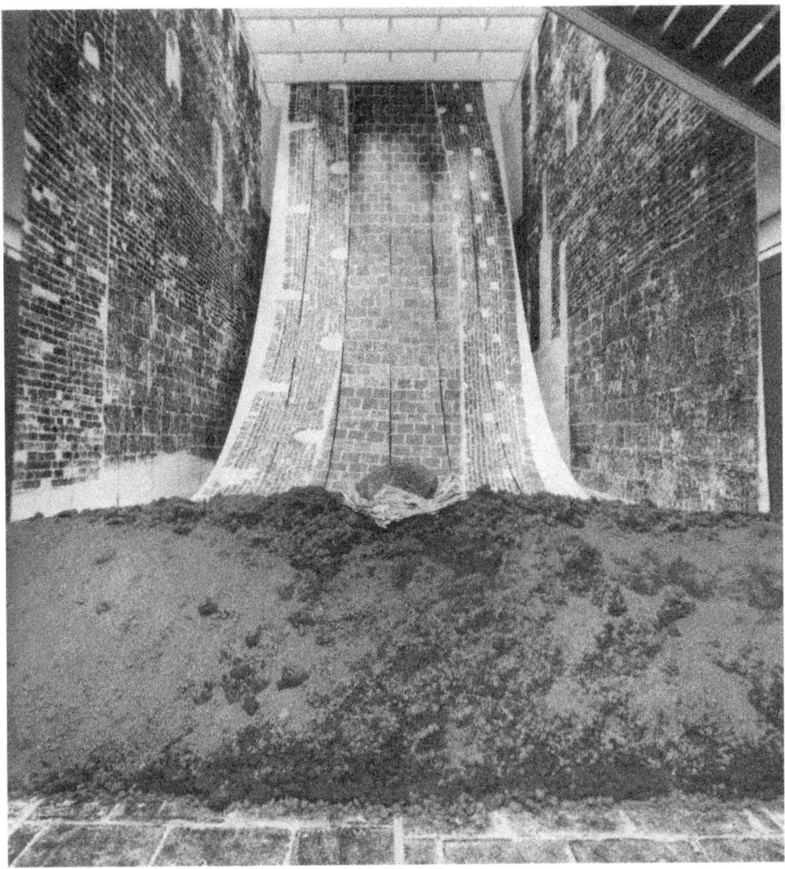

Figure 10.5. Xu Bing, *Ghosts Pounding the Wall*, 1991. From Erickson, *Three Installations by Xu Bing*, 27.

Locality

Ever since its initial construction in the third century BCE, the Great Wall has often been featured in literature, especially poetry; but it has seldom been the subject of pictorial representation.[11] The Ming Dynasty painter and calligrapher, Wang Fu 王紱 (1362–1416), delineated a separate image of the Wall's Cloud Terrace at the Juyong Pass in his *Eight Views of Beijing*, but the terrace would be represented as part of the Great Wall only later, in the sixteenth century.[12] The only other pre-twentieth-century example is an illustration associated with the ancient legend of Meng Jiang crying over her husband, who died building the Great Wall, produced during the Jiajing reign

(1522–1566) of the Ming Dynasty.[13] Not until China became a republic in 1911 did the situation change, when Liu Kuiling 劉奎齡 (1885–1967), a professional painter in Tianjin, pioneered the incorporation of the Great Wall into traditional Chinese painting.

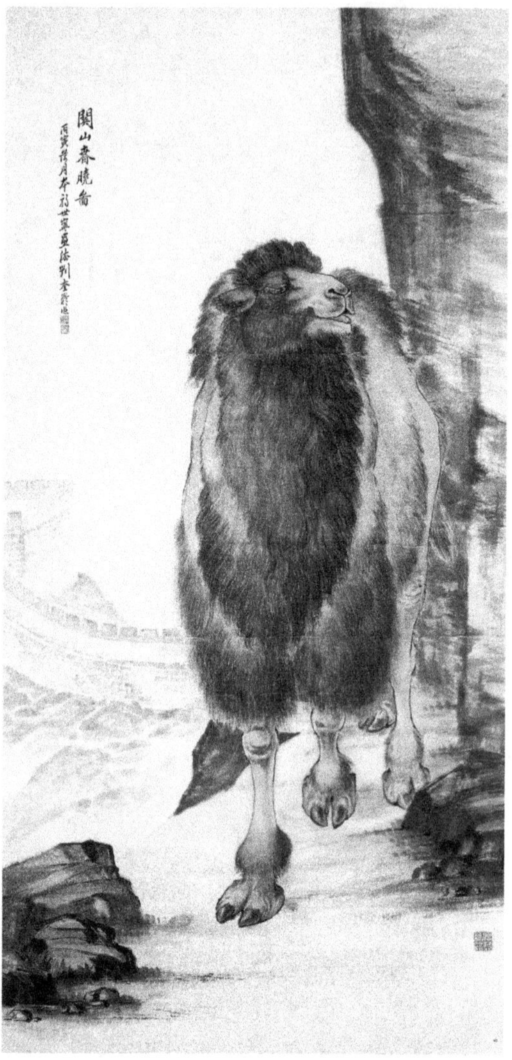

Figure 10.6. Liu Kuiling, *Spring Coming to the Pass and Mountains*, 1926. Ink and color on paper. 136.5 × 66.5 cm. From Liu Jianping, ed., *Liu Kuiling huaji*, Tianjin: Tianjin renmin meishu chubanshe, 1995, vol. 2, pl. 15.

In his 1926 painting entitled *Spring Coming to the Pass and the Mountain*, Liu Kuiling portrayed a discrete section of the Great Wall, including a tower and a walkway (Figure 10.6).[14] Unlike Xu Bing, however, the wall was not Liu's main focus. He merely sketched the tower and the walkway with light ink as a background for the camel he much more carefully depicted and colored. Never a landscape painter, Liu Kuiling was celebrated for his mastery of bird and animal painting. Depicting the Great Wall as a background for a camel was, for Liu, the rough equivalent of including a pasture in a rendering of sheep and goats, as he does in a painting executed in 1927.[15]

Portraying camels was nothing new in the Chinese pictorial tradition, but no one prior to Liu Kuiling had ever tried the combination of camels and the Great Wall. Previously, painters had tended to arrange camels with yurts or fur-coated nomads to indicate the frontier. Hua Yan 華喦 (1682–1756),

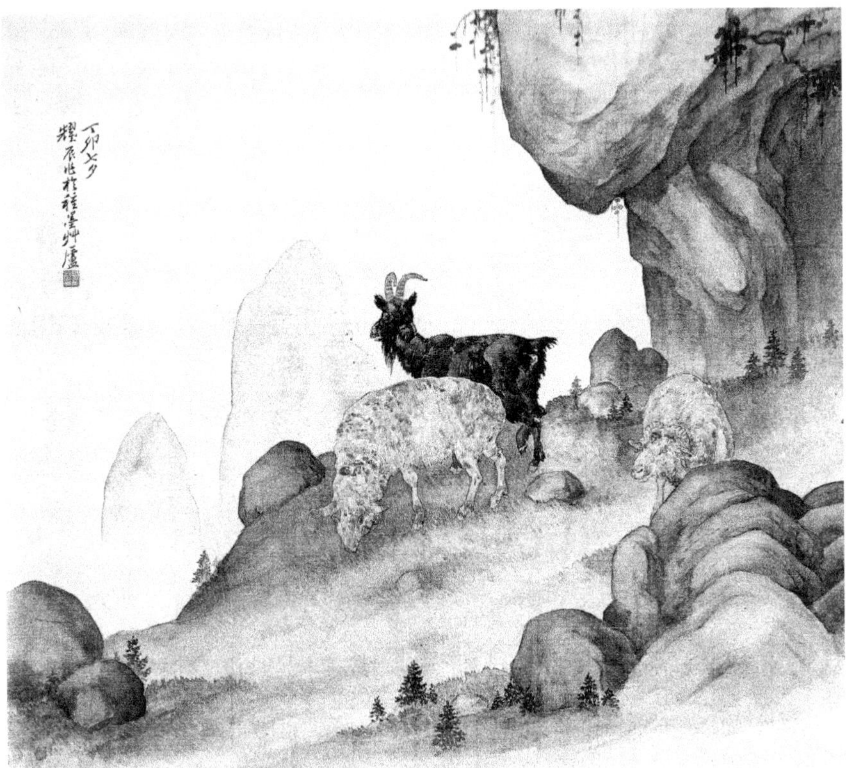

Figure 10.7. Liu Kuiling, *Harmonious Landscape*, 1927. Ink and color on silk. 35 × 39 cm. From Liu, *Liu Kuiling huaji*, vol. 2, pl. 22.

one of the Eight Eccentric Masters of Yangzhou, painted yurts in his 1746 hanging scroll *Snowy Landscape with Camel*,[16] and Liu Kuiling himself used nomads in his 1929 painting *The Boat of the Desert About to Depart.*[17] More often than not, painters simply highlighted skillful riders hunting on galloping horses to signal a border scene. Liu's 1942 painting *Autumn Wind at the Northern Frontier* followed this convention.[18]

In contrast with the reticence displayed by artists in China, Europeans had begun producing pictorial representations of the Great Wall long before Liu Kuiling's experiment. A member of the diplomatic delegation from the Dutch East India Company to China, Johannes Nieuhof, provided the earliest known Western illustration in 1665: a depiction of the Great Wall showing a gateway with its two-story tower positioned at the center.[19]

A hundred years later, in 1797, H. W. Parish, who accompanied a British delegation to China, produced the first panoramic view of the Great Wall, which unexpectedly came to shape the visual memory of this Far Eastern wonder.[20] Not only did later illustrators, such as Thomas Allom, appropriate Parish's composition (Figure 10.9),[21] but so did early photographers, including Romyn Hitchcock.[22]

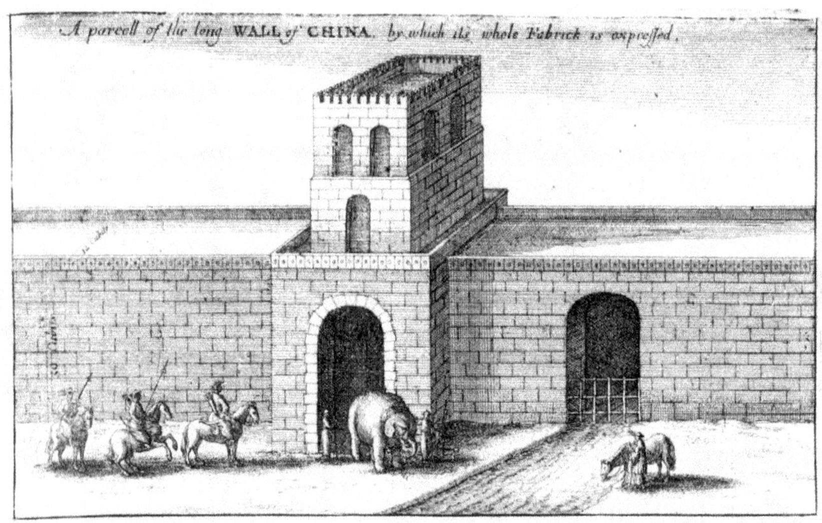

Figure 10.8. *A Parcel of the Long Wall of China.* Engraved illustration. From Johannes Nieuhof, *Embassy from the East-India Company of the United Provinces, to the Grand Tartar Cham, Emperour of China* (1669), 101.

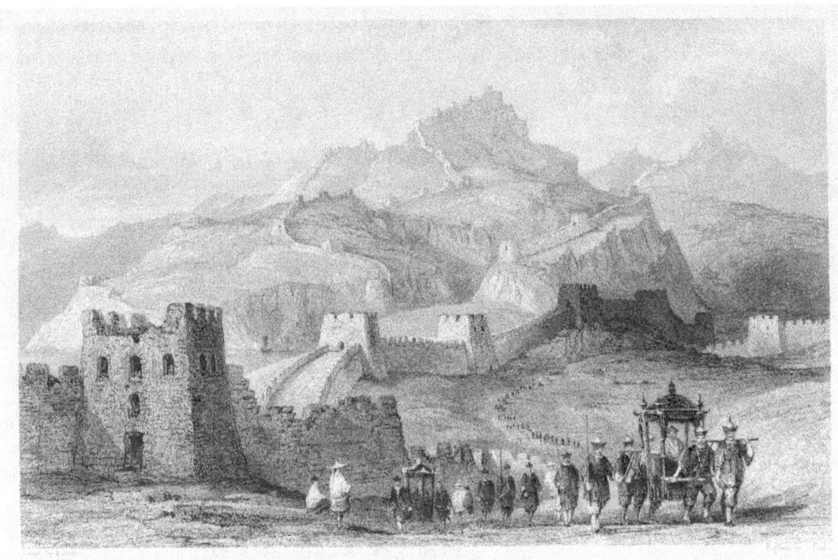

Figure 10.9. *The Great Wall of China.* Drawn by Thomas Allom and engraved by J. Sands. From Allom, *China, in a Series of Views, Displaying the Scenery, Architecture, and Social Habits of that Ancient Empire,* 1834.

To what extent the Western drawings and photographs of the Great Wall may have influenced Liu Kuiling is unclear. A self-taught painter, Liu appears to have been in the conservative camp: he relied on a traditional medium (ink and color on silk or paper), studied the masters of past dynasties, especially those of the Song (960–1279) and the Yuan (1279–1368), and painted in the stale genre of birds and animals. Yet Liu was born and grew up in Tianjin, the most cosmopolitan city in north China at the time, so he must have been exposed at a young age to foreign cultures. He began to radiate enthusiasm for art when he studied in Jingye High School, a private institution run by the influential advocates of Western education.[23]

Liu Kuiling, while attending this short-lived but new-fashioned school in his early teens, learned about perspective, chiaroscuro, and anatomy. Even though he chose to be a traditional painter, his interest in European art never waned.[24] In his colophon for *Spring Coming to the Pass and Mountain,* he declared that he was indebted to Giuseppe Castiglione (1688–1766), an Italian Jesuit painter at the Qing court for five decades who demonstrated the use of perspective and chiaroscuro to court painters and who created his individual style by meshing European technology with Chinese aesthetics.[25] It occasioned no surprise when Liu, who may have paid attention to Western prints and photographs circulating in Tianjin, decided to give the combination of camels and the Great Wall a try.

Liu Kuiling's use of perspective and chiaroscuro is more palpable in his 1932 painting *Spring Wind at the Northern Frontier* (Figure 10.10) than in *Spring Coming to the Pass and Mountain*.[26] The structure of the Great Wall is more definitely described, especially the way the rampart joins the tower,

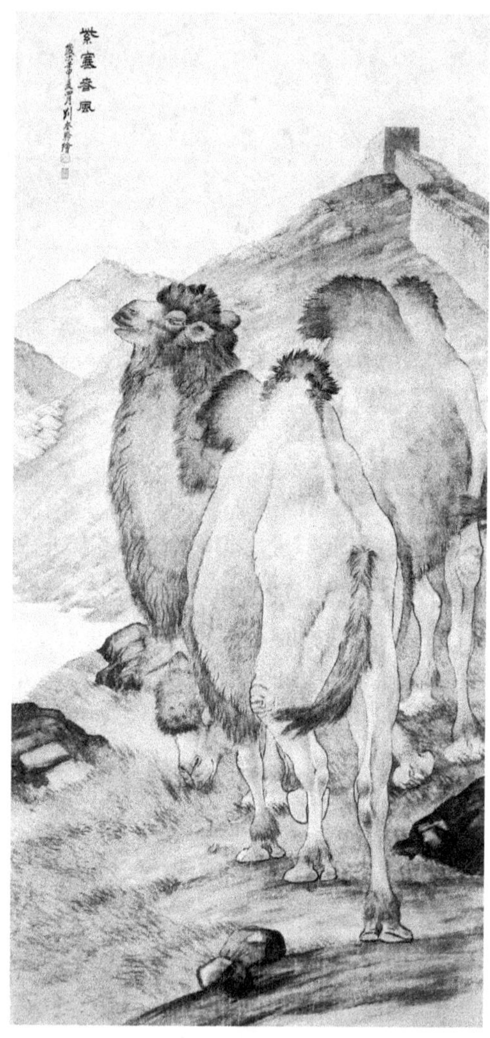

10.10. Liu Kuiling, *Spring Wind at the Northern Frontier*, 1932. From Liu, *Liu Kuiling huaji*, vol. 1, pl. 8.

which is ambiguous in his 1926 work. The connection between the Great Wall and its surroundings is also more naturally rendered, with the walkway winding along the mountain ridge and receding in the distance. Although the sources of light in the painting are multiple, the light cast on the Great Wall is consistently from the left, which gives the monument volume. A traditional Chinese painter would have been oblivious to the depth of the pictorial plane and would have inserted the Great Wall into the landscape like a paper-cut silhouette, as in the 1929 gazetteer of Linyu County (Figure 10.11).[27] Liu, in contrast, was not confined by the traditional mode of representation. Clearly he borrowed the Western view of the Great Wall popularized by prints and photographs and juxtaposed it with the camel, an animal motif he favored.

Liu Kuiling intended the grouping of camels and the Great Wall to represent the frontier, as the title he gave the 1932 painting indicates. In early dynasties, when the capital was in Chang'an, Luoyang, Kaifeng, or a southern city, both camels and the Great Wall had functioned as signs of the frontier in the minds of those Chinese who dwelled far from the northern border. After the capital had been moved to Beijing, the "northern capital," in the late thirteenth century, however, the symbolism changed dramatically. Camels and the

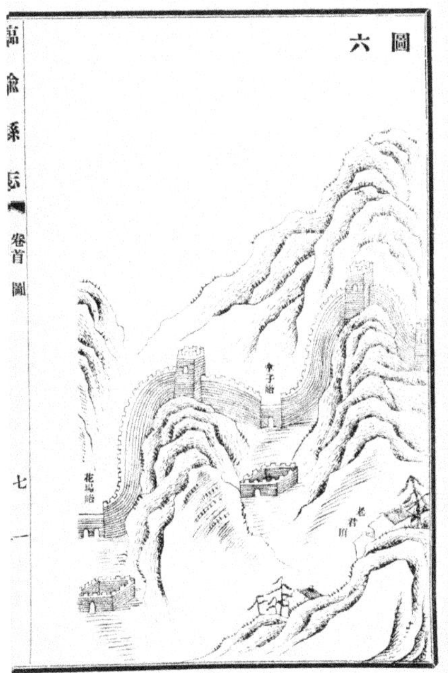

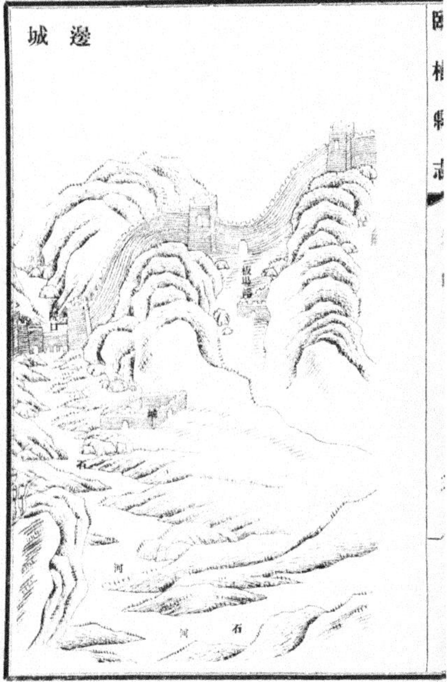

Figure 10.11. *The Border Town.* Engraved illustration. From Gao Zeyu, *Linyu xianzhi* (1929), 1.6b–7a.

Great Wall were not exotic to the residents of the great metropolises of Beijing (Beiping) and Tianjin, the likely viewers of Liu's paintings and his potential patrons. The Great Wall's Juyong Pass was only forty-five miles from Beijing. It had been included in the conventional Eight Views of Yanjing since the Qianlong period (1736–1795). Many photographs show that camel caravans still frequented Beijing, the terminus of the classical Silk Road, even in the early twentieth century. Since Liu never specified a location, the Great Wall and the camels in his paintings could have referred to a place as near as the Juyong Pass or as remote as the Jiayu Pass, the location of the westernmost fort on the Great Wall, at the end of the Hexi (Gansu) Corridor. By presenting the Great Wall while obscuring its locality, Liu's paintings inadvertently suggested the impossibility of capturing it in its entirety. They also exposed the absurdity of continuing to equate the Great Wall with the frontier.

China's claim to Mongolia since the seventeenth century, be it Inner, Outer, or both, makes the equation of the Great Wall and the frontier even more ludicrous. After Liu Kuiling, Shi Lu 石魯 (1919–1982) was one of the few traditional painters who depicted the Great Wall. Like Liu, Shi did not specify locality, as we can see in his 1954 painting *Beyond the Ancient Great Wall* (Figure 10.12).[28] Shi was much bolder than Liu, however: he went so

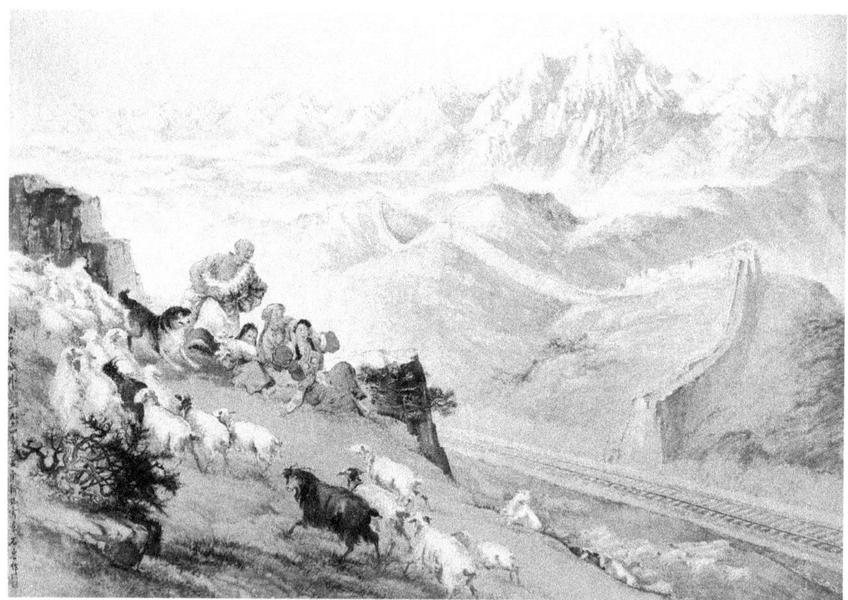

Figure 10.12. Shi Lu, *Beyond the Ancient Great Wall*, 1954. Ink and color on paper. 127 × 89 cm. From Wang Yushan, ed., *Shi Lu*, Beijing: Renmin meishu chubanshe, 1996, 16.

far as to proclaim the death of the Great Wall. He painted a railway cutting through it to indicate the defenselessness of the ancient fortification against modern technology. He exhibited a happy and contented Mongolian family with their goats and sheep in the foreground to suggest the superfluousness of the Great Wall in a country that already possessed vast Inner Mongolia. To the artist, the Great Wall was no more than a relic, vulnerable and quaint.

Identity

In 1934, soon after Liu Kuiling finished his *Spring Wind at the Northern Frontier*, Zhao Wangyun 趙望雲 (1907–1977), an artist working for a newspaper, presented a very different series of sketches of the Great Wall. Employed by *L'Impartial* (*Dagong bao*), the largest newspaper in north China, Zhao Wangyun depicted what he saw and specified where he was when he sketched. The ancient monument was no longer an abstract motif to be toyed with in a studio.

The shift of artistic interest toward the Great Wall came during the prelude to the second Sino-Japanese War, which would quickly be subsumed into World War II.[29] In 1932, Japan established Manchuria as its puppet state, and in 1933 it annexed China's Rehe Province, west of Manchuria and north of the

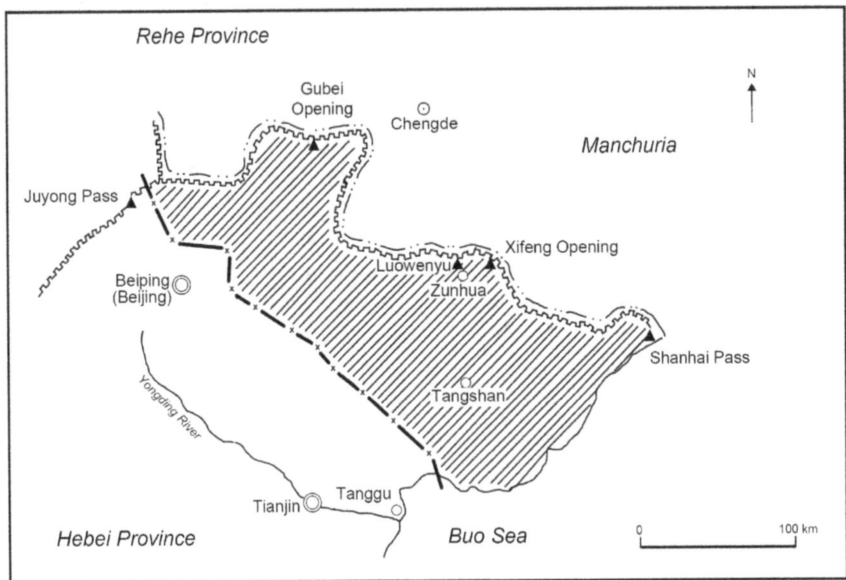

Figure 10.13. Map showing the noncombat zone under the Tanggu Armistice in 1933. Modified by the author from Wang Fu, *Rijun qinhua zhanzheng*, fig. 1–17.

Great Wall, without much military resistance. The Chinese were stunned when the Japanese army breached the Great Wall from the northeast in March 1933. The government sent troops to major forts along the wall, from the Shanhai Pass all the way to the Gubei Opening, to repel the invasion.

For two months, the battle seesawed back and forth along the Great Wall where it bordered Manchuria, Rehe, and Hebei. The Chinese claimed some victories, but the Japanese gradually gained ground, and the Chinese signed a humiliating armistice at Tanggu in May. They conceded the northeastern part of Hebei Province as a noncombat zone and agreed that Chinese forces would not march beyond a pathetic defensive line that barely included Beijing and Tianjin. The Japanese army thereby also acquired the right to station itself outside the Great Wall and to patrol the neutral zone.[30]

Zhao Wangyun was, like Liu Kuiling, a self-taught painter active in Beijing and Tianjin. He clung to the traditional medium, ink and color on paper, but was open to modern theories and Western ideas. It was through diligent practice in drawing from life that he forged his own style. Though not a political activist, he had a deep concern for marginalized members of society, and liked to represent their lives. His paintings of poverty and injustice did not have much market value; the bourgeoisie did not eagerly buy his pictures. However, his social realism attracted the attention of *L'Impartial* owners and editors, who recruited Zhao as a special correspondent in 1933, asking him to report the truth about the neglected rural villages in southern Hebei with his sketches. Functioning as a news photographer, Zhao traveled to remote areas to observe and depict the living conditions of peasants, and sent his sketches back to the press for daily publication. His "pictorial correspondence" about rural villages, which spanned four months, received an enthusiastic welcome from the public and greatly boosted the circulation of *L'Impartial*.[31]

After the Japanese and the Chinese became involved in military confrontations along the Great Wall, *L'Impartial* gave Zhao another commission: to use his sketches as a means of reporting on the impact of war. He embarked on the assignment with another journalist, Yang Ruquan 楊汝泉, in the spring of 1934, during the period before transportation services had again become available to the public. Zhao was to focus on painting while Yang worked on captions. Starting from Tangshan, they approached the Great Wall at Luowenyu, where fierce fighting had taken place months earlier (see Fig. 10.13).[32] Zhao produced four sketches here, all entitled *Luowenyu After the War*.

Without exception, the sketches re-present the conventional impression of the Great Wall as it was first produced by Parish: its ramparts sweeping through the mountains, with towers at intervals (Figure 10.14). Yang's captions, however, immediately guide readers from the *sight* of the Great Wall to the *sites* of recent battles. He notes the slogan left by China's 29th Army on the north wall: "Vow to fight to the death to recover the lost land!" He describes the gunnysacks the Chinese troops used to fill breaches in the east wall. He comments on the trench dug outside the Great Wall. Image and text thus work together to describe the Great Wall as the locale of the war.[33]

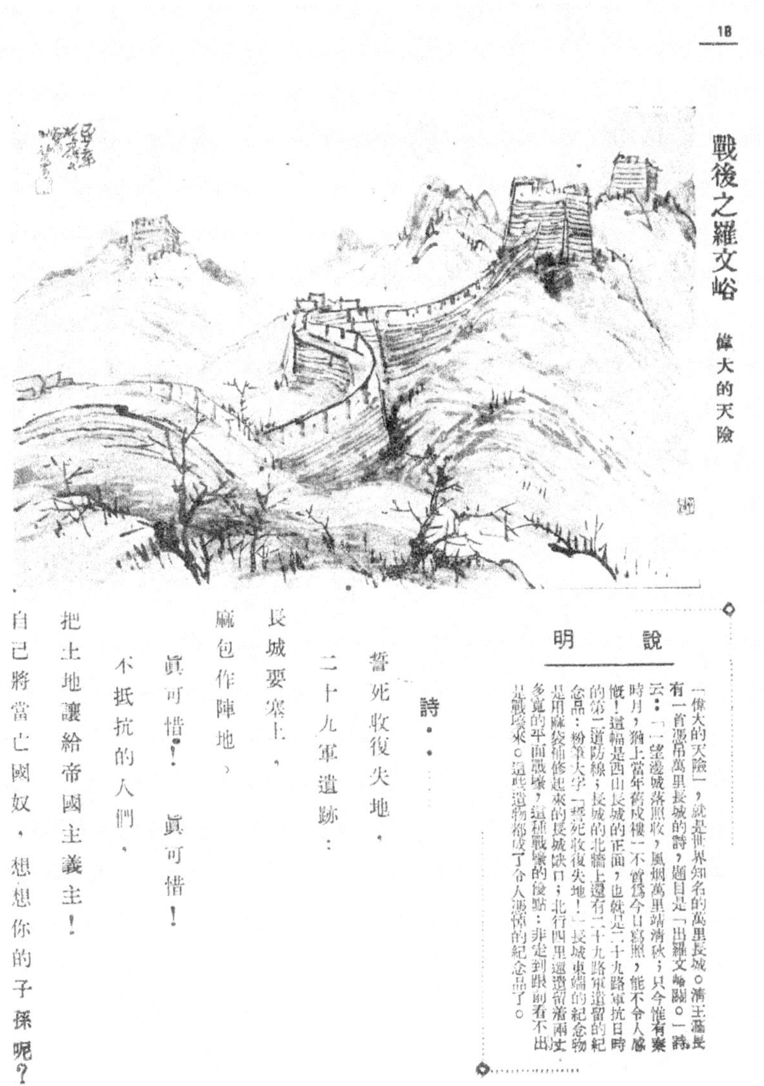

Figure 10.14. Zhao Wangyun, *Luowenyu After the War: The Grand Terrain Feature that Strongly Enhances Defense*, 1934. From *Zhao Wangyun saishang xiesheng ji*, 18.

Zhao Wangyun's pictorial representations placed the Great Wall in the context of the battles that raged around it. In two sketches, for example, he introduced the city being defended at Luowenyu. One shows the dilapidated city wall (Figure 10.15). Yang's caption explains that the city had been worn down over the years and had gone without repairs; one could only view its ruins and lament its ancient glory.

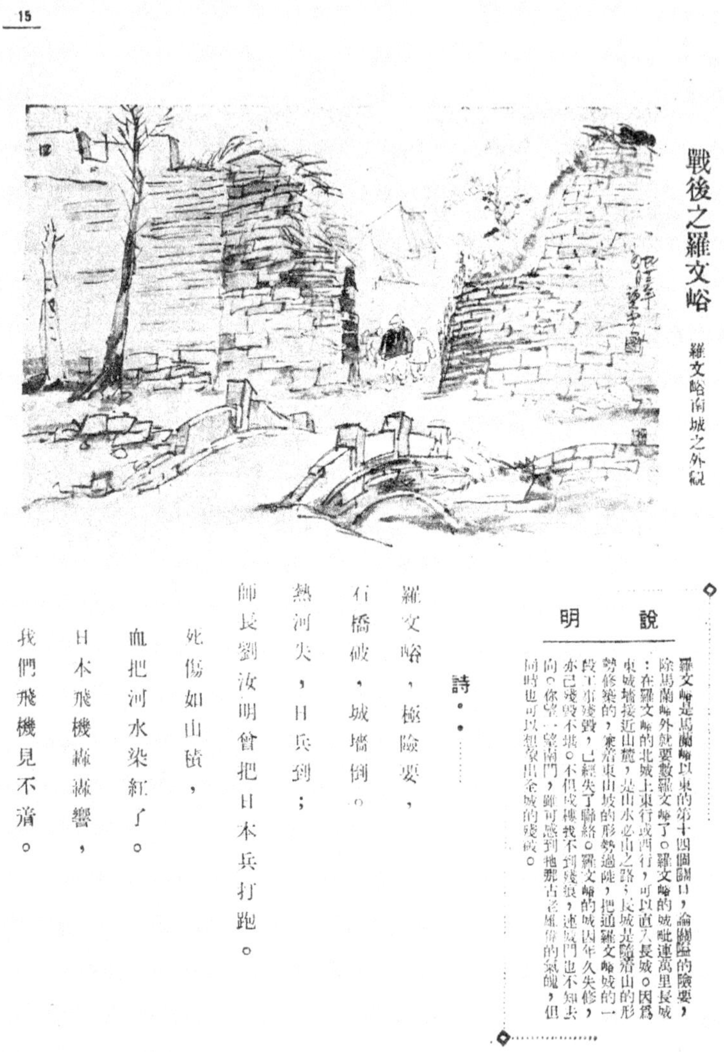

15

戰後之羅文峪

羅文峪南城之外貌

說明

羅文峪是馬蘭峪以東的第十四個關口，論關隘的險要，除馬蘭峪外就要數羅文峪了。羅文峪的城毗連萬里長城：在羅文峪的北城上東行或西行，可以直入長城。因為東城墻接近山麓，是出水必由之路；長城是隨着山的形勢修築的，順着東山坡的形勢過陡，把通羅文峪城的一段工事殘毀，已經失了聯絡。羅文峪的城因年久失修，亦已殘毀不堪。不但戍樓找不到殘痕，連城門也不知去向。你望一望南門，雖可感到她那古老雄偉的氣魄，但同時也可以想象出全城的殘破。

詩

羅文峪，極險要，
石橋破，城墻倒。
熱河失，日兵到；
師長劉汝明曾把日本兵打跑。
死傷如山積，
血把河水染紅了。
日本飛機轟轟響，
我們飛機見不着。

Figure 10.15. Zhao Wangyun, *Luowenyu After the War: The Town in Its South*, 1934. From *Zhao Wangyun saishang xiesheng ji*, 15.

The other sketch, which illustrates the strategic connection of the city to the Great Wall, shows three mountainside forts without linking ramparts and a group of abandoned houses at the mountain's foot (Figure 10.16). The ramparts to the northwest of the city had long been destroyed, noted Yang, although they were supposed to provide an additional defensive line south of the Great Wall. And a deserted architectural complex within the northern city

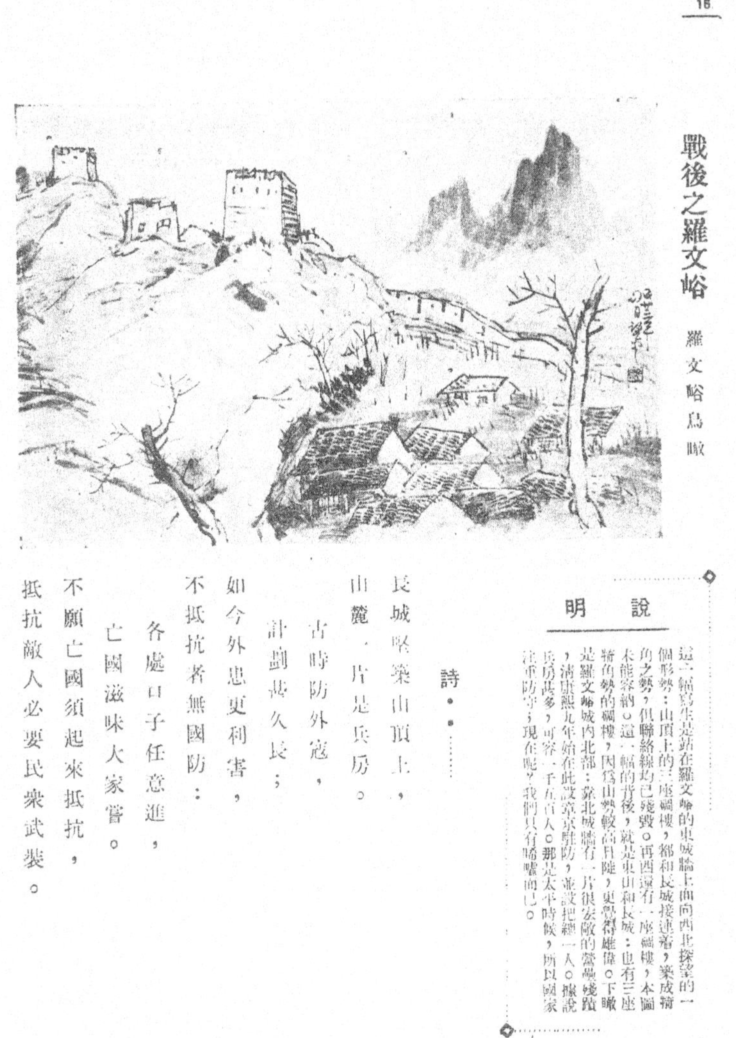

Figure 10.16. Zhao Wangyun, *Luowenyu After the War: A Bird's Eye View*, 1934. From *Zhao Wangyun saishang xiesheng ji*, 16.

wall had once served as barracks; it was said to have accommodated 1,500 soldiers during the Kangxi reign (1662–1722).[34]

Zhao's and Yang's sketched and written reports rectified the general impression that the Great Wall, with its ramparts and towers, stood alone in the mountains, a false image perpetuated by the Western prints and photographs that focused exclusively on the wall. Their reports also expressed alarm at the slackness of national security measures: the damage to the Great Wall had been caused more by long negligence than by recent battles.

The Great Wall had in fact long since lost its significance as a military defense, after Mongolia became part of China's territory in the seventeenth century.[35] It was Japan's aggression and military strategy that placed the Great Wall in the spotlight in the twentieth century. All of a sudden, China's national border in the northeast was pushed back from Manchuria to the line demarcated by the Great Wall. The Tanggu Armistice provided only temporary relief from the fighting, for the Japanese army was soon waging a full-scale war against China; in 1937 it crossed the Great Wall and quickly occupied north China. But the truce was already in place in the spring of 1934, when Zhao Wangyun conducted his pictorial correspondence.

The Grand Terrain Feature That Strongly Enhances Defense, the subtitle of one of Zhao's sketches (see Figure 10.14), probably added by Yang Ruquan, expresses a different assessment of the Wall. The subject of the praise was the Chinese troops bravely engaged in combat along the Great Wall, not the Wall itself.[36] One of the four sketches that Zhao produced at Luowenyu in 1934 shows donkeys and travelers beyond the Great Wall (Figure 10.17). As Yang explains in his caption, only a strip of land outside the Great Wall still belonged to Zunhua County, which was under Chinese government. The land farther to the north, which used to be China's Rehe Province, had fallen into Japanese clutches. To engage in trade or visit relatives on either side of the wall, local people had to pass through it. They would, Yang says, always remember the valiant resistance of Chinese soldiers, the 29th Army in particular, with deep emotion and profound gratitude.[37]

Zhao Wangyun's sketches may not compete with Xu Bing's installation in creativity or with Liu Kuiling's paintings in exquisiteness, but they enjoyed a much wider audience. Zhao's pictorial correspondence about rural villages in 1933 reached more than 90,000 readers through *L'Impartial*. In comparison, the exhibition of his paintings held in Zhongshan Park in 1928 attracted only 2,000 visitors. Because of the popularity of Zhao's pictorial correspondence about rural villages, the sketches were soon republished in book format, which expanded their audience. The book quickly sold out, and it was reprinted five times. Some credited the success of the book to the participation of the noted warlord Feng Yuxiang 馮玉祥 (1882–1948). It was Zhao's social realism that first caught Feng's eye when his pictorial correspondence was appearing in *L'Impartial.* After seeing the book with the sketches, Feng wished to add his own vernacular poems. He invited the painter to his retreat at Mount Tai and worked with him on the revision he proposed. Feng even financially supported the republication of the book in a new edition that included both Zhao's sketches and Feng's poems. This proved to be a mutually beneficial project: the young painter won the endorsement of a powerful figure, while the warlord used the popularity of the sketches to spread his own political views, specifically, his furor against the Japanese invasion.[38] The two collaborated again when Zhao's pictorial correspondence on the northern frontier was ready for publication in book form.

Feng Yuxiang's participation in the republication of Zhao Wangyun's sketches along the Great Wall was significant politically because he was anxious to avenge Japanese aggression. After Japan took possession of Rehe, Feng went to the Zhangjia Opening, an important Great Wall pass in Chahar Province, to mobilize an army to keep Japan from further nibbling at north China.[39] The much-admired 29th Army, which showed great valor at Luowenyu, had once been under his command. When the Chinese government, then headquartered in Nanjing, signed the Tanggu Armistice, Feng was commander-in-chief of the Chahar People's Anti-Japanese Army Alliance, with more than 100,000 followers. Even though he had conducted several victorious battles, Feng was compelled to give up his military efforts in the summer of 1933, when his forces were surrounded by both Japanese and Nanjing troops, for the Nanjing government favored negotiation and compromise with the Japanese rather than aggressive policies.[40] One can imagine how frustrated Feng must have felt when he composed poems for Zhao Wangyun's sketches of the northern frontier in 1934. Feng sighed, for instance, in his poem for Figure 10.17, "Today Japanese attacked us, [but] high and low no one interfered. Who dared to air his grievances?!"

Zhao Wangyun's journey along the Great Wall started at Luowenyu and ended at Zhangjia Opening, covering a distance of approximately 300 miles. Only the section from the Juyong Pass westward fell within the newly drawn Chinese defensive line; none of the wall east of Beijing was included (see Figure 10.13). Many northerners may have believed that after the Tanggu Armistice, China was still protected by the Great Wall, the "grand terrain feature that strongly enhances defense." To Feng Yuxiang, however, the Great Wall east of the Juyong Pass, where Chinese troops were not allowed and where the Japanese troops had every right to patrol, was no better than a lost land. In his poems, Feng repeatedly emphasized the loss and warned of the dire consequences if

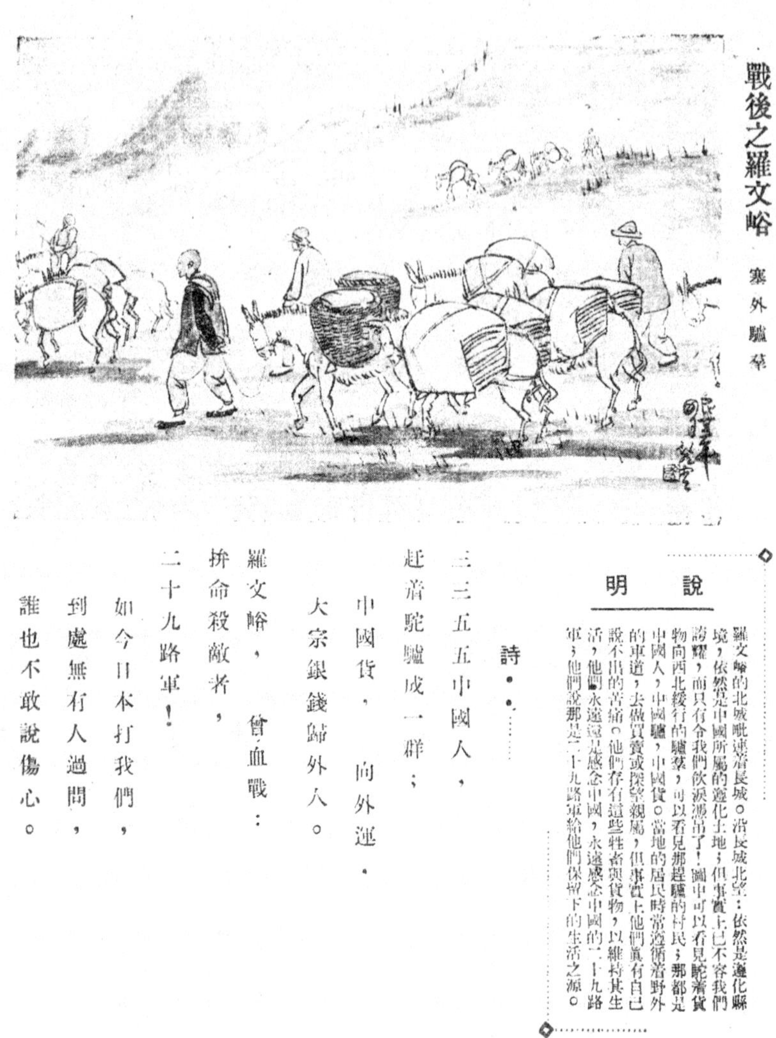

17

戰後之羅文峪

塞外驢羣

說明

羅文峪的北城毗連着長城。沿長城北望：依然是遵化縣境，依然是中國所屬的遵化土地；但事實上已不容我們誇耀，而只有令我們飲淚憑弔了！圖中可以看見駝着貨物向西北緩行的驢羣，可以看見那趕驢的村民；那都是中國人，中國驢，中國貨。當地的居民時常遵循着野外的車道，去做買賣或探望親屬，但事實上他們眞有自己說不出的苦痛。他們存有這些牲畜與貨物，以維持其生活，他們永遠還是感念中國，永遠感念中國的二十九路軍；他們說那是二十九路軍給他們保留下的生活之源。

詩

三三五五中國人，
赶着駝驢成一群；
中國貨，向外運．
大宗銀錢歸外人。
羅文峪，曾血戰：
拚命殺敵者，
二十九路軍！
如今日本打我們，
到處無有人過問，
誰也不敢說傷心。

Figure 10.17. Zhao Wangyun, *Luowenyu After the War: Donkeys Beyond the Great Wall*, 1934. From *Zhao Wangyun saishang xiesheng ji*, 17.

China failed to resist Japanese aggression.[41] Like Yang Ruquan's captions, Feng Yuxiang's poems also attempted to frame Zhao Wangyun's pictorial representations. But Feng, hailed as an anti-Japanese war hero, added stature to the book through his contributions, while Zhao's sketches were so popular that they carried Feng's hawkish viewpoint to readers far and wide.

In the end, history proved the uselessness of the Great Wall in modern warfare. The Japanese army swept across north China in 1937. It was precisely at this time, during the Sino-Japanese War, that the Great Wall began to emerge as an icon, not just of China's territorial claims, but of the Chinese as a people. A tangible, visible reminder of both the first Chinese military resistance against invasion and the lost Chinese territory to be recovered, it was readily marshaled to invigorate the Chinese resistance in the eight-year war. The renowned playwright Tian Han 田漢 (1898–1968) crystallized the wartime perceptions of the Great Wall into one concise sentence in the lyrics of the song, *March of the Volunteers*: "For those who do not want to be enslaved, let us build our new Great Wall with our flesh and blood!" A theme song of the patriotic film *Sons and Daughters in a Time of Storm* (1935), *March of the Volunteers* became one of the most popular songs of the war.[42] The song was promoted as the national anthem of Communist China in 1949. The promotion, in turn, officially enshrined the Great Wall as a national icon.

Zhao Wangyun produced ninety-nine sketches along the northern frontier in 1934. He was not only the first Chinese painter to produce images of the Great Wall in such great quantity but also the first Chinese artist to present the Great Wall in its historical and geographical context, blending views of the isolated and seemingly indifferent monument with depictions of the people living near it and events happening around it. His pictorial correspondence in *L'Impartial* and its republication in book form helped to shape the collective memory of the Great Wall and to establish its new identity as a national icon. But there is no denying that the renewed interest in the Great Wall arose as a result of a shared sense of its imminent loss—or its partial loss, depending on how one perceived the Tanggu Armistice. The presence of the Great Wall in Zhao's sketches in the spring of 1934 can thus be thought of as demarcating the "almost-absence" of the Great Wall in Chinese territory.

Boundary

If the presence of the Great Wall in Zhao Wangyun's 1934 sketches corresponded to, and perhaps even referred to, its effective near-absence, the absence of the Great Wall in the pictorial art of the Han dynasty (207 BCE–220 CE) may be read as a reflection of its indomitable, unencompassable presence.

According to the court historian Ban Gu (32–92), the First Emperor of Qin built the "Long Wall" to mark the boundary of China after he had defeated the Xiongnu, his northern neighbors. But the Qin boundary in the west did not go beyond Lintao (south of present-day Lanzhou, Gansu), near the Great Bend of the Yellow River.[43] It was only later, when Emperor Wu of the Han (r. 141–87 BCE) started to retaliate against the Xiongnu for pillaging in Han territory, that the Qin fortifications along the Great Bend were reinforced and expanded. After pushing the Xiongnu westward, Emperor Wu seized the Hexi Corridor to sever the ties between the Xiongnu and the Qiang, and ordered the establishment of administrative units and the construction of defensive forts along the corridor. The "Outer Wall" linked ramparts and beacon towers from Zhangyi to Dunhuang. It ended at the Yumen Pass, more than 800 miles northwest of Lintao. The Han Great Wall went deep into the 600-mile Hexi Corridor.[44]

The compelling practical motivations behind the Great Wall's construction notwithstanding, even long before the expansion of the empire, the Han court had already formulated a discourse of the Great Wall as something a bit less concrete and tangible: as a cultural boundary. Spurred by raids south of the Wall, in 162 BCE Emperor Wen (r. 179–157 BCE) issued a letter to the Xiongnu reminding them of an agreement that had been reached during the reign of Emperor Gao (r. 206–195 BCE): "The land north of the Great Wall, where men wield the bow and arrow, was to receive its commands from the Shanyu [the highest ruler of the Xiongnu], while that within the wall, whose inhabitants dwell in houses and wear hats and girdles, was to be ruled by us."[45]

Emperor Wen's diplomatic protest suggests that he knew the Han were not yet strong enough to force a military showdown; likewise, in 8 CE, when the Xiongnu became the weaker party, their leaders adopted the same rhetoric to dispute the border.[46] The verbal evocation of the Great Wall to delineate distinct cultures continued on into the Eastern Han period (25–220), as made evident in a statement by the erudite scholar-official Cai Yong 蔡邕 (132–192) during a court debate on frontier defenses held in 177. Cai plainly wrote that "the reason for the Qin to build the Long Wall and for the Han to erect the frontier ramparts was to discriminate between the inside and the outside and to set apart different customs."[47]

It is difficult, to say the least, to summon visual documentary evidence of an absent presence. Yet, in light of the texts cited here, it seems possible to interpolate an invisible Great Wall as cultural boundary in some of the pictorial documents handed down to us. One battle scene, for example, carved on the west wall of the shrine at Xiaotangshan, Shandong, is traditionally dated to the mid–first century.[48]

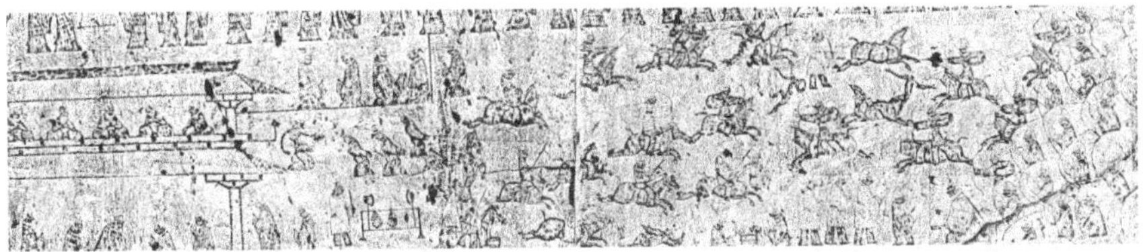

Figure 10.18. *The combat between the Hu and the Han.* Mid–first century. Stone carving on the west wall of the shrine at Xiaotangshan in Changqing, Shandong. L: 218 cm. Inverted from a rubbing by the author.

It portrays two forces engaged in combat. Cavalry regiments apparently dominate the battlefield. Beheaded riders falling from horses and the dying soldier on the ground indicate the fierceness of the fighting. The seated figure to the right of the central battle scene is identified by the nearby cartouche as the "King of the Xiongnu." Behind him, mountains, from which emerge more riders with pointed caps, are suggested by incised curves. In stark visual contrast, left of the battle scene is the Han camp, depicted as an architectural structure. The victory clearly belongs to the encamped Han army: captives are led leftward, and a rack on the left exhibits their foes' decapitated heads.

Another stone carving, retrieved from a Han tomb in Zouxian, Shandong (and probably also produced in the mid-first century), is composed around a similar contrast (Figure 10.19): the fight occurs between mountains on one side and buildings on the other.[49] The striking similarities between the two carvings suggest the existence of a pictorial formula that emphasized the contest between the nomadic Xiongnu people, who were believed to have come from mountainous areas, and the Han people, who lived in buildings. It is evident

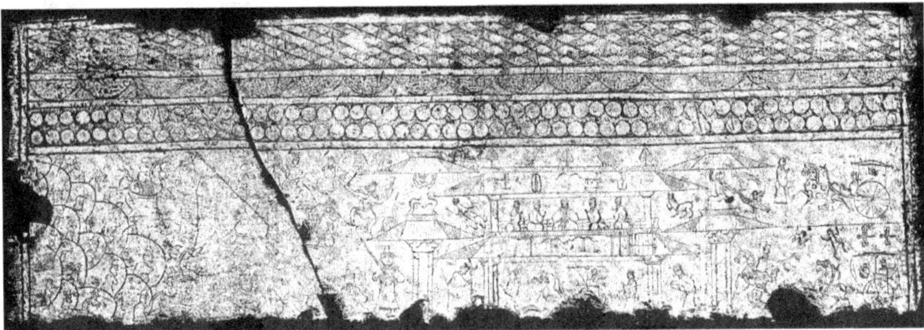

Figure 10.19. *The combat between the Hu and the Han.* Mid–first century. Stone carving in a tomb at Chengguan in Zouxian, Shandong. 270 × 85 cm. Inverted from a rubbing by the author.

that the artisan who carved the Zouxian tomb was especially interested in portraying the contrasting settlement styles.

The pictorial formula may not have applied to a specific battle, but it certainly was inspired by the recurring and sometimes frequent conflicts between the Han and the Xiongnu. That Emperor Gao, the founder of the Han Dynasty, was once trapped by the Xiongnu did not bode well for relations between the two. The later policy of marrying the Han princesses to the Xiongnu leaders only reinforced the Han's compromised position. Emperor Wu finally pushed the Xiongnu far back to their steppe, but it took him three decades to achieve that goal, and it inevitably exhausted the national resources.[50] Although the threat from the Xiongnu was eased after Emperor Wu's successful campaigns, troubles with the Qiang, who resided between the Hexi Corridor and the Tibetan Plateau, plagued the Chinese during the entire Eastern Han period.[51] The Xiaotangshan and the Zouxian carvings were both produced in the Eastern Han, but they did not ostensibly depict the current reality of battles with the Qiang; rather, they portrayed the old memory of conflicts with the Xiongnu. It seems fair to say that this is partly because the visual formula invented when the Xiongnu were the greatest threat to the Han Empire remained the most compelling expression of the cultural significance of the Great Wall: a pounded-earth construction that, while pictorially invisible, exercised an inescapable structuring force.

In the Han mind, then, the Great Wall was both the territorial boundary that marked off China from the lands of the Xiongnu and the cultural boundary that separated civilization from barbarism. The pictorial formula seen in the Xiaotangshan and Zouxian carvings expresses this dichotomy. The multistoried buildings represented civilized China, an agricultural society whose people "dwelled in houses and wore hats and girdles." The mountains symbolized the barbaric Xiongnu, whose people lived a nomadic existence and "wielded the bow and arrow." The battle that took place between the buildings and the mountain signified the inevitable conflict between the two sides: the nomadic Xiongnu forever coveted the rich products of its southern neighbor, while the agricultural Chinese strove to fend off forays by its bellicose enemy. The depiction of a Chinese victory was wishful thinking, however. At any rate, the absence of the Great Wall in the pictorial formula did not stop the carvings from conveying what the presence of the Great Wall meant in the Han world.

Notes

1. The length of the present Great Wall, built in the Ming Dynasty, is controversial. Here I use the figure given by Luo Zhewen 羅哲文: 7,300 km (4,536 miles).

See Luo Zhewen, *Changcheng* 長城 (The Great Wall) (Beijing: Qinghua University Press, 2008), 68.

2. Gao Minglu has tackled issues surrounding the Great Wall in twentieth-century Chinese art in his exhibition catalog, *The Wall: Reshaping Contemporary Chinese Art* (Buffalo, NY: Albright-Knox Art Gallery & University at Buffalo Art Gallery, 2005), 191–207. However, he did not pay attention to two key figures, Liu Kuiling and Zhao Wangyun, whose works I will discuss in length in this paper.

3. Romyn Hitchcock, "The Great Wall of China," *The Century Illustrated Monthly Magazine* 45, no. 3 (1893): 327–32.

4. William Edgar Geil, *The Great Wall of China* (New York: Sturgis & Walton, 1909).

5. Lillian Lan-ying Tseng, "Between Printing and Rubbing: Chu Jun's Illustrated Catalogues of Ancient Monuments in Eighteenth-Century China," in *Reinventing the Past: Archaism and Antiquarianism in Chinese Art and Visual Culture*, ed. Wu Hung (Chicago: Paragon Books, 2010), 269–71.

6. The earliest such example known to us is the rubbing of the *Inscription on a Hot Spring*, written by Emperor Taizong of the Tang dynasty (r. 626–649) and transferred onto a stele in 628. Retrieved from the Cave Library in Dunhuang, the rubbing had been rearranged as a nine-inch-high hand scroll and had a colophon dated to 653. Shimonaka Yasaburo 下中彌三郎, *Shodō zenshū* 書道全集 (The complete collection of calligraphy). 10 vols. (Tokyo: Heibonsha, 193012), 7: 175, pls. 90–95.

7. Britta Erickson, *Three Installations by Xu Bing* (Madison: Elvehjem Museum of Art, University of Wisconsin–Madison, 1991), 18–31. For further discussion of the installation, see Gao Minglu, "Meaninglessness and Confrontation in Xu Bing's Art," in *Fragmented Memory: The Chinese Avant-Garde in Exile*, eds. Julia Andrews and Gao Minglu (Columbus: Wexner Center for the Arts, the Ohio State University, 1993), 28–31; Wu Hung, *Transience: Chinese Experimental Art at the End of the Twentieth Century* (Chicago: The David and Alfred Smart Museum of Art, the University of Chicago, 1999), 31–34.

8. Erickson, *Three Installations by Xu Bing*, 19–20.

9. Modern critics are in awe of Xu's project partly because his team made rubbings of the tower on wooden scaffolds forty to forty-five feet off the ground; but the vertical challenge in a gentle, open terrain may not have intimidated early artisans. After all, artisans in the eighteenth century produced rubbings of the twenty inscriptions of the Longmen Grottos on steep walls as high as eleven feet in a narrow cave with a small entrance. They also made rubbings of the *Hymn of the Western Passage* incised on a cliff ten feet above dangerous torrents pouring through a deep gorge.

10. Erickson, *Three Installations by Xu Bing*, 10–17; Robert E. Harrist, "*Book from the Sky* at Princeton: Reflections on Scale, Sense, and Sound," in *Persistence/Transformation: Text as Image in the Art of Xu Bing*, eds. Jerome Silbergeld and Dora Ching (Princeton, NJ: P. Y. and Kinmay W. Tang Center for East Asian Art, 2005), 25–45.

11. For just a sample of traditional poems treating the Great Wall, see *Changcheng cidian* 長城詞典 (Dictionary of the Great Wall), eds. Lin Yan 林岩 and Li Yiran 李益然 (Shanghai: Wenhui, 1999), 346–563. It introduces 26 poems from the Qin to the

Southern and Northern Dynasties, 91 poems in the Sui and the Tang, 66 poems from the Five Dynasties to the Yuan, 58 poems in the Ming, and 61 poems in the Qing.

12. Arthur Waldron, *The Great Wall of China* (Cambridge, UK: Cambridge University Press, 1990), 144–45.

13. Ibid., 198.

14. Liu Jianping 劉建平 and Liu Zheng, eds., *Liu Kuiling huaji* 劉奎齡畫集 (Collected paintings of Liu Kuiling) (Tianjin: Tianjin renmin meishu, 1995), vol. 2, pl. 15.

15. Ibid., pl. 22.

16. Ginger Cheng-chi Hsü, *A Bushel of Pearls: Painting for Sale in Eighteenth-Century Yangchow* (Stanford, CA: Stanford University Press, 2001), 218–23.

17. Liu and Liu, eds., *Liu Kuiling huaji*, vol. 2, pl. 81.

18. Liu and Liu, eds., *Liu Kuiling huaji*, vol. 1, pl. 25.

19. Johannes Nieuhof, *Embassy from the East-India Company of the United Provinces, to the Grand Tartar Cham, Emperour of China* (London: Printed by John Macock for the author, 1669), 101. Its Dutch version was first published in Amsterdam in 1665.

20. Waldron, *The Great Wall of China*, Fig. 9a.

21. Thomas Allom, *China, in a Series of Views, Displaying the Scenery, Architecture, and Social Habits, of that Ancient Empire* (London: Fisher, Son, & Co., 1843), 29–33.

22. For further discussion of the Western interest in the Great Wall, see Waldron, *The Great Wall of China*, 203–14.

23. Jingye High School was established by Yan Xiu (1860–1929) and Zhang Boling (1876–1951), who later established Nankai University. Having denounced the civil exam even before its abolishment, Yan Xiu was famous for advocating modern education. He recruited Zhang Boling, who was trained first at the Academy of Beiyang Fleet in Tianjin and later at St. John's University in Shanghai, to promote Western academic disciplines. They both went to Japan in 1904 to inspect the development of modern education and together founded Jingye High School that year when they came back. Jingye High School, also called Tianjin First High School, lasted about two years before the campus was moved to Nankai, where it became known as Nankai High School. Gao Lingwen 高凌雯 et al., eds., *Yan Xiu xiansheng nianpu* 嚴修先生年譜 (Mr. Yan Xiu's chronological biography) (Ji'nan: Qilu shushe, 1990); Zheng Zhiguang 鄭致光 et al., eds., *Zhang Boling zhuan* 張伯苓傳 (The biography of Zhang Boling) (Tianjin: Tianjin renmin, 1989).

24. He Yanzhe 何延喆 and Qi Jue 齊珏, *Liu Kuiling* 劉奎齡 (Shijiazhuang: Hebei jiaoyu, 2003), 24–28.

25. Cécile and Michel Beurdeley, *Giuseppe Castiglione: A Jesuit Painter at the Court of the Chinese Emperors*, trans. Michael Bullock (Rutland, VT: C. E. Tuttle Co., 1972).

26. Liu and Liu, eds., *Liu Kuiling huaji*, vol. 1, pl. 25.

27. Gao Zeyu et al., eds., *Linyu xian zhi* (Gazetteer of Linyu County) (1929). The Great Wall was portrayed in the seven pictures of the border towns in the beginning volume. The Shanhai Pass, the east end of the Great Wall, was then in Linyu County.

28. Wang Yushan 王玉山 et al. eds., *Shi Lu* 石魯 (Beijing: Renmin meishu, 1996), 16; Gao Minglu, *The Wall*, 194.

29. For more visual depictions of the Great Wall during the Sino-Japanese war, see Gao, *The Wall*, 192–94.

30. Wang Fu 王輔, *Rijun qinhua zhanzheng* 日軍侵華戰爭 (1931–1945) (Japanese aggressions and wars against China) (Shenyang: Liaoning renmin, 1990), 1:294–316. The area was not stabilized until much later. Public transportation resumed in the summer of 1934. Postal communication returned to normal at the beginning of 1935.

31. Lillian Lan-ying Tseng, "Tuxiang zaixian yu lishi shuxie: Zhao Wangyun lianzai yu Dagong bao de nongcun xiesheng tongxin" 圖像再現與歷史書寫：趙望雲連載與大公報的農村寫生通信 (Pictorial representation and historical writing: Zhao Wangyun's visual reports on rural north China for *L'Impartial*), in *Huazhong you hua: jindai Zhongguo de shijue biaoshu yu wenhua goutu* 畫中有話：近代中國的視覺表述與文化構圖 (Visual representation and cultural mapping in modern China), ed. Ke-wu Huang 黃克武 (Taipei: Institute of Modern History, Academia Sinica, 2003), 63–122; republished in *Zhongguo xiangcun yanjiu* 中國鄉村研究, no. 3 (2005): 152–230.

32. For an account of the fighting at Luowenyu, see Guoshiguan shiliaochu 國史館史料處, ed., *Changcheng zhanyi* 長城戰役 (Battles along the Great Wall) (Taipei: Guoshiguan, 1980), 243–47.

33. Zhao Wangyun 趙望雲, Yang Ruquan 楊汝泉, and Feng Yuxiang 馮玉祥, *Zhao Wangyun saishang xiesheng ji* 趙望雲塞上寫生集 (Collection of Zhao Wangyun's sketches from the northern frontier) (Tianjin: Dagong bao, 1934), 18.

34.Ibid., 15–16.

35. For Qing's conquest of Mongolia, see Peter C. Perdue, *China Marches West: The Qing Conquest of Central Eurasia* (Cambridge, MA: Belknap Press of Harvard University Press, 2005), 133–73.

36. For discussion of the modern Chinese positive attitude toward the Great Wall, see Waldron, *The Great Wall of China*, 214–226; Arthur Waldron, "The 'Great Wall of China': An Author's Reflections after Twenty Years," in *Chinese Walls in Time and Space*, eds. Roger des Forges et al. (Ithaca, NY: Cornell University, 2009), 27–28.

37. Zhao, Yang, and Feng, *Zhao Wangyun saishang xiesheng ji*, 17.

38. Tseng, "Tuxiang zaixian yu lishi shuxie," 106–14.

39. Chahar Province no longer existed after 1949. It was merged into Hebei Province and the Inner Mongolia Autonomous Region. The Zhangjia Opening is now in Hebei Province.

40. Feng Yuxiang, *Feng Yuxiang huiyi lu* 馮玉祥回憶錄 (A memoir by Feng Yuxiang) (Shanghai: Wenhua, 1949), 30–36; James E. Sheridan, *Chinese Warlord: The Career of Feng Yü-hsiang* (Stanford, CA: Stanford University Press, 1966), 268–76.

41. Zhao, Yang, and Feng, *Zhao Wangyun saishang xiesheng ji*, 40–47.

42. Tian Haiyong, "Wode fuqin Tian Han yu Nie Er de zhandou youqing" 我的父親田漢與聶耳的戰鬥友情 (The wartime friendship between Nie Er and my father Tian Han), in *Tian Han: jinian Tian Han tongzhi dansheng bashiwu zhounian* 田漢：紀念田漢同志誕生八十五週年 (Tian Han: in commemoration of Tian Han's eighty-fifth birthday), ed. 中國人民政治協商會議委員會 (Chinese People's Political Consultative Standing Committee) (Beijing: Wenshi ziliao, 1985), 121–28.

43. Ban Gu 班固, *Han shu* 漢書 (Standard history of the Former Han) (Beijing: Zhonghua shuju, 1962), 69a.3872.

44. For the Han construction of the Great Wall, see Luo Zhewen, *Changcheng*, 47–58.

45. Sima Qian 司馬遷, *Shi ji* 史記 (Record of the Grand Historian) (Beijing: Zhonghua shuju, 1959), 110.2902–3; Ban Gu, *Han shu*, 94a.3762–63. Translation from Burton Watson, *Records of the Grand Historian of China* (New York: Columbia University Press, 1961), 2:173.

46. Ban Gu, *Han shu*, 94b.3810, 3818–19.

47. Fan Ye 范曄, *Hou Han shu* 後漢書 (Standard history of the Later Han) (Beijing: Zhonghua shuju, 1965), 90.2992.

48. For information about the shrine and its carvings, see Luo Zhewen, "Xiaotangshan Guo shi mu shici" (The Guo stone shrine at Xiaotangshan), *Wenwu* 文物 1961.4/5: 44–51; Xia Chaoxiong, "Xiaotangshan shici huaxiang niandai ji zhuren shitan" (A preliminary study of the date of the stone carvings in the Xiaotangshan shrine and its owner), *Wenwu* 1984.8: 34–39. For research on the motif of Hu-Han combats, see Xing Yitian, "Han dai huaxiang Hu Han zhanzheng tu de goucheng, leixing yu yiyi" 漢代畫像胡漢戰爭圖的構成, 類型, 與意義 (Meaning, typology, and composition of the depiction of Hu-Han combats in the Han Dynasty), *Taida meishushi yanjiu jikan* 臺大美術史研究 no. 19 (2005): 63–132.

49. Shandong sheng bowuguan 山東省博物館 et al., eds., *Shandong Han huaxiang shi xuanji* 山東漢畫像石選集 (Selected Han carved stones in Shandong) (Ji'nan: Qilu shushe, 1982), 20, fig. 102.

50. For the Han and Xiongnu conflicts, see Nicola di Cosmo, *Ancient China and Its Enemies: The Rise of Nomadic Power in East Asian History* (Cambridge, UK: Cambridge University Press, 2002), 161–252.

51. For the Han and Qiang conflicts, see Ying-shih Yü, "Han Foreign Relations," in *The Cambridge History of China*, Vol. 1, *The Ch'in and Han Empires, 221 B.C.–A.D. 220*, eds. Denis Twitchett and Michael Loewe (Cambridge, UK: Cambridge University Press), 422–35.

The Languages of Synecdoche

11

Synecdoche of the Imaginary

STEPHEN OWEN

Zhao Zhixin's 趙執信 (1662–1744) "Discussion on Dragons," *Tan long lu* 談龍錄, begins with an exchange that gives the little book its name:

> Hong Sheng (1645–1704) 洪昇 of Qiantang had long been a follower of Wang Shizhen 王士禛 (1634–1711) of Xincheng and was a friend of mine. One day we were all together discussing poetry at the residence of the Minister of Justice [Wang Shizhen]. Hating the lack of structure in contemporary work, Hong Sheng said: "A poem is just like a dragon, with head, tail, claws, horns, scales and fins. If any one of these is missing, it is not a dragon." Wang Shizhen scoffed at this and said: "A poem is like the divine dragon. When you see its head, you don't see its tail. Sometimes only a claw or a scale is revealed in the clouds—how can you ever get the whole body. What you are talking about is for carvers or painters."
>
> I said: "The divine dragon expands and contracts in its transformations and has no fixed form at all. Those who gaze and see it in a blur only can point to one scale or one claw, yet the dragon's head and tail are complete, thus it is there right before you. If one is restricted to what one sees, one thinks the dragon is entire in these parts, even carvers and painters will have cause to refute you."[1]

This famous debate on poetic representation begs the question of whether any of these three famous writers actually believed in the empirical existence of dragons.[2] This makes it a most unusual metaphor for poetic representation, a peculiar fictionality whose existential status is guaranteed by blurred and partial appearance. It is certain, however, that these men did believe in clouds. Clouds and the blur of transformation were, moreover, necessary to make the dragon "appear" more perfectly than the patently mimetic art of the carver or sculptor. This parable of poetic representation is not really about dragons; it is about clouds, which I will join with other nebulous forms of *qi* 氣 that occlude vision—mist, fog, haze, misty rain, cloud, and so on.

If you look up "fog" (*wu* 霧) in the medieval "encyclopedia" (*leishu* 類書), you will find a topic much like others, and one that was not particularly popular. In the Six Dynasties and early Tang, fog and mist seem to have had no particular poetic charge. By the ninth century, however, the "nebulous" had become a quintessentially poetic signifier. In later centuries the evocative commonplace was translated into painting to produce what was, I believe, a unique visual idiom in which part and sometimes most of the painting was washed over to create a blur, or simply left blank to signify visual erasure of something notionally present.

The Play of Absence and Presence

I do not know when and how "thick *qi*" acquired its poetic charge, but the process was clearly underway in the poems of Wang Wei 王維 (701–760), as in his famous exchange with Pei Di 裴迪 (b. 716).

"At Wangkou Meeting Rain and Recalling South Mountain, Thus I Presented This to Wang Wei"[3]
裴迪, 輞口遇雨憶終南山因獻王維

Continuous rain obscures the deserted bends,
from the level sands the drifting glitter vanishes.
The Wang's waters go on and on,
but where now is South Mountain?

積雨晦空曲　　平沙滅浮彩
輞水去悠悠　　南山復何在。

Wang Wei, "Answering Pei Di"[4]
王維, 答裴迪

Darkly flooding, the cold stream broadens,
gray-green, the autumn rain obscures.

You ask about South Mountain—
in my mind I know it lies beyond the white clouds.

淼淼寒流廣　蒼蒼秋雨晦
君問終南山　心知白雲外

The exchange is clearly underwritten by Buddhism, in which all sensuous percepts are in the mind; but Wang Wei's response, affirming the massive presence of the invisible mountain through mind, is something of the negative image of Buddhist ideology. The flooding stream, fed by rain on the mountain, is evidence of the mountain's continued existence; but Wang Wei calls the absent mountain into presence through mind. The title, apparently given by Pei Di, uses the word *yi* 憶, translated as "recalls," thinking back fondly, often nostalgically on something or someone absent. Here, as in other forms of *yi*, an absence to the empirical senses makes it all the more effectively present to the mind.

Though it lacks the intimacy of ninth-century poetic mist, Wang Wei's "About to Set Sail Where the Yangzi Meets the Han" 漢江臨汎 is an early case of visual half presence.[5] If South Mountain was visually erased in his poetic exchange with Pei Di, here mind brings the mountain (or mountains) back into half presence:

The River flows out beyond Heaven and Earth,
the mountain's colors, between being there and not.

江流天地外　山色有無中

As we often see later, a scene of visual clarity is paired with a scene of misty blurring. The open space, the scene of the river, extends to the horizon and speculatively beyond. As in later painting, the mountain does not have a *xing* 形, a delineated shape corresponding to line drawing, but is rather a *se* 色, a faint color space without sharp demarcation of its borders. Even that color space is uncertain, hanging between presence and absence. By naming it "the *mountain's* color space," the mind affirms the presence of a known object, even though the claim of the line is that its presence is uncertain. The hidden mountain of the earlier quatrain is partially appearing, its identity confirmed by mind rather than the uncertain senses.

The relation between hiddenness and meaning is one way to think of "literariness" in the Chinese tradition. I take this image of "thick *qi*" as a way to suggest the relation between representations and theory, a link that returns as a metaphor in the passage from the Zhao Zhixin passage above.

In their discussions of the "Yinxiu" 隱秀 (latent and out-standing) chapter of *Wenxin diaolong* 文心雕龍, scholars tend to be more interested in the "hidden" *yin*, and don't quite know what to do with the fully transparent, hypervisible *xiu*. Wang Wei's famous couplet above reminds us that Chinese literature works through the binary, in contrast with our disposition toward the "hidden," our local cultural version of the literary, "saying one thing and meaning another." The second line ("the mountain's colors, between being there and not") depends on the first, and also on the visual movement from openness to blockage of vision, a blockage that blurs into the uncertain presence of massive physical form. Like enlightenment, the couplet marks a shift of attention that is a significant event—but the significance lies in the shift and not in the single line of hiddenness. If the lines are reversed, the movement of attention is likewise reversed. We will see this movement, from *xiu* (the hyper-visible) to *yin* (the hidden), in Du Mu's 杜牧 (803–ca. 853) "Spring in the Southland," though in a less philosophically inflected way.

Mist can completely hide things, but more often, as with the dragon, it half-hides things, lending force by semiconcealment. Poetic mist is a cliché, but every cliché invites an archeology, to uncover the promise that was so compelling that it generated an excess of reproduction.

As is clear from Zhao Zhixin's account of his discussion with Hong Sheng and Wang Shizhen, mist is the ground of visual synecdoche, the part representing or embodying the whole. In the language of visual arts, with its terms "figure" and "ground," mist makes it possible for the secondary ground to erase the primary ground. Images are detached from their totality. The early modern European painter will often fill his canvas with tiny details far in the background to situate the figure in a complete, contiguous world, achieving with the brush what even the eye could not clearly see. Chinese painters too sometimes represented distant detail, but often erased the majority of the scene in mist and cloud so that the eye was drawn to the detail as an isolate rather than part of a contiguous whole.

In Tang imperial geography, where the whole land was mapped, inventoried, administratively partitioned, crisscrossed by post stations to facilitate desired movement and checked by barriers and authorizing officials to impede undesired movement, mist may even have had political as well as poetical significance. Misty scenes poetically resist imperial space, where everything is illuminated and perspicuous. The capital is *rixia* 日下, "beneath the sun" of the imperial presence that both "illuminates" and "comprehends," *ming* 明, the world. On reaching Chengdu, Du Fu's patron Yan Wu, invites his underlings to a party to look at maps of the region; cartography is control. Figures who withdraw from public life, however, habitually go off into the "misty waves," *yanbo* 煙波, or into the "mists and auroras," *yanxia* 煙霞. It is difficult to tax misty geography; it is not clear how one gets from "here" to "there"; one often gets lost, which is a motif of the poetry of mist. The government cannot regulate movement there; people disappear from the public eye.

While darkness simply erases space, mist attenuates the visible world, which gradually recedes into invisibility. Unlike darkness, mist articulates depth, allowing percepts not only to recede into invisibility but also to emerge. When Wang Wei does his version of the ultimate space outside the perspicuous polity, "Ballad of Peach Blossom Spring" 桃源行, the first thing the fisherman sees after going through the cave is misty trees: "Afar he looked at a place where trees massed with cloud" 遙看一處攢雲樹.[6] Only upon nearer approach does he find people, and at the end of the poem, when he tries to return to the idyllic community, all he sees are trees in the clouds.

That process by which things gradually appear in the mist as one grows closer and attenuate as one gets farther may help explain why things of the past (so often treated in terms of spatial "distance") are so often shrouded in mist. In recent years scholars have taken up the question of ruins, whose aesthetic played such a prominent role in the European tradition. There aren't many ruins in Chinese poetry, but old sites tend to appear in the mist, either as muted presences or uncertain absences. Mist operates in the visible world much as Nature works in the tangible world: integrals dilapidate and fade away or appear in pieces.

Du Mu was very much a poet of mists, which figure in some of his most famous poems.

Du Mu, "Spring in the Southland: A Quatrain"[7]
杜牧, 江南春絕句

For a thousand leagues orioles sing, green half-hides the red,
river hamlets, mountain towns, wind on the tavern banners.
Four hundred and eighty temples of the Southern Dynasties,
how many towers and terraces in the misty rain?

千里鶯啼綠映紅　　水村山郭酒旗風
南朝四百八十寺　　多少樓臺煙雨中

Within this thousand *li* of Jiangnan are the expected generic markers of spring—orioles everywhere, the green of leaves against the red of flowers. *Ying* 映, translated here as "half-hides," is a good visual foil for the blurring of mist; *ying* juxtaposes two phenomena, such that each illuminates the other through (rather than despite) their overlapping. Such juxtaposition is often an overlap, by which one thing is "half-hidden" by the other, as is the case here with the growing leaves partially hiding the last spring flowers. It has its "mountains," *shan* 山, and its "waters," *shui* 水, with dwellings everywhere.

The whole opening couplet, however, with its empirically impossible clarity of vision, is only a foil for the ending. In the third line, the past and book knowledge enter his vision, as the poet invokes the number of temples built in the Southern Dynasties. When a poet spends an entire seven-syllable line of a four-line poem giving the exact number, that poetic act foregrounds the number, making it far more definite than his vague "thousand *li*." The generic becomes specific, and measuring book knowledge against the scene in the mind's eye provokes the question "how many?" Faced with the problem of knowledge, Du Mu washes over the bright and breezy scene of the opening couplet with misty rain, hiding the answer. Some temples may vaguely appear in the misty rain, while others might not. He invokes these blurred and ghostly presences from the past to save us from having to measure the present against the book knowledge of what once was.

This poem cannot be dated. In good Chinese historical fashion, knowledge of the date could be crucial to reading the poem. If the poem dates from the spring of 846 or later, it follows the suppression of Buddhism in the Huichang reign of Wuzong, which saw the large-scale dissolution of the Buddhist establishment and the destruction of most of the temples in the empire. As prefect of Chizhou, Du Mu himself would have had to oversee the closing—and often physical dismantling—of the temples in his prefecture. In this context Du Mu's evocation of the old temples of the Southern Dynasties and the question "how many?" would have an edge—those temples are destroyed, or in ruins, or their remaining quarters have been sparsely repopulated when the edict was revoked after Wuzong's death. The ability to clearly see all the temples is the ability to count them with precision, to register them, and thus the ability to destroy them; they exist in the emperor's vision. There are, in any case, no longer four hundred and eighty temples. What history has erased Du Mu calls back poetically into half-presence, protectively misted over.

I began with Zhao Zhixin to suggest that such scenes are not simply emotive decoration, but have something essential to do with poetic representation, how the poet brings things into presence "poetically." If we return to the opposition between *yin* 隱 and *xiu* 秀, Du Mu starts off with a hypervisible *xiu* scene of the present, eternally recurring spring in Jiangnan. Then, in the second couplet, we have an ostensibly literal *yin* which is also a figurative *yin*, the history that makes loss possible, the erasure of the past, and its poetic restoration as neither entirely present nor entirely lost—existing ambiguously in the misty rain.

Let me return to an old argument that Pauline Yu and I made a long time ago in different ways. Chinese representations tend to synecdoche. They may be conventionally metaphorical, but their status as synecdoche bears the weight of interest. The dragon produced by the painter or carver may represent the emperor. The dragon fragmentarily emerging in cloud, the version of poetic representation supported by Wang Shizhen and Zhao Zhixin, may also represent the emperor, but all interest is focused on how it appears. The efficacy and adequacy of the representation is the question, not whether the dragon does or does not represent the emperor.

The flash of a claw in the clouds—did I see a dragon or did I not? A color space seen wandering in the misty rain—is that one of the temples of the Southern Dynasties or not? The misty scene is not more "poetic" than the sunlit vistas, as when Wang Wei's eyes follow the river to the horizon and out "beyond Heaven and Earth" or when Du Mu sees spring over all the Southland in the mind's eye. Mist, however, reserves space and the things it contains from the hard light of imperial vision.

Du Mu found one of those 480 temples in the mist in Xuanzhou—clearly before the Huichang suppression of Buddhism. It was designated as a "Kaiyuan temple," of which there were a great many spread through the empire, but an old note—presumably by Du Mu himself—identifies it as having been founded in the Eastern Jin. Du Mu's poems are often not empirically coherent scenes; the couplets are snapshots put together into a collage. The way mist and rain are used in the collage is interesting.

Du Mu, "The Kaiyuan Temple in Xuanzhou"[8]
杜牧, 題宣州開元寺

Xie Tiao's tower of the Southern Dynasties,
the most remote spot in eastern Wu.
The fallen dynasty, gone like a swan,
the temple left behind, hidden in a misty vale.
The tower flies up ninety feet,
a porch rings it with four hundred columns.
Between the high heights and lowest depths
the breeze winds round pine and cassia.
Green mosses shine on red pavilions,
white birds talk to each other in pairs.
The creek's sounds enter the dreams of monks,
the moon's color glows on plaster walls.
I view the scenes, regardless of dawn and evening,

leaning on a railing, past and present is here.
A cup of ale makes me linger
watching spring rain in the mountains ahead.

南朝謝朓樓　　東呉最深處
亡國去如鴻　　遺寺藏煙塢
樓飛九十尺　　廊環四百柱
高高下下中　　風繞松桂樹
青苔照朱閣　　白鳥兩相語
溪聲入僧夢　　月色暉粉堵
閱景無旦夕　　憑欄有今古
留我酒一樽　　前山看春雨

Couplet collage is itself like mist. If many poems are unified by a sequence of percepts representing linear experience through synecdoche, collage breaks the pieces apart and rearranges them in ways that resist an experientially linear reading. In the penultimate couplet Du Mu thematizes collage, with dawn and evening views thrown together, past and present existing together. Even here, however, we must start out from imperial geography in order to leave it. Du Mu begins by "identifying" the temple in the title, in the attached note, and in the opening lines naming it by its poet, its period, and location. At last it is located on the very margin of imperial space, "the most remote spot."

The second couplet, with its dazzling simile, removes the past like a bird taking flight. The dynasty (or dynasties) flies off, leaving a temple in the mist. The scene here is one of approach, discovering what is hidden. In the rest of the poem, the poet is present in the temple, looking from it rather than toward it. In place of the horizontal space of imperial geography and discovery, we have vertical space, "the high heights and lowest depths." Within temple space there is communication—of breeze, moonlight, and sound, a collage of scenes and moments, until the end with the poet lingering there, ale in hand, gazing out—not gazing at any of the scenes of preceding couplets but gazing into the blur of the rain.

The Boat in the Mist

The viewer may look into misty space with the thought that something is hidden and may emerge. Mist was gathering its poetic charge in the second half of the eighth century.

Sikong Shu, "Huangzi Embankment"[9]
司空曙, 黃子陂

Fragrant plants on the shore, dawn of spring colors,
light on the water grows faint in the evening sun.
In the deep mist, which is so quiet and still,
the fishing boat does not return by night.

岸芳春色曉　　水影夕陽微
寂寂深煙裏　　漁舟夜不歸

The clear scene of the first couplet marks the interval of daytime; the presence of mist suggests time continues, confirmed by "night" in the last line. The time sequence implicit in the percepts implies a subject who looks at the water continuously, though we do not know what he or she is looking for. The melancholy stillness of the third line is the ground for the possibility of sound that would announce the return of the fishing boat in the darkness.

The real question is: since the darkness of night is adequate for the basic thematics of the poem, what is the function of adding "in the deep mist?" Let me suggest that while the rest of the poem is made up of empirical signifiers, the "deep mist," while not at all empirically impossible, functions as a purely poetic signifier, creating a three-dimensional space within which the boat could potentially emerge.

This brings us to another boat that might emerge in the mist, even after more than a millennium. The story is well known. Fan Li 范蠡 (fl. fifth c.) was the architect of the king of Yue's revenge on the kingdom of Wu. He sent the beautiful Xi Shi 西施 to the king of Wu, whose infatuation made her a literal *qingguo* 傾國, "toppler of kingdoms." After the kingdom of Wu was destroyed, the king of Yue offered Fan Li great rewards. Fan Li refused these, instead setting sail as a wanderer in the lakes region. Some versions of the story have him taking Xi Shi with him.[10] In some versions he became an immortal.

If figures in the mist can link past and present, then Fan Li on his boat on the misty lakes is a possible presence, a possible absence, and a poetic figure of desire for someone who wants to go off and leave the world. To imagine his boat still out there, drifting in Tang Dynasty mist, unites the power of mist to link past and present and a route to leave perspicuous imperial space. Fan Li's boat in the mist recurs with some frequency in the second quarter of the ninth century. Poets were obviously reading one another, though with undatable poems we cannot say who is emulating whom.

Zhang Hu (fl. 853), "Meditation on the Past at Songjiang"[11]
張祜, 松江懷古

Emerald trees, Wu's isles afar,
green mountains, Thunder Marsh remote.
No one can follow the tracks of Fan Li—
in twilight misty waters engulfing.

碧樹吳洲遠　青山震澤深
無人蹤范蠡　煙水暮沈沈

The movement from clear scenes to mist is so frequent that it deserves some reflection, however much it may, in some cases, be an empirical function of the local weather. If Fan Li were out sailing in the perspicuous scene of the first couplet, we could find him. According to the suggestion of the poem, the reason we cannot follow him is the scene of misty waters at twilight. If one set out to find him in the first couplet, one would be visible in the far distance; if one set out at twilight, one too would disappear.

Variations on this poem recur in the poetry of the period. The eyes that can see a single egret flying over thousands of acres of the richest farmland in the empire become lost in the mist when they look for Fan Li:

Wen Tingyun (812–ca. 870), "The South Crossing at Lizhou"[12]
溫庭筠, 利州南度

Still and empty waters face the sinking glow of the sun,
a vast expanse of winding isles touching the azure haze.
A horse whinnies over the waves, I watch the oars depart,
beside the willows people are gone, I await the boat's return;
several clumps of plants in the sand, a flock of gulls scatters.
Over thousands of acres of river fields a single egret flies,
Who is able to take a boat and seek out Fan Li?—
in misty waters on the Five Lakes, alone free of motive.

澹然空水對斜暉　曲島蒼茫接翠微
波上馬嘶看櫂去　柳邊人歇待船歸
數叢沙草群鷗散　萬頃江田一鷺飛
誰解乘舟尋范蠡　五湖煙水獨忘機

Few poems so perfectly enact the movement from clarity to misty occlusion than this poem framed with "empty waters" in the first line and "misty waters" in the final line.

The link between mist and being "free of motive" deserves some reflection and brings us back to poetics. If poetry is *yan zhi* 言志, "saying what is intently on one's mind," then it is the very antithesis of freedom from motive.[13] In the perspicuous world of light, everything is open to motive; lost in the mist, unable to locate yourself, you can only arrive somewhere by chance. Fan Li broke the cycle by refusing reward and going away. Wen Tingyun proposes to seek him out, but that departure means entering the mist where one can neither be found nor find another. Finding Fan Li is a motive, but in the mist the discovery of the ancient statesman-recluse can only be by accident.

This prepares us for the great Fan Li poem, again by Du Mu. We thought that, from the earlier poem, the Kaiyuan temple in Xuanzhou was isolated. Actually it was not. There were people all around.

Du Mu, "On the Water Tower of the Kaiyuan Temple in Xuanzhou: below the tower is Wan Creek, with people living on both sides"[14]
杜牧, 題宣州開元寺水閣閣下宛溪夾溪居人

Cultural works of the Six Dynasties, plants stretching to the sky,[15]
the heavens calm, clouds at ease, the same in present and past.
Birds go off, birds come, in the colors of the mountain,
people sing and people weep in the sound of the waters.
Deep in autumn, curtains, rain on a thousand homes,
in the setting sun terrace and tower, a single flute in the wind.
Depressed that I have no way to meet Fan Li—
scattered unevenly, misty trees west of the five lakes.

六朝文物草連空　　天澹雲閒今古同
鳥去鳥來山色裏　　人歌人哭水聲中
.深秋簾幕千家雨　　落日樓臺一笛風
惆悵無因見范蠡　　參差煙樹五湖東

Here is the same technique of collage as in "The Kaiyuan Temple in Xuanzhou"; but instead of a serene, enclosed world of beauty, here the couplets stress the ground of sameness on which human changes occur—laughing, weeping, and eventually returning to the earth and the "plants stretching to the sky." This variation is punctuated by the sound of a flute, which leads to thoughts of Fan Li and a scene of the five lakes in the mind's eye, trees in the mist—or perhaps one of them is a mast.

By this point it should be clear that Fan Li in the mist of the five lakes had become something of an icon in the poetry of the second quarter of the ninth century. We should add one more in Xu Hun's peculiar impressionistic style.

Xu Hun, "Passing By Eastgrove Temple on Mount Lu"[16]
許渾, 經行廬山東林寺

The soul of one parted, on and off, wilderness by the river in Chu,
leaves tumbling, just reddened, sky of the tenth month.
On the purple lanes many concerns, hard to count them all,[17]
green mountains are always here, good for sleeping in peace.
Still scurrying in the capital, hoping to get a salary,
I never found an empty hall to learn to sit in meditation.
If someday it could work out that I be like Fan Li,
then I too would certainly go off into the mist of the five lakes.

離魂斷續楚江壖　　葉墜初紅十月天
紫陌事多難數悉　　青山長在好閑眠
方趨上國期幹祿　　未得空堂學坐禪
他歲若教如范蠡　　也應須入五湖煙

Mist is the last word in the poem, the space into which the poet dreams of disappearing, once he has achieved his hopes of public life. One leaves this world, the hopes and perils of public life, the laughter and weeping, and heads off into the misty waves.

The Mist of Jinling

We cannot entirely ignore the possibility that in the history of global climate, Jinling, the Tang term for the old city of Jiankang, the capital of the Southern Dynasties, was particularly misty in the ninth century. If, however, mist is a poetic signifier, then its special association with scenes of Jinling may have some significance. Unlike the misty five lakes, which made it possible for Fan Li and later hopefuls to leave public life, to disappear and perhaps become immortal, the mist of Jinling is melancholy, inscribed with vanished splendor.

Let us recall first the tendency of poets to begin with a scene of vast perspicuity, then to present a scene hidden in mist. Second, let us recall the political dimension of mist, its capacity to create a space of hiddenness outside imperial perspicuity. If we map those two principles onto history, we have Jinling, with its dynasties that flew off like swans, leaving places in the mist. The misty scene is thus both outside the present imperial order and the remnant of a lost imperial order (keeping in mind that in the Tang the succession of legitimate dynasties passed through the North, rather than, as now, the South).

Once Jinling had been a site of power. Legend had it that its "royal atmosphere," *wangqi* 王氣, was such that an anxious Qin Shihuang 秦始皇, the First Emperor, had the Qinhuai River dug so that this aura could drain away. When the famous minister of the Shu-Han kingdom, Zhuge Liang 諸葛亮 (181–234), saw it as the capital of Wu, he was reputed to have commented that Zhong Mountain was a "dragon coiling," and the Rock, Shitou 石頭, the fortress near the Yangzi, was a "tiger crouching."

By Wen Tingyun's time the poetic mistiness of the site was well established, and Wen explained its transformation from power to pathos through a change in the quality of its *qi*.

> Its force, crouching and coiling, after three centuries gone;
> the southland's atmosphere of killing became melancholy mist.[18]
>
> 盤踞勢窮三百年　　朱方殺氣成愁煙・

The "atmosphere of killing," *shaqi* 殺氣, was a rather violent aura to choose for this city of culture and poetry, but Jiankang had been a potent military force, appropriate to the "royal atmosphere" of which Qin Shihuang was warned. That violent energy wore out over the centuries of the Southern Dynasties; that "atmosphere," *qi*, thickened, lost energy, and became mist. By Wen Tingyun's time mist was already potentially melancholy and poetic, but here that quality of melancholy is explained as loss of earlier vigor.

If the space of mist can contain the effective political figure Fan Li, who disappeared long ago, it can also contain a lost, once-vigorous polity. It is a painting of absence, as Wu Rong 吳融 (*jinshi* 889) wrote in the second half of the ninth century (Jianye is Jiankang, Tang Dynasty's Jinling).

> **Wu Rong, "Autumn Colors"**[19]
> 吳融, 秋色
>
> Dyed but not fully dried, painting not yet faded away,
> so hazy, swaying, so deep-set as well.
> Once I went along the road by the walls of Jianye,
> wild creepers and cold mist locked the Six Dynasties in.
>
> 染不成乾畫未銷　　霏霏拂拂又迢迢
> 曾從建業城邊路　　蔓草寒煙鎖六朝

The phrase "locked the Six Dynasties in" gives pause, though it is a characteristically Late Tang locution. How can a visible space "lock in" a historical era? It is easy to amplify: the mist encloses a space where the central events of the Six Dynasties occurred—but to see that space may be to see the past.

Perhaps the most famous of these Jinling poems is one that begins with mist and moonlight, a favorite combination.

Du Mu, "Mooring on the Qinhuai"[20]
杜牧, 泊秦淮

Mist veils the cold waters, moonlight veils the sands,
by night I moored on the Qinhuai near a tavern.
The merchant girl does not understand the bitterness of a ruined kingdom—
across the river still she sings "Flowers in the Rear Courtyard."

煙籠寒水月籠沙　　夜泊秦淮近酒家
商女不知亡國恨　　隔江猶唱後庭花

The moment begins in mist and moonlight, both lighting up the night scene and blurring it, creating a distinct space for the old poetic motif of "when on a boat hearing music in the darkness." In the usual version of this motif the poet either wonders about the feeling and identity of the musician or singer, or, as in Bai Juiyi's (772–846) 白居易 "Ballad of the Pipa" 琵琶行, goes and meets the person. But this is the Qinhuai River in Jinling, where the past is "locked in" by the mist. What he hears is the ghostly return of the past in the famous song "Flowers in the Rear Courtyard" by the Last Ruler of Chen 陳後主 ([Chen Shubao 陳叔寶] 553–604), the song whose sensuality foretold the fall of the dynasty to the Sui and the subsequent obliteration of the city.

The song comes from "across the river," through the moonlit mist. He knows it is a tavern singer, which enables him to deliver the "message" of the poem: to her it is just a sensual song; to him it is a song with a heavy freight of history; if she knew what he knows, she would not sing *this* song. The important word is *you* 猶, "still" singing, the continuity of past and present in this place where the "royal atmosphere" turned into "melancholy mist." That transformation happened after three centuries of Southern power, when the Last Ruler composed this song. Like the "still," the mist connects past and present, calling it back into a half-presence.

A few decades later the poet Luo Yin 羅隱 (833–910) also moored near a tavern on the Qinhuai. The scene does not cohere as well as Du Mu's (mist and strong wind are hard to reconcile), but the mist is there at the beginning, as a poetic signifier for the place so imbued with its past. Luo Yin, too, calls the past back into presence, but in the immaterial spirits (*jingling* 精靈) of its former inhabitants in the moonlight.

Luo Yin, "Mooring By Night at Jinling"[21]
羅隱, 金陵夜泊

Cold mist light and pale by dying clumps of plants,
on this evening at the Qinhuai the rootless tumbleweed halts.
Roosting geese are startled afar by fires where ale is sold,
high up a tangled flock of crows avoids the wind that lowers sails.
From this land has melted the royal aura, the sound of the
 waves swift,[22]
mountains are lined with autumn shadow, outlines of trees bare.
The spirits of the Six Dynasties, the people not to be seen—
thinking it over I'm sure they're here in the bright moonlight.

冷煙輕澹傍衰叢　　此夕秦淮駐斷蓬
棲雁遠驚沽酒火　　亂鴉高避落帆風
地銷王氣波聲急　　山帶秋陰樹影空
六代精靈人不見　　思量應在月明中

Although poets continued to balance perspicuous scenes and misty scenes in the ninth century, the misty scene became the very icon of the "poetic." Fortunately Tang poets often tell us explicitly what is "poetic." We have a late-eighth-century statement from Wei Yingwu 韋應物 (737–ca. 792), who went to visit Censor Wang.

Wei Yingwu, "On My Day Off Going to Visit Censor Wang and Not Finding Him In"[23]
韋應物, 休暇日訪王侍御不遇

Nine days of hustle and bustle, one day of leisure,
I looked for you, didn't find you, and went back home in vain.
Remarkable, how poetic thoughts are clear right to the bone[24]
where your gate faces a cold stream and snow fills the mountains.

九日驅馳一日閑　　尋君不遇又空還
怪來詩思清入骨　　門對寒流雪滿山

This cold, perspicuous scene may be contrasted with what in the 830s or 840s was probably thought to be a "poetic scene."

Yong Tao, "On Recluse Wei's Dwelling Outside the City"[25]
雍陶, 韋處士郊居

The scene of a poem fills the yard, red leaves tossed in wind,
circling stairs a zither's notes, an unseen fountainhead trickling.
Outside your gate a clear evening, colors of autumn grow old,
thousands of strips of cold jade, mist all along the creek.

滿庭詩境飄紅葉　　繞砌琴聲滴暗泉
門外晚晴秋色老　　萬條寒玉一溪煙

The famous statement on poetics and mist is attributed to Dai Shulun 戴叔倫 (732–789) by Sikong Tu 司空圖 (837–908): "The scene given by a poet is like the sun being warm on Indigo Fields and the fine jade there giving off a mist; you can gaze on it but you can't fix it before your eyes" 詩家之景, 如藍田日暖, 良玉生煙, 可望而不可置於眉睫之前也.[26]

Dai Shulun's poetics of mist is mere haze. There is nothing in it but the jade that generates it. It lacks the flash of the dragon claw, the "dragon coiling" that was Mount Zhong by Jinling. The mist was once the "royal atmosphere"; Fan Li, lost in the mist of the Five Lakes, once destroyed the then most powerful kingdom in China, whose ruler was making a bid to be hegemon even as his capital was falling. The dragon may not be real, but it is a necessary possibility, potentially emergent, for the clouds to be more than just shapes of mere cloud.

Notes

1. Zhao Zhixin 趙執信, *Tanlong lu* 談龍錄 (Beijing: Renmin wenxue chubanshe, 1981), 5–6.

2. For a discussion of the passage that leads smoothly from the representation of dragons to the representation of more empirical percepts, see Zhou Zhenfu 周振甫, *Shici lihua* 詩詞例話 (Beijing: Zhongguo qingnian chubanshe, 1962), 12–14.

3. Yang Wensheng 楊文生, ed., *Wang Wei shiji jianzhu* 王維詩集箋注 (Chengdu: Sichuan renmin chubanshe, 2003), 262.

4. Ibid.

5. Ibid., 464–65.

6. Ibid., 61.

7. Feng Jiwu 馮集梧, ed., *Fanchuan shi jizhu* 樊川詩集注 (Beijing: Zhonghua shuju, 1962), 201.

8. Feng Jiwu, *Fanchuan shi jizhu*, 100–1.

9. *Quan Tang shi* 全唐詩 (Beijing: Zhonghua shuju, 1960), 3322.

10. This legend of Fan Li going off with Xi Shi first appears in Du Mu's "Du Qiuniang" 杜秋娘詩. See Feng Jiwu, *Fanchuan shi jihzu*, 35–46. This is the same period in which we find these poems on Fan Li's boat in the mist.

11. Yin Zhanhua 尹占華, ed. *Zhang Hu shiji jiaozhu* 張祜詩集校注 (Chengdu: Ba Shu shushe, 2007), 258–59.

12. Zeng Yi 曾益, et al., eds. *Wen Feiqing shiji jianzhu* 溫飛卿詩集箋注 (Shanghai: Shanghai guji chubanshe, 1980), 80.

13. One can, of course, say that going off into the mist is an "aim," *zhi* 志; but since *zhi* is so commonly associated with political aims for service and advancement, this is the "aim" that negates other "aims."

14. Feng Jiwu, *Fanchuan shi jizhu*, 202–3.

15. "Cultural artifacts" is an imperfect translation of *wenwu* 文物, which refers to things that represent high culture, particularly ceremonial paraphernalia.

16. Luo Shijin 羅時進, ed., *Dingmao ji jianzheng* 丁卯集箋證 (Nanchang: Jiangxi renmin chubanshe, 1998), 283.

17. Of the capital.

18. "The Song of Cockcrow Locks" 雞鳴埭歌, in *Wen Feiqing shiji jianzhu*, 1–3.

19. *Quan Tang shi*, 7882.

20. Feng Jiwu, *Fanchuan shi jizhu*, 273.

21. Li Zhiliang 李之亮, ed., *Luo Yin shiji jianzhu* 羅隱詩集箋注 (Changsha: Yuelin shushe, 2001), 55.

22. The "royal aura" is the "royal atmosphere." In this case the *qi* has congealed into water.

23. Sun Wang 孫望, ed., *Wei Yingwu shiji xinian jiaojian* 韋應物詩集繫年校箋 (Beijing: Zhonghua shuju, 2002), 52.

24. *Ru* 入 is the *Youxuan ji* 又玄集 reading. The standard text reads 人 (*ren*), which violates the tonal pattern.

25. Zhou Xiaotian, ed., 周嘯天, *Yong Tao shi zhu* 雍陶詩注 (Shanghai: Shanghai guji chubanshe, 1988), 50.

26. Zu Baoquan 祖保泉 and Tao Litian 陶禮天, eds., *Sikong Biaosheng shiwenji jianjiao* 司空表聖詩文集箋校 (Hefei: Anhui daxue chubanshe, 2002), 215.

12

"The Disarrayed Hills Conceal an Old Monastery"

The Dynamics of Poetry and Painting in the Northern Song

EUGENE WANG

"Hiddenness" is not of our own making; it was a Northern Song (960–1127) problem. The term *cangyi* 藏意, a reasonable equivalent, appears in a well-known twelfth-century account of an imperial examination during the Huizong reign (1100–1125). Students of painting who were sitting for that exam were given a poetic line as a prompt for a composition: "The disarrayed hills conceal an old monastery" 亂山藏古寺. Practically all of the candidates visualized the line literally by picturing a pagoda mast or a rooftop peeping over the mountain ridges. Some even presented front halls—a decision apparently considered to be in bad taste, precisely because the resulting paintings lacked the quality of "hints of concealment" (*cangyi*). One candidate, however, showed a monastic flagpole peeping over rustic hilltops. His composition clinched the top prize.[1]

Why was this relatively obscure poetic line—"the disarrayed hills conceal an old monastery"—considered particularly amenable to painting, more so than many other better-known lines?[2] The seemingly random choice of this poetic line, in fact, spoke to a pictorial trend in the Northern Song. The kind of composition it solicited belonged to a recognized subgenre gaining currency at that time, known as the "landscape of the forlorn monastery" 蕭寺圖. The imperial catalog of 1120, *Xuanhe huapu* 宣和畫譜, lists twenty-odd such paintings, all attributed to well-known masters.[3] The *Forlorn Monastery*

Amidst Autumn Hills 秋山蕭寺圖 (Figure 12.1) at the Yurinkan Collection, Kyoto,[4] is a typical example. Desolate trees on a hill conceal a nearly obscured monastery signaled by the faint contours of a pagoda and a pavilion barely observable between the trees.

The growing popularity of this subgenre raises some questions. Why is an *old monastery* in the disarrayed hills of any interest? If it holds appeal, why *hide* it? The successful candidate's decision to opt for a flagpole instead of a pagoda to signal a monastery only testifies to the pagoda as a visual cliché in such compositions at the time. The more inventive painter excelled by avoiding the cliché. In our search for answers, we find ourselves treading the well-trodden terrain of poetry/painting interactions. Our standard account tends to assume an unproblematic parity. We commonly cite the eleventh-century scholars' call for a poetic turn in painting, and then present a fourteenth-century literati landscape painting as visual evidence that the call was heeded. The glaring anachronism does not seem to bother us. Nor do we appear to mind the dissonance between the scholar-official's discursive proposition and the so-called "prosaic artisans'" formal solution.

To set the record straight, we need to focus exclusively on the Northern Song period, the initial moment when the scholar-officials and the so-called "prosaic artisans" first attempted to cross the divide between poetry and painting. Until that time, poetry had been the scholar-official's pursuit; painting, the artisans' profession. Some time around the mid–eleventh century, scholars' newly acquired cultural authority emboldened them to "force the issues" on artisan-painters and advocate for a poetic turn in painting. In so doing, they intervened in the art of painting, concerning which they had little expertise. The plot thickened when the artisan painters actually began to heed the scholar-official's changing taste, and landscape paintings showed signs that artisan-painters were warming up to the scholar-official's theoretical advocacy. There was certainly enough pressure for them to do so. The poetic turn was after all integral to the wholesale civilian turn under the Northern Song. Success in the

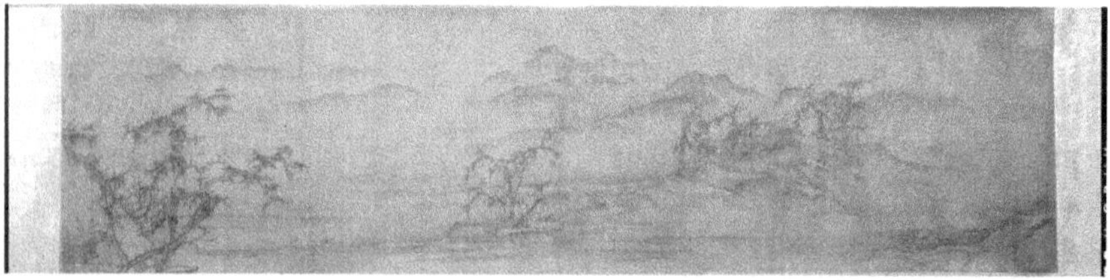

Figure 12.1. *Forlorn Monastery Amid Autumn Hills*, eleventh century. Handscroll. 38.3 × 147.5 cm. Ink on silk. Fujii Yurinkan, Kyoto.

imperial exam required poetic competence, for to possess a poetic sensibility was part of being a cultured gentleman. Thus, if the painting were to speak to the increasingly refined taste of the time, it, too, had to turn poetic.

How is one to make painting look poetic? Different periods would respond with different answers. By the early twelfth century, a landscape showing a hazy mist-veiled horizon was considered to inspire thoughts in the same way a lyrical poem does.[5] Such a misty landscape is "sufficient to facilitate the poets' and song writers' lyrical rumination."[6] In other words, to make a painting look poetic is to resort to suggestive concealment, *cang* 藏: to use vaguely inked forms as an atmospheric smokescreen to hide whatever is to be hidden. This accounts, for example, for the vogue of the Xiao-Xiang riverscape. Once the painter puts in "the semblance of *concealing* haze and forlorn faintness" 掩靄慘淡之狀, he "defines the conception" 命意, often too elusive to be named.[7] Eventually, the practice of suggestive concealment became so commonplace that even the previously cited twelfth-century critic, who once insisted on the presence of *cangyi*, "hint of concealment," would eventually have enough of it: "[These evening scenes] are hard to figure out. It is impossible to paint the bell sound, to begin with. And to show the Xiao-Xiang [riverscape] at night! And then to add rain on top of that! What can one see?" Worse still, everyone followed suit, especially those "prosaic artisans."[8]

The provenance of our sources is understandably lopsided, with many more coming from scholar-officials than from the painters themselves. Those in the mid–eleventh century who issued the call—with few exceptions—rarely painted anything more serious than bamboos and rocks, and those who produced landscapes—with few exceptions—hardly theorized. History has been written by scholars; little is known about the mid–eleventh century nonscholar painters responsible for the greatest number of Northern Song paintings. Yet it is precisely in these paintings that we detect a pictorial sensibility being increasingly dictated, infused, and fine-tuned by a poetic consciousness. In our critical reappraisal of the poetry/painting exchange under the Northern Song, we need to be mindful of the gap between the social groups on both sides of the divide—a gap that both groups were seeking to bridge. Our challenge comes from the dearth of documentation about, and statements by, the Northern Song artisan-painters. What we lack in documented statements from them, however, is largely made up through their pictorial eloquence.

The hermeneutical complexity we confront in attempting to account for the poetic "message" manifest in their paintings requires treading a thin line between what we perceive and what we know. On the one hand, we want to confirm and comprehend the apparent consonance between the scholar-officials' pronouncement of cultural values and the professional painters' endeavor to visualize these values. On the other hand, we need to be aware of the very real communication gap between the pontificating scholar and the taciturn, convention-bound painter, each comfortable in his own medium. The scholar's most eloquent pontification does not translate into the painter's composition without glitches. The painter may feel the pressure of the scholar-official breathing down his neck, and so attempt to comply; but there is no guarantee that the values—verbalized in discursive propositions—remain the same after they are integrated into the pictorial text. Misprision may occur; ways of modeling images may signal unexpected and often unintended messages; circumstantial contingencies may leave their indelible imprint on the final product. If poetry is what is lost in translation, then there is surely some lost-and-found going on in this period. This essay therefore sets out to chart the dynamics of this volatile situation, so as to better understand how poetic and pictorial mediums work out their effects differently. One painting in the subgenre of "landscape of the forlorn monastery," called *Disarrayed Hills Concealing an Old Monastery*, presents a fitting case study.

From Pathos to Stillness: A Mental Theater in Two Acts

It is hard to pinpoint when the "landscapes of the forlorn monastery" first gained popularity.[9] It can be surmised, however, that by Ouyang Xiu's 歐陽修 (1007–1072) time, the trend had picked up momentum. Ouyang Xiu, the most eminent scholar-official of his time, humbly professed his ignorance concerning the art of painting in his essay, "On Looking at Paintings" (*Jian hua* 鑑畫).[10] Such humility and modesty were largely obligatory as befitting a gentleman of his time; in the next breath, he does not hesitate to pontificate on the subject. This pontification, as it turns out, changed the face of Chinese painting for good. Ouyang calls here for a poetic turn in painting. If poetry aims to capture the ineffable, painting should do the same:

> Desolation-*cum*-austerity (*xiaotiao danbo* 蕭條淡泊) is the pictorial conception [or mood] hardest to capture in painting. Even when the painter gives shape to it, the beholder does not necessarily get it. Whereas it is easy to portray the surface impression of the varying rates of speed of birds and animals, it is difficult to give shape to the far-reaching consciousness of leisurely harmony and solemn stillness. As for the effects of height and depth, distance and recession, these uniquely pertain to the skills of the artisan-painter and are not the concern of refined connoisseurship. I do not know

> whether or not this discourse has any merit. Not knowing much about painting, I venture to say it nonetheless. Indeed, it may be that none of it is true. Still, those who are currently thought to be painting aficionados may not even be aware of this possibility. I only hope that these words are not so crass as to be hurtful.[11]

Ouyang here proposes two key pictorial modes: first, "desolation-*cum*-austerity" (*xiaotiao danbo* 蕭條淡泊); second, "leisurely harmony and solemn stillness" (*xianhe yanjing* 閒和嚴靜). He has good reason to specifically favor them. Seemingly disconnected, their link, latent in Ouyang's statement, becomes manifest once seen in their respective pictorial realizations.

A remarkable synergy exists between the hypothetical pictures Ouyang Xiu verbally commended and the surviving Northern Song specimens of the "landscape of the forlorn monastery." Not that painters specifically pressed Ouyang's stated ideas into their compositions (although at least one Northern Song author did explicitly recognize the resonance of Ouyang Xiu's "Ode to Autumnal Sound" in some contemporary landscapes[12]). The situation is one where the same cultural aspiration finds different expressions in verbal and pictorial mediums. Ouyang verbalized an aesthetic and cultural aspiration shared by a cultured community; painters, sensitive to shifting psychological needs, pictured it—albeit with some unintended dissonances due to the differences in the properties of their respective mediums. The *Forlorn Monastery Amid Autumn Hills*, mentioned earlier, is a good example of this synergy-cum-dissonance (Figure 12.1). Desiccated trees sparsely punctuate a barren landscape that stretches into a "level-distance." The trees pointedly convey the mood of "desolation" (*xiaotiao* 蕭條). A combination of pictorial features spells out the mood of "austerity" (*danbo* 淡泊); among them is the scantily treated spatial recession, which leaves much to the vast emptiness. This feature in particular resonates well with the loaded notion of "blandness" (*dan* 淡), which had gained wider acceptance in the eleventh century, with Ouyang Xiu as its chief exponent.[13]

Both Ouyang Xiu and the painter of this work make a virtue out of the mood of "desolation-*cum*-austerity." Its embedded human value is one of rejecting plenitude and excess and aestheticizing scarcity and poverty. And, given the changing social picture of the times, it is fair to say that this was no accident. The civil service examination system instituted under the Northern Song had done much to redraw the map of social stratification. This situation made it possible for people with humble origins to advance their careers exclusively through the civil service recruitment system. Members of this newly empowered scholar-official class—many of them of modest family background—cultivated an aesthetic taste befitting their roots. They rejected the culture of ornamentation and excess as the trappings of aristocratic nobility. In its stead, they promoted an aesthetic of poverty.

This climate is crystallized in the symbolic representation of the scholar as a donkey-rider in the landscapes of the "forlorn monastery," as exemplified by the figure in the center of the left portion of the Yurinkan scroll (Figure 12.1). The implicit rejection of the ostentatious aristocratic stance of horseback-riding in favor of setting astride the humble donkey speaks to the literati's deliberate molding of his own image.[14] The humbleness, however, is a mitigated one: the donkey-rider is usually accompanied by a zither-toting attendant, signaling the traveler's elegant cultural disposition even in the face of his material deprivation.

The Buddhist monastery adds the final touch to this contrived picture of austerity. Traditionally, poverty had *not* been the public face of the Buddhist monastery. The growing impulse to aestheticize poverty and austerity gradually found in Buddhist monasteries an ideal imaginary space on which to project such sensibilities. The monk's empty begging bowl, the tattered and patched robe, the austere diet, and the secluded monastic environment all evoke the sensory condition of material deprivation. The monastery was envisioned as a pristine world of *austerity*, to be relished aesthetically. The poetry of Jia Dao 賈島 (779–843), in particular, supplies the set scenarios.[15] The Song scholars were well-exercised in creating such poetic scenarios, using Buddhist monasteries and their perceived austerity. It is fitting, then, that the eremitic journey depicted in the Yurinkan scroll features a Buddhist monastery, partially hidden behind the cluster of old trees atop a hill in the middle of the right portion of the scroll (Figure 12.1).

The force of the landscape of the "forlorn monastery" derives primarily from the sensory effect of the "cold" 寒. The desiccated trees are a staple feature of the "cold grove" 寒林, a related landscape convention that also gained currency during the Northern Song. A "forlorn monastery" landscape often combines a "cold grove" with a Buddhist monastery, to provide a kind of double dose of desolation and austerity. The intended effect is to produce chill in the beholder.

Unlike earlier landscapes, the typical "landscape of the forlorn monastery" is designed to touch the viewer by way of poetry. That is, particular elements in the painting resonate with certain poetic conventions, and so function as visual cues to the viewer that he should recognize, and respond to, a distinct lyric voice colored with distinct lyric feelings. Among the typical cues we find: (1) the donkey-rider crossing a bridge, (2) desiccated trees, and (3) spatial recession.

The donkey-rider, a recurrent motif in Northern Song landscape painting, is a generic portrait of the poverty-stricken scholar, an eccentric nonconformist given to inebriation, eschewing the material comforts of an official career and seeking poetic inspiration and spiritual solace in the natural landscape.[16] The scenario of the donkey-rider crossing a bridge here is a visual formula of poverty-inspired pathos. The bridge to be crossed by the donkey-rider has its origin in the legendary Ba Bridge near the Tang capital city Chang'an,[17] a wind-swept snowy topography allegedly conducive to poetic thoughts.[18] The chill scene had long since lost its geographic specificity and become a general symbolic ambience or backdrop. The donkey-rider at the bridge here therefore plays its generic role of an *impoverished* scholar-poet on an eremitic journey, and so inspires poetic sentiment.

Ouyang Xiu's formulation of the aesthetics of poverty gives us an example of a typical string of associations. For Ouyang, poverty is a stimulus to expression. It can serve as a circumstantial or at times even a causal condition for the artful and cathartic release of inner tension. It leads to a gentleman scholar's "self-exile to the mountaintop and water margin" 自放於山巔水涯.[19] The myriad forms of nature that he encounters in this wilderness awaken the scholar's curiosity, and their evocation provides a means of venting the "pent-up sad thoughts and rankling frustrations" 憂思感憤之鬱積 in his mind.[20] "It is not that poetry impoverishes the poet; rather, poverty enriches poetry" 然則非詩之能窮人. 殆窮者而後工也.[21] In other words, poverty, especially when set in its normative natural landscape, inspires poetry; it is a situational framework for poetry.

The desolate landscape highlighted by the desiccated trees (the "cold grove") provides the poverty-stricken poet with yet another cue to poeticize. The cold grove suggests the advent of autumn and winter. As Su Shi wrote: "When tree leaves fall, the poet already resents the autumn, / And cannot bear how the 'Level Distance' [landscape] provokes poetic sorrow" 木落騷人已怨秋, 不堪平遠發詩愁.[22] The sorrow inspired by the advent of autumn leads to lamentation. The Song Dynasty scholars were well versed in Song Yu's *sao*-style poem, "Jiubian," which set the precedent for the autumn-inspired lamentation:

Alas for the breath of autumn!
Wan and drear! Flower and leaf fluttering fall and turn to decay.
Sad and lorn! As when on journey far one climbs a hill and
  looks down on the water to speed a returning friend.
Empty and vast! The streams have drunk full and the waters are
  clear.

> Heartsick and sighing sore! For the cold draws on and strikes into a man.
> Distraught and disappointed! I leave the old and turn toward the new.
> Afflicted! The poor esquire has lost his office and his heart rebels.
> Desolate! On his long journey he rests with never a friend.
> Melancholy! . . . and secretly pities himself.
> . . . .
> I have left home and country, and gone a traveler to distant places.
> Far have I wandered; where now can I stop?[23]

Song Yu's rhapsody sets the pattern, one that was later famously mediated by Du Fu[24]: a disgruntled, unemployed "poor esquire" on the road, finding the desolate autumn scene a fitting objective correlative to his own circumstances, and an apt occasion for sorrow.

The mist-shrouded distance completes the construction of a subjective, poetic view. The desiccated trees in the "cold grove" landscape typically serve as the lookout point, offsetting the spatial recession. In the case of the Yurinkan scroll, three clusters of desiccated trees mark respectively three different distances to accentuate the spatial recession. The hills, half-shrouded in mist and fog, terminate the depth of the field. The foregrounded trees and the hazy distance work out a pull-and-push sequence to simulate the casting about of the eye. The desolation of the trees colors the perception of the hazy vistas.

Moreover, one can see that the Tang and Song poetic values of conciseness and "lingering flavor" (*yuwei* 餘味)—the premise that poetry works by inspiring an infinite chain of thoughts through the precious finiteness of limited words—incite the painters to attempt to do the same through images. The richly suggestive "semblance of *concealing* haze and forlorn faintness" 掩靄慘淡之狀 became a pictorial device to "facilitate the poets' and song writers' lyrical rumination" 助騷客詞人之吟思[25]: a blank plane on which the poetic-minded beholder could project any number of thoughts.[26] The hazy distance has both spatial and temporal resonances; poor visibility figures the inaccessibility of both places and times, remembered and anticipated. Hence Su Shi's line: "When tree leaves fall, the poet already resents the autumn, / And cannot stand 'Level Distance' [landscape] provoking poetic sorrow."[27] This also explains Ouyang Xiu's taste for works that capture "far-reaching consciousness" (*qu yuan zhi xin* 趣遠之心), which the "Level Distance" landscape facilitates or solicits.[28]

To return to the template provided by Ouyang Xiu, he takes the semblance of "desolation-*cum*-austerity" to be only part of the hypothetical painting he commends; it is complemented by the mood of "leisurely harmony and solemn stillness." While he does not make explicit how the two are related, paintings such as *Forlorn Monastery Amid Clearing Peaks* (Figure 12.2) fully spell out the inner logic between the two.[29]

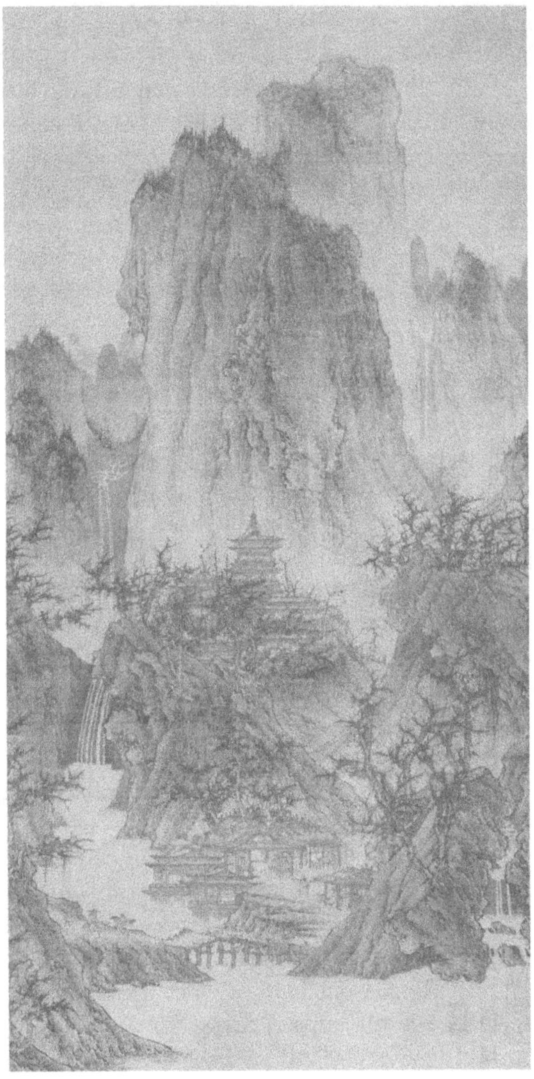

Figure 12.2. *Forlorn Monastery Amid Clearing Peaks*, eleventh century. Attributed to Li Cheng, Chinese (919–67 CE). [*A Solitary Temple Amid Clearing Peaks*], Northern Song Dynasty. Hanging scroll. Ink and slight color on silk. 44 × 22 in. (111.8 × 55.9 cm). The Nelson-Atkins Museum of Art, Kansas City, Mo. Purchase: William Rockhill Nelson Trust, 47-71.

In this particular painting, the mood of "desolation-*cum*-austerity" constitutes a cue for a response conditioned by knowledge of literary conventions: "When tree leaves fall, the poet already resents the autumn, / And cannot stand how the 'Level Distance' [landscape] provokes poetic sorrow."[30] The lyric voice being summoned by such lines is that of the "poor esquire" who has "lost his office," or the poverty-stricken poet lamenting the withering force of autumn. The donkey-rider who embodies the voice has come to a broken bridge, in a scene that is well rehearsed in such Northern Song accounts of landscape paintings as appear in the *Xuanhe huapu*: "Therefore, all of the conditions pictured in [Li Cheng's] paintings—the mountains, forests, marshes, waters, level-distant [recessions], rugged and easy [roads], *tumbling waterfalls*, precarious plank paths, the *broken bridge*, the precipitous valley, rapids, boulders, wind, rain, obscurity, light, mist, cloud, snow, and fog—are *disgorged from within his breast and released through his brush* (一皆吐其胸中, 而寫之筆下), much as Meng Jiao gives utterance through his poetry."[31] Sure enough, there are four "tumbling waterfalls" in the painting. Following the logic here, these landscape features externalize the subject's inner agitation as he seeks a cathartic outlet. Han Yu 韓愈 (768–824), in his "Preface to 'Seeing off Meng Jiao,' " supplies the grammar of the train of thought underlying such landscapes: wind causes trees to cry out and water to resound; likewise, humans, when stirred, lose their "inner equilibrium" and emit sound. For Han Yu, his friend Meng Jiao 孟郊 (751–814) is among the poets to have done just that.[32]

This discourse on poetic emotion is only part of what I would describe as an oft-rehearsed Northern Song mental theater. The psychological process it dramatized often consists of two acts. Act One, "desolation-*cum*-austerity"; autumnal scenes—withering trees, waterfalls, and the like—induce pathos and agitation, the "sighs" and "moans" of loyal ministers and "bitter men or lonely women."[33] Act Two, "leisurely harmony and solemn stillness"; "stillness," as Su Shi puts it, "ends all motions" 靜故了群動.[34] The rhapsodic southern-style poets' gushing "sound of the valley waterfalls" is consequently deemed inferior to the pregnant silence of the "metal, stone, strings and bamboo" in the elegant register of the *Classic of Poetry*.[35] The two moods—"desolation-*cum*-austerity" and "leisurely harmony and solemn stillness"—as Ouyang Xiu envisions in his ideal landscape, precisely spell out these two acts in a sequence.

The Nelson-Atkins scroll maps out this mental theater. We observe two distinct and contrasting moods. The tilting rock outcroppings and agitated "crab claw" tree branches in the foreground emanate a mood that Mi Fu has elsewhere described as the demonic "manners of dragons, serpents, ghosts, and spirits,"[36] and produce an effect of chill, agitation, restlessness, and anxiety. The soaring peaks in the background, especially the central one, convey, in general, a majestic stability, august grandeur, lordliness, sturdiness, and composure, as the vertical form recapitulates the monumental landscape convention that gained ground in the Northern Song. The monumentality is, however, marred by a disturbing sign of instability, most notably manifested in the left-inclining craggy rock face that threatens to collapse onto the central pagoda beneath it.[37]

The stage is thus set for Act Two, in which the central pagoda rises up to the occasion. Interposed between the agitated tilting rock outcroppings capped by monstrously gesticulating trees in the foreground and the dominant, precarious central peak in the background, the pagoda remains unfazed in its calm architectonic composure. Its structural stability dramatically offsets the agitation of the surrounding landscape forms. This visual drama is characterized by modern scholars as an interplay between "the obvious energy seen in the trees" and "a classical equipoise."[38] Ouyang Xiu's formula, "leisurely harmony and solemn stillness," perfectly captures the architectonic majesty of the otherwise hidden pagoda-dominated monastic precinct. In the eleventh-century parlance of Guo Ruoxu 郭若虛 (fl. 1070–1075), the best architectural drawing conveys the "flavor of sublime majesty and leisurely elegance" 莊麗閑雅之意.[39] Furthermore, the Buddhist monks and, by extension, the monastery they occupied, were thought of during this period as embodying the dispassionate qualities of "subdued austerity" 淡泊 and "emptiness and tranquility" 空且靜 that overcome earthly motions and commotions.[40]

Monastery and Cognitive Dissonance

With a deftness integral to the pictorial medium, the Nelson-Atkins' scroll, at first glance, seems to perfectly, and inadvertently, encapsulate and diagram a typical Northern Song scholar's rhetorical thought process, at least as described (or prescribed) by Ouyang Xiu and Su Shi. However, the apparent conceptual consonance between the scholar-official's thought process and its ingenious pictorial staging by the artisan-painter actually belies a cognitive dissonance. It seems likely that even Ouyang himself would have balked at a landscape painting like this one. This is because in the context of the pictorial trend we have been describing, this composition is decidedly an anomaly.

The fact is, no other extant Northern Song scroll gives the pagoda such central prominence. True, it is not uncommon for Northern Song landscape paintings to feature architectural images, mostly palatial towers, terraces, and pavilions, in keeping with the classification of architectural painting in the early twelfth-century imperial catalog as the generic category of "palaces and chambers" (*gong shi* 宮室). Yet, of the seventy-one *architectural* paintings listed in the imperial catalog, only one pertains to Buddhist monastery.[41] That is to say, if one were to do architectural painting, a monastery is the last thing one would have taken up, for the subgenre of the "forlorn monastery" falls into the category of landscapes.[42]

Looking at the imperial catalog, we find that it lists about twenty-four of them.[43] On the basis of the catalog, it is notable that (1) with the exception of the one painting of a Buddhist monastery listed in the architectural painting category mentioned above, these paintings belong exclusively to the landscape genre; (2) they are mostly entitled the *Painting of a Forlorn Monastery [in the mountains]*, with a consistent emphasis on the "*xiao*" or "solitary-*cum*-desolate" mood; (3) the setting is invariably mountains or hills.[44] It therefore becomes apparent that the pictorial interest vested in the monasteries stems largely from the desolate-*cum*-austere mood associated with them. As a result, a monastery is often treated cursorily as a notational sign or marker that points to something beyond itself. Surviving Northern scrolls testify to this. The few scrolls that feature a pagoda push it to the recessed depth where it is all but lost or veiled in the hazy horizon of clouds and mist, or registered as an apparition in the far distance (Figure 12.1).

The pagoda in the Nelson-Atkins scroll, by contrast, is taken on its own structural or architectonic terms and treated fully with care. Drawn in the manner of the "ruler-lined painting" (*jiehua* 界畫), the architectural members and structural features—the eaves, railings, mast, finial, and so on—are all rendered with sharp precision in correct proportion and spatial modeling. It is presented as an expansive, squat, octagonal timber structure.

The sight of the dominant pagoda would have completely turned Ouyang Xiu off, and for good reason. Pagodas do not hold pride of place in the Northern Song scholar-officials' mindscape. While the pagoda is the most conspicuous architectural landmark of a Buddhist monastery, it is also the most expensive to build. The heavy cost incurred in its construction often drew ire from Confucian scholar-officials. The pagoda in the Kaibao Monastery in the Northern Song capital is a notable example. Standing outside the northeast corner of the Inner City, the pagoda was the most conspicuous landmark in the capital city. Built in 989 at Taizong's decree, the structure allegedly radiated golden light in 1013. It thereby received more imperial patronage and became a ritual platform for the imperial state. However, the grandiose edifice was an eyesore to the frugal Confucian scholar-officials. One scholar-official did not mince words when counseling the emperor: "whereas the public hails the [pagoda] as a gold-and-green splendor, this minister thinks [the pagoda] has [people's] sweat and blood written all over it!"[45] The pagoda's detractors were vindicated when the timber structure was struck by lightening and burned down in 1044.[46] The emperor's intention to rebuild it caused loud protests from the scholar-officials on the grounds of the heavy financial burden and labor cost. Ouyang Xiu was among the most vocal opponents, pointing to the fire as an omen of heavenly disapproval of the extravagant building.[47] The emperor went ahead with the rebuilding anyway.[48] As his remonstration against the rebuilding fell on the deaf ear of Emperor Renzong, Ouyang Xiu never mentioned the rebuilt pagoda again—not even once in his writing. He was not alone. The entire scholar-official community showed their collective indifference to the rebuilt pagoda, resulting in a glaring lacuna in the Northern Song writing on the site.

The Northern Song scholars preferred only certain types of architecture. The pavilion—with its modest structure, smooth integration into landscape, and open views—caught the literary imagination and became a favorable topos in the Northern Song.[49] But when it comes to choosing architectural structures as signposts for imaginary compositions or landscapes, the pagoda—fraught as it is with ambiguities and baggage—is something they would rather not deal with. The Leifeng—or "Thunder Peak"—pagoda, for example, had stood on the South Screen Hill south of West Lake since the tenth century. Quite a few eminent scholar-officials are known to have visited the picturesque site, but none of them bothered to take note of the looming pagoda in their writing.[50] Qisong 契嵩 (1007–1071), an eminent monk-scholar of the Lingying Monastery in the lake area, left us with a detailed description of his climb of the South Screen Hill. On scaling to the top, he commanded a sweeping view of the four quarters and was overcome with elevated sentiments. Yet he spent not a drop of ink on the Thunder Peak Pagoda, even as he took care to mark and punctuate his itinerary with *pavilions*. As he documents it, his trek began with the Cloud-Clearing Pavilion, and then took him to the Green-Gathering Pavilion, the Seclusion-Commencing Pavilion, and the White-Cloud Pavilion. He made a point of recording his trip "so that the future generation may admire [him] as a traveler."[51]

If pavilions are generally favored during this period, the interest in them stems not from the architectural form itself, but from the views it affords the beholder. Again, here is Ouyang Xiu: "When it comes to the splendid forms of the mountains and rivers *around the pavilion*, the blurring haze of plants, trees, clouds, and mist coming into view and disappearing in the broad and empty expanse, hanging between presence and absence, which can fully satisfy the gaze of a poet as he climbs these heights and writes his own 'Li Sao'—it is best that each viewer find such things for himself. As for the frequent ruin and repair of the pavilion, either accounts already exist or the details do not merit close examination. I will say nothing more."[52] This is why Ouyang Xiu would have balked at the pagoda-dominated landscape of the Nelson-Atkins scroll. Or at least he would have felt ambivalent about it.

So, here is the paradox. The painting, as we have thus far demonstrated, neatly parses and diagrams the twin moods of the ideal landscape envisioned by Ouyang Xiu. Through the cold grove, donkey-rider at the broken bridge, the waterfall, and so on, it visualizes "desolation-*cum*-austerity" to a fault; it even finds an effective way of projecting the mood of "leisurely harmony and solemn stillness" through the architectonic stability of a pagoda. The orderliness of architecture counteracts the disorder of the agitated landscape. Seen in this way, it is a pictorial tour de force.

But, by the standards of Ouyang Xiu, a nonpainter, it fails where it succeeds most. The pagoda undoes it all: for its architectonic grandeur is precisely what Ouyang Xiu and his like-minded frugal Confucian scholars would abhor. *Conceptually*, the monastery embodies austerity and eremitism. However, the *formal* aggrandizement of the monastery through the oversized depiction of the pagoda betrays this ideal with its extravagant overtone.

This is what can happen when values expressed in discursive propositions get lost in the process of convention-bound picture-making; the visualizing painter and the verbalizing scholar may talk past each other. The painter may have simply acted on the generic impulse of the "forlorn monastery": he pictures architecture as the embodiment of "leisurely harmony and solemn stillness" to counteract the agitations caused by "desolation-*cum*-austerity" of the "cold grove." These were notions much bandied about, abuzz in the air, in his time—whether he read Ouyang Xiu or not. Trying to be *with it* and pressing these formulas into service in composing his landscapes, however, he gets the concepts right and the form wrong—at least in the eyes of his contemporary scholar-officials. The architectural painting, which would send wrong messages to the likes of Ouyang Xiu, backfires on him. Giving primacy to the formal grandeur of the pagoda, the painter ostensibly runs afoul of the Confucian scholar-official's deep-seated wariness of architectural extravagance. The painter thereby inadvertently "deconstructs" the aesthetics of austerity he set out to capture in the first place.

This tension partly explains the short-lived parity between the scholar's aesthetics of "desolation-cum-austerity" and the "forlorn monastery" landscape around the mid–eleventh century. The aesthetics of this subgenre would have to wait until the fourteenth century to be unambiguously captured in landscape painting. In the Northern Song, the pagoda was a thorny issue. If it was too much to handle, it was a safe bet simply to hide it. This is why the subgenre of the landscape of the "forlorn monastery" never had a place in the *architectural* painting. Safely ensconced as a *landscape* subgenre, the pagoda could be pointedly scaled down or reduced to a sketchy affair, or spirited away by veiling or concealing it. The *Autumn Colors of the Streams and Mountains* 溪山秋色圖, an early twelfth-century scroll (Figure 12.3),[53] plays out the endgame of this subgenre. The painting amounts to a compositional palimpsest. The compositional precedent in the Nelson-Atkins scroll (Figure 12.2) is reworked to its exhaustion in *Autumn Colors* (Figure 12.3). The central pagoda is pushed back, mist-veiled, until it becomes no more than an apparitional signpost in the distance.

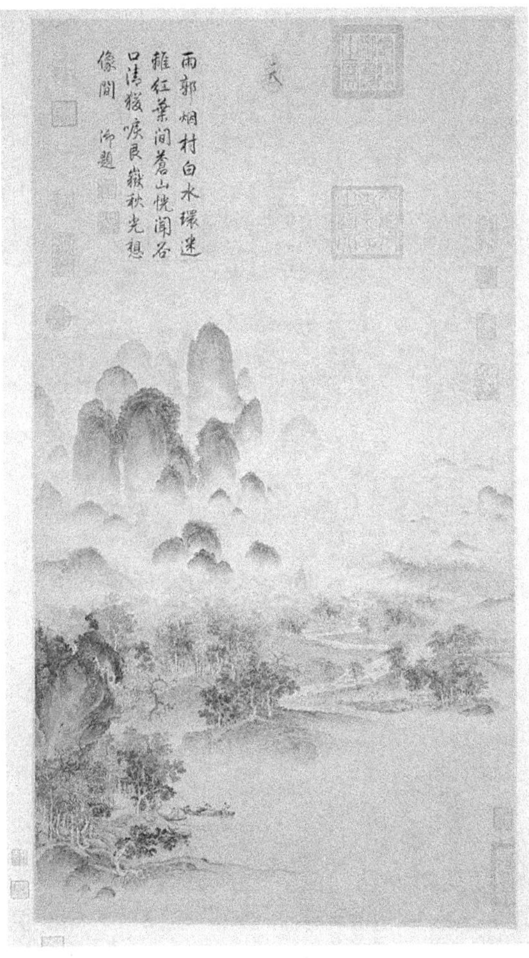

Figure 12.3. *Autumn Colors of the Streams and Mountains*, early twelfth century. Hanging scroll. Ink and light color on paper. 97 × 53 cm. National Palace Museum, Taipei.

This development takes a different turn in the early twelfth-century *Winter Evening Landscape* (Figure 12.4). It is a curious painting. The composition itself is relatively familiar. Desiccated trees in the vein of the "cold grove" gesticulate in the foreground.

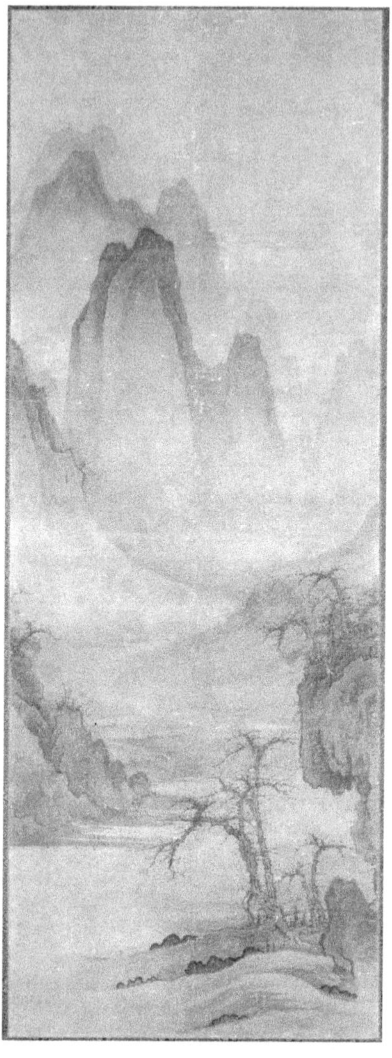

Figure 12.4. Li Gongnian (twelfth century CE), *Winter Evening Landscape*, ca. 1120. China, Northern Song Dynasty. Hanging scroll. Ink and light colors on silk. 129.6 × 48.3 cm. Mount: 202.5 × 62.2 cm (79¾ × 24½ in.). Gift of DuBois Schanck Morris, Class of 1893. y1946-191. Photo: Bruce M. White, Princeton University Art Museum. Photo credit: Princeton University Art Museum/Art Resource, NY.

Whatever agitation they cause is stabilized by the towering mountains in the distance. What is curious is the miniscule pavilion at the foot of the distant monumental mountain. So tiny is it that it is barely discernible. It is apparent that the composition still recalls the convention of the "landscape of the forlorn monastery." Yet out goes the pagoda; in comes the pavilion. Its relative centrality is iconic, yet its reduced size is the message. Extravagance is eschewed; humbleness and openness are the new order of this universe.

This brings us back to the examination for Northern Song imperial painting academy.[54] Both the *Autumn Colors of the Streams and Mountains* and the *Winter Landscape* are close in date to the examination. By the late Northern Song, the increasing reluctance to paint a full-scale pagoda in landscape is palpable. It is perhaps no coincidence that, in assessing the submitted paintings for the imperial examination on the topic of "disarrayed hills conceal an old monastery," the jury favored the flagpole over the pagoda mast in the composition. Innocuous and unwitting as it appears, the verdict inadvertently registers the endpoint of a historical change. The genre of the Landscape of the Forlorn Monastery had run its course. The pagoda—or its replacement, the flagpole—is merely the tip of the iceberg. There is more to the "disarrayed hills conceal an old monastery" than meets the eye.

Abbreviations

YWSQ: *Yingyin wen'ge siku quanshu* (Taipei: Taiwan shangwu chubanshe, 1983).
ZSQ: *Zhongguo shuhua quanshu*, eds. Lu Fusheng et al. (Shanghai: Shanghai shuhua chubanshe), 1993. 14 vols.

Notes

1. Deng Chun 鄧椿 (twelfth c.), *Huaji* 畫繼, in ZSQ, 2:704b.

2. A lyrical song by Yang Wujiu 楊無咎 (1097–1169), "New Jade Candle" 玉燭新, contains the line: "The desolate peaks conceal an old monastery" 荒山藏古寺. *Taochanci* 逃禪詞, YWSQ edition, 1487: 33. A poem by Wang Shipeng 王十朋 (1112–1171), "Wuhou xinci" 武侯新祠, contains the line: "Mountains hide an old monastery amidst verdant cypress" 山藏古寺柏青青. In *Meixi ji houji* 梅溪集後集, YWSQ edition, 1151: 12.10.

3. *Xuanhe huapu* 宣和畫譜, ZSQ, 2:90–99.

4. The scroll has traditionally been attributed to Xu Daoning 許道寧 (ca. 970–1051), without much basis.

5. *Xuanhe huapu*, ZSQ, 2:97a.

6. 足以助騷客詞人之吟思. *Xuanhe huapu*, ZSQ, 2:91a.

7. Deng Chun, *Huaji*, ZSQ, 2:716b.

8. Ibid.

9. According to the *Xuanhe huapu*, ZSQ, 2:92b, Li Cheng is among the first to produce a "landscape of forlorn monastery." since the tenth-century painter was subject to later generations' reconstruction, it is not clear if Li Cheng did indeed start the generic trend or if the painting attributed to him was recognized as such when the trend started posthumously.

10. Ouyang Xiu, "Jian hua," in *Ouyang Xiu quanji* 歐陽修全集 (Beijing: Zhonghua shuju, 2001), 5:1976.

11. 此難畫之意。畫者得之,鑑者未必識也。故飛走遲速意淺之物易見,而閒和嚴靜趣遠之心難形。若乃高下嚮背,遠近重複,此畫工之藝爾,非精鑒者之事也。不知此論為是否。余非知畫者,強為之說,但恐未必然也。然世謂好畫者,亦未必能知此也。此字不乃傷俗耶。 Ouyang Xiu, "Jian hua," in *Ouyang Xiu quanji*, 5:1976.

12. The landscape chapter of the 1120 imperial catalog *Xuanhe huapu* contains an entry regarding an inner palace eunuch named Feng Jin, a native of Kaifeng, who excelled in painting both hazy atmospheric landscapes and "towers in forest shades." His painting, the *Golden Wind [or Phoenix] and Sounds of Nature*, according to the catalog author, made one feel as if one could hear the piping of wind instruments. "The depth of the thought and sentiments embedded therein can be compared to Ouyang Xiu's 'Rhapsody on the Sounds of Autumn.'" *Xuanhe huapu*, in ZSQ, 2:98.

13. François Jullien and Graham Parkes, "The Chinese Notion of 'Blandness' as a Virtue: A Preliminary Outline," *Philosophy East and West* 43, no. 1 (Jan., 1993): 107–11.

14. Peter Sturman, "The Donkey Rider as Icon: Li Cheng and the Early Chinese Landscape Painting," *Artibus Asiae* 55, nos. 1/2 (1995): 43–97.

15. See Xiao Chi 蕭馳, *Fofa yu shijing* 佛法與詩境 (Beijing: Zhonghua shuju, 2005), 207–33.

16. It originally alludes to Meng Haoran 孟浩然 (689–740) or other well-known eremitic poets. See Sturman, "The Donkey Rider as Icon."

17. The Ba Bridge is located east of modern Xi'an. The association of the bridge with "winds and snow" results from the topographic lore that the banks along the Ba River used to be lined with willow trees whose catkins were perceived figuratively as "snow flakes."

18. Zheng Qi 鄭綮, a late Tang official, is said to have observed that "poetic thought lodges on the back of the donkey in the winds and snow of the Ba Bridge" 詩思在霸橋風雪中驢子上. See Dong You 董逌 (fl. 1111–1118), *Guangchuan huaba* 廣川畫跋, ZSQ, 1:822.

19. Ouyang Xiu, "Mei Shengyu shiji xu 梅聖俞詩集序," in *Ouyang Xiu quanji*, 2:612.

20. Ibid.

21. Ibid.

22. Su Shi, "Guo Xi Qiushan pingyuan ershou" 郭熙秋山平遠二首 in Su Shi, *Su Shi quanji* 蘇軾全集 (Shanghai: Shanghai guji, 2000), 355. Translation following Murck, *Poetry and Painting*, 124.

23. Song Yu 宋玉, "Jiubian 九辯," in Hong Xingzu 洪興祖 (1090–1155), *Chuci buzhu* 楚辭補注 (Taipei: Tiangong shuju, 1989), 182. Translation from David Hawkes, *Ch'u Tz'u: The Songs of the South* (Boston: Beacon Press, 1959), 92–3.

24. See, for just one salient, multilayered example, his "Eight Autumn Laments" (Qiuxing bashou 秋興八首). Chou Zhaoao 仇兆鰲 (1638–1717), ed. *Du shi xiangzhu* 杜詩詳註. 5 vols. (Beijing: Zhonghua shuju, 2004), 4:1484–1499. See, too, Stephen Owen's complete translation in his *An Anthology of Chinese Literature: Beginnings to 1911* (New York: W. W. Norton and Company, 1996), 434–38.

25. *Xuanhe huapu*, ZSQ, 2:91a.

26. Deng Chun, *Huaji*, ZSQ, 2:716b.

27. Su Shi, "Guo Xi Qiushan pingyuan ershou," in Su Shi, *Su Shi quanji*, 355. Translation following Murck, *Poetry and Painting*, 124.

28. Ouyang Xiu, "Jian hua," in *Ouyang Xiu quanji*, 5:1976.

29. See Eugene Y. Wang, "Response: 'Picture Idea' and Its Cultural Dynamics in Northern Song China," *The Art Bulletin* 89, no. 3 (2007): 463–81.

30. Su Shi, "Guo Xi Qiushan pingyuan ershou," in Su Shi, *Su Shi quanji*, 355. Translation following Murck, *Poetry and Painting*, 124.

31. *Xuanhe huapu*, ZSQ, 2:92a.

32. Han Yu, "Preface Seeing Off Meng Jiao" 送孟郊序, in *Quan Tang wen* 全唐文, eds. Dong Gao 董誥 et al. (Beijing: Zhonghua shuju, 1983), 555.5612–13. Translation from Charles Hartman, *Han Yü and the T'ang Search for Unity* (Princeton, NJ: Princeton University Press, 1986), 230–32.

33. Ouyang Xiu, "Song Yangzhi xu," in *Ouyang Xiu quanji*, 2:629. Translation from Ronald Egan, "The Controversy Over Music and 'Sadness' and Changing Conceptions of the Qin in Middle Period China," *Harvard Journal of Asiatic Studies* 57, no. 1 (June 1997): 63.

34. Su Shi, "Song Canliao shi" 送參廖師, in *Su Shi quanji*, 17.212.

35. Huang Tingjian 黃庭堅, "Hu Zongyuan shiji xu," *Shangu ji* 山谷集, YWSQ edition, 1113:16.19.

36. Mi Fu, *Huashi*, in ZSQ, 1: 979; *Xuanhe huapu*, in ZSQ, 2:92.

37. Jonathan Hay, "Interventions: The Mediating Work of Art," *The Art Bulletin* 89, no. 3 (Sept. 2007): 444, first observes this visual drama.

38. Lawrence Sickman and Marc F. Wilson, "A Forlorn Monastery Amid Clearing Peaks," in *Eight Dynasties of Chinese Painting* (Cleveland, OH: Cleveland Museum of Art; Bloomington: Indiana University Press, 1980), 15.

39. Guo Ruoxu, *Tuhua jianwen zhi* 圖畫見聞志, in ZSQ, 1:467b; see also Alexander Soper, trans. and annot., *Kuo Jo-Hsü's Experiences in Painting: An Eleventh Century History of Chinese Painting* (Washington, DC: American Council of Learned Societies, 1951), 12.

40. Su Shi fully expects a Buddhist monk to possess these qualities. He therefore had a hard time reconciling this image of even-keeled Buddhist disposition with the ninth-century monk Gao Xian's dashing cursive-script calligraphy. See Su Shi, "Song Liaocan shi," in *Su Shi quanji*, 212.

41. *ZSQ*, 2:83. It is also known as "jiehua" 界畫. For studies of the genre, see Robert Maeda, "Chieh-Hua: Ruled-Line Painting in China," *Ars Orientalis* 10 (1975):

123–41; Heping Liu, " 'The Water Mill' and Northern Song Imperial Patronage of Art, Commerce, and Science," *Art Bulletin* 84, no. 4 (Dec., 2002): 566–95.

42. They can also be called "lanruo tu" 蘭若圖 (such as those painted by Juran 巨然 (tenth c.), see *Xuanhe huapu*, in *ZSQ*, 2:99a), or "fancha tu" 梵剎圖 (as those by Fan Tan, ZSQ 2:96b), or simply "sengshe tu" 僧舍圖 (2:93b). The Chinese character *si* 寺 has sometimes been translated as "temple." I translate it as "monastery."

43. *Xuanhe huapu*, ZSQ, 2:90b–99b.

44. *Xuanhe huapu* lists twenty-five or so paintings featuring Buddhist monasteries. Eleven of them are titled *Xiaositu* (painting of Forlorn Monastery [in the mountains]); the rest have various titles, such as *Painting of Aranya* (*lanruotu*) or *Painting of Buddhist Monastery* (*fochatu*; *fanchatu*). See ZSQ, 2:90–99. The Chinese character "*cha*" 剎 is derived from Sanskrit "laksatā" (banner post).

45. Li Tao 李燾, *Xu zizhi tongjian changbian* 續資治通鑑長編 (Beijing: Zhonghua shuju, 1979–), 30.686; Qian Yueyou 潛說友, *Xianchun Lin'an zhi* 咸淳臨安志 (Beijing: Zhonghua shuju, 1990), 89.4181.

46. *Song shi* 宋史 (Beijing: Zhonghua shuju, 1977), 63.1378; *Fayun tongsai zhi*, in T49:410b. Wang Pizhi 王闢之, *Shengshui yantan lu* 澠水燕談錄 (Beijing: Zhonghua shuju, 1981), 5.

47. For Yu Jing's remonstration, see *Song shi*, 320.10408; Zhao Ruyu 趙汝愚, ed., *Song mingchen zouyi* 宋名臣奏議, edition, 431:84.3. For Cai Xiang's remonstration, see *Song shi*, 320.10398; Zhao, *Song mingchen zouyi*, YWSQ 432:128.8–9. For Ouyang Xiu's remonstration, see *Ouyang Xiu quanji*, 4:1639–40.

48. The new pagoda was a thirteen-story octagonal masonry structure built of glazed tile. Li Lian 李濂, *Bianjing yiji zhi* 汴京遺蹟志 (Beijing: Zhonghua shuju, 1999), 10.155. It retained the height of the old timber structure that had gone down in fire: 360 Chinese feet (now more than 55.08 m.) tall, still standing today. Liu Chunying 劉春迎, *Bei Song dongjingcheng yanjiu* 北宋東京城研究 (Beijing: Kexue chubanshe, 2004), 238. Another source gives a different measurement: 55.60 m. in height. See *Zhongguo lidai yishu, jianzhu yishu bian* 中國歷代藝術建築編 (Beijing: Zhongguo jianzhu gongye chubanshe, 1994), 343, no. 248.

49. Notable examples include the Pavilion of the Bounty and Joy (Fengle ting 豐樂亭), the Pavilion of the Drunkard Old Man (Zuiweng ting 醉翁亭), and the Pavilion on Mount Xian, made famous through its description by Ouyang Xiu and his contemporaries. Ouyang, *Ouyang Xiu quanji*, 2:575–77; 2:588–89.

50. Eugene Wang, "Tope and Topos: The Leifeng Pagoda and the Discourse of the Demonic," in *Writing and Materiality in China*, eds. Judith Zeitlin and Lydia Liu (Cambridge, MA: Harvard University Press, 2003): 488–552.

51. Seng Qisong, "Touring the South Screen Mountain," in *Xihu youji xuan* 西湖遊記選, eds. Cao Wenqu 曹文趣 et al. (Hangzhou: Zhejiang wenyi chubanshe, 1985), 224–25.

52. Ouyang Xiu, "Xianshan ting ji" (An Account of the Pavilion on Mount Xian) (1070), in *Ouyang Xiu quanji*, 2:589. Translation from Stephen Owen, ed. and trans., *An Anthology of Chinese Literature: Beginnings to 1911* (New York: W.W. Norton, 1996), 630.

53. The scroll, which bears Huizong's (1082–1135) seal, *yushu* 禦書, has traditionally been attributed to the emperor. According to Cai Tao 蔡絛, *Tieweishan congtan* 鉄圍山叢談 (Beijing: Zhonghua shuju, 1983), 2, Emperor Huizong deployed numerous distinguished painters in the palace to produce paintings in his name. So the scroll very likely comes from the hand of a court painter. The dating remains a matter of contention. The scroll *Flowing Clouds over Clearing Hills* 晴麓橫雲圖 in the Osaka City Museum of Art contains a similar composition; it bears an inscription (the title) 晴麓橫雲 rendered in the emperor's calligraphic style. The Osaka scroll is likewise from the hand of a professional artist ghost-painting for or copying an alleged painting by the emperor. For a study of the paintings traditionally attributed to Huizong, see Xu Bangda 徐邦達, "Song Huizong Zhao Ji qingbihua yu daibihua de kaobian" 宋徽宗趙佶親筆畫與代筆畫的考辨, in *Gugong bowuyuan yuankan* 故宮博物院院刊 1 (1979): 62–67; 50.

54. Deng Chun, *Huaji*, in *ZSQ*, 2:704.

Just Words

13

Manifesting Sagely Knowledge

Commentarial Strategies in Chinese Late Antiquity

MICHAEL PUETT

Allow me to begin by quoting a famous set of lines from the *Laozi* 老子:

> Thirty spokes join together at one hub; the usefulness of the cart resides in its nothingness (*wu* 無).
> Clay is pulled to make vessels; the usefulness of the vessel resides in its nothingness.
> One cuts doors and windows to make dwellings; the usefulness of the dwelling resides in its nothingness.
> Something (*you* 有) is what makes them beneficial; nothing (*wu*) is what makes them useful.[1]
>
> 三十輻共一轂, 當其無, 有車之用。埏埴以為器, 當其無, 有器之用。鑿戸牖以為室, 當其無, 有室之用。故有之以為利, 無之以為用。

The lines are written in a characteristically paradoxical style, with characteristically counterintuitive examples. In the case at hand, the text implies that we tend to assume that the usefulness of implements resides in their constituent parts, but in fact their usefulness resides in nothingness: the emptiness of a wheel hub, the emptiness in a vessel, the emptiness between the walls of a dwelling. Such an argument is part of the *Laozi*'s overall valuation of *wu* 無,

"nothingness," which is itself associated with the Way, *dao* 道. The text calls on the reader to focus on nothingness, with far-reaching implications that the text explores through its many chapters.

But let us now turn to the *Xiang'er* 想爾 commentary to the *Laozi*,[2] a commentary probably written in the late second century of the common era.[3] The *Xiang'er* commentary begins with the first line of the same passage, the translation of which I will change to reflect the commentator's reading:[4]

> "Thirty spokes join together at one hub, but the usefulness of the cart resides in *whether it exists or not*."
>
> *Commentary:* When in antiquity there were not yet carts, the people were isolated. The Way sent down Xi Zhong to invent them [carts]. When foolish people obtained the carts, they desired benefits from them, and that is all. They did not think to practice the Way; and they were not aware of the spirits of the Way. But when the worthy saw them [the carts], they understood the kindness of the Way. They quietly trained themselves, and put an emphasis on obtaining the truth of the Way.[5]
>
> "卅輻共一轂，當其無，有車之用。"
>
> 古未有車時，退然，道遣奚仲作之。愚者得車，貪利而已，不念行道，不覺道神。賢者見之，乃知道恩，默而自厲，重守道眞也。

The Way is here defined as a deity who intervenes to help humanity. The Way sends down sages to help humanity, and also calls on humanity to follow its precepts. In the case at hand, the Way saw that humans were isolated from each other without carts, so the Way sent down the sage Xi Zhong to invent carts and thus allow humans to have more interaction with each other. However, most humans, on seeing these newly invented carts, simply desired to gain benefits from them. Only those who were worthy focused on what really mattered, namely that the Way had sent down the carts as an act of kindness. They accordingly focused on training themselves according to the precepts of the Way.

In other words, the commentator is reading the word *wu* here not as "nothingness" but rather as "when they did not exist." The worthy understood that their coming into existence was due to the Way, so they focused properly on the Way's kindness; others only focused on the benefits of the carts themselves. In such a reading, there is no valuation of nothingness at all.

Before discussing the implications of such a reading, let us first continue with the commentary. The commentary reads the example of the clay in the same way:

> "Clay is pulled to make vessels, but the usefulness of the vessel resides in *whether it exists or not.*"
>
> *Commentary:* The same explanation as with the carts. (*Xiang'er*, line 128)
>
> "埏殖爲器, 當其無, 有器之用。" 亦與車同説。

And the same argument continues with the example of dwellings. The text attributes the invention of dwellings to the sage Huangdi, who was also sent by the Way:

> One drills doors and windows to make dwellings, but the usefulness of the dwelling resides *in whether it exists or not.*
>
> *Commentary:* The Way sent Huangdi to make them. This is also the same explanation as with the carts. (*Xiang'er*, lines 128–29)
>
> "鑿戸牖以爲室, 當其無, 有室之用。" 道使黃帝爲之, 亦與車同説。

The commentator then elaborates on the argument in the discussion of the final line of the chapter. I translated the line above as "Something (*you* 有) is what makes them beneficial; nothing (*wu*) is what makes them useful." Here I will again change the translation to reflect the commentator's reading:

> "*Those who have them* take them as beneficial; *those who do not have them* take them as useful."
>
> *Commentary:* These three things were at their basis difficult to invent. If there were no Way, they would not have been completed. When the common people obtained them, they merely desired their benefits but did not understand their origins. When the worthy people saw them, they turned back to [to their origins] and held fast to their usefulness. As for their usefulness, the Way is the basis. The minds of the worthy and foolish are like south and north, completely

> dissimilar. The meaning of these three [lines] simply refers to the fact that it is like this. (*Xiang'er*, lines 130–133)
>
> "有之以爲利, 無之以爲用。"
>
> 此三物本難作, 非道不成。俗人得之, 但貪其利, 不知其元。賢者見之, 還守其用。用道爲本, 賢愚之心, 如南與北, 萬不同。此三之義指如是耳。

The distinction between something (*you*) and nothing (*wu*) that animates the line is read throughout this passage as being between having (*you*) the created implements and not having them (*wu*). Gone is the entire argument contrasting the things that are there (the spokes of the wheel, the clay of the vessel, the walls of the dwelling) with the nothingness inside. The issue here is simply that there was a time before the implements existed, and now, thanks to the Way, sages have been sent down to create them for humanity. So humanity should now revere the Way for what it has done and should listen to the teachings of the Way.

As many scholars have noted, this is, to say the least, a rather odd interpretation of the *Laozi* lines. Stephen Bokenkamp, one of the leading analysts of the *Xiang'er* commentary, puts it beautifully:

> It is difficult to escape the impression that the commentator has here misunderstood, or willfully suppressed, the meaning of this and the following lines of the *Laozi*, which argues that the utility of such things resides as much in emptiness as in substance. The more standard reading is: The utility of a wheel derives from the empty spot where the spokes join; the utility of a pot, from where there is no clay; and the utility of windows and doors, from the space within. The commentator seems to be reading "where they are not" as "when they were not," which is equally possible grammatically, but nonsensical in this case. The reason for the commentator's insistence on a historical explanation of these passages becomes clear once we realize the sorts of glosses he wishes to refute.[6]

To see what Bokenkamp is referring to here, let us return to the commentary:

> Now, in the false arts practiced among the current generation, they accord with and follow the true text [i.e., the *Laozi*] to set up deceptive and clever words. [According to these practitioners,] the Way has a Heavenly hub, and human bodies also have a hub.

> If one concentrates one's breath, it will become soft. The "spokes" refer to the form acting as the linchpin. They also [say] that one should nourish the embryo and refine the form, just like making the earth into pottery. They also say that there are doors and windows to the Way that reside within the human body. All of these are false teachings that cannot be used. Those who use them will be greatly deceived. (*Xiang'er*, lines 133–137)

The *Laozi* is the true text, but unfortunately false teachings have emerged that use "deceptive and clever words" to read metaphysical understandings into the text.

This refutation of metaphysical readings of the text makes it quite clear that the *Xiang'er* commentator is aware of other interpretations and rejects that particular approach. In contrast to these other readings, the approach taken here—and it is an approach repeated throughout the commentary—is to provide extremely concrete, mundane, almost deadening readings of the *Laozi* chapters, in which the words are read in such a way as to deny all of the paradoxes, puns, and counterintuitive twists: *wu* is simply read as "not existing," and references to the importance of the Way are read as calls to follow the dictates of a deity called the "Way."

Why, one might ask, would the *Xiang'er* commentary read the *Laozi* in this way?

Reading in Chinese Late Antiquity

This paper will be an exploration of one particular strand among the commentarial strategies that developed in Chinese late antiquity in response to what many perceived to be a crisis of textual authority.[7] Authors during the first centuries of the Common Era felt themselves to be confronted with an enormous body of earlier texts. Some of these texts were presumably written by sages, but which texts were the sagely ones? And of those written by sages, how should one interpret them, given that there was an ever-proliferating set of competing reading strategies being developed for each text? Were the texts written clearly, so that even nonsages could understand them? Or are there hidden meanings embedded in the sagely texts, requiring a careful hermeneutic to bring their esoteric messages to the surface? Or, to give yet another option, were the sages of the past themselves limited and occasionally flawed, in which case the interpreter must himself be a sage willing to correct the errors of the original or perhaps even creatively and intentionally misread the original to bring out what ought to have been its proper meaning? In this latter strategy, the goal is not so much to uncover a hidden meaning provided by the earlier sage as to establish a hidden truth that had eluded even the earlier sage himself.

All of these problems were greatly exacerbated by the fact that the pre-Han texts were also being applied to a period and set of concerns dramatically different than the ones for which they were originally written—a fact frequently referred to in the debate. To give one example that will be significant for the *Xiang'er*: a concern with immortality arose very late and became particularly pronounced during the first centuries of the Common Era—yet it is something rarely if ever even mentioned in the pre-Han textual corpus.

The arguments in the *Xiang'er* commentary will make much more sense once we place them within this larger debate concerning how to read the earlier texts.

How to Read a Text

One of the most extreme positions in this debate was also one of the earliest. During the early Han period, it became common for a number of authors to claim themselves to be greater sages than the authors of the vast body of pre-Han material.[8] Usually this was implicit—as with Sima Qian's implicit claim to superiority vis-à-vis Confucius.[9] But in texts such as the *Huainanzi* 淮南子, it was quite explicit.[10] The *Huainanzi* claims that earlier authors only wrote in response to specific situations,[11] whereas the *Huainanzi* is an all-encompassing work in which everything is placed into a single comprehensive system that will be true for all time:

> The book of Mister Liu observes the images of Heaven and Earth, penetrates the affairs of ancient times and the present, weighs affairs and establishes regulations, measures forms and puts forth what is fitting. . . . It thereby unifies all under Heaven, gives pattern to the myriad things, and responds to alternations and transformations. . . . It does not follow a path from one trace, nor hold fast to instructions from one corner. . . . Therefore, one can establish it regularly and constantly and never be blocked; one can promulgate it throughout all under Heaven and never make a mistake.[12]
>
> 若劉氏之書, 觀天地之象, 通古今之論, 權事而立制, 度形而施宜。 . . . 以統天下, 理萬物, 應變化 . . . 非循一跡之路, 守一隅之指 。 . . . 故置之尋常而不塞, (市)〔布〕之天下而不窕。

As I have argued elsewhere, this results in the *Huainanzi*'s strategy of a "violent misreading" of earlier texts, in which earlier texts would be twisted, altered, or intentionally misread in order to place them into this enduring comprehensive system. In one striking example, the *Huainanzi* authors quote a set of lines from the *Zhuangzi* about the absurdity of trying to work out a cosmogony; the *Huainanzi* authors then provide a line-by-line commentary to that same *Zhuangzi* passage, in which each line is read as part of a grand cosmogony. This commentary is then used to provide the opening argument of a lengthy chapter on the importance of cosmogony for understanding how everything is ultimately interrelated in a single comprehensive system. The *Zhuangzi* passage is not only read in a manner contrary to its obvious point, it is also then used as an opening piece for a chapter devoted to doing precisely what the *Zhuangzi* passage was arguing ought not be done.[13]

This level of sagely arrogance was characteristic of the culture of the early Han, but in a less extreme form, the approach would continue to play a crucial role in later Chinese hermeneutic traditions as well. Indeed, the interpretive technique of the great Southern Song scholar, Zhu Xi, in part came out of this tradition of creative misreading, if in a much less arrogant form and with much less debasement of the earlier sages. For example, he would argue that the Four Books are correct—but only after he had altered them, rearranged them, added characters, and provided a cosmological framework wholly lacking in the original texts. None of this editing is based on a claim to have found philological evidence supporting the rewriting—the claim is simply that the rewritten texts are the proper ones. If the early sages really were true sages, this is what they must have written. And if they did not actually write the proper texts—well, that need not concern the reader who now has them.

Despite the continued application of the violent misreading approach, its history immediately following the Han was not so successful. The kind of arrogance vis-à-vis the past that was so common in the very early Han gave way soon thereafter to a reaction against such claims of surpassing the ancients. By the end of the Western Han, the dominant mode at court was to call for an end to what was seen as the imperial hubris of the Qin and early Han courts. Instead, calls were made to return to the culture of the Western Zhou—including a return to the simplicity of style associated with the Zhou as well as a return to those texts written during or written about the Zhou period. This ultimately resulted in, among other things, the claim that a proper explication of sagely knowledge was to be found in the Five Classics—a set of texts that were seen as having been written and edited well before the sagely arrogance of the Qin and early Han.

But, if this body of texts—the Five Classics as well as other pre-Qin works—ought to contain true knowledge, interpreters still faced the basic problem of how to read them—particularly since they did not often clearly speak to contemporary concerns. And if they were not a full repository of true knowledge, then what was? By the time one gets into the Eastern Han, these concerns became increasingly acute.

One way out of this problem was to make a distinction between the esoteric and exoteric: the pre-Han corpus, by such a definition, is simply a product of exoteric writing, and the commentary would claim to be laying out an esoteric doctrine—usually based on a claimed oral transmission. One of the best examples of this approach is found in the Han Dynasty Chenwei 讖緯 materials, the so-called apocryphal texts, which provided an esoteric reading of the Classics.[14] What is hidden is therefore simply what was esoteric, and the commentary consists of making manifest this hidden, esoteric knowledge.

Others, such as the Eastern Han scholar Wang Chong 王充 (27–ca. 100), opposed any attempt to claim that a true body of knowledge was to be found in any corpus of previous texts or oral transmissions. Wang Chong's position was that all sages are imperfect and limited. Thus, what the world needs is an endless number of new sages arising, to build on the good work of the previous sages and to correct the previous sages' errors. Wang Chong accordingly spent a great deal of time both pointing out the errors of earlier sages like Confucius, and arguing against any restrictions on the recognition of new sages as such. Thus, although he certainly does not claim, as did the *Huainanzi* authors, to be a sage superior to those in the past, he does strongly assert the need for the emergence of new sages to continue writing new texts and building on the past. Each of these texts will be imperfect and limited, but the proliferation of new texts will allow an accumulation of knowledge and an ongoing correction of previous errors.[15]

Yet another move was that attempted by the Eastern Han commentator Zheng Xuan 鄭玄 (127–200). Zheng Xuan's solution was essentially to argue that authority should be granted not to a single text but rather to a time period. It was the Western Zhou that was correct, rather than a single corpus of texts. The texts that are of primary interest, then, are those that maintain some record or remnant of the practices of the Western Zhou. The goal of the interpreter is thus to work through these remnants and shards from the Western Zhou and from them to develop a sense of what the Western Zhou was like. Confucius, as a supporter of the Western Zhou and as a sage who edited works on that period, is obviously given a privileged position, but it is not the texts themselves that are authoritative. What matters is the degree to which they reflect, or could be read as shedding light on, the Western Zhou. Zheng Xuan's resulting hermeneutic consisted of working to reconstruct the

Western Zhou system by connecting and synthesizing the remnants found in the various texts associated with the dynasty.

One of the implications of such an approach is that new sages were, in fact, unnecessary: a period had already existed in which things operated properly. Thus, the goal of the reader is to understand this period and the texts that discuss it, not to have new sages claiming to create something better than what existed in the past.

One of the most ingenious solutions to the problem of where to locate true authority in the earlier textual tradition was provided by a section of the *Taiping Jing* 太平經 that probably belongs to the late Eastern Han.[16] The section explicitly calls on people not only to stop recognizing new sages but to not even try to decide which of the earlier texts are by sages and which are not. The section is also against interpretation: there is no reason to interpret texts at all. The call instead is for contemporaries simply to assemble absolutely *all* texts. Once they are assembled together, it will be clear what is sagely and what is not, and in their collectivity the assembled texts will yield a single sagely truth:

> If the sages of higher antiquity missed something, the sages of middle antiquity may have obtained it. If the sages of middle antiquity missed something, the sages of lower antiquity may have obtained it. If the sages of lower antiquity missed something, the sages of higher antiquity may have obtained it. If one arranges these by category so they thereby supplement each other, then together they will form one good sagely statement.[17]
>
> 上古聖人失之，中古聖人得之；中古聖人失之，下古聖人得之；下古聖人失之，上古聖人得之。以類相從，因以相補，共成一善聖辭矣。

In a sense, then, there is nothing hidden: all knowledge is present in the texts, without any interpretation necessary. The problem is simply that the knowledge is partial in any one text, and there is no way to know when a text is right and when it is not. So the key is just to put all texts together. All knowledge will be manifest once everything is assembled.

Thus, in just this brief summary, we have seen several different options opening up in the Eastern Han. The kind of extreme sagely arrogance seen in the *Huainanzi* is largely absent—in fact, opposition to the extreme claim that a present-day author can provide a full summation of all knowledge is one of the few topics on which there is relatively wide agreement in the Eastern Han. But there was a consensus on little else. Does one need an endless number of new sages to continue writing an endless number of new texts? Or has knowledge already been achieved at a certain time in the past, or in the sum of all texts already written? And if the latter, how does one read such material? How, in short, does one make manifest the hidden truth when there is no clear authority in the past or present to make such a determination?

Following the Way in the *Xiang'er*

Within this production of texts and interpretive claims about earlier texts, the *Xiang'er* commentary makes a number of fascinating moves. Not unlike the *Huainanzi*, the authors of the *Xiang'er* commentary are interested in reading a number of things into an earlier text that would not obviously appear to be there; unlike the *Huainanzi*, however, it will not claim to be reinterpreting or providing any kind of new reading of the text—or even to be interpreting the text at all. Rather, it claims full subordination to the earlier text. It will also not appeal to any esoteric tradition; indeed, it will claim that the only reason the truth is hidden from other readers of the text is that they have foolishly tried to be overly clever in interpreting the text. While thus providing what could be construed as a strong misreading of the host text, it will on the contrary claim for itself complete subordination to the obvious meaning of the original, arrived at without any interpretation at all. It is simply a paraphrase of a straightforward, clear, and completely correct text.

Let us turn to a closer reading of the *Xiang'er* commentary. And let us look at another of the classic lines from the *Laozi*:

> The Way constantly does nothing, yet nothing is not done.
>
> If lords and kings are able to hold fast to it, the myriad things will transform themselves. (*Laozi*, chapter 37)
>
> 道（常）〔恒〕無為,而無不為。侯王若能守之,萬物將自化。

The power of these opening lines of the chapter would appear to lie in their paradox, in which the Way is doing nothing (*wuwei* 無為) but nonetheless (or, perhaps, consequently) still having nothing not done (*wu buwei* 無不為).

The *Xiang'er* commentary, on the contrary, reads the line a bit differently:

> The nature of the Way is that it never does bad things. Therefore it is able to be spiritual, and there is nothing it cannot cause to occur. The person of the Way always patterns himself on this. (*Xiang'er*, lines 572–73)
>
> 道性不爲惡事, 故能神無所不作, 道人當灋之。

Gone is any sense here that the Way does nothing—*wuwei*. On the contrary, the Way simply does not do anything that is bad. As Bokenkamp has argued, probably the best way to translate the original line, if one is to make it accord with this reading, would thus to be read *wei* 為 as *wei* 偽—"artifice, falsity": "The Way is without falsity, and nothing is not done."[18]

The commentary continues:

> "If the kings and lords are able to hold fast to it."
>
> Even though the king is revered, he must always fear the Way, and the precepts must be followed. (*Xiang'er*, line 574)
>
> "王侯若能守。" 王者雖尊, 猶常畏道, 奉誡行之。

The Way is something that should be feared and whose precepts should be followed.

> "The myriad things will transform themselves."
>
> If the king rules by patterning himself on the Way, the officials, people, and bad elements will all transform to the Way. (*Xiang'er*, lines 575–76)
>
> "萬物將自化。" 王者灋道爲政, 吏民庶孽子, 悉化爲道。

Here again, the Way is the source of good, and if the ruler will follow it, the populace will turn to the Way as well. The Way is not a technique of rulership based on nothingness, nor is it a cosmic force. It is rather a deity handing down proper precepts.

Indeed, as we are told in the commentary to another chapter, the Way comes down from on high, appoints rulers, and provides all the guidelines for how to rule. When these are followed, the Way sends down omens to signal the coming of Great Peace:

"Grasp the great image and all under Heaven will proceed."

The ruler grasps the correct method and models himself on the great Way. All under Heaven returns to him. . . . As for the Way's transformation, it descends from on high. When it indicates the one to be called the ruler, it distinguishes the one man. In ruling there are not two rulers. That is why the thearchs and kings always practice the Way. Only thus will it reach the officials and people. It is not that only nobles of the Way (*dao shi* 道士) can practice it, with the ruler being excluded. Rather, the great sage ruler follows the Way and fully puts it into practice so as to educate and transform. Once all under Heaven is thus ordered, the omens of Great Peace will accumulate in response to the merit of humans. The one who brings this about is a ruler of the Way. (*Xiang'er*, lines 527–33)

"執大象天下往。"

王者執正灋，像大道，天下歸往。 . . . 道之爲化，自高而降，指謂王者，故貴一人。製無二君，是以帝王常當行道，然後乃及吏民。非獨道士可行，王者棄捐也。上聖之君，師道至行以教化。天下如治，太平符瑞，皆感人功所積，致之者道君也。

And even the spirits are also arrayed on behalf of the Way:

"Auspicious and not harmful."

When rulers put in practice the Way, the Way comes back to them. Rulers also rejoice in the Way, knowing the spirits and celestial beings cannot be cheated or turned away from. They do not fear regulations and statutes, but do fear the Heavenly spirits. They do not dare engage in wrongdoing. (*Xiang'er*, lines 541–43)

"佳而不害。"

王者行道，道來歸往。王者亦皆樂道，知神明不可欺負。不畏灋律也，乃畏天神，不敢爲非惡。

In terms of statecraft, therefore, the key is for the ruler to follow the precepts handed down by the Way. Absent here entirely is the vision of statecraft that played such a crucial role in the *Han Feizi* reading of the *Laozi*, and that would later interest Wang Bi—namely that the sage creates an order that the people come to think of as natural.[19] The *Xiang'er* commentary on the contrary reads such passages as simply saying that the successful ruler is one who follows the precepts. Take, for example, the following *Laozi* lines, which I will first translate as a Han Feizi or Wang Bi would read them:

> When his achievements are completed and tasks finished,
>
> The hundred families say: "We (*wo* 我) are like this spontaneously (*ziran* 自然)." (*Laozi*, chapter 17)
>
> 功成事遂,〔而〕百姓皆謂我自然。

The ruler sets up an order that the hundred families come to think of as simply natural. The *Xiang'er* commentary on the contrary reads the (*wo* 我) in the first person—as referring not to the hundred families but rather to the transcendent noble who has completed great achievements:

> "The hundred families say that I (*wo* 我) was like this spontaneously (ziran 自然)."
>
> "I" refers to the transcendent noble. The hundred families do not study the fact that I had to value and have faith in the words of the Way to bring about this accomplishment. They think I was like this spontaneously. One must make known to those not conscientious that they are expected to do as I have done. (*Xiang'er*, lines 242–43)
>
> "百姓謂我自然。"
>
> 我,僊士也。百姓不學我有貴信道言,以致此功,而意我自然,當示不肯企及效我也。

According to the commentary, it is not that the people believe the system created by the sage to be spontaneous. The text is instead referring to a problem—that the follower of the Way, the "transcendent noble," is incorrectly perceived by the people to have brought forth his accomplishments spontaneously. To the contrary, says the *Xiang'er*, the people need to be convinced to work hard in following the teachings of the Way and to have faith in the words of the Way.

In short, the commentary argues that the cosmos is a moral one, ruled over by a moral deity called the Way, who creates precepts for humanity, designates rulers to follow them, and offers rewards to those who do well and inflicts punishments on those who do not. The Way also organizes the various spirits in the cosmos to reward and punish as well.

Morality in the *Xiang'er*

Such a moral reading of the *Laozi* is rather surprising, given that it contains several chapters that would appear to argue for a distinctly nonmoral reading of the Way. Let us look at a few of these passages, as well as the *Xiang'er* commentary to them.

> "When the great Way was discarded, there was humaneness and propriety." (*Laozi*, chapter 18)
>
> 大道廢,〔安〕有仁義。

Humaneness and propriety, the line appears to be saying, emerged only when the Way was discarded.

The *Xiang'er*, on the contrary, reads the line in precisely the opposite manner:

> When the Way was used in high antiquity, it relied on the [conduct of the] people to establish names [of categories of conduct]. Since all practiced humaneness and propriety, all were of the same type, and the humane and proper were not distinguished. Now, the Way is not used, and the people are all dishonest and stingy. When there is a person who practices propriety, all uphold and distinguish him. Therefore it is now said that there are the qualities of [humaneness and propriety]. (*Xiang'er*, lines 244–46)
>
> 上古道用時,以人爲名,皆行仁義,同相像類,仁義不別。今道不用,人悉弊薄,時有一人行義,便共表別之,故言有也。

According to this reading, when the precepts of the Way were practiced in high antiquity, everyone was humane and proper, and thus there was no reason to distinguish particular people as having such attributes. It was only after the Way stopped being followed that those few who acted morally needed to be deemed as being humane and proper.

But what about those lines of the *Laozi* that would at least appear to state explicitly that Heaven and Earth are not moral? Take, for example:

> "Heaven and Earth are inhumane. They take the myriad things as straw dogs." (*Laozi*, chapter 5)
>
> 天地不仁，以萬物為芻狗。

The *Xiang'er* comments:

> Heaven and Earth model themselves on the Way. They are humane to those who do good, and inhumane to those who do bad. Therefore, when they bring to an end the badness of the myriad things, they do not love them but see them as grass and as dogs. (*Xiang'er*, lines 32–4)
>
> 天地像道，仁於諸善，不仁於諸惡，故煞萬物惡者不愛也，視之如芻草。

Far from being a provocative claim that the Way is amoral, the line is read as an affirmation of the rigorous morality of the Way, in which the good are rewarded and the bad are punished. The statement that "Heaven and Earth are inhumane" is thus only in reference to those who act wrongly—such people are treated as straw dogs. But those who act properly, the commentary claims, are treated humanely.

The *Laozi* goes on to state the inhumaneness of the sage:

> "The sage is inhumane, treating the hundred families as if they were straw dogs."
>
> 聖人不仁，以百姓為芻狗。

The *Xiang'er* commentary reads the passage in the same manner as it did the previous line. The sage is humane to the good and inhumane to the bad:

> The sage patterns himself on Heaven and Earth. He is humane to the good and inhumane to the bad. When it comes to the ruler correcting and bringing the bad to an end, he also sees them as if they were straw dogs. This is why when the people accumulate good merit, their essence and spirit communicate with the Way. If there are those who wish to attack and injure one, Heaven will

> then save one. The common people are all just followers of straw dogs. Their essences and spirits are unable to communicate with Heaven. (*Xiang'er*, lines 35–7)
>
> 聖人灋天地，仁於善人，不仁惡人。當王政煞惡，亦視之如芻苟也。是以人當積善功，其精神與天通。設欲侵害者，天卽救之。庸庸之人，皆是芻苟之徒耳，精神不能通天。

In short, a rigorously moral cosmos is read into the text. The Way is moral, rewarding the good and punishing the bad. Heaven and Earth pattern themselves on the Way and do the same. Proper sages model themselves on Heaven and Earth and thus also do the same.

This same point is reiterated again and again in the commentary:

> For those who themselves achieve sincerity, Heaven will itself reward them. As for those who do not achieve sincerity, Heaven will itself punish them. Heaven's discernment is greater than any human's. It always knows who reveres the Way and fears Heaven. (*Xiang'er*, lines 280–81)
>
> 自當至誠，天自賞之；不至誠者，天自罰之。天察必審於人，皆知尊道畏天。

Revere the Way, and you will be rewarded. As the reader has probably realized by now, the commentary makes this point many times.

Sages

But this raises a problem. If the loss of the Way was not coincident with the emergence of human artifice (including morality distinctions), then why has a decline occurred? One of the reasons is that people listen to false texts, written by false sages. Let us return to the commentary to chapter eighteen of the *Laozi*:

> "When wisdom and intelligence emerged, there was the great falsity." (*Laozi*, chapter 18)
>
> 智慧出，〔安〕有大偽。

Although the line might appear to be yet another statement of how human craft has resulted in a loss of the Way, the *Xiang'er* commentary reads the line as simply referring to the emergence of false texts:

> The true Way was hidden, and aberrant texts emerged. In the present age, the proliferating false arts are proclaimed as teachings of the Way. All of these are great falsities and cannot be used. What are these aberrant texts? Of the Five Classics, half fall under [this category] of aberrance. Apart from the Five Classics, all books, transmissions, and records are aberrant texts created by corpses. (*Xiang'er*, lines 246–48)
>
> 眞道藏,耶文出。世間常僞伎稱道教,皆爲大僞不可用。何謂耶文?其五經半入耶,其五經以外,衆書傳記,尸人所作悉耶耳。

We will return to the statement about the corpses momentarily. The point to emphasize here is that the emergence of false texts was one of the causes of humanity's failure to follow the Way. And the problem of the present day is that these false teachings have continued to proliferate. The Five Classics themselves are only half-correct, and all of the other books and records are false teachings of this sort.

This is indeed a recurrent argument throughout the commentary: fraudulent sages, writing false texts that the populace follows, are one of the central causes of decline. True sages, on the contrary, are sent by Heaven. We have already seen this latter theme in the passages quoted at the beginning of this paper: major innovations for humanity were created by sages who, like Xi Zhong and Huangdi, were sent down by Heaven.

This same theme is read into passages of the *Laozi* that would appear to be against sages altogether. The *Xiang'er* instead reads the passages as being against fraudulent sages only:

> "If one cut off the sages and discarded knowledge, the people would benefit a hundred times over."
>
> This refers to fraudulent sages who know aberrant texts. [True] sages are put forward by Heaven. When they are born, there will always be signs made manifest. The Yellow River and Luo River announce their names. And so, [the sages] constantly proclaim the truth, never reaching the point of accepting what is false. (*Xiang'er*, lines 266–68)

"絶聖棄知，民利百倍。" 謂詐聖知耶文者。夫聖人天所挺，生必有表，河雒著名，然常宣眞，不至受有誤。

Sages are sent by Heaven, which also therefore provides signs to humanity that these are in fact true sages. Unlike the sages discussed by Wang Chong, true sages are infallible. They are human, but they are sent by Heaven, and thus cannot be wrong.

Unfortunately, people often do not follow the words of true sages:

> Those who practice aberrant ways do not trust the words of enlightened sages. Thus, for thousands and hundreds of years the great sages have expounded the truth and cleared away repeatedly the aberrant texts. (*Xiang'er*, lines 268–69)
>
> 耶道不信明聖人之言，故令千百歲大聖演眞，滌徐耶文。

The true sages have appeared repeatedly to clear away the aberrant texts, since, once people start practicing the aberrant ways, they do not listen to the true sages. Thus, as we have seen, the sages have given humans the basic inventions they need to thrive, and have continued to appear to save humanity from the endless growth of new, aberrant texts written by false sages.

Such work is necessary in the present day as well:

> The people of today are not in their proper state. They copy in their entirety the classics and, without hearing the truth of the Way, proclaim themselves sages. They do not cleave to the underlying sense [of the text as a whole], but gauge their own [ideas] by the texts' chapters and sections. They are not able to obtain the Way. (*Xiang'er*, lines 269–70)
>
> 今人無狀，載通經藝，未貫道眞，便自稱聖。不因本而章篇自揆，不能得道。

Sages have emerged throughout history to teach humanity to stop following the aberrant ways, and the commentary would appear to be making the same claim for itself: the present age is one dominated by aberrant texts, the followers of which proclaim themselves to be sages. They cannot obtain the Way, and the aberrant texts thus need to be cleared away by a true sage.

And what would this Way consist of? The commentary continues:

> They speak of themselves first and do not guide the people in the true Way so that they can obtain long life, practicing the good and striving [to perfect] themselves. They instead say that transcendents naturally have bones that are inscribed [for long life]; and that this is not something one can arrive at through practice. They say that there is no Way of life, and that the books of the Way only take advantage of the people. . . . Thus, you must cut off the false sages and their aberrant knowledge; do not cut off the true sages and their knowledge of the Way. (*Xiang'er*, lines 270–77)
>
> 言先爲身; 不勸民眞道可得僊壽, 修善自勤, 反言僊自有骨録; 非行所臻, 云無生道, 道書欺人。 . . . 是故絶詐聖耶知, 不絶眞聖道知也。

If humans were to listen to the true sages, they would be able to obtain the Way of life, meaning that they actually could become transcendents and live forever. The people of the present day argue that long life is only due to fate—something inscribed in the bones of some people at birth. The true Way, on the contrary, teaches that people can indeed become transcendents.

Life and Death

And here we arrive at another point in the argument: not only is the true Way the way of life; the aberrant teachings are of death:

> The Way is life; aberrance is death. The dead belong to the earth; the living belong to Heaven. (*Xiang'er*, line 295)
>
> 道生耶死, 死屬地, 生屬天。

Indeed, life and death were established by the Way as part of the same moral cosmos that the commentary discusses repeatedly: life was established by the Way in order to reward the good, and death was established by the Way in order to punish the bad.

> The Way established life in order to reward the good, and established death in order to punish the bad. As for death, this is what all men fear. The transcendent rulers and nobles, like the common people,

know to fear death and enjoy life; it is what they practice that is different. . . . Although the common people fear death, they do not try to trust in the Way, and they enjoy committing bad acts. Is it surprising that they are not yet trying to escape from death? The transcendent nobles fear death, trust in the Way, and hold fast to the precepts. Therefore they join with life. (*Xiang'er*, lines 299–303)

道設生以賞善，設死以威惡，死是人之所畏也。僊王士與俗人，同知畏死樂生，但所行異耳 . . . 俗人雖畏死，端不信道，好爲惡事，奈何未央脫死乎！僊士畏死，信道守誡，故與生合也。

As the commentary states bluntly, those who follow the Way will live, and those who do not will die:

Those who practice the Way live; those who lose the Way die. (*Xiang'er*, lines 374–75)

行道者生，失道者死。

Indeed, the text goes so far as to see those who do not follow the Way as simply moving corpses:

The bodies of those who do not understand the Way of long life are all just corpses that move. It is not the Way that moves them; theirs is entirely the motion of corpses. The reason that people of the Way are able to obtain the long life of transcendents is that theirs is not the movement of corpses. They are different from the vulgar. Thus, they are able to fulfill the potential of their corpse and command themselves to become transcendent nobles. (*Xiang'er*, lines 72–4)

不知長生之道。身皆尸行耳，非道所行，悉尸行也。道人所以得僊壽者，不行尸行，與俗別異，故能成其尸，令爲僊士也。

This clarifies a sentence we saw earlier: "Apart from the Five Classics, all books, transmissions, and records are aberrant texts created by corpses." Those not following the Way are moving corpses—and soon they will die and stop moving altogether.

Here again, we are dealing with an argument that would appear not only to have little textual support in the *Laozi*, but in fact seems to contradict directly one of the primary arguments of the text. The fact that everything that lives will ultimately die would appear to be a basic aspect of the *Laozi*'s cosmology:

> "The myriad things become active together,
> And I thereby watch them turn back.
> All of the things are teeming and multifarious,
> But each returns to its root." (*Laozi*, chapter 16)
>
> 萬物並作，吾以觀〔其〕復。夫物芸芸，各復歸其根。

Things live, things die; things become active, things decline. The true follower of the text is one who can understand these processes and act accordingly, seeing where true strength lies, and seeing the inevitable moment when things, at the height of their power, will begin their decline.

Now, the *Xiang'er* reading. To reflect how it impinges on the original lines of the *Laozi*, I will again modify slightly the translation, changing the translation of *fu* (復) from "turn back" to "come back":

> "The myriad things become active together,
> And I thereby watch them come back.
> All of the things are teeming and multifarious,
> But each returns to its root."
>
> The myriad things contain the essence of the Way. "Becoming active together" refers to when they are first born and arise. "I" is the Way. When it watches the essences [of the myriad things] come back [to it], they are "returning to their root." Thus, it commands people to treasure and be careful with their root. (*Xiang'er*, lines 216–18)
>
> "萬物並作，吾以觀其復。夫物云云，各歸其根。" 萬物含道精，並作，初生起時也。吾，道也。觀其精復時，皆歸其根，故令人寶慎根也。

The "I" is not the follower of the Way; it is rather the Way itself. The Way gives each thing its essence—its life force. The Way watches things as they emerge with this essence, and commands them to treasure it. When they fail to do so, they die.

At this point, the reader may plausibly begin wondering if the commentary simply misunderstood the *Laozi* altogether. But the fact that the commentary critiques other commentaries to the text, while clearly understanding their meaning, makes this a dubious argument. As seen in the first passage from the text discussed in this paper, the *Xiang'er* clearly understood the metaphysical reading of the *Laozi*, but is arguing explicitly against it.[20]

So, then, how are we to understand such a reading of the *Laozi*?

The Revelation of the Way

The overall argument of the *Xiang'er* is in many ways remarkably like that seen in the writings of the Mohists. As with the Mohists, an active deity has created the cosmos, organized spirits to reward the good and punish the bad, sent down sages to create things needed by the populace, and designated figures to act as rulers.[21] The Mohists called this deity Heaven, while the *Xiang'er* commentary calls it the Way (to which Heaven is subordinate), but otherwise the argument is remarkably similar.[22]

Indeed, just as the argument of the text reads like early Mohism, so does the writing style. The writing contains no elusive prose, no poetry, no subtle allusions. It exemplifies extremely straightforward argumentation, provided in clear, almost boring prose, with basic points being repeated over and over again. It reads, in other words, like early Mohist writings. And the commentary itself defends such clear prose as itself the style of the Way:

> "When the Way emits words, they are tasteless and without flavor."
>
> The words of the Way are opposed to the extreme cleverness of the vulgar. [Circulated] among the vulgar people, they are truly without flavor. [Passed around] among the flavorless (i.e., the sages), they harbor the flavor of great life. Thus the flavor of the sages is the flavor of the flavorless. (*Xiang'er*, lines 549–50)
>
> "道出言，淡無味。" 道之所言，反俗絶巧，於俗人中，甚無味也。無味之中，有大生味，故聖人味無味之味。

The vulgar use cleverness to express themselves, and only appreciate clever words; the words of the Way are flavorless, without rhetorical embellishment, and thus can only be fully apprehended by those who are attuned to their essence.

Such a statement could almost serve as a self-description of the style and claims of the commentary itself. The *Xiang'er* commentary is strongly opposed to the view that the *Laozi* requires subtle or complex interpretation. On the contrary, the power of the *Xiang'er* commentary comes from the claim that the text is in fact perfectly clear, and that others have obfuscated this clear message by reading a complex metaphysics into it.

Even the evocative, pregnant puns in the *Laozi* are denied: as we saw above, the famous line "of doing nothing but leaving nothing undone" simply becomes a statement that the Way always acts properly. Neither literary style nor metaphysical claims are allowed to be present in the text at all.

It is also clear that the commentary presents itself as the product of a sage who does understand the Way, and who is therefore trying to eradicate the vulgar and demonic texts and interpretations that are dominant in the present age. Since humans do listen to false sages, the world is filled with such aberrant texts and false teachings. As the *Xiang'er* makes clear, only sages sanctioned by the Way are to be listened to, and thus only texts produced by Way or by sages sanctioned by the Way should be followed. The commentary itself is such a work.

But then what about the text is the commentary explicating? What is the *Laozi* itself? We have already seen the hint of the answer in a passage quoted above. I will quote it again, here focusing on a different element:

> "The myriad things become active together,
> And I thereby watch them come back.
> All of the things are teeming and multifarious,
> But each returns to its root."
>
> The myriad things contain the essence of the Way. "Becoming active together" refers to when they are first born and arise. "I" is the Way. When it watches the essences [of the myriad things] come back [to it], they are "returning to their root." Thus, it commands people to treasure and be careful with their root. (*Xiang'er*, lines 216–18)
>
> "萬物並作，吾以觀其復。夫物云云，各歸其根。" 萬物含道精，並作，初生起時也。吾，道也。觀其精復時，皆歸其根，故令人寶慎根也。

The "I" in the text is the Way itself.

This is not just a passing statement. To give another example:

> The reason I can suffer great calamity is that I have a body. When I reach the point of no longer having a body, how could I suffer calamities? (*Laozi*, chapter 13)
>
> 吾所以有大患者，為吾有身〔也〕。及吾無身，吾有何患？

The *Xiang'er* commentary explains:

> "I" refers to the Way. It desires to be without a body. It simply desires to nourish spirits; that is all. And it desires to compel humans to model themselves on this. (*Xiang'er*, lines 154–55)[23]
>
> 吾我，道也。誌欲無身，但欲養神耳。欲令人自瀍。

"I," again, is the Way.

So why should we trust the words of the text? Because the author of the *Laozi* was not a human at all. The text was rather a revelation issued by the Way itself, and Laozi is not a (possibly limited) human sage but, rather, a god.[24] And once the *Xiang'er* defines the *Laozi* as a divine revelation, there is no possibility of seeing the text as anything other than containing accurate knowledge. The commentary thus restricts, if it does not obviate, the possibility of self-proclaimed sages creating anew, creating wrong texts, or interpreting the text: the Way has already stated its views, in clear language, and the commentary is sweeping away all clever interpretations to highlight the clear, straightforward words of the revelation itself.

It is as if, in order to work around the debates of the time concerning sages and textual authority, the *Xiang'er* commentary opted out of the entire problem by appealing to a Mohist vision of a deity handing down true knowledge, sending down sages, and rewarding the good and punishing the bad.[25] But the *Xiang'er* has done the Mohists one better: here, that deity has in fact handed down a revelation.

This claim of divine revelation as a basis for legitimacy—thus stepping completely outside of the debates concerning sagely authorship that were so pervasive in Chinese late antiquity—would become increasingly significant over the ensuing centuries. Increasingly, the debate would concern not just who was a sage, but whether the author was human or divine.

Conclusion

As we have seen, the Han and immediately post–Han Dynasty debate over textual and sagely authority, with its consequent concerns over how to read earlier writings, revolved around the issue of sagehood. Barring the existence of a single, perfect sage who had written a text that contained all knowledge—an arrogant claim that only a few figures like the *Huainanzi* authors would make—then all of our previous texts are at best written by limited, imperfect sages. And even if there had been a sage who one could claim was perfect, there would still exist the problems of whether that sage's texts had survived in perfect form and, even if they had, whether and how the latter-born could understand that sage's texts. The resulting debate generated a plethora of increasingly complex hermeneutic strategies.

The *Xiang'er* commentary takes a distinctive position within this debate. It opts out of the problem of sagely authorship altogether by reading Laozi as the Way itself, and reading the text of the *Laozi* as a revelation of this Way. It also opts out of the problem of providing criteria for deciding which earlier sages were truly sages worth following by simply stating that the true sages were those sent down by the Way. And, finally, it opts out of the problem of interpretation by arguing that the message of the text is straightforward and clear—not only is subtle interpretation unnecessary, but the habit of complex interpretation is precisely why the other commentators have misunderstood the clear meaning of the work.

What makes this commentary surprising is precisely that such a hermeneutic is applied to, of all things, the *Laozi*, a text that would appear to provide a highly elusive argument, relying heavily on a range of subtle rhetorical devices, paradoxes, and puns. Thus, the consistent approach of the *Xiang'er* commentary is to deny the paradoxes, ignore the puns, and read the text as giving a clear, straightforward argument. The Way is a deity that sends down sages to guide humanity and sends down moral precepts for humanity to follow, and that rewards those who follow the precepts and punishes those who do not. It is a perfect Mohist system, with a perfect Mohist style of writing, applied to one of the most subtle and elusive texts in the entire tradition. Indeed, with the possible exception of the *Zhuangzi*, there are few if any other texts from the pre-Han period that are less amenable to such a framework.

When one reads Han commentaries to the *Spring and Autumn Annals*, one sees an incredibly complex hermeneutic applied to a seemingly simple annal. With the *Xiang'er*, one sees the opposite move: a seemingly mundane hermeneutic applied to an incredibly elusive and subtle text. And that this is an intentional hermeneutic—as opposed to, well, a bad reading—is clear from the type of critique this commentary applies to the hermeneutic strategies of other commentaries to the same text.

One could call the *Xiang'er* commentary as violent a misreading as anything attempted in the *Huainanzi*. But in contrast to the sagely arrogance that characterizes the *Huainanzi*, the *Xiang'er* presents itself as anti-interpretive, simply paraphrasing the revealed teachings of the text. If the *Huainanzi* proclaims its superiority to the text being commented on, the *Xiang'er* proclaims its complete subordination to a text that is absolutely correct (being the result of divine revelation). In other words, if it is a misreading, it is a misreading that legitimates itself by claiming to be the precise opposite: a clear paraphrase of a clear text. The author of the commentary is thus himself a sage, or at the very minimum, the equivalent of the worthies who, after the Way sent Xi Zhong to create carts, recognized the significance of those carts. Under this latter interpretation, the author would be a worthy who has recognized the significance of what the Way has handed down and is now explaining it to others. Instead of presenting itself as a grand sagely corrective of an earlier great but perhaps flawed text, this commentary claims to be simply a paraphrase of a divine revelation—a revelation that, by definition, cannot be flawed in any way.

The *Xiang'er* commentary is an audacious response to the problem of hiddenness. Truth is not hidden in earlier texts—even, or especially, in those that seem most abstruse—and they do not require a complex hermeneutic to bring it to the surface; it does not lie buried in an esoteric teaching that can be unmasked through the discovery of an oral transmission or a secret code. The truth is rather hidden in plain sight, missed simply because there are too many self-proclaimed sages who refuse to subordinate themselves to the obvious meaning of a very straightforward and clear text.

Notes

1. *Laozi*, chapter 11.

2. The *Xiang'er* commentary was discovered at Dunhuang (S 6825). It is unfortunately only a portion of the full text, consisting of commentary to chapters 3 through 37. The text is attributed in the received tradition to either Zhang Daoling 張道陵 (34–156), who purportedly received revelations from the god Laozi in 142, or to his grandson Zhang Lu 張魯, who founded the Celestial Masters movement.

For excellent studies of the *Xiang'er* commentary, see Rao Zongyi 饒宗頤, *Laozi Xiang'er zhu jiaojian* 老子想爾注校牋 (Shanghai: Guji chubanshe, 1991); Ôfuchi Ninji 大淵忍爾, *Shoki no dôkyô* 初期の道教 (Tokyo: Sôbunsha, 1991); Stephen Bokenkamp, "Traces of Early Celestial Master Physiological Practice in the *Xiang'er* Commentary," *Taoist Resources* 4.2 (Dec., 1993): 37–51; Bokenkamp, *Early Daoist Scriptures* (Berkeley: University of California Press, 1997), 29–77; William G. Boltz, "The Religious and Philosophical Significance of the 'Hsiang Erh' Lao-tzu in Light of the Ma-wang-tui Silk Manuscripts," *Bulletin of the School of Oriental and African Studies* 45 (1982): 95–117. For a discussion of the cosmology of the *Xiang'er* commentary, see Michael Puett, "Forming Spirits for the Way: The Cosmology of the *Xiang'er* Commentary to the *Laozi*," *Journal of Chinese Religions* 32 (2004): 1–27.

3. For helpful summaries of the scholarship on the dating of the *Xiang'er* commentary, see Bokenkamp, *Early Daoist Scriptures*, 58–62; Barbara Hendrischke, "Early Daoist Movements," in *Daoism Handbook*, ed. Livia Kohn (Leiden: Brill, 2000), 146.

4. My translations of the *Xiang'er* commentary, here and throughout this paper, have been aided tremendously by the superb translation by Stephen Bokenkamp in his *Early Daoist Scriptures*, 78–148. I have also learned enormously from the studies collected in Rao Zongyi 饒宗頤, *Laozi Xiang'er zhu jiaojian* 老子想爾注校牋 (Shanghai: Guji chubanshe, 1991); and William G. Boltz, "The Religious and Philosophical Significance of the 'Hsiang Erh' Lao-tzu in Light of the Ma-wang-tui Silk Manuscripts," *Bulletin of the School of Oriental and African Studies* 45 (1982): 95–117.

5. *Xiang'er*, lines 124–27. I follow Bokenkamp in referencing the line number of the commentary as given in the photographic copy of the manuscript in Ôfuchi Ninji 大淵忍爾, *Tonkô dôkyô: Zurokuhen* 敦煌道經: 圖錄編 (Tokyo: Fukutake, 1979), 421–34. This will allow the reader to easily find both the original and Bokenkamp's excellent translation.

6. Bokenkamp, *Early Daoist Scriptures*, 91n.

7. For excellent discussions of hermeneutic strategies in early and medieval China, see John B. Henderson, *Scripture, Canon, and Commentary: A Comparison of Confucian and Western Exegesis* (Princeton, NJ: Princeton University Press, 1991); Rudolf G. Wagner, *The Craft of a Chinese Commentator: Wang Bi on the* Laozi (Albany: State University of New York Press, 2000); Cai Zong-qi, *A Chinese Literary Mind: Culture, Creativity, and Rhetoric in* Wenxin diaolong (Stanford, CA: Stanford University Press, 2001); Cai Zong-qi, *Chinese Aesthetics: The Ordering of Literature, the Arts, and the Universe in the Six Dynasties* (Hawaii: University of Honolulu Press, 2004); Ming Dong Gu, *Chinese Theories of Reading And Writing: A Route to Hermeneutics and Open Poetics* (Albany: State University of New York, 2006).

8. Michael Puett, "The Temptations of Sagehood, or: The Rise and Decline of Sagely Writing in Early China," in *Books in Numbers*, ed. Wilt Idema (Cambridge, MA: Harvard-Yenching Library, 2007), 23–47.

9. Puett, "Review of Stephen Durrant's *The Cloudy Mirror: Tension and Conflict in the Writings of Sima Qian*," *Harvard Journal of Asiatic Studies* 57.1 (June 1997): 299–301.

10. For a superb analysis of the *Huainanzi* argumentation, see Griet Vankeerberghen, *The Huainanzi and Liu An's Claim to Moral Authority* (Albany: State University of New York Press, 2001). For excellent analyses of the *Huainanzi* postface, which strongly asserts the text's superiority over previous texts, see Sarah Queen, "Inventories of the Past: Rethinking the 'School' Affiliation of the *Huainanzi*," in *Asia Major*, Third Series, 14.1 (2001): 51–72; Judson Murray, "A Study of 'Yaolüe,' (A Summary of the Essentials): Understanding the *Huainanzi* from the Point of View of the Author of the Postface," *Early China* 29 (2004): 45–108. For a brief discussion of the implications of such claims in the postface, see Puett, *The Ambivalence of Creation: Debates Concerning Innovation and Artifice in Early China* (Stanford: Stanford University Press, 2001), 159–60.

11. *Huainanzi*, "Yaolüe," Chinese University of Hong Kong, Institute of Chinese Studies, Ancient Chinese Text Concordance Series (hereafter, *ICS*), 21/227/20–21/228/26.

12. *Huainanzi*, "Yaolue," *ICS*, 21/228/28–31.

13. Michael Puett, "Violent Misreadings: The Hermeneutics of Cosmology in the *Huainanzi*," *Bulletin of the Museum of Far Eastern Antiquities* 72 (2000): 29–47;

Puett, "The Temptations of Sagehood, or: The Rise and Decline of Sagely Writing in Early China," in Idema, *Books in Numbers*, 23–47.

14. See the outstanding work of Jack Dull, *A Historical Introduction to the Apocryphal (Ch'an-Wei) Texts of the Han Dynasty* (PhD diss. University of Washington, 1966) and Hans Van Ess, "The Apocryphal Texts of the Han Dynasty and the Old Text/New Text Controversy," *T'oung Pao*, Second Series 85.1/3 (1999): 29–64.

15. Puett, "The Temptations of Sagehood"; and Puett, "Listening to Sages: Divination, Omens, and the Rhetoric of Antiquity in Wang Chong's *Lunheng*," *Oriens Extremus* 45 (2005–2006): 271–281.

16. My understanding of the *Taiping jing* has been aided tremendously by Max Kaltenmark, "The Ideology of the *T'ai-p'ing ching*," in *Facets of Taoism: Essays in Chinese Religion*, eds. Holmes Welch and Anna Seidel (New Haven, CT: Yale University Press, 1979), 19–45; Xiong Deji 熊得基, "Taiping jing de zuozhe he sixiang ji qi yu Huangjin he Tianshidao de guanxi" 太平經的作者和思想及其與黃巾和天師道的關係, in *Lishi yanjiu* 歷史研究 4 (1962): 8–25; Jens Østergård Petersen, "The Early Traditions Relating to the Han Dynasty Transmission of the *Taiping jing*, Part One," *Acta Orientalia* 50 (1989): 133–71; Petersen, "The Early Traditions Relating to the Han Dynasty Transmission of the *Taiping jing*, Part Two," *Acta Orientalia* 51 (1990): 173–216; Petersen, "The Anti-Messianism of the *Taiping jing*," *Studies in Central and East Asian Religions* 3 (Autumn 1990): 1–41; Barbara Hendrischke, "The Daoist Utopia of Great Peace," *Oriens Extremus* 35 (1992): 61–91; Barbara Hendrischke, "The Concept of Inherited Evil in the *Taiping Jing*," *East Asian History* 1991 (2): 1–30.

The section under discussion here concerns the dialogues between a Celestial Master and the Perfected. Most scholars of the text agree that this portion of the text belongs the late Eastern Han. See the excellent summary by Barbara Hendrischke, "Early Daoist Movements," in Kohn, *The Daoism Handbook*, 143–145. For an outstanding translation of significant portions of this section of the text, see Hendrischke, *The Scripture on Great Peace: The* Taiping jing *and the Beginnings of Daoism* (Berkeley: University of California Press, 2006).

For a fuller discussion of how the arguments of the section may fit into the Eastern Han contexts, see my "Temptations of Sagehood," and "The Belatedness of the Present: Debates over Antiquity during the Han Dynasty," in *Perceptions of Antiquity in Chinese Civilization*, eds. Dieter Kuhn and Helga Stahl (Heidelberg: Würzburger Sinologische Schriften, 2008), 177–90.

17. Wang Ming 王明, *Taiping jing hejiao* 太平經合校 (Beijing: Zhonghua shuju, 1992), 132.352.

18. Bokenkamp, *Early Daoist Scriptures*, 140.

19. See the excellent discussion by Rudolf G. Wagner, *The Craft of a Chinese Commentator: Wang Bi on the* Laozi (Albany: State University of New York Press, 2000), 187.

20. For another such critique, see *Xiang'er*, line 98.

21. Puett, *The Ambivalence of Creation: Debates Concerning Innovation and Artifice in Early China* (Stanford, CA: Stanford University Press, 2001), 51–56.

22. I have argued elsewhere that a number of the texts associated with millenarian movements in Chinese late antiquity appealed to Mohist views. The Mohists were the only major community from the pre-Han period that wrote texts claiming Heaven to be a moral deity who had created a moral cosmos and who presided over a pantheon of spirits directed toward rewarding the good and punishing the bad. A number of millenarian movements, many of which would later be characterized as Daoist, embraced such a cosmology, with the added view that this moral deity was now, in the midst of a general social crisis, handing down revelations to help humanity. One of these movements was the Celestial Masters, which was founded by Zhang Lu, to whom the authorship of the *Xiang'er* has traditionally been assigned. See Puett, "Forming Spirits for the Way," 9; Puett, "Sages, Gods, and History: Commentarial Strategies in Chinese Late Antiquity," *Antiquorum Philosophia* 3 (2009): 75; Puett, "Becoming Laozi: Cultivating and Visualizing Spirits in Early Medieval China," *Asia Major*, Third Series, 23.1 (2010): 227–38, 249–52; and Puett, "Sages, the Past, and the Dead: Death in the *Huainanzi*," in *Mortality in Traditional Chinese Thought*, eds. Amy Olberding and Philip J. Ivanhoe (Albany: State University of New York Press, 2011), 244–46.

23. For a fuller discussion of this passage, see Puett, "Forming Spirits for the Way."

24. For an excellent discussion of the deification of Laozi, see Anna Seidel, *La Divinisation de Lao Tseu dans le Taoisme des Han* (Paris: École Française d'Extrême-Orient, 1992); Livia Kohn, *God of the Dao: Lord Lao in History and Myth* (Ann Arbor, MI: Center for Chinese Studies, 1998).

25. This is not meant to imply that the entire cosmology of the *Xiang'er* is similar to the Mohists. We have already seen that the *Xiang'er* contains an entire vision of transcendent immortality—something completely foreign to the Mohists. And elsewhere I have discussed the *Xiang'er* argument for humans producing spirits—certainly not something the Mohists would have argued. See Puett, "Forming Spirits for the Way."

14

The *Yi-Xiang-Yan* Paradigm and Early Chinese Theories of Literary Creation

ZONG-QI CAI

Yi 意, *xiang* 象, and *yan* 言 are three key terms that Chinese philosophers have used from very early on to explore the interplay of the hidden and the manifest in language and signs, human cognition, and cosmological transformations. The three terms are commonly and conveniently translated, respectively, as "idea," "image," and "words." But these translations can at best capture a tiny fraction of the rich polysemy the three terms have accrued in Chinese philosophical discourse. Broadly speaking, *yi* denotes what is "hidden": the immaterial referents of spoken or written words; authorial or readerly intent; the mind's fathoming, speculative thinking; or the sages' intuitive cognizance of the Dao.[1] *Yan* represents what is "manifest"—words spoken, names, inscribed or written characters, or the act of speaking or using language. *Xiang* denotes what lies in between the hidden and the manifest. Depending on how closely it is associated with one pole or another, *xiang* has been variously construed as a suprasensory manifestation of the Dao (e.g., Laozi's *daxiang* 大象 or "Great Image"; Zhuangzi's *xiangwang* 象罔 or "Image Shadowy"); an intermediary that partakes of both poles and miraculously embodies the hidden Dao in the trigrams, hexagrams, and texts of the *Book of Changes*; or, simply, the appearance of physical things. As they continually evolved and accrued new philosophical significance, *yi*, *xiang*, and *yan* became ever more intertwined until Wang Bi 王弼 (226–249) codified them as a grand linguistic-cognitive-cosmological paradigm.

A study of the evolution of the three terms is essential to understanding the rise and development of Chinese theories of literary creation. Together and individually, these polysemous terms provide a reservoir of concepts needed to differentiate the complex mental and linguistic activities considered to comprise the different stages of literary creation. Indeed, this was not lost on the early Chinese critics, who consistently exploited the polysemy of the three terms as they sought to theorize literary creation. Once Wang Bi established the *yi-xiang-yan* triad as a paradigm, it would provide the frame by which Chinese critics would conceptualize the creative process for well over a millennium.

Within the limited space of this article, I shall trace the evolving philosophical concepts of *yi*, *xiang*, and *yan* from the earliest times through the Six Dynasties, the formative era of Chinese literary criticism, and demonstrate how the most prominent literary thinkers of this period, Lu Ji 陸機 (261–303) and Liu Xie 劉勰 (ca. 460s–520s), deftly appropriated those concepts to develop their comprehensive theories of literary creation. Notably, both of them explored the creative act as a dynamic process beginning with the hidden yi, and leading through the intermediary xiang to the manifest yan.

Divergent Concepts of *yi* and *yan* in Early Philosophical Discourse

The relationship of *yan*, or language, to the various realities—sociopolitical actualities (*shi* 實), heaven's will, the cosmological Dao—was a subject of intense debate among early Chinese philosophers. As this debate continued into the Wei-Jin period, it came to be formulated as a debate on the specific relationship between *yan* and *yi*, aptly articulated by these two opposing statements: "*Yan* fully expresses *yi*" 言盡意 and "*Yan* cannot fully express *yi*" 言不盡意. These two well-known statements crystallize what I will term the "essentialist" and "deconstructive" views of *yan* formulated, respectively, by early Confucian and Daoist thinkers.

"*Yan* Can Fully Express *Yi*": Confucius's, Xunzi's, and Dong Zhongshu's "Essentialist" Views of Language

The term "essentialist," if cleansed of its baggage of Western ontotheological subjectivity, may be taken as the common denominator of early Confucian views of language and reality. Confucius and his followers share a common belief in the potential for perfect correspondence between names (*ming* 名) on the one hand and external actualities (*shi* 實) and internal thought (*yi* 意) on the other. Whatever gaps may actually exist between names and their referents, they believed it is possible to close those gaps through a rectification of names, such that names become the unmediated representation or even embodiment of the external actualities or internal thoughts to which they refer.

In the *Analects*, we can discern this essentialist view of *yan* (language) in Confucius's discussion of names (*ming* 名) and phrases (*ci* 辭). When asked by his disciple, Zilu, what his first task would be if he were to govern a country, Confucius said:

> §1 It would certainly be to correct names. . . . If names are incorrect, what is said does not accord with what was meant; and if what is said does not accord with what was meant, what is to be done cannot be effected. If what is to be done cannot be effected, then rites and music will not flourish. . . . Therefore the Gentleman uses only such names as are proper for speech, and only speaks of what it would be proper to carry into effect. The Gentleman, in what he says, leaves nothing to mere chance.[2]
>
> 必也正名乎。 . . . 不正。則言不順。言不順。則事不成。事不成。則禮樂不興。禮樂不興。 . . . 故君子、名之必可言也。言之必可行也。君子於其言。無所苟而已矣。

Here Confucius identifies the rectification of names as the paramount task of his government. To him, names constitute the basis of human speech and action. The correct use of names will ensure an unimpeded, effective use of speech, and the right speech will in turn guarantee proper application of rituals and the laws. This passage clearly reveals Confucius's belief in an indissoluble bond between *yan* (language) and sociopolitical realities. Only because he sees names as bound up with ethico-sociopolitical realities does he believe that a rectification of names almost automatically guarantees the success of his sociopolitical endeavors.

Confucius also believes in an inherent bond between *yan* and what lies in the human mind, or *yi*: §2 "The master said, 'Phrases are to get [things] across—there is nothing more to it.'" 子曰。辭達而已矣。[3] In this statement, "phrases" may be seen as synonymous with *yan;* what they "get across" (*da* 達) is in all likelihood one's idea, intent, will—all of which can be subsumed by *yi*. Judging by the tone of this statement, Confucius apparently believes that *yan* can fully express *yi*.

The task of explaining the grounds for seeing the use of names as intimately linked with sociopolitical realities is left to Xunzi 荀子 (ca. 313–238 BCE), who wrote the lengthy essay, "Rectification of Names" (*zhengming* 正名), to accomplish this task. He begins the essay by showing the paramount importance of the correct use of names, invoking two complementary pieces of historical evidence to prove his point. The first, a positive example, is the peace and prosperity of the early Zhou, which he identifies as stemming from its rulers' correct employment of names. The second, a negative example, is the collapse of sociopolitical order, which he attributes to the rise of "flamboyant phrases to undermine correct names" (*qici yi luan zhengming* 奇辭以亂正名). He then proceeds to the more difficult task of proving the possibility of uniting names and realities:

> §3 Names have no correctness of their own. Their correctness is given by convention. When the convention is established and the custom is formed, they are called correct names. If they are contrary to convention, they are called incorrect names. Names have no corresponding actualities by themselves. The actualities ascribed to them are given by convention. When the convention is established and the custom is formed, they are called names of such-and-such actualities. But some names are felicitous in themselves. When a name is direct, easy to understand, and self-consistent, it is called a felicitous name.[4]
>
> 名無固宜，約之以命。約定俗成謂之宜，異於約則謂之不宜。名無固實，約之以命實，約定俗成謂之實名。名有固善，徑易而不拂，謂之善名。

Xunzi first concedes that names have no inherent correspondence to actualities in and of themselves, but then asserts that correct, felicitous names are assigned corresponding actualities by virtue of convention. He calls this wedding of names with actualities "the establishment of names" (*chengming* 成名) and considers it the key to the successes of the so-called "late kings," the rulers of the early Zhou. He contends that a ruler "cannot afford not to examine the late kings' establishment of names." 後王之成名，不可不察也.[5] This leads him to pursue a detailed analysis of how language interacts with actualities on several different levels:

> §4 When names are heard, actualities are made known. This is the function of names. When names combine to form refined phrases,

> we have the beauty of names. When both the function and beauty of names are achieved, it indicates one's "understanding of names." Names are what one uses to differentiate among closely linked actualities. Phrases are what one uses to combine differentiating names to elucidate one meaning (*yi*). Argument and discourse are that which avoids estranging actuality and name, while making known the *dao* of action and inaction.[6]
>
> 名聞而實喻, 名之用也。累而成文, 名之麗也。用、麗俱得, 謂之知名。名也者, 所以期累實也。辭也者, 兼異實之名以論一意也。辨說也者, 不異實名以喻動靜之道也。

Xunzi depicts the "interfacing" of language with actualities as taking place on three levels. On the first level, names are correctly employed to the effect that they become practically wedded to external actualities. On the second level, the combination of such names produces a refined phrase or statement, which illuminates an otherwise hidden internal, psychological (or cognitive) reality—one particular meaning or thought (*yiyi* 一意). This pairing of *ci* with *yi* provides a good answer to the question of what Confucius thinks *ci* is supposed to convey (see §2). On the third level, argument and discourse (*bianshuo* 辨說), made up of names and phrases, makes known the *dao* of action and inaction. To reiterate his quasi-essentialist view of *yan*, Xunzi retraces this chain of links between *yan* and actualities from the top down: §5 "What lies in the heart accords with the Dao; argument and discourse accord with what lies in the heart; and phrases accord with argument and discourse" 心合於道, 說合於心, 辭合於說.[7]

If Xunzi seeks to close the gap between language and realities, we find a culmination of this endeavor in the unabashed reification of language by Dong Zhongshu 董仲舒 (179–134 BCE). In "Shen cha ming hao" 深察名號 (An in-depth examination of names and appellations), a chapter of his *Chunqiu fan lu* 春秋繁露 (*Luxuriant gems of the Spring and Autumn Annals*), he writes:

> §6 The correctness of names and appellations is derived from heaven and earth. Heaven-and-earth is the great meaning of names and appellations. The ancient sages, in howling, patterned themselves on (*xiao*) heaven and earth; and so, this is called *hao* or appellation. They, in calling out (*ming*), issued an order; and so, this is called *ming* or name. As a word, "name" (*ming*) means calling out (*ming*) and issuing an order (*ming*). As a word, "appellations" (*hao*) means howling (*xiao* [a near homophone of *hao*]) and patterning oneself

on (*xiao*) [something]. Therefore, howling and patterning oneself on heaven and earth is called "appellation"; and calling out and issuing an order is called "naming." "Name" and "appellation" are different in pronunciation but have the same basic sense. They both make sounds to convey heaven's will. Heaven does not speak, but lets man express his will; heaven does not act, but lets man act under it. So names are that by which the sages expressed heaven's will, and they must be subjected to a thorough examination.[8]

名號之正, 取之天地, 天地為名號之大義也。 古之聖人, 譹而效天地謂之號, 鳴而施命謂之名。 名之為言, 鳴與命也, 號之為言, 譹而效也。譹而效天地者為號, 鳴而命者為名。 名號異聲而同本, 皆鳴號而達天意者也。 天不言, 使人發其意; 弗為, 使人行其中。 名則聖人所發天意, 不可不深觀也。

Dong unequivocally seeks to reify the words *ming* (name) and *hao* (appellation), making them the embodiment of *yi* or, more precisely, *tianyi* 天意 (heaven's will). To this end, Dong employs a fairly complicated, if common, scheme of phonological gloss (*yinxun* 音訓), evident even in the modern pronunciations I indicate here. First, he locates an onomatopoetic homonym for *ming* 名 (name): *ming* 鳴 (to call out, to crow); and an onomatopoetic near-homonym for *hao* 號 (appellation): *xiao* 譹 (to howl).[9] Then, by glossing each pair as interchangeable synonyms, Dong traces the origins of "name" and "appellation" to the ancient sages' howling and calling.

As howling and calling are, first and foremost, sounds of nature, Dong contends that names and appellations derived from those sounds are not arbitrary man-made signs, but the natural utterances of Heaven. To make this point absolutely clear, Dong stresses that "Heaven does not speak, but lets man express His will." In other words, names and appellations are nothing less than the expression of Heaven's will through the mouths of the sages. Having completed this radical reification of name and appellation, Dong proceeds to reify a set of key Confucian names and appellations in order to divinize the Confucian sociopolitical hierarchy.

Thanks to the concerted efforts by Xunzi, Dong Zhongshu, and other Confucian thinkers to endow names, or simply *yan*, with actualities or even divinity, the entire Confucian sociopolitical system eventually came to be codified under a system of thought known as *mingjiao* 名教 (the Teaching of Names). Thus, upholding the endowed actualities of names or *yan* (language) means, in practical terms, defending the Confucian sociopolitical system. So, when *mingjiao* came under intense attack during the Wei-Jin period, Ouyang Jian 歐陽建 (?–300) rose up to defend the substantiality of *yan*, composing his famous essay "Yan jin yi lun" 言盡意論 (A discourse on *yan* fully expressing *yi*).

"Yan Does Not Fully Express Yi": Laozi's and Zhuangzi's "Deconstructive" Views of Language

The term "deconstructive," if cleansed of its original Derridean significance, may be seen as the common denominator of early Daoist theories of language. Since the Confucian hierarchal sociopolitical system rests in large measure on the reification of *yan*, it is only natural that the Daoists, their archrivals, seek to dereify *yan* by stressing the gap that separates it from both external realities (ranging from the hidden Dao to perceptible, concrete things) and internal *yi*. This anti-Confucian stance, however, is generally kept in the background in most Daoist expositions on the insubstantiality of *yan*. It seems that they prefer to explore the relationship of *yan* with the Dao and *yi* on a lofty philosophical plane. §7 "The way that can be spoken of / Is not the constant way; / The name that can be named / Is not the constant name" 道可道, 非常道; 名可名, 非常名.[10]

This famed opening statement of the *Laozi* 老子 (*Dao de jing* 道德經) spells out the best known Daoist perspective on *yan*—an emphasis on the inability of names to embody realities, especially the Dao. The fact that Laozi goes on to use language, and even names, to depict the Dao reveals the concomitant, paradoxical Daoist perspective on *yan*—a recognition of its indispensability in suggesting what lies beyond itself. An elucidation of these two Daoist perspectives on *yan*—its inadequacy and its necessity—is given in the *Zhuangzi*:

> §8 We can speak of the coarseness or fineness of a thing only if it has some form. If it has no form, then numbers cannot define its dimensions, and if it cannot be encompassed, then numbers cannot completely account for it. What words (*yan*) describe is the coarseness of things and what the mind (*yi*) fathoms (*zhi*) is the fineness of things. But what words cannot describe and the mind cannot fathom has nothing to do with coarseness and fineness.[11]
>
> 夫精粗者, 期於有形者也; 無形者, 數之所不能分也; 不可圍者, 數之所不能窮也。可以言論者, 物之粗也; 可以意致者, 物之精也; 言之所不能論, 意之所不能察致者, 不期精粗焉。

This passage tells us that *yan* can only reveal crude appearances while *yi*—the mind's fathoming[12]—can capture the refined essence of things. It also identifies something hidden beyond the reach even of *yi*, that transcends the distinction between the crude and refined. The use of *yi* to represent the required mental effort to locate something hidden can be traced to its etymology (see note 1); and here, Zhuangzi does indeed foreground the idea of hiddenness. According to him, *yi* not only reveals the refined essence of things, otherwise hidden from the senses and inaccessible to language, but also points—by virtue of its very limitations—to what lies hidden beyond that refined essence. This notion of a three-stage progression from the obvious to the hidden to the most hidden is reiterated in the following passage:

> §9 Men of the world who value the Way all turn to books. But books are nothing more than words. Words have value; what is of value in words is meaning (*yi*). Meaning is pursuing something, but the thing that it is pursuing cannot be put into words and handed down. The world hands down books because it values words but, though the world values them, I do not think them worth valuing. What the world takes to be value is not real value.[13]
>
> 世之所貴道者書也。書不過語，語有貴也。語之所貴者意也，意有所隨。意之所隨者，不可以言傳也，而世因貴言傳書。世雖貴之，我猶不足貴也，為其貴非其貴也。

What does Zhuangzi have in mind when he says "Meaning has something it is pursuing" (*yi you suo sui* 意有所隨)? Zhuangzi does not explicitly tell us, but we can easily infer that it is the ultimate reality of the Dao. So this three-stage progression denotes an epistemological process from tangible *yan* through inward cognizance (*yi*) to the suprasensible Dao. Having deconstructed the essentialist views of *yan*, it is out of the question for Zhuangzi to see *yan*, *yi*, and the Dao as progressively linkable or "mergeable." So he depicts this progression as a series of leaps from one separate category of existence to another.

> §10 The fish trap exists because of the fish; once you've gotten the fish, you can forget the trap. The rabbit snare exists because of the rabbit; once you've gotten the rabbit, you can forget the snare. Words exist because of meaning; once you've gotten the meaning, you can forget the words. Where can I find a man who has forgotten words so I can have a word with him?[14]
>
> 荃者所以在魚，得魚而忘荃；蹄者所以在兔，得兔而忘蹄；言者所以在意，得意而忘言。吾安得夫忘言之人而與之言哉！

The famous metaphors of the fish trap and rabbit snare underscore the role of *yan* as a springboard from which to attain higher realities, even as they reaffirm *yan*'s own insubstantiality and deficiency. Although these two metaphors somewhat alleviate the tension between the two Daoist perspectives—characterizing it as fundamentally inadequate, on the one hand, and extremely practical (even necessary) on the other—true resolution of this tension was to be attempted in *Xici zhuan* 繫辭傳 (Commentary on the attached phrases) (§14–15).

Divergent Concepts of Xiang in Early Philosophical Discourse

The emergence and evolution of *xiang* as a key philosophical term have much to do with the ongoing debates on the *yan-yi* relationship. As I shall demonstrate below, "*xiang*" denotes a wide range of images: the appearance of physical things (*wuxiang* 物象), the images produced in the mind (*Xinxiang* 心象), the suprasensory "Great Image" (*daxiang* 大象) or "Image Shadowy" (*xiangwang* 象罔) of the Dao, and the trigrams and hexagrams of the *Book of Changes* (*Yixiang* 易象), which purportedly embody the ancient sages' intuitive envisagement of cosmic secrets. As a philosophical term, *xiang* has almost always been conceived of as a third term mediating between *yan* and *yi.*

What is the nature of the boundary separating this third term from *yi* on the one hand and *yan* on the other? This is a question that has long divided Chinese thinkers and has given rise to two influential opposing perspectives—which, again, I characterize as the deconstructive and the essentialist—on *xiang*'s relationship to the other two terms. Pre-Han philosophers tended to espouse either of these two opposing perspectives while the more syncretic-minded thinkers of later periods sought to reconcile the two in some fashion.

A Deconstructive Perspective on *Xiang*: Laozi and Zhuangzi

The notion of *xiang* was first introduced by Laozi, and picked up by Zhuangzi, for the dual purpose of rendering the metaphysical Dao "palpable" (and, thereby, accessible in some measure) and demonstrating the inability of *yan* to "presence" the Dao. In the *Dao de jing*, Laozi identifies the suprasensory *xiang* with the Dao itself: §11 "As a thing the Way is / Shadowy, indistinct. / Indistinct and shadowy, / Yet within there is an image; / Shadowy and indistinct, / Yet within there is a substance." 道之為物，惟恍惟惚。惚兮恍兮，其中有象，恍兮惚兮，其中有物.[15] To differentiate this shadowy and indistinct image of the Dao from ordinary visual images, he calls it the "Great Image": §12 "The Great Note is rarefied in sound, / The Great Image has no shape. / The Way conceals itself in being nameless. / It is the Way alone that excels in bestowing and in accomplishing" 大音希聲, 大象無形。道隱無名, 夫唯道善貸且成.[16]

With Laozi having thus established a particular kind of image, the supra-sensory image of the Dao, Zhuangzi now identifies the particular human faculties required for perceiving it:

> §13 The Yellow Emperor went wandering north of the Red Water, ascended the slopes of Kun-lun, and gazed south. When he got home, he discovered he had lost his Dark Pearl. He sent Knowledge to look for it, but Knowledge couldn't find it. He sent Keen-Eye to look for it, but Keen-Eye couldn't find it. He sent Wrangling Debate to look for it, but Wrangling Debate couldn't find it. At last he tried employing Image Shadowy, and Image Shadowy found it. The Yellow Emperor said, "How odd!—in the end it was Image Shadowy who was able to find it."[17]
>
> 黃帝遊乎赤水之北, 登乎崑崙之丘而南望, 還歸, 遺其玄珠。使知索之而不得, 使離朱索之而不得, 使喫詬索之而不得也。乃使象罔, 象罔得之。黃帝曰:「異哉, 象罔乃可以得之乎?」

This fable tells of four ways of knowing: conceptual thought (Knowledge, *zhi* 知), verbal argument (Wrangling Debate, *chigou* 喫詬), visual perception (Keen-Eye, *lizhu* 離朱), and intuitive envisagement (Image Shadowy, *xiangwang* 象罔). It explains that the Dao (Dark Pearl, *xuanzhu* 玄珠) is accessible only to Image Shadowy. Two of these four ways, Keen-Eye and Image Shadowy, seem similar but are rather different. According to Zhuangzi, intuitive envisagement is far more powerful and penetrating than visual perception. If "Keen-Eye" merely brings forth the outer appearances of things, "Image Shadowy" reveals the Dao (Dark Pearl). In creating the allegorical noun, *Image* Shadowy, Zhuangzi gives a new meaning to *xiang*. If Laozi describes his "Great Image" (*daxiang*) as primordial, undifferentiated existence, Zhuangzi portrays his "Image Shadowy" as intuitive "imaging" or envisagement. Later, following this new direction initiated by Zhuangzi, Han Fei 韓非 (ca. 280 BCE–ca. 233 BCE) describes how Laozi's sages, using their intuitive envisagement, "perceived" the Dao:

> §14 People rarely see a live elephant (*xiang*). So, when they obtain the bones of a dead elephant, they rely on them to conjure up what it looked like while alive. Therefore, whatever people use their minds to conjure is called *xiang* (image). Now even though

> the Dao cannot be heard or seen, the sage seizes upon the manifest accomplishments of the Dao to envisage its shape. This is why [Laozi] says it is a "shape without shape, a thing without image."

In explaining Laozi's notion of "shape without shape and image without image," Han Fei stresses the dynamic role of *yixiang* 意想 (or 臆想), an act of conjuring up or imagining something absent.

While Confucius dismisses this type of mental activity as speculative and unreliable,[18] Laozi and Zhuangzi rely on it to leap beyond the boundaries of time and space toward the Dao. According to Han Fei's explanation, this act of "imaging" begins with the stimuli of the actual world (the bones of a dead elephant) and ends with a mental image of what is not or cannot be seen (a living elephant). If common people are able to conjure up absent objects, Han Fei explains, then certainly the sages could envisage the Dao as "shape without shape and image without image" or simply the "Great Image."

An Essentialist Perspective on *Xiang*: "Commentary on the Attached Phrases"

An essentialist perspective on *xiang* was later introduced by the anonymous author of "Commentary on the Attached Phrases," arguably the most important of the so-called Ten Wings (*shi yi* 十翼) or the Ten Commentaries on the *Book of Changes*. This commentary is traditionally attributed to Confucius, but most modern scholars have dismissed this attribution as legend and now consider it to be an anonymous work composed later on during the Warring States period. Some scholars, such as Chen Guying, have even questioned its status as a canonical Confucian text on account of its embrace of many distinctly Daoistic ideas. One may not want to go so far as to call it a Daoist text, but one cannot but recognize its syncretic blending of Confucian and Daoist ideas.[19] Its blend of what we have heretofore considered to be distinct Confucian and Daoist views on the *yan-yi* relationship is particularly noteworthy in the following two passages attributed to Confucius, the first leaning close to Daoist views and the second to those traditionally associated with Confucian thought:

> §14 The Master said, "Writing does not exhaust words, and words do not exhaust ideas. If this is so, does it mean that the ideas of the sages cannot be discerned?"[20]
>
> 子曰。書不盡言。言不盡意。然則聖人之意。其不可見乎。

This first passage begins with a distinctly Daoistic statement: "Writing does not exhaust words, and words do not exhaust ideas." This statement lies in tension with Confucius's declaration of *ci*'s vaunted capacity to convey ideas as recorded in the *Analects* (see §2); at the same time, it would seem to accord nicely with Laozi's opening assertion that language is not up to the task of conveying the Dao (see §7). Furthermore, the ensuing question attributed to Confucius by the authors of the "Appended Phrases," "If it is so, does this mean that the ideas of the sages cannot be discerned?" tacitly points to the second Daoist perspective—the indispensability of *yan*. Insubstantial though it is, *yan* is a useful tool, just like Zhuangzi's fish trap, for conveying the ideas (*yi*) of the sages.

The immediately ensuing passage, offered in response to this fundamental question, however, sets us firmly back on the path of Confucian thinking:

> §15 The Master said, "The sages established images in order to express their ideas exhaustively. They established the hexagrams in order to treat exhaustively the true innate tendency of things and their countertendencies to spuriousness. They attached phrases to the hexagrams in order to exhaust what they had to say. They let change occur and achieve free flow in order to exhaust the potential of the benefit involved. They made a drum of it, made a dance of it, and so exhausted the potential of its numinous power."[21]
>
> 子曰。聖人立象以盡意。設卦以盡情偽。繫辭焉以盡其言,。變而通之以盡利。鼓之舞之以盡神。

While the first passage uses the negative phrase "*bu jin*" 不盡 (does not exhaust [in the sense of fully express]) twice, this second passage takes the discussion into a more affirmative direction, emphasizing the efficacious instrumentality of the images, hexagrams, and phrases deployed by the sages. It contains a series of five neatly parallel statements, each containing an auxiliary clause of purpose led by the phrase "*yi jin*" 以盡 × (in order to exhaust the potential of X). In short, the five auxiliary clauses set forth the sages' goals in constructing and employing the trigrams and hexagrams:

1. To fully express their cognizance (*jinyi* 盡意) of the cosmic secrets by "imaging" the workings of the universe (*lixiang* 立象);
2. To fully reveal the innate tendencies and countertendencies of things (*jin qing wei* 盡情偽) by devising trigrams and hexagrams based on that image (*shegua* 設卦);

3. To fully express the purport of the trigrams and hexagrams by appending phrases to them (*xici* 系辭);
4. To fully yield the benefits of the *Changes* (*jinli* 盡利) by allowing changes to occur and flow smoothly;
5. To fully exploit its numinous power (*jinshen* 盡神) by making full use of the *Changes*.[22]

This series of five "*yi jin*" phrases underscores a Confucian belief in the numinous power of language and the trigrams and hexagrams to make manifest all realities, including the Dao, the cosmic ultimate. Of the five statements, the first is the most noteworthy, as it ingeniously appropriates the Daoist views on *xiang* (image). If Laozi's "Great Image" and Zhuangzi's "Image Shadowy" have no inherent connection with *yan* (language), the "Commentary on the Attached Phrases" seeks to establish just such a connection. Through parallel phrasing, the authors link *xiang* (the sages' intuitive envisagement), first with the graphic signs of the trigrams and hexagrams and then with actual written words (appended phrases). In this way, the authors endow *yan* with the same divine power as Laozi and Zhuangzi did *xiang*. Indeed, they extol the trigrams and hexagrams as being capable of "exhausting the inner tendencies and countertendencies" of things. Elsewhere in the "Commentary on the Appended Phrases," its authors attempt an even more explicit reification of *yan*.

> §16 To plumb the mysteries of the world to the utmost is dependent on the hexagrams; to drum people into action all over the world is dependent on the phrases.[23]
>
> 極天下之賾者。存乎卦。鼓天下之動者。存乎辭。
>
> §17 As a book, the *Changes* is something which is broad and great, complete in every way. There is the Dao of Heaven in it, the Dao of Man in it, and the Dao of Earth in it. It brings these three powers together and doubles them. This is the reason for there being six lines. What these six lines embody is nothing other than the Dao of the three powers.[24]
>
> 易之為書也。廣大悉備。有天道焉。有人道焉。有地道焉。兼三才而兩之。故六。六者非他也。三才之道也。

Since this reification of *yan* is entirely premised on its intrinsic link with *xiang*, it speaks to the authors' feat in blending the Daoist notions of the suprasensory *xiang* with the Confucian belief in the numinous power of graphic signs and language.[25]

Codification of the *Yi, Xiang, Yan* Triad as an Onto-Epistemological Paradigm: Wang Bi

If the *yi-xiang-yan* triad in the "Commentary on the Appended Phrases" can be considered a prototype of a paradigm, we observe its codification as a grand onto-epistemological paradigm in the writings of Wang Bi. In the "Ming xiang" 明象 (Clarifying image) section of his *Zhou yi lüe li* 周易略例 (*General remarks on the Book of Changes*), Wang gives a clear exposition of this onto-epistemological paradigm:

> §18 Images are the means to express ideas. Words are the means to explain the images. To fully express ideas, there is nothing better than images, and to fully explain the meaning of the images, there is nothing better than words. The words are generated by the images, thus one can ponder the words and so observe what the images are. The images are generated by ideas, thus one can ponder the images and so observe the ideas there. The ideas are yielded up completely by images, and the images are made explicit by the words.[26]
>
> 夫象者，出意者也。言者，明象者也。盡意莫若象，盡象莫若言。言生於象，故可尋言以觀象；象生於意，故可尋象以觀意。意以象盡，象以言著。

Judging by the repeated use of the word *jin* (to yield up completely), this opening paragraph is most likely inspired by the account of the making of the *Book of Changes* in the "Commentary on the Attached Phrases" (see §15). However, if we compare this passage with §15, we notice two important differences. In §15, *yi*, *xiang*, and *yan* pertain to a series of actions by the sages—the intuition of the Dao, the envisagement of the Dao, the devising of trigrams and hexagrams, and the attachment of phrases. But with Wang Bi, the three terms become broad philosophical categories that seem to indicate three main stages in the ontological transformation from the hidden to the manifest. Second, while the authors of the "Commentary on the Attached Phrases" merely imply a causal connection linking the sages' sequential actions, Wang Bi explicitly describes the triad in terms of one producing another. If *yan* is produced by *xiang*, it must follow that *yan* partakes in the divine power of both *xiang* and *yi* and thus possesses a good measure of ontological essence. This essentialist conclusion, however, is subverted by what Wang says in the very next paragraph:

> §19 Thus, since the words are the means to explain ideas, once one gets the ideas, he forgets the images. Similarly, "the rabbit snare exists for the sake of the rabbit; once one gets the rabbit, he forgets the snare. And the fish trap exists for the sake of fish; once one gets the fish, he forgets the trap." If this is so, then the words are snares for the images, and the images are the traps for the ideas. Therefore someone who stays fixed on the words will not be one to get the images, and someone who stays fixed on the images will not be one to get the ideas.[27]
>
> 故言者所以明象, 得象而忘言; 象者, 所以存意, 得意而忘象。猶蹄者所以在兔, 得兔而忘蹄; 筌者所以在魚, 得魚而忘筌也。然則, 言者, 象之蹄也; 象者, 意之筌也。是故, 存言者, 非得象也; 存象者, 非得意者也。

If the preceding paragraph reiterates the essentialist view of the "Commentary on the Appended Phrases," this paragraph presents a deconstructive argument. Indeed, here Wang goes all out to demonstrate the gaps among the three terms. To begin with, he recasts Zhuangzi's metaphors of the fish trap and the rabbit snare (§10) by inserting *xiang* in between *yan* and *yi*. As *yan* is merely the fish trap or the rabbit snare for *xiang*, so is *xiang* for *yi*. Consequently, *yan* cannot be one and the same as *xiang*. The same goes for *xiang*'s relationship with *yi*. To take this desconstructive exercise one step further, Wang Bi contends that only by successively forgetting or disposing of *yan* and *xiang* can one hope to become cognizant of *yi*, the ontological hidden.

Why does Wang Bi present two mutually contradictory views in the same breath? We may point to his eclectic turn of mind as a simple answer. In my opinion, his eclecticism springs from practical needs of different kinds. As he is elaborating on the meaning of the *Book of Changes*, the essentialist view of the "Commentary on the Attached Phrases" is simply too influential for him to ignore. Hence he feels compelled to reiterate that view in §18. Of course, the necessity of invoking the "Commentary on the Attached Phrases" does not necessarily preclude the possibility of a genuine though qualified embrace of that essentialist view. By the same token, Wang Bi's dramatic switch to the deconstructive argument may have much to do with his aim to attack the rigid obsession with concrete images among the Han *Yijing* exegetes, especially those of the Images and Numbers School (*xiangshu pai* 象數派). Of Wang's essentialist and deconstructive strains of thought, it is definitely the latter that have wielded the greatest influence in his and later times. In fact, the weaker essentialist strain of thought, inherited from the "Commentary on the Attached Phrases," is very seldom acknowledged in either traditional or modern studies of Wang Bi's philosophical thought. In the course of the development of theories of literary creation, however, it is precisely this forgotten tradition of essentialist thinking that wields the greater and more productive influence.

Thinking about Literary Creation through the *Yi-Xiang-Yan* Paradigm: Lu Ji and Liu Xie

Both Lu Ji's and Liu Xie's theories of literary creation, crafted in the context of debates concerning the very value of literary writing, manifest their thinking about the creative process through the *yi-xiang-yan* paradigm. Lu Ji's appropriation of what had by then become an onto-epistemological paradigm is clearly evident in the prose preface to his "Wenfu" 文賦 (Rhapsody on Literary Writing), the first Chinese work devoted solely to the subject of literary creation.

> §20 Whenever I myself compose a literary work, I keenly perceive the state of the creative mind (of talented writers). I constantly fear that my conception (*yi*) does not match the actual things and that my writing (*wen*) does not capture my conception (*yi*). To understand (literary creation) is not difficult, but to acquire competence for it is. Therefore, I compose "Rhapsody on Literary Writing": to transmit earlier writers' craft of elegant writing and thereby discuss the reasons for success and failure in literary composition. I hope that some day it will be known for having exhausted the subtleties of the subject.[28]
>
> 每自屬文，尤見其情，恆患意不稱物，文不逮意。蓋非知之難，能之難也。故作《文賦》，以述先士之盛藻，因論作文之利害所由，佗日殆可謂曲盡其妙。

This preface introduces us to a new concept of literary creation unseen in earlier writings on literature. Literary creation is now depicted as an externalization of *yi*, rather than *zhi* 志 (heart's intent).[29] In many pre-Han and Han texts, however, while *yi* and *zhi* share etymological roots denoting "the movement of the heart"[30] and are often used interchangeably or even merged into a compound (*zhiyi* 志意), the two terms are used to indicate two very different kinds of movement in poetry-making. In pre-Han and Han texts, the statement "*Shi yan zhi*" 詩言志 (Poetry expresses the heart's intent) occurs often. If we look at the numerous occurrences of that statement, we can surmise that *zhi* usually denotes a volitional intent provoked by certain sociopolitical events or conditions. Furthermore, as I have shown elsewhere, in most cases the expression of *zhi* is itself depicted as a sociopolitical act, usually performed on public occasions, that praises or criticizes the state of governance or delivers a diplomatic message.[31]

In contrast, the word *yi* does not appear in early discussions on literature and had accrued few sociopolitical connotations. So by substituting this neutral *yi* for the sociopolitically loaded *zhi*, Lu Ji effectively gets rid of what he would have considered to be so much sociopolitical baggage, and paves the way for his rethinking of the creative process in terms of a conscious, private act of pure artistic creation. To Lu Ji, this de-sociopoliticization of the creative process is not the only benefit of substituting *yi* for *zhi*. By reconceptualizing the creative process as an externalization of *yi* in the form of *yan*, he is able to explore the roles played by *xiang* in the externalization of *yi*, and apply various philosophical analyses of *yi-yan*, *yi-xiang*, and *xiang-yan* relationships to plumb all the subtleties of literary creation.

The next important issue that arises when reading Lu Ji's preface concerns the antecedents of his *yi-xiang-yan* paradigm. His statement "I constantly fear that my conception (*yi*) does not match the actual things and that my writing (*wen*) does not capture my conception (*yi*)" has been generally traced to Zhuangzi's remarks about the incommensurability of *yi* and *yan* (§8, 9).

In my opinion, the two may seem the same but are actually diametrically opposed to each other. Zhuangzi's remarks are deconstructionist insofar as they stress the inherent gaps separating *wu* (things) from *yi*, and *yi* from *yan*. By contrast, Lu Ji's statement that he fears he cannot close those gaps when composing a literary piece belies his belief in the possibility of doing so. Indeed, while acknowledging in his preface the limit of his endeavor to capture the subtle secrets of literary creation, he expresses the hope that someday his present work "will be known for having exhausted the subtleties of the subject." In light of this statement alone, it seems safe to argue that Lu Ji's *yi-xiang-yan* paradigm is grounded, not in Zhuangzi's desconstructive view, but in the "essentialist" views of the *yan-xiang* and *xiang-yi* relationships expressed in the "Commentary on the Attached Phrases."

After the preface, Lu Ji proceeds to depict two primary stages of literary creation: the envisagement of the process leading to the formation of the work-to-be and the transformation of that envisagement into a tangible work of language. According to him, the intentional act of artistic envisagement begins, somewhat ironically, with a self-forgetting transcendental contemplation.

§23
This is how it begins: perception is held back and listening is
  reverted.
Engrossed in thought, one searches all sides.
His essence galloping to the world's eight boundaries,
One's mind roaming across ten thousand yards.[32]

其始也，皆收視反聽，耽思傍訊，精騖八極，心遊萬仞.

Lu tells us that transcendental contemplation begins with a suspension of all sense perception, followed by a daimonic flight of one's essence or spirit, or in his own words, the act of "[one's] mind roaming" (*xinyou* 心遊). Notably, Lu's "*xinyou*" is an inversion of Zhuangzi's "*youxin*" 游心 with essentially the same meaning. "Just go along with things and let your mind roam freely (*youxin*)," writes Zhuangzi, "Resign yourself to what cannot be avoided and nourish what is within you—this is best."[33] Commenting on the effects of *youxin*, Zhuangzi says, "Let your mind roam in simplicity and blend your *qi* with the vastness, follow along with things the way they are, and make no room for personal views—then the world will be governed" 汝游心於淡，合氣於漠，順物自然而無容私焉，而天下治矣.[34] There is little doubt that Lu Ji's description of the daimonic flight of the literary mind is modeled on Zhuangzi's account of *xinyou*. Like Zhuangzi, Lu stresses that such a daimonic flight is primed by one's well-concentrated essence and that it transcends all limitations of time and space to reach the ends of the universe.

Unlike a Daoist adept striving to perpetuate his blissful flight in the Great Empyrean (*taiqing* 太清), however, a writer does not seek to achieve the permanent transcendence of time and space. His daimonic flight of spirit is only momentary and always ends in a return to this world. Immediately after describing the outbound flight "to the world's eight boundaries," Lu describes how it ends by returning to the world of emotions, images, and words:

§24
And when it is attained: light gathers about moods (*qing*) and
  they grow in brightness,
Things (*wu*) become luminous and draw one another forward;
I quaff the word-hoard's spray of droplets,

> And roll in my mouth the sweet moisture of the Classics;
> . . .
> Then, phrases from the depths emerge struggling as when the swimming fish, hooks in their mouths, emerge from the bottom of the deepest pool . . .
>
> 其致也，情曈曨而彌鮮，
> 物昭晣而互進；
> 傾群言之瀝液，
> 漱六藝之芳潤；
> . . .
> 於是沉辭怫悅，若游魚銜鉤而出重淵之深 . . .

The *wu* (things) mentioned here are not real physical objects; their existence is insubstantial or virtual, images of the mind. Likewise, *qing* (emotion) does not mean crude emotional responses to external stimuli, but denotes feelings that have been sublimated by the contemplative mind into "moods." Again, refined phrases (*wen*) described here are not yet actual words coming out of the tip of a writing brush, but their virtual, as-yet-hidden existence in the writer's mind.

Lu Ji's description of transcendental contemplation and the ensuing interplay of emotions, images, and words seems to trace a process that parallels the linear progression from hidden to manifest—from *yi* to *xiang* to *yan*—described by Wang Bi. Lu's transcendental contemplation strikes us as a literary analogue to the sages' *yi* or intuitive cognizance of the mysteries of the universe (see §15). Just as the sages' intuitive cognizance (*yi*) is completed in and fully expressed by *xiang* (images), Lu's transcendental contemplation culminates in the upsurge of plentiful images in the mind; "Things (*wu*) become luminous and draw one another forward." Indeed, Wang Bi's statement, "Images are generated by the ideas" (see §18), serves as an antecedent for Lu Ji's conception of the role of images. The only significant difference may lie in the fact that Lu blends images with emotions. This modification is imperative for one who would promote the importance of the lyric endeavor, the very seed of which is emotion. Similarly, Wang's statement "Words are generated by images" (see §18) applies equally well to the birth of refined words and phrases vividly described by Lu. As mental constructs, these refined words arise right alongside the images and provide the linguistic "grid" through which the images are mediated and with which they are eventually fused as the envisaged work-to-be.

The next stage of literary creation is that of composition. According to Lu Ji, the writer must now work hard to transform his insubstantial envisagement into an actual text. If the preceding stage of envisagement involves the use of *yan* only on a rarefied mental level, this compositional stage entails a conscious handling of *yan* in all its practical aspects, ranging from structure, phrasing, and rhetoric, to style.

Like Lu Ji, Liu Xie traces the entire process of literary creation from initial transcendental contemplation through the final act of composition in "Spirit Thought" (Shensi 神思), an important chapter of his magnum opus *Literary Mind and the Carving of Dragons* (*Wenxin diaolong* 文心雕龍). If we carefully compare this chapter point by point with Lu Ji's "An Exposition on Literature," we shall clearly see Liu Xie's tremendous debt to Lu Ji as well as his unique contributions.[35] Like Lu Ji's, his description of initial contemplation is focused on the suspension of the senses, the roaming of the daimon and its return to the world of images and words. To him as to Lu Ji, this contemplation gives rise to a sustained interplay, and ultimately a fusion, of emotions and images as the envisagement of the work-to-be. It is true that Liu Xie did not say a great deal that had not already been said by Lu Ji, but he surely compensated for this weakness with his conceptual clarity. In the following passage, for example, we note the extraordinary clarity of his argument.

> §25 Thus *yi* (conception) is received from *si* (contemplation), and *yan* (language) in turn is received from *yi*. *Yi* and *yan* may be so close that no boundary can be found between them, or so far apart that there seem a thousand leagues between them. Sometimes the principle (*li*) can be found in a spot of one's mind, yet one goes beyond the world to seek it; sometimes a truth lies merely a foot away, but one's thought is separated from it by mountains and rivers.[36]
>
> 是以意授於思，言授於意；密則無際，疏則千里; 或理在方寸而求之域表，或義在咫尺而思隔山河。

This passage recapitulates his description of the creative process in terms of a progression from *si* to *yi* to *yan*. The term *si* denotes, not conscious rational exercise of the mind, but its unconscious daimonic flight, or "spirit thought." The first statement, "Thus *yi* (conception) is received from *si* ('spirit thought' or transcendental contemplation)," underscores the crucial importance of the initial daimonic flight of mind. This "spirit thought" gives birth to *yi*, as it brings forth a plenitude of emotions, images, and words and interfuses them as an envisagement of a work-to-be. Just as Liu's *si* does not mean ordinary but "spirit" thought, his term "*yi*" means no ordinary concept or idea, but an envisagement of a work-to-be. In this summary paragraph, the term *yi* is undoubtedly used as short for "*yixiang*" 意象 (idea-image), just as *si* is used as short for *shensi* 神思 (spirit thought). Earlier in the chapter, by merging the *Yizhuan* concepts of *yi* and *xiang* (see §15), Liu has coined the term "*yixiang*" 意象 (conception-image) to capture the virtual reality of artistic envisagement, a term that would become an aesthetic ideal in Chinese poetry and arts.

The next statement, "*yan* (language) in turn is received from *yi*," accentuates the crucial role played by envisagement in the genesis of a fine literary work. Only after a writer has formed the insubstantial or virtual "idea-image" of his work-to-be, can he hope to create a true work of art in the medium of words. To Liu, to transform the envisagement into an actual text—or in his own words, "to observe the idea-image and wield the axe of writing (to shape it)" 窺意象而運斤—is the most challenging task in literary creation. While acknowledging the possibility of the two being far apart, Liu expresses his abiding faith that *yi* and *yan* can be seamlessly merged into one by a good writer: "*Yi* and *yan* may be so close that no boundary can be found between them."

Liu Xie's *yi-xiang-yan* paradigm exhibits an enormous influence from the essentialist view of the "Commentary on the Attached Phrases," as does Lu Ji's. Just as the author of the "Commentary on the Attached Phrases" conceives of *yi*, *xiang*, and *yan* as progressively generative, Liu Xie traces a similar progressive chain of causation through *si*, *yi* (or *yixiang*), and *yan*. Moreover, that chain of causation leads him to a similar essentialist conclusion. Just as the author of the "Attached Phrases" regards *yan* as capable of fully expressing *yi* (through the intermediary *xiang*), Liu contends that *yi* and *yan* can become one at the hands of a literary master. It seems that both Lu Ji and Liu Xie could not but adopt the essentialist *yi-xiang-yan* paradigm in theorizing the creative process. Their theories were crafted in defense of the value of both reading and writing poetry. Without the promise of a perfect fusion of *yi* (*yixiang*) and *yan* in a great work of art, their theorization of the creative process—and literature in general—would be meaningless.

The impact of Lu's and Liu's essays is truly profound in the realm of Chinese literary criticism. Instead of attempting to write a comprehensive essay on the subject to rival Lu's and Liu's, later critics choose to dwell on certain mental activities in a particular stage of literary creation. While most of them gladly emulate Lu and Liu and conceptualize the creative process within the broad *yi-xiang-yan* paradigm, some rebel against this paradigm by advocating a return to the early *yanzhi* traditions or by embracing the new Buddhist ideal of spontaneous creativity. In the case of either emulation or rebellion, Lu's and Liu's essays provide the very frame of reference for thinking about literary creation by later critics. In the end, far from expunging hiddenness from literary expression, the successful model of the relationship between meaning and language was the one that saw it as central—that attributed to hiddenness its all-important role as the generative seed of the literary process.

Notes

1. In at least one example, the two characters *yi* and *yin* 隱 (hiddenness) appeared to be interchangeable. The name of Jisun Yiru, a person mentioned several times in the *Spring and Autumn Annals*, is written as 季孫意如 in the *Zuozhuan* 左傳 *(Zuo commentaries)* and the *Guliang zhuan* 穀梁傳 (*Guliang commentaries*), but as 季孫隱如 in the *Gongyang zhuan* 公羊傳 (*Gongyang commentaries*). This seems to indicate an etymological bond between the two words. See Gao Heng 高亨 (1900–1986), comp., *Gu zi tong jia hui dian* 古字通假字典 (A dictionary of interchangeable ancient characters) (Jinan: Qi-Lu chubanshe, 1987), 374.

2. *Lunyu yinde* 論語引得 (*Concordance to the "Analects"*), Harvard-Yenching Institute Sinological Index Series, supp. 16 (Rpt. Shanghai: Shanghai guji chubanshe, 1986), 25/13; Arthur Waley, trans., *The Analects of Confucius* (New York: Random House, 1938), 171–72. To be more faithful to the original, I have replaced "language" (Waley's choice) with "names" as the English translation of the term *ming.*

3. *Lunyu yinde*, 33/15/41.

4. Wang Xianqian 王先謙 (1842–1917), annot., *Xunzi jijie* 荀子集解 (Works of Xunzi, with collected commentaries). 2 vols. (Beijing: Zhonghua shuju, 1988), 2:22.420; Wing-tsit Chan, *A Source Book in Chinese Philosophy* (Princeton, NJ: Princeton University Press, 1963), 126.

5. Wang Xianqian, annot., *Xunzi jijie*, 2:22.420.

6. Wang Xianqian, annot. *Xunzi jijie*, 2:22.422–23. My translation is based on the textual notes collected in *Xunzi jijie.*

7. Wang Xianqian, annot., *Xunzi jijie*, 2:22.423. *He* 合, the key word of this passage, is very hard to translate. It seems to suggest a degree of integration somewhere between "being matched" and "being fused." In Xunzi's view, appropriate language and actualities are closer to each other than just being matched, but are not yet fused into one. There seems to be no English word that exactly captures this degree of integration, and the phrase "accord with" is an imperfect choice.

8. Su Yu 蘇輿 (d. 1914), annot., *Chun Qiu fanlu yizheng* 春秋繁露義證 (Luxuriant gems of the Spring and Autumn Annals, with an investigation of its meanings) (Beijing: Zhonghua shuju, 1992), 10.285.

9. On *hao* 號 and *xiao* 謞 as onomatopoetic near-homonym, see Su Yu, annot., *Chun Qiu fanlu yizheng*, 285.

10. Wang Bi 王弼, annot., *Laozi Daodejing zhu* 老子道德經注 (Laozi's classic of the way and its power, with commentaries), in *Wang Bi ji jiaozhu* 王弼集校注

(The works of Wang Bi, with collations and commentaries), ed. Lou Yulie. 樓宇烈 2 vols. (Beijing: Zhonghua shuju, 1980), 1:1; D. C. Lau, trans., *Lao Tsu: Tao Te Ching* (London: Penguin, 1963), 57.

11. Guo Qingfan 郭慶藩, comp., *Zhuangzi jishi* 莊子集釋 (Works of Zhuangzi, with collected annotations). 4 vols. (Beijing: Zhonghua shuju, 1961), 3:17.572; my translation. Cf. Burton Watson, trans., *The Complete Works of Chuang Tzu* (New York: Columbia University Press, 1968), 178.

12. Here, Zhuangzi uses *yi* in the verbal sense of fathoming, visualizing, or conjuring up something. There is no hint of rational thinking in the exercise of *yi* described in this passage. In fact, when the word *yi* is used as a verb, it often indicates a nonrational use of the mind. See, for instance, Han Feizi's use of 意想 in §14.

13. Guo Qingfan, comp., *Zhuangzi jishi*, 2:13.488; Burton Watson, trans., *Complete Works of Chuang Tzu*, 152. Slightly modified.

14. Guo Qingfan, comp., *Zhuangzi jishi*, 4:26.944; Watson, trans., *Complete Works of Chuang Tzu*, 302.

15. Wang Bi, annot., *Laozi Daodejing zhu*, ch. 21 in *Wang Bi ji jiaozhu*, 1:52; D. C. Lau, trans. *Lao Tsu: Tao Te Ching*, 78.

16. Wang Bi, annot., *Laozi Daodejing zhu*, ch. 41 in *Wang Bi ji jiaozhu*, 1:112; D. C. Lau, trans. *Lao Tsu: Tao Te Ching*, 102.

17. Guo Qingfan, comp., *Zhuangzi jishi*, 2:12.414; Watson, trans., *Complete Works of Chuang Tzu*, 302. Translation slightly modified.

18. Confucius does use *yi* 意 and its variant *yi* 億 as a verb (to fathom, to speculate) a total of three times in the *Analects*. Each and every time he dismisses speculative thinking (*yi*) as unworthy of a gentleman. (See *Lunyu yinde*, 16/9/4; 29/14/31, 21/11/18). This seems a logical stance for Confucius to take. Since he refrains from probing the supernatural, he naturally finds little use for any speculative flight of thought ungrounded in external realities.

19. For a summary of the debate on the character of the "Commentary on the Attached Phrases" from the Song to the late 1950s, see Willard J. Peterson, "Making Connections: 'Commentary on the Attached Verbalizations' of the *Book of Changes*," *Harvard Journal of Asiatic Studies* 42, no. 1 (1982): 77–9. For an account of recent works on the "Commentary on the Attached Phrases," see Chen Guying 陳鼓應, *Yi zhuan yu Daojia sixiang* 易傳與道家思想 ("Commentaries on the Changes" and Daoist thought) (Beijing: Sanlian shudian, 1996), 232–76. Chen seeks to establish the Daoist character of this commentary through textual collations. Comparing the commentary's standard text with the oldest extant silk text unearthed in the Mawangdui Tomb in the 1970s, Chen notes the absence in the latter of several passages expounding on Confucian ideas and regards those passages as latter-day interpolations into a text of Daoist origins. To demonstrate the commentary's Daoist origins, Chen also traces its key philosophical concepts to a broad array of Daoist texts and presents the results of his textual collations in a convenient chart (Chen, *Yizhuan*, 225–31).

20. *Zhou yi zhengyi* 周易正義, commentary by Wang Bi 王弼 (226–249), in Ruan Yuan 阮元 (1764–1849), comp., *Shisan jing zhu shu* 十三經注疏 (*Commentaries and Subcommentaries on the Thirteen Classics*; hereafter *SSJZ*),1:70; Richard John Lynn,

trans., *The Classics of Changes: A New Translation of the* I Ching *as Interpreted by Wang Bi* (New York: Columbia University Press, 1994), 67.

21. *Zhou yi zhengyi*, in *SSJZ*,1:70; Lynn, *Classics of Changes*, 67.

22. See my discussion on the term *shen* in "The Conceptual Origins and Aesthetic Significance of '*Shen*' in Six Dynasties Texts on Literature and Painting," in *Chinese Aesthetics: The Orderings of Literature and Arts, and the Universe in the Six Dynasties*, ed. Zong-qi Cai (Honolulu: University of Hawaii Press, 2004), 310–432.

23. *Zhou yi zhengyi*, in *SSJZ*,1:71; Lynn, trans, *Classics of Changes*, 68.

24. *Zhou yi zhengyi*, in *SSJZ*,1:78; Lynn, trans. *Classics of Changes*, 92.

25. Compare this praise of the *Book of Changes* with Zhuangzi's denunciation of words and books in §9.

26. Lou Yulie, annot., *Wang Bi ji jiaozhu*, 2:609; Lynn, trans., *The Classics of Changes*, 31. Slightly modified.

27. Lou Yulie, annot., *Wang Bi ji jiaozhu*, 2:609; Lynn, trans., *The Classics of Changes*, p. 31.

28. Zhang Shaokang 張少康, *Wen fu jishi* 文賦集釋 ("An Exposition on Literature," with collected annotations) (Beijing: Renmin wenxue chubanshe, 2002), 1; my translation. See also Stephen Owen, *Readings in Chinese Literary Thought* (Cambridge, MA: Council on East Asian Studies, Harvard University: 1992), 77, 80, 84.

29. The word *zhi* has been translated as "earnest thought" in James Legge, *The Shoo King or the Book of Historical Documents, The Chinese Classics*, vol. 3. (rpt. Taibei: Wenxin, 1971), 48, and as "the heart's intent" in James J. Y. Liu, *Chinese Theories of Literature*, 75. Liu's translation seems to be more appropriate because it avoids the rationalistic connotations of "earnest thought" and yet subtly implies moral inclination. However, the word *zhi* can take on a wide range of different meanings depending on the historical periods and particular contexts in which it is used. For this reason, Liu finds it necessary to render it as "emotional purport," "moral purpose," or "heart's wish" in other contexts (p. 184). For a discussion of the translation of *zhi*, see Owen, *Readings*, 26–9.

30. Xu Shen 許慎, in the *Shuowen*, glosses *yi* in terms of *zhi*, the entry that immediately precedes it: "*Yi* means *zhi*. It is constituted of the parts *xin* (heart) and *yin* (sound). By observing words one can get to know *yi*" 意, 志也。从心音。察言而知意. Xu points out *yi*'s etymological connection with *yan* (word) as revealed in its character formation—音 (sound) +心 (heart). Because *yi* can therefore be thought of as the "sound in—or of—the heart," Xu maintains that "it can be known through an examination of words (*yan*)." In addition, he describes *yi* as synonymous with the word *zhi*, a word that literally means the movement of the heart and, by extension, intent and volitional or moral preference. See Xu Shen, *Shuo wen jie zi [zhu]* 說文解字[注] (Explanations of simple and compound characters, with commentaries), ann. Duan Yucai 段玉裁 (1735–1815) (Rpt. Yangzhou, Jiansu: Jiangsu Guangling chubanshe, 1997), 10.502.

31. See the detailed discussion of the early "*Shi yan zhi*" tradition in my *Configurations of Comparative Poetics: Three Perspectives on Western and Chinese Literary Criticism* (Honolulu: University of Hawaii Press, 2002), 35–49.

32. Zhang Shaokang, *Wen fu jishi*, 20; translation from Owen, *Readings in Chinese Literary Thought*, 96.

33. 且夫乘物以游心，託不得已以養中，至矣。Guo Qingfan, ed., *Zhuangzi jishi*, 1/4/160; trans. Watson, *Complete Works of Chuang Tzu*, p. 61.

34. Guo Qingfan, ed., *Zhuangzi jishi*,1/7/294; trans. Watson, *Complete Works of Chuang Tzu*, p. 94, slightly modified.

35. For English-language studies of this chapter, see Owen, *Readings in Chinese Literary Thought*, 201–210; Ronald Egan, "Poet, Mind, and World: A Reconsideration of the 'Shensi' Chapter of *Wenxin diaolong*," and Shuen-fu Lin, "Liu Xie on Imagination"; both in Zong-qi Cai, ed., *A Chinese Literary Mind: Culture, Creativity, and Rhetoric in* Wenxin diaolong (Stanford, CA: Stanford University Press, 2001), 101–26; 127–60.

36. Zhu Yingping 朱迎平, ed., *Wenxin diaolong suoyin* 文心雕龍索引 (Indexes to *Wenxin diaolong*) (Shanghai: Shanghai guji chubanshe, 1987) [hereafter, *WXDL*], 26/55–60 (i.e., chapter 26/lines 55–60). The edition of *WXDL* in this book is that of Fan Wenlan 范文瀾, ed., *Wenxin diaolong zhu* 文心雕龍注 (Commentaries on *Wenxin diaolong*) (Beijing: Renmin wenxue chubanshe, 1958). My translation; see also Owen, *Readings in Chinese Literary Thought*, 206.

Contributors

Zong-qi Cai is professor of Chinese and comparative literature at the University of Illinois at Urbana-Champaign, and the Lee Wing Tat Chair Professor of Chinese Literature, Lingnan University, Hong Kong. Among his books in English are *The Matrix of Lyric Transformation: Poetic Modes and Self-Presentation in Early Chinese Pentasyllabic Poetry* (Michigan, 1996), and *Configurations of Comparative Poetics: Three Perspectives on Western and Chinese Literary Criticism* (Hawaii, 2002). In addition, he has edited *A Chinese Literary Mind: Culture, Creativity, and Rhetoric in* Wenxin dialong (Stanford, 2001), *Chinese Aesthetics: The Ordering of Literature, the Arts, and the Universe in the Six Dynasties* (Hawaii, 2004), *How to Read Chinese Poetry: A Guided Anthology* (Columbia, 2008), and *Sound and Sense of Chinese Poetry* (Duke, 2015). He is also the cofounding editor-in-chief of the *Journal of Chinese Literature and Culture* and editor-in-chief of *Lingnan Journal of Chinese Studies* 嶺南學報.

Shigehisa Kuriyama is Reischauer Institute Professor of Cultural History at Harvard University. His book, *The Expressiveness of the Body and the Divergence of Greek and Chinese Medicine* (Zone, 1999), received the 2001 William H. Welch Medal of the American Association for the History of Medicine, and has been translated into Chinese, Greek, Spanish, and Korean. Kuriyama has also been actively engaged in expanding the horizons of teaching and scholarly communication through the creative use of digital technologies both at Harvard and at other universities in the United States and abroad.

Wai-yee Li is professor of Chinese literature at Harvard University. She is the author of *Enchantment and Disenchantment: Love and Illusion in Chinese Literature* (Princeton, 1993); *The Readability of the Past in Early Chinese Historiography* (Harvard University Asia Center, 2007); and *Women and National Trauma in Late Imperial Chinese Literature* (Harvard University Asia Center, 2014). Her annotated translation of *Zuozhuan*, in collaboration with Stephen Durrant and David Schaberg, was published by the University of Washington Press (2016), and she is the coeditor and contributing translator of *The Columbia Anthology of Yuan Drama,* with C. T. Hsia and George Kao (Columbia, 2014).

Michael Nylan is professor of history at the University of California, Berkeley. Among her many publications in the field of early Chinese history and thought, she has written *"The Canon of Supreme Mystery" by Yang Hsiung* (SUNY, 1993); *The Five "Confucian" Classics* (Yale, 2001); and *Lives of Confucius* (eight chapters plus an epilogue, three coauthored with Thomas A. Wilson) (Random House, 2011); *Yang Xiong and the Pleasures of Reading and Classical Learning* (The American Oriental Society, 2011); and *Exemplary Figures: A Complete Translation of Yang Xiong's* Fayan (University of Washington Press, 2013).

Stephen Owen is James Bryant Conant University Professor at Harvard University. He is the author of such works as *Traditional Chinese Poetry and Poetics: Omen of the World* (Wisconsin, 1985); *Mi-lou: Poetry and the Labyrinth of Desire* (Harvard 1989); *Remembrances: The Experience of the Past in Classical Chinese Literature* (Harvard, 1992); *Readings in Chinese Literary Thought* (Harvard, 1992); *The End of the Chinese "Middle Ages"* (Stanford, 1996); *The Late Tang: Chinese Poetry of the Mid-Ninth Century* (Harvard, 2006); and *The Making of Early Chinese Poetry* (Harvard, 2006). He most recently published *The Complete Poetry of Du Fu* (de Gruyter, 2015).

Michael Puett is the Walter C. Klein Professor of Chinese History in the Department of East Asian Languages and Civilizations, Harvard University. He is the author of *The Ambivalence of Creation: Debates Concerning Innovation and Artifice in Early China* (Stanford, 2001); *To Become a God: Cosmology, Sacrifice, and Self-Divinization in Early China* (Harvard, 2002); and *Ritual and Its Consequences: An Essay on the Limits of Sincerity,* coauthored with Robert Weller, Adam Seligman, and Bennett Simon (Oxford, 2008). He also coedited, with Sarah A. Queen, *The Huainanzi and Textual Production in Early China* (Brill, 2014).

James Robson is the James C. Kralik and Yunli Lou Professor of East Asian Languages and Civilizations at Harvard University. He is the author of *Power of Place: The Religious Landscape of the Southern Sacred Peak [Nanyue] in Medieval China* (Harvard, 2009), which was awarded the Stanislas Julien Prize for 2010 by the French Academy of Inscriptions and Belles-Lettres and the 2010 Toshihide Numata Book Prize in Buddhism; "Signs of Power: Talismanic Writings in Chinese Buddhism" (*History of Religions* 48, no. 2); "Faith in Museums: On the Confluence of Museums and Religious Sites in Asia" (PMLA, 2010); and the forthcoming *The Daodejing: A Biography* (Princeton). He is the editor of the *Norton Anthology of World Religions: Daoism* (W. W. Norton & Company, 2014), and the coeditor of *Images, Relics and Legends—The Formation and Transformation of Buddhist Sacred Sites* (Toronto, 2011) and *Buddhist Monasticism in East Asia: Places of Practice* (Rutledge, 2010).

David Schaberg is a professor of classical Chinese literature and thought in the Department of Asian Languages and Cultures, as well as dean of humanities, at UCLA. He is the author of *A Patterned Past: Form and Thought in Early Chinese Historiography* (Harvard 2005), which won the Joseph Levenson Prize of the Association of Asian Studies (pre-1900 category). He has also published numerous articles and book chapters, including "Playing at Critique: Indirect Remonstrance and the Formation of *Shi* Identity," in *Text and Ritual in Early China*, edited by Martin Kern (2005), and "Platitude and Persona: Junzi Comments in *Zuozhuan* and Beyond," in *Historical Truth, Historical Criticism, and Ideology: Chinese Historiography and Historical Culture from a New Comparative Perspective*, edited by Helwig Schmidt-Glintzer et al. (2005). His annotated translation of *Zuozhuan*, in collaboration with Stephen Durrant and Wai-yee Li, was published by the University of Washington Press (2016).

Xiaofei Tian is professor of Chinese literature in the Department of East Asian Languages and Civilizations at Harvard University. Among her most recent English publications are *Tao Yuanming and Manuscript Culture: The Record of a Dusty Table* (University of Washington, 2005), *Beacon Fire and Shooting Star: The Literary Culture of the Liang (502–557)* (Harvard, 2007), *Visionary Journeys: Travel Writings from Early Medieval and Nineteenth-Century China* (Harvard, 2011), and the translation of a late-nineteenth-century memoir, *The World of a Tiny Insect: A Memoir of the Taiping Rebellion and Its Aftermath*, with notes and a critical introduction (University of Washington, 2014).

Lillian Lan-ying Tseng is associate professor at the Institute for the Study of the Ancient World at New York University. She is the author of *Picturing Heaven in Early China* (Harvard, 2011), as well as numerous articles and book chapters on subjects such as history and memory, visual replication and political persuasion, and pictorial representation and historical writing. These include "Funerary Spatiality: Wang Hui's Sarcophagus in Han China," in *Res: Journal of Anthropology and Aesthetics*, nos. 61/62 (2012), and "Positioning the Heavenly Horses on Han Mirrors," in *The Lloyd Cotsen Study Collection of Chinese Bronze Mirrors*, Vol. II: *Studies*, ed. Lothar von Falkenhausen (Los Angeles: UCLA Cotsen Institute of Archaeology Press, 2011).

Paula M. Varsano is associate professor in the Department of East Asian Languages and Cultures at the University of California, Berkeley. She is the author of *Tracking the Banished Immortal: The Poetry of Li Bo and Its Critical Reception* (Hawaii, 2003) as well as a number of articles and book chapters on Chinese poetry and poetics. Her current research focuses on constructions of subjectivity in Chinese literary writing, with a focus on the role of the senses.

Sophie Volpp is associate professor in the Department of East Asian Languages and Cultures, as well as in the Department of Comparative Literature, at the University of California, Berkeley. She is the author of *Worldly Stage: Theatricality in Seventeenth Century China* (Harvard, 2011), as well as a number of articles and book chapters. Her current research examines the depiction of material objects in late-imperial literature.

Eugene Wang is the Abby Aldrich Rockefeller Professor of Asian Art at Harvard University. His book, *Shaping the Lotus Sutra: Buddhist Visual Culture of Medieval China* (2005) received the Academic Excellence Award from Japan in 2006. His extensive publications cover the entire range of Chinese art history from ancient funerary art to modern and contemporary Chinese art and cinema. He serves on the advisory board of the Center for Advanced Studies at the National Gallery of Art in Washington, D.C., and the editorial board of *The Art Bulletin*.

Index

Note that alphabetical sorting ignores the word "the."
Thus, "The disarrayed hills conceal an old monastery" is found under "D."

www.ingramcontent.com/pod-product-compliance
Lightning Source LLC
LaVergne TN
LVHW010347080826
844660LV00003B/213
9781438463032